ane & Hana

18

STORY AND ART BY

Yuki Shiwasu

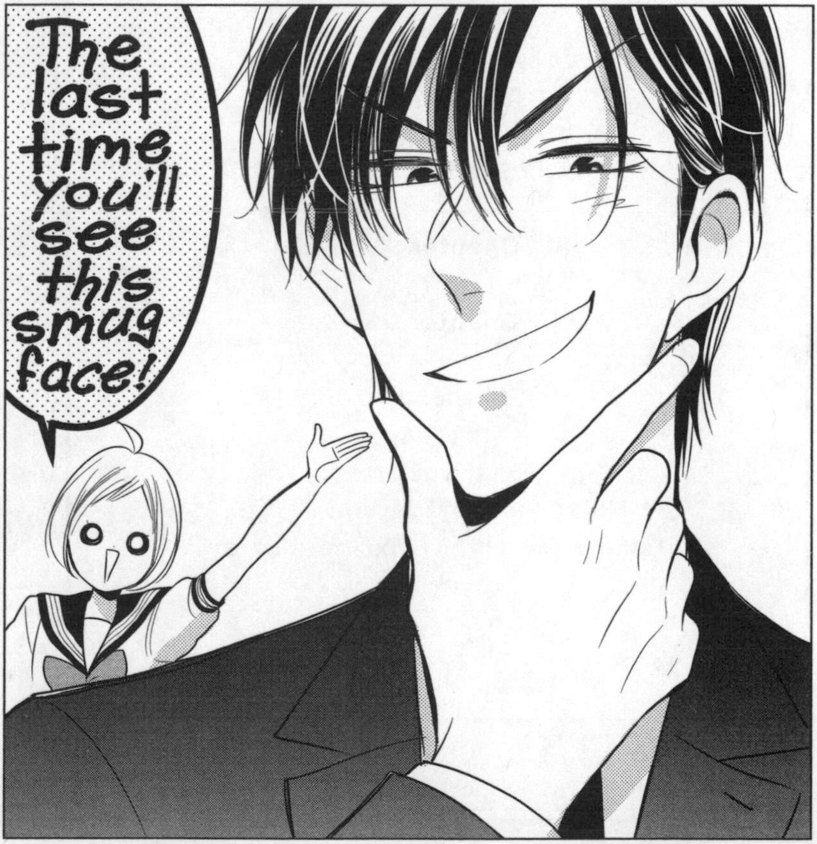
The last time you'll see this smug face!

Takane &Hana

18

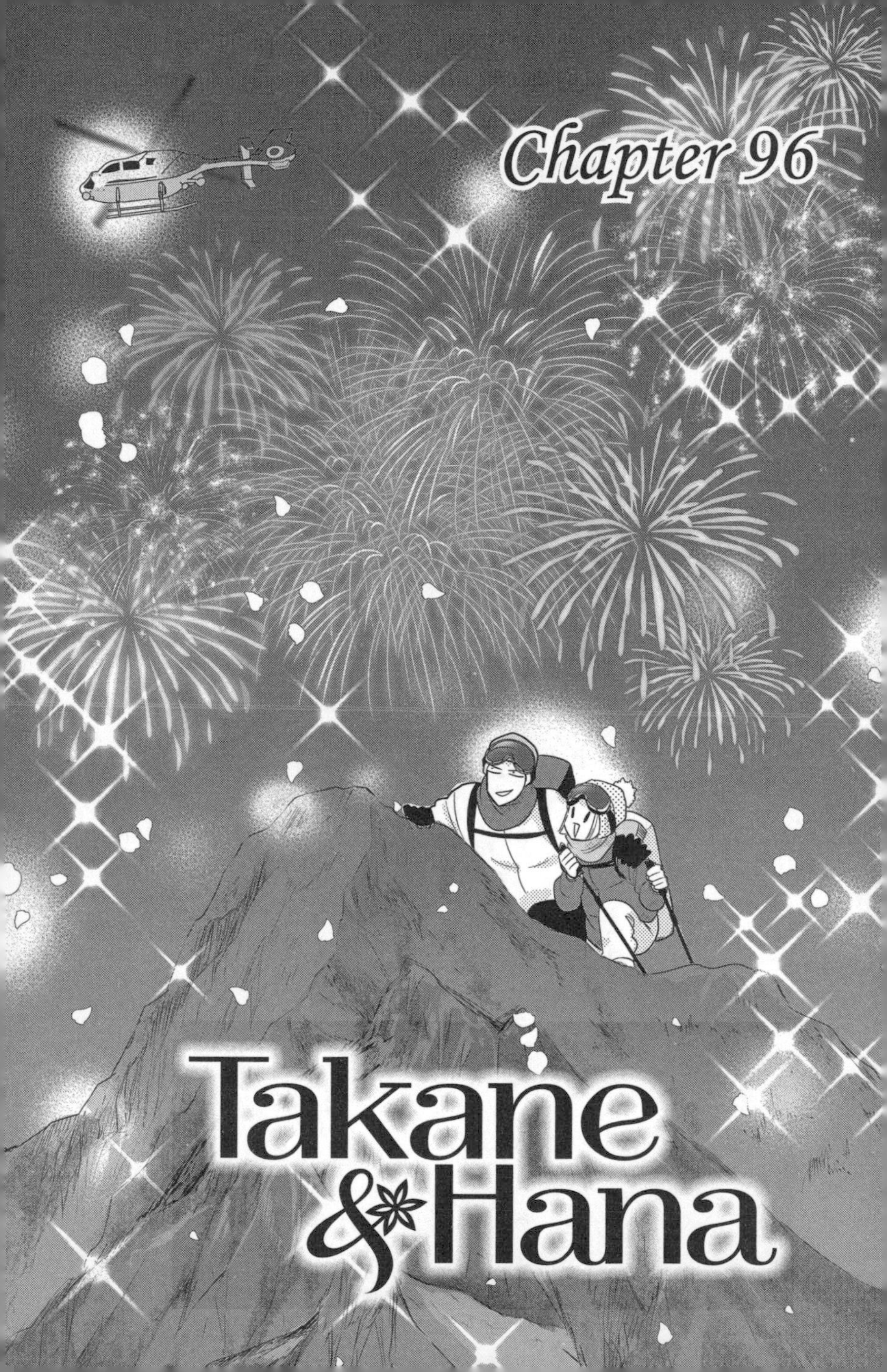
Chapter 96
Takane & Hana

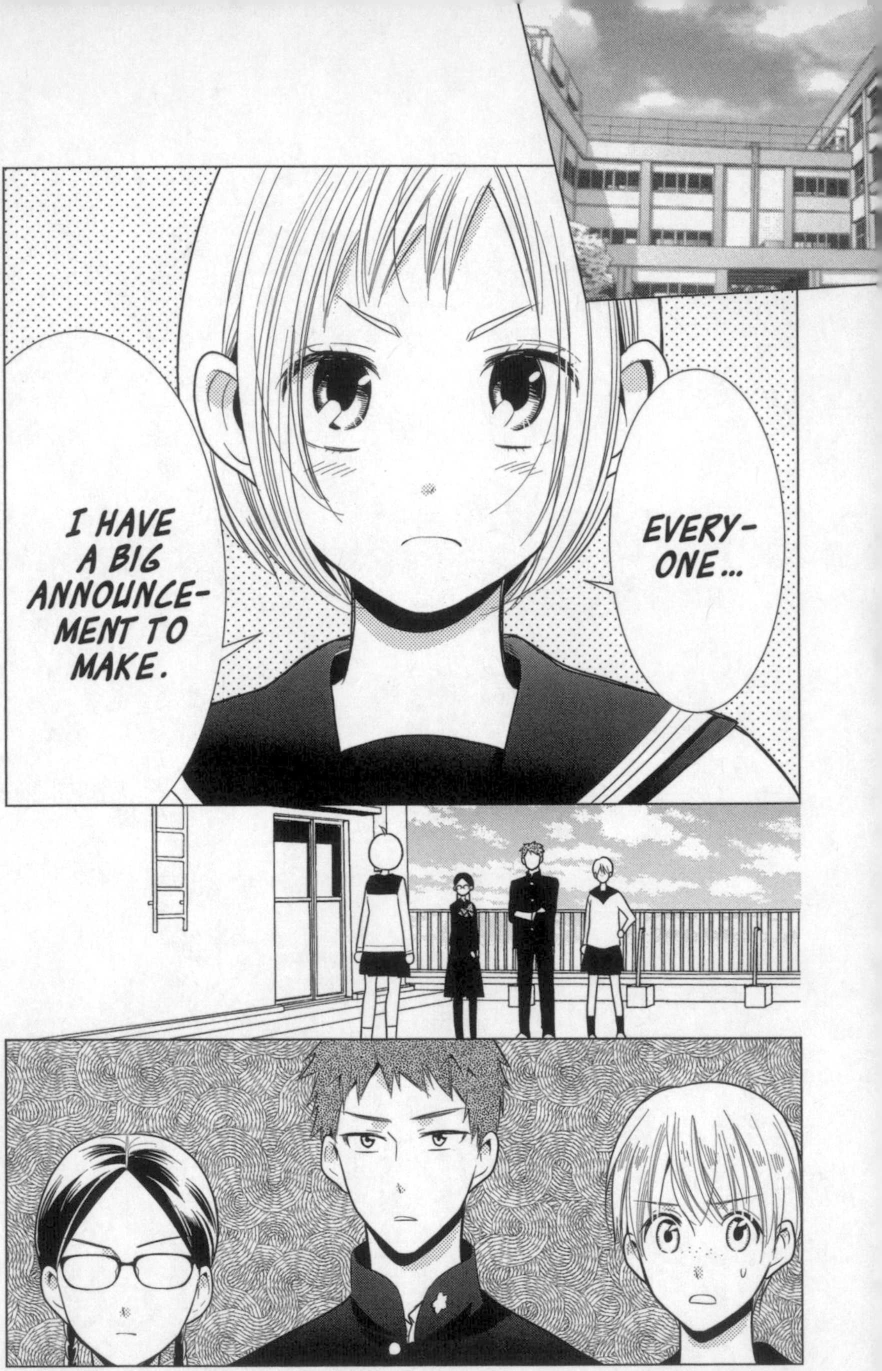
EVERY-ONE...
I HAVE A BIG ANNOUNCE-MENT TO MAKE.

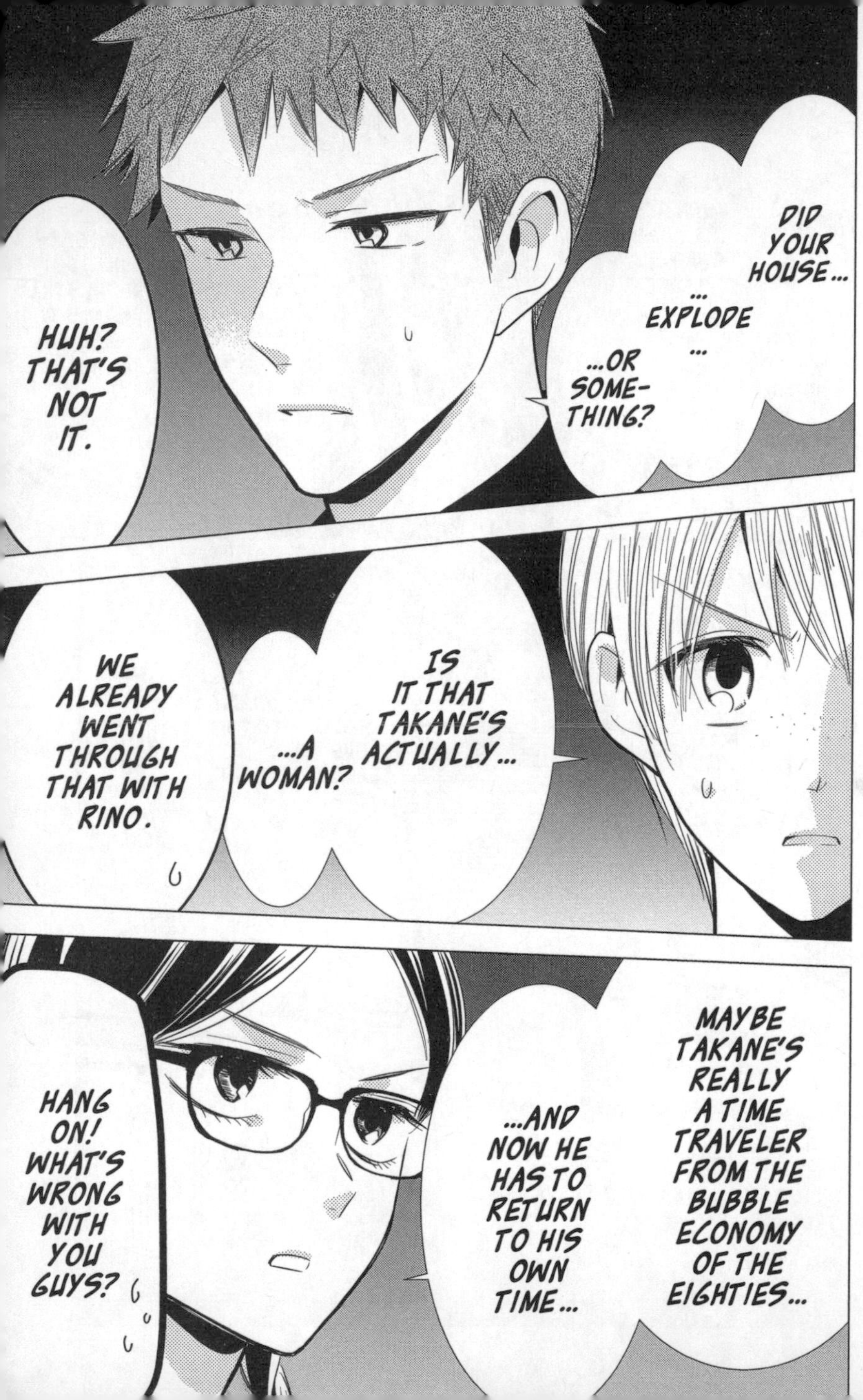
DID YOUR HOUSE... ...EXPLODE... ...OR SOMETHING?
HUH? THAT'S NOT IT.
IS IT THAT TAKANE'S ACTUALLY... ...A WOMAN?
WE ALREADY WENT THROUGH THAT WITH RINO.
MAYBE TAKANE'S REALLY A TIME TRAVELER FROM THE BUBBLE ECONOMY OF THE EIGHTIES...
...AND NOW HE HAS TO RETURN TO HIS OWN TIME...
HANG ON! WHAT'S WRONG WITH YOU GUYS?

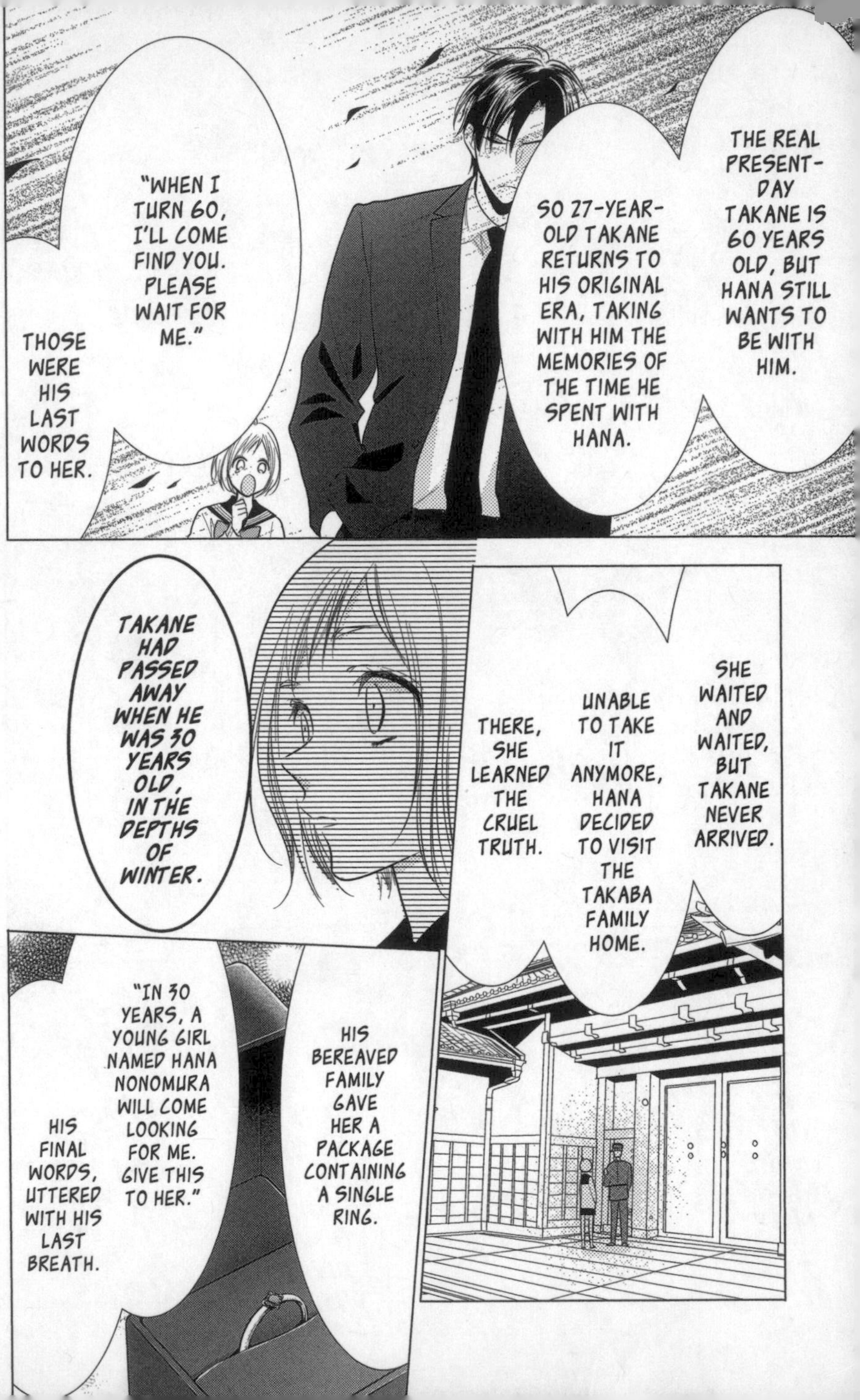
THE REAL PRESENT-DAY TAKANE IS 60 YEARS OLD, BUT HANA STILL WANTS TO BE WITH HIM.
SO 27-YEAR-OLD TAKANE RETURNS TO HIS ORIGINAL ERA, TAKING WITH HIM THE MEMORIES OF THE TIME HE SPENT WITH HANA.
"WHEN I TURN 60, I'LL COME FIND YOU. PLEASE WAIT FOR ME."
THOSE WERE HIS LAST WORDS TO HER.
SHE WAITED AND WAITED, BUT TAKANE NEVER ARRIVED.
UNABLE TO TAKE IT ANYMORE, HANA DECIDED TO VISIT THE TAKABA FAMILY HOME.
THERE, SHE LEARNED THE CRUEL TRUTH.
TAKANE HAD PASSED AWAY WHEN HE WAS 30 YEARS OLD, IN THE DEPTHS OF WINTER.
HIS BEREAVED FAMILY GAVE HER A PACKAGE CONTAINING A SINGLE RING.
"IN 30 YEARS, A YOUNG GIRL NAMED HANA NONOMURA WILL COME LOOKING FOR ME. GIVE THIS TO HER."
HIS FINAL WORDS, UTTERED WITH HIS LAST BREATH.

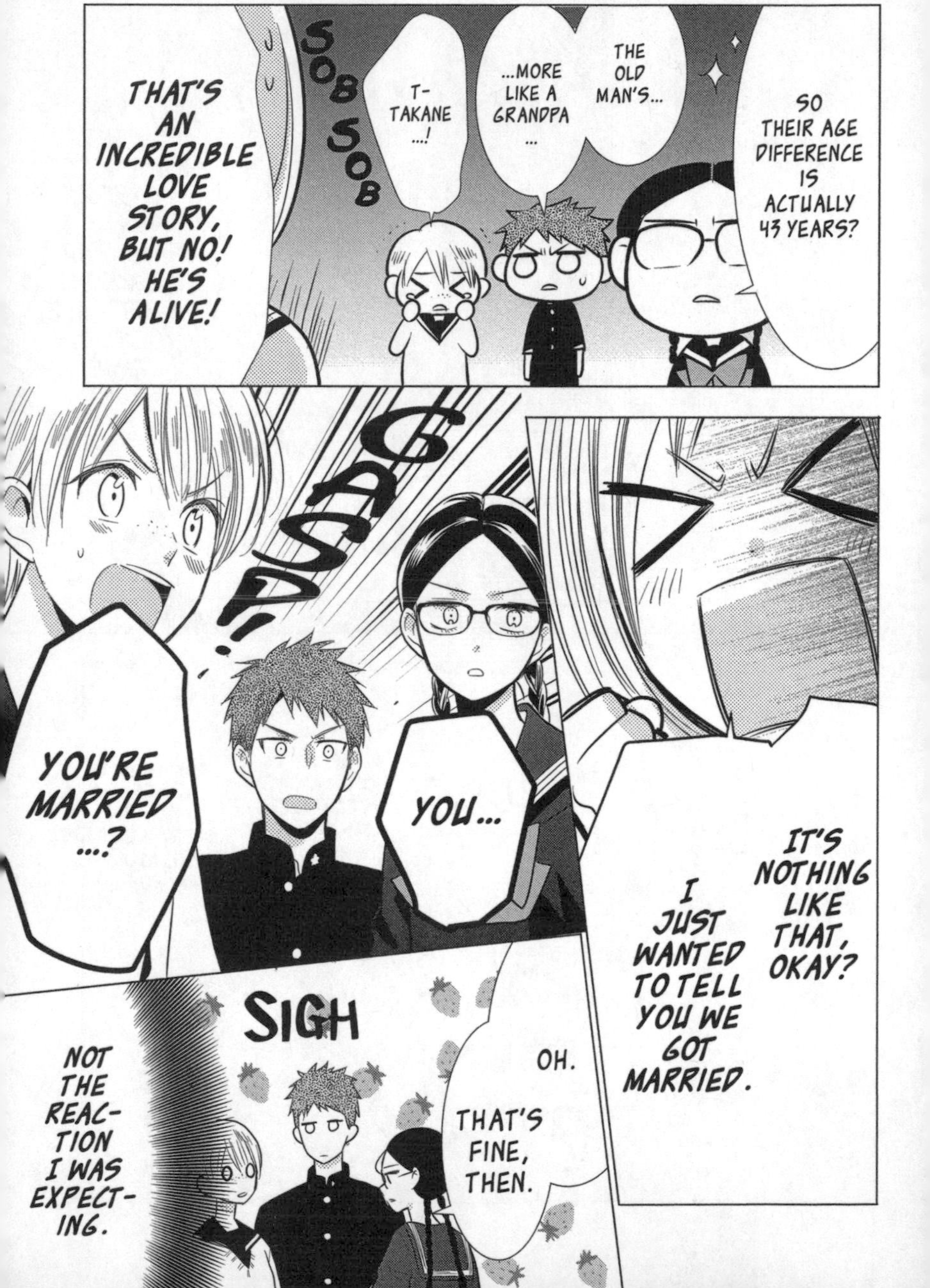
SO THEIR AGE DIFFERENCE IS ACTUALLY 43 YEARS?
THE OLD MAN'S...
...MORE LIKE A GRANDPA ...
T-TAKANE ...!
SOB SOB
THAT'S AN INCREDIBLE LOVE STORY, BUT NO! HE'S ALIVE!
IT'S NOTHING LIKE THAT, OKAY?
I JUST WANTED TO TELL YOU WE GOT MARRIED.
GASP!!
YOU...
YOU'RE MARRIED ...?
OH.
THAT'S FINE, THEN.
SIGH
NOT THE REACTION I WAS EXPECTING.

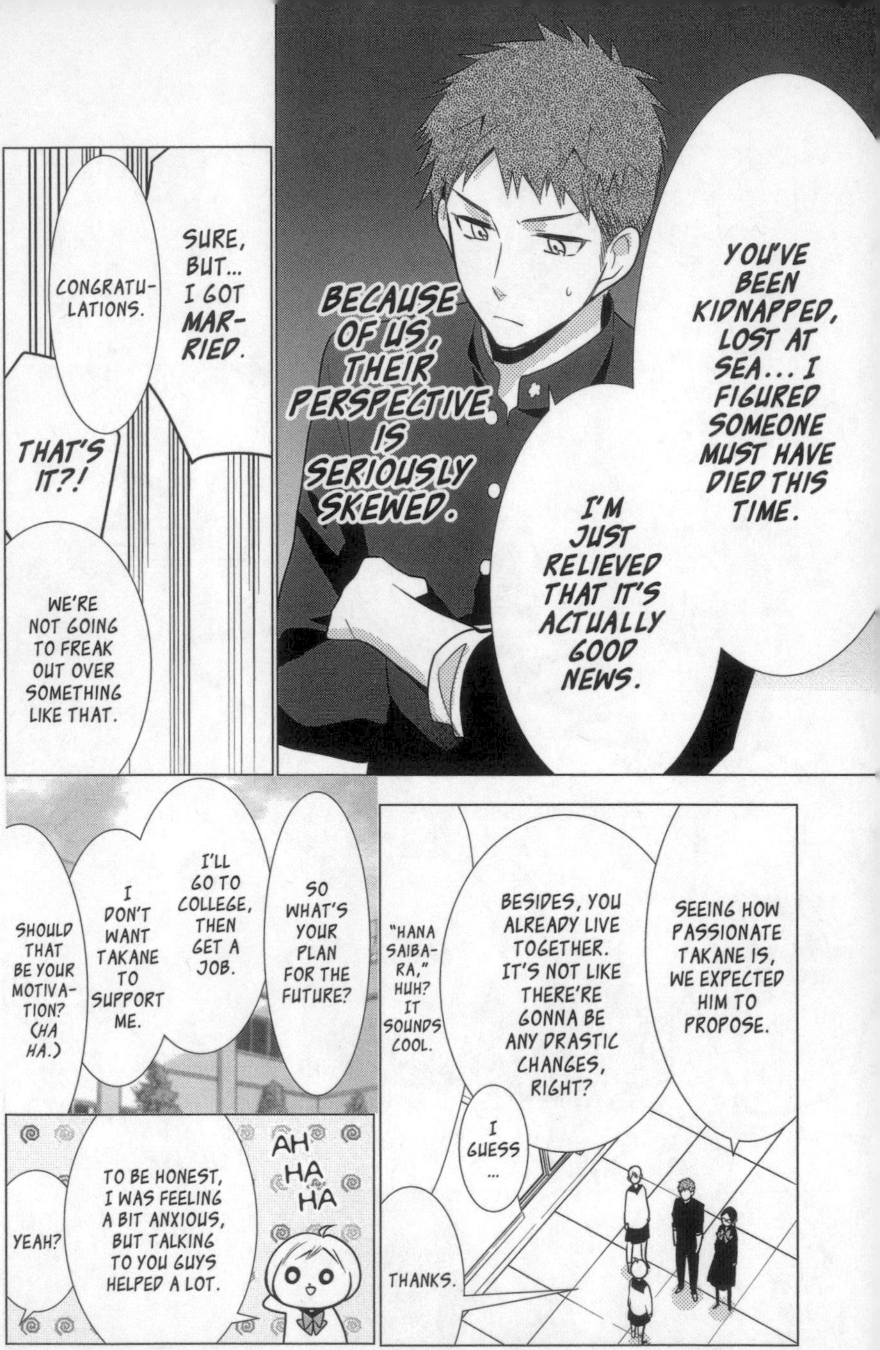
YOU'VE BEEN KIDNAPPED, LOST AT SEA... I FIGURED SOMEONE MUST HAVE DIED THIS TIME.
I'M JUST RELIEVED THAT IT'S ACTUALLY GOOD NEWS.
BECAUSE OF US, THEIR PERSPECTIVE IS SERIOUSLY SKEWED.
SURE, BUT... I GOT MAR-RIED.
CONGRATU-LATIONS.
THAT'S IT?!
WE'RE NOT GOING TO FREAK OUT OVER SOMETHING LIKE THAT.
SEEING HOW PASSIONATE TAKANE IS, WE EXPECTED HIM TO PROPOSE.
BESIDES, YOU ALREADY LIVE TOGETHER. IT'S NOT LIKE THERE'RE GONNA BE ANY DRASTIC CHANGES, RIGHT?
"HANA SAIBA-RA," HUH? IT SOUNDS COOL.
I GUESS...
THANKS.
SO WHAT'S YOUR PLAN FOR THE FUTURE?
I'LL GO TO COLLEGE, THEN GET A JOB.
I DON'T WANT TAKANE TO SUPPORT ME.
SHOULD THAT BE YOUR MOTIVA-TION? (HA HA.)
AH HA HA
TO BE HONEST, I WAS FEELING A BIT ANXIOUS, BUT TALKING TO YOU GUYS HELPED A LOT.
YEAH?

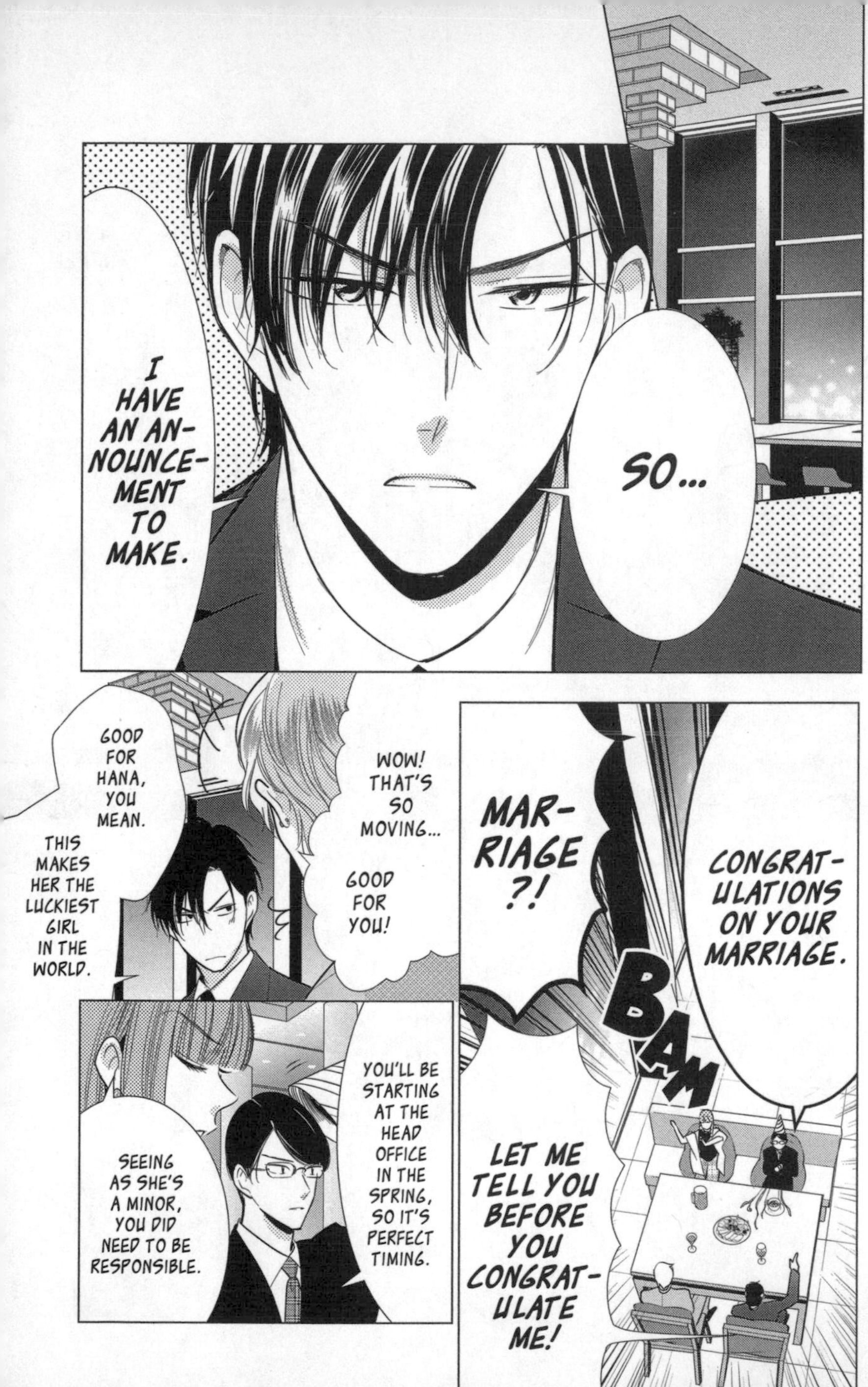
SO...
I HAVE AN ANNOUNCEMENT TO MAKE.
CONGRATULATIONS ON YOUR MARRIAGE.
BAM
MARRIAGE?!
LET ME TELL YOU BEFORE YOU CONGRATULATE ME!
WOW! THAT'S SO MOVING...
GOOD FOR YOU!
GOOD FOR HANA, YOU MEAN.
THIS MAKES HER THE LUCKIEST GIRL IN THE WORLD.
YOU'LL BE STARTING AT THE HEAD OFFICE IN THE SPRING, SO IT'S PERFECT TIMING.
SEEING AS SHE'S A MINOR, YOU DID NEED TO BE RESPONSIBLE.

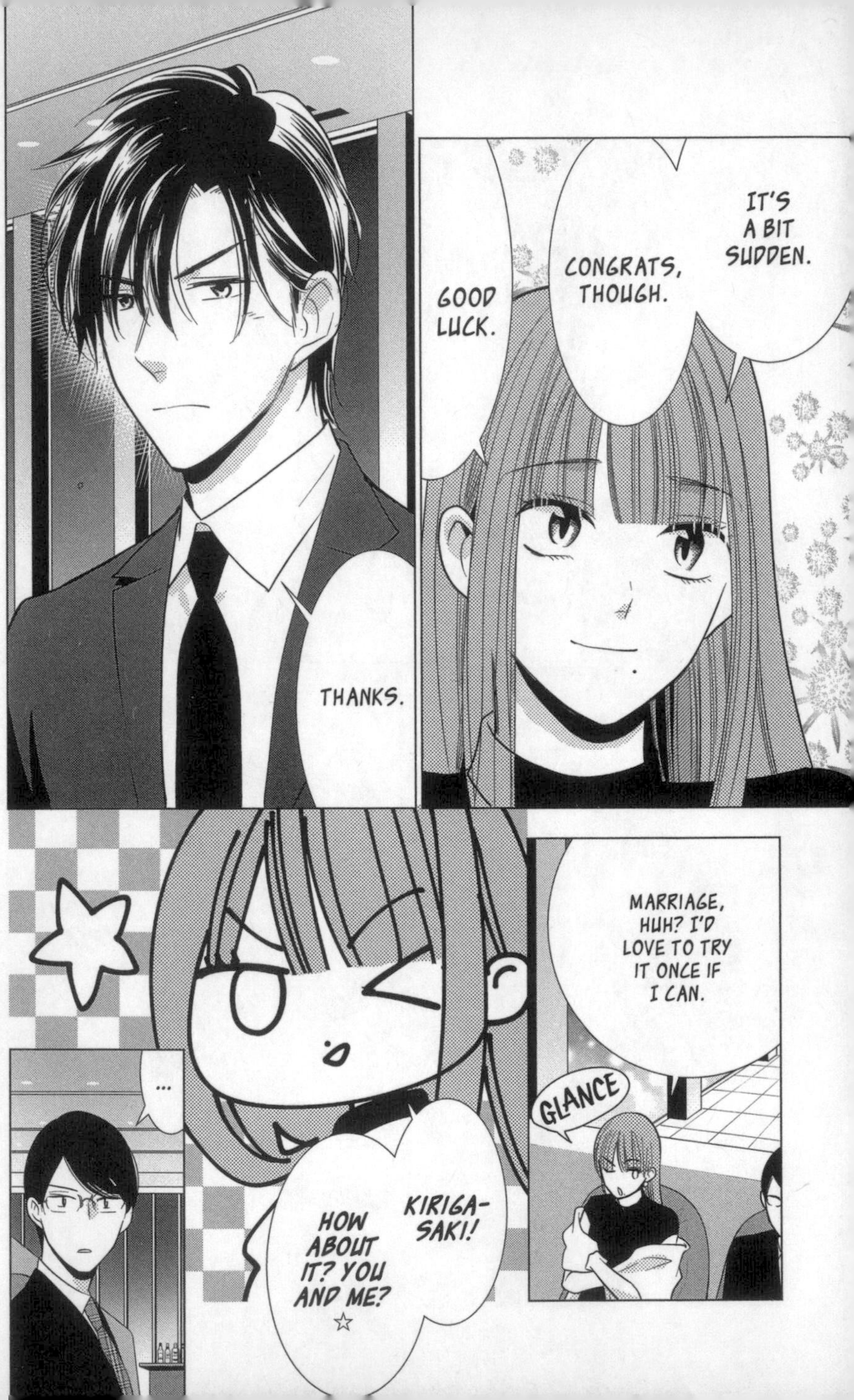
IT'S A BIT SUDDEN.
CONGRATS, THOUGH.
GOOD LUCK.
THANKS.
MARRIAGE, HUH? I'D LOVE TO TRY IT ONCE IF I CAN.
GLANCE
KIRIGA-SAKI!
HOW ABOUT IT? YOU AND ME? ☆
...

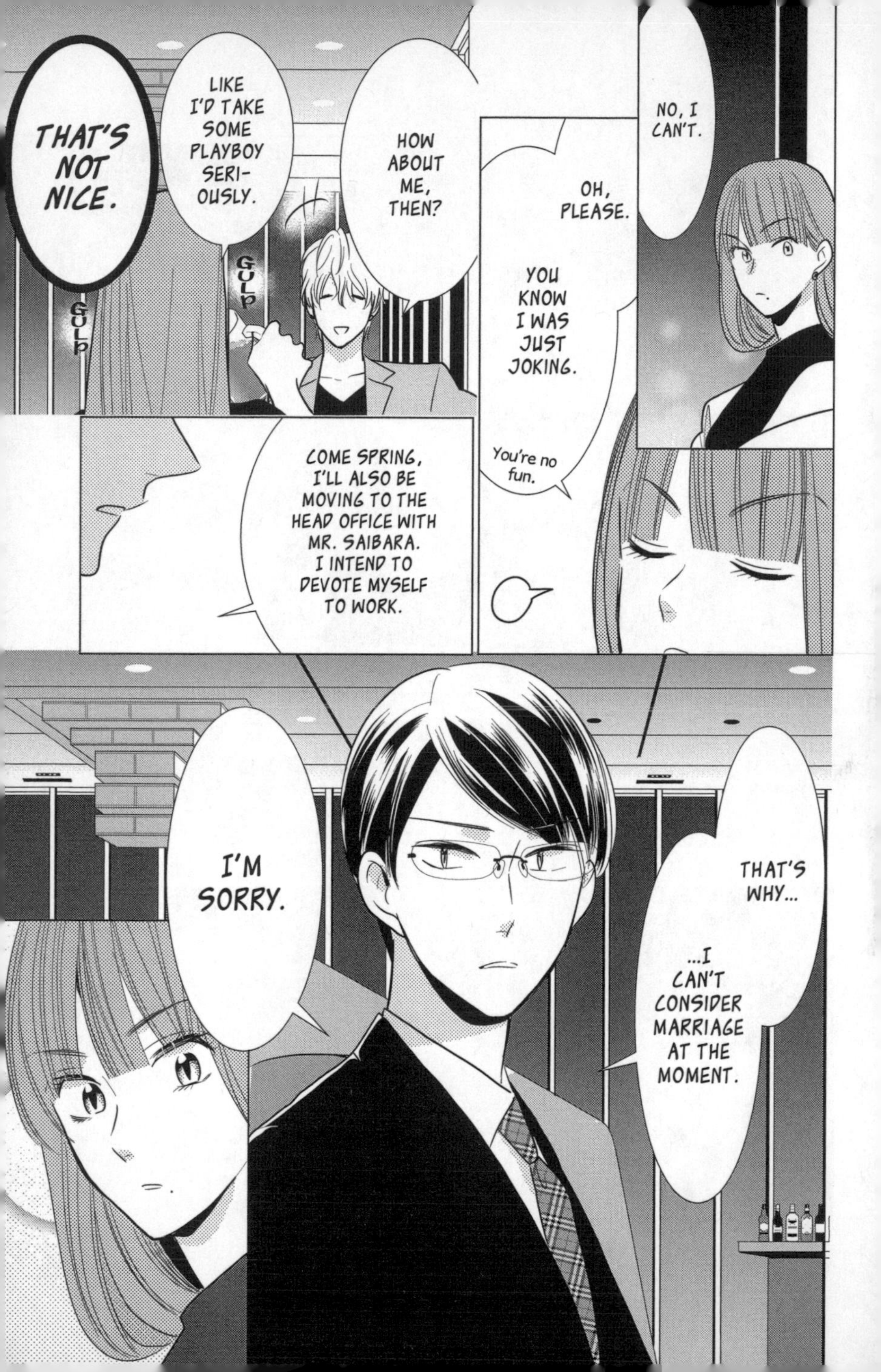
NO, I CAN'T.
HOW ABOUT ME, THEN?
LIKE I'D TAKE SOME PLAYBOY SERI-OUSLY.
GULP
GULP
THAT'S NOT NICE.
OH, PLEASE.
YOU KNOW I WAS JUST JOKING.
You're no fun.
COME SPRING, I'LL ALSO BE MOVING TO THE HEAD OFFICE WITH MR. SAIBARA. I INTEND TO DEVOTE MYSELF TO WORK.
THAT'S WHY...
...I CAN'T CONSIDER MARRIAGE AT THE MOMENT.
I'M SORRY.

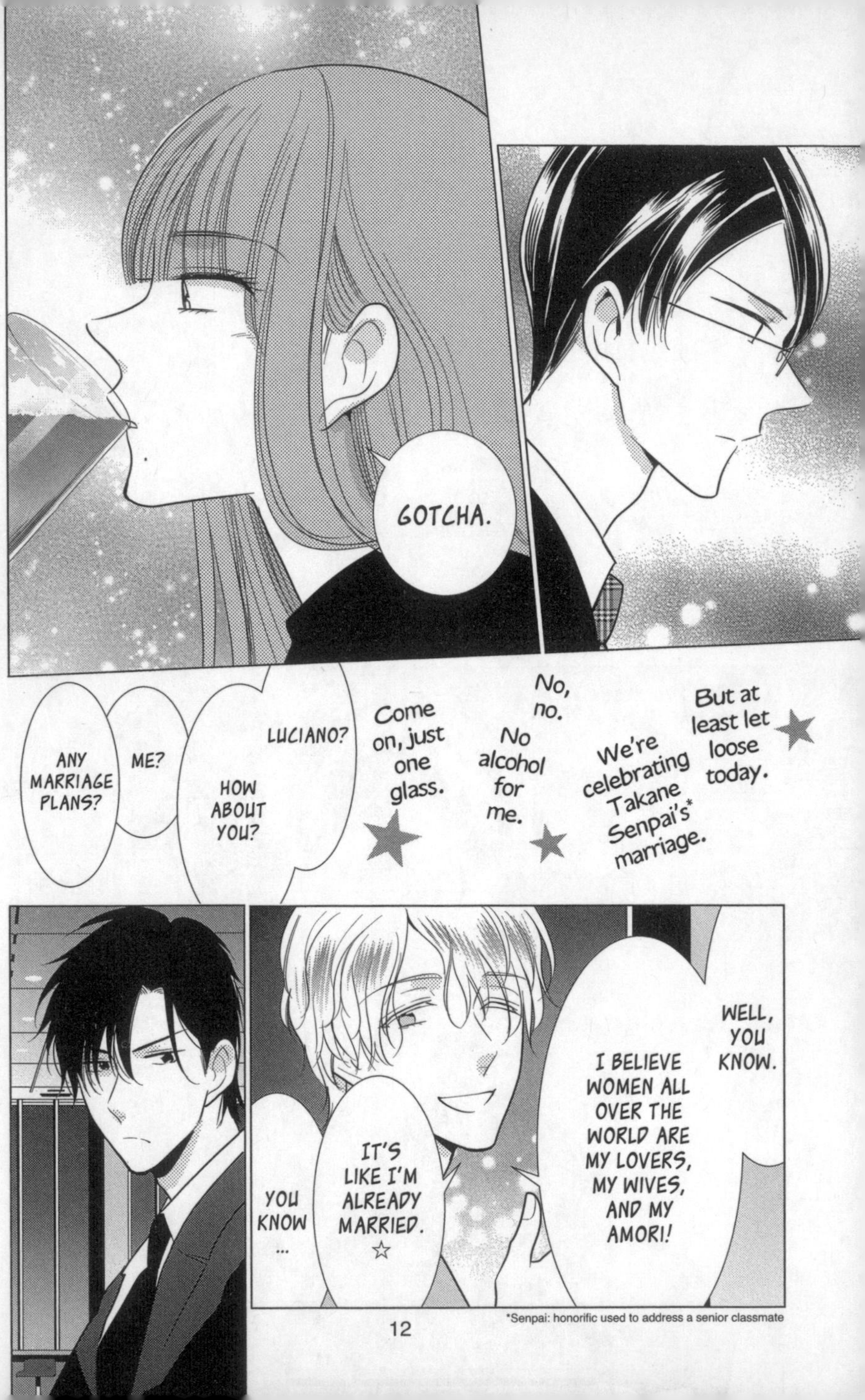
GOTCHA.
But at least let loose today.
We're celebrating Takane Senpai's* marriage.
No, no.
No alcohol for me.
Come on, just one glass.
LUCIANO?
HOW ABOUT YOU?
ME?
ANY MARRIAGE PLANS?
WELL, YOU KNOW.
I BELIEVE WOMEN ALL OVER THE WORLD ARE MY LOVERS, MY WIVES, AND MY AMORI!
IT'S LIKE I'M ALREADY MARRIED. ☆
YOU KNOW ...

*Senpai: honorific used to address a senior classmate

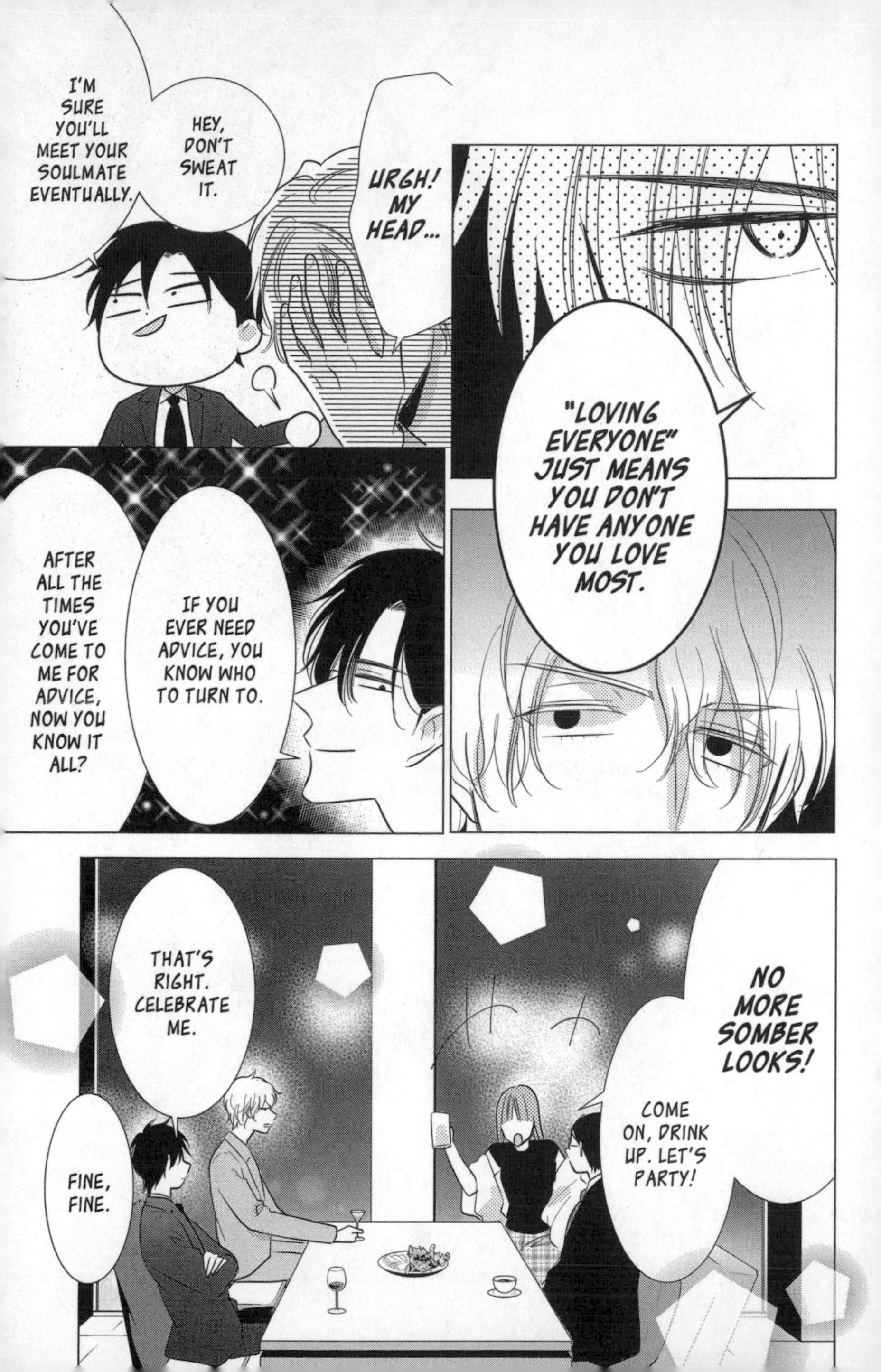
HEY, DON'T SWEAT IT.
I'M SURE YOU'LL MEET YOUR SOULMATE EVENTUALLY.
URGH! MY HEAD...
"LOVING EVERYONE" JUST MEANS YOU DON'T HAVE ANYONE YOU LOVE MOST.
IF YOU EVER NEED ADVICE, YOU KNOW WHO TO TURN TO.
AFTER ALL THE TIMES YOU'VE COME TO ME FOR ADVICE, NOW YOU KNOW IT ALL?
NO MORE SOMBER LOOKS!
COME ON, DRINK UP. LET'S PARTY!
THAT'S RIGHT. CELEBRATE ME.
FINE, FINE.

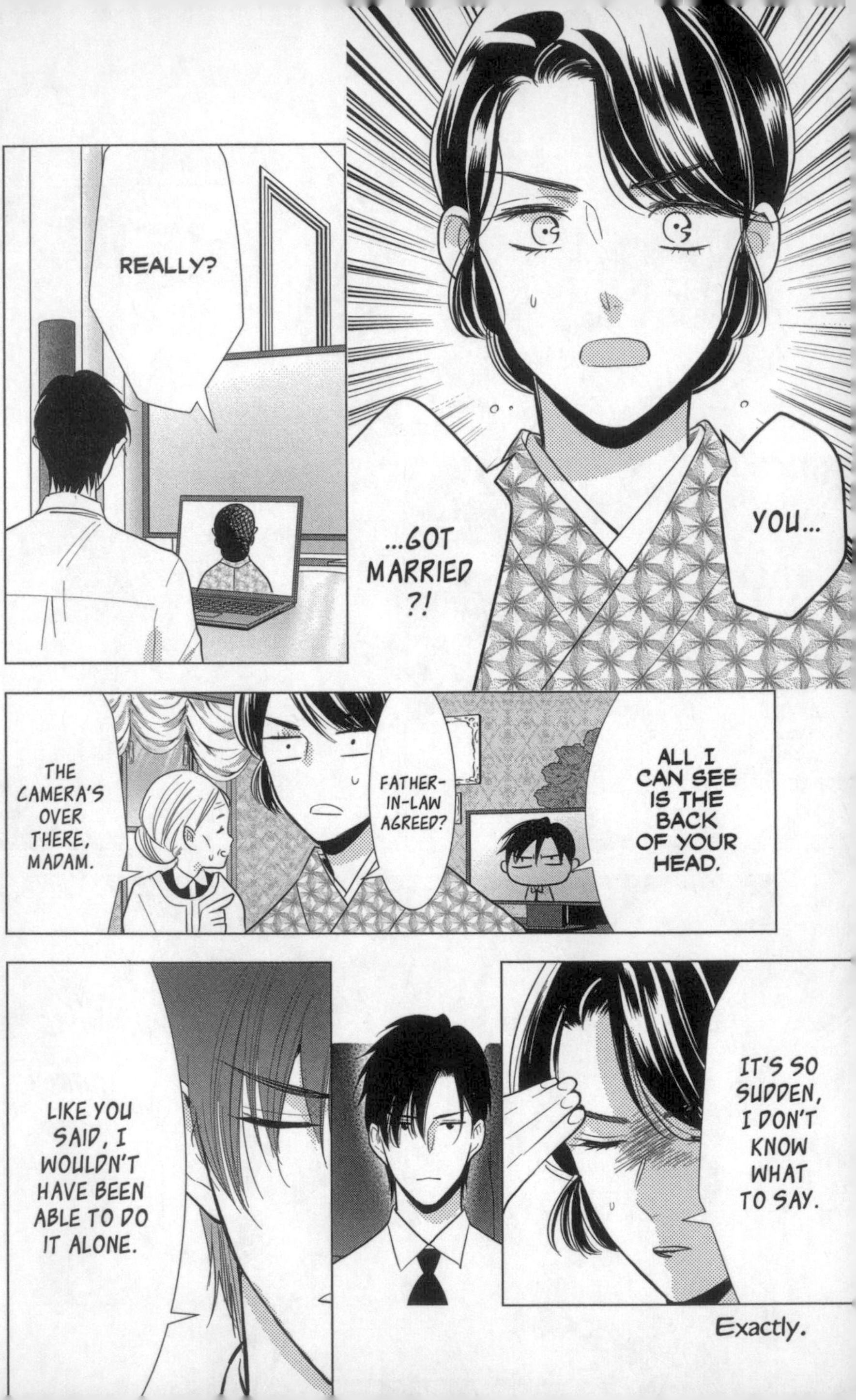
YOU...
...GOT MARRIED?!
REALLY?
ALL I CAN SEE IS THE BACK OF YOUR HEAD.
FATHER-IN-LAW AGREED?
THE CAMERA'S OVER THERE, MADAM.
IT'S SO SUDDEN, I DON'T KNOW WHAT TO SAY.
Exactly.
LIKE YOU SAID, I WOULDN'T HAVE BEEN ABLE TO DO IT ALONE.

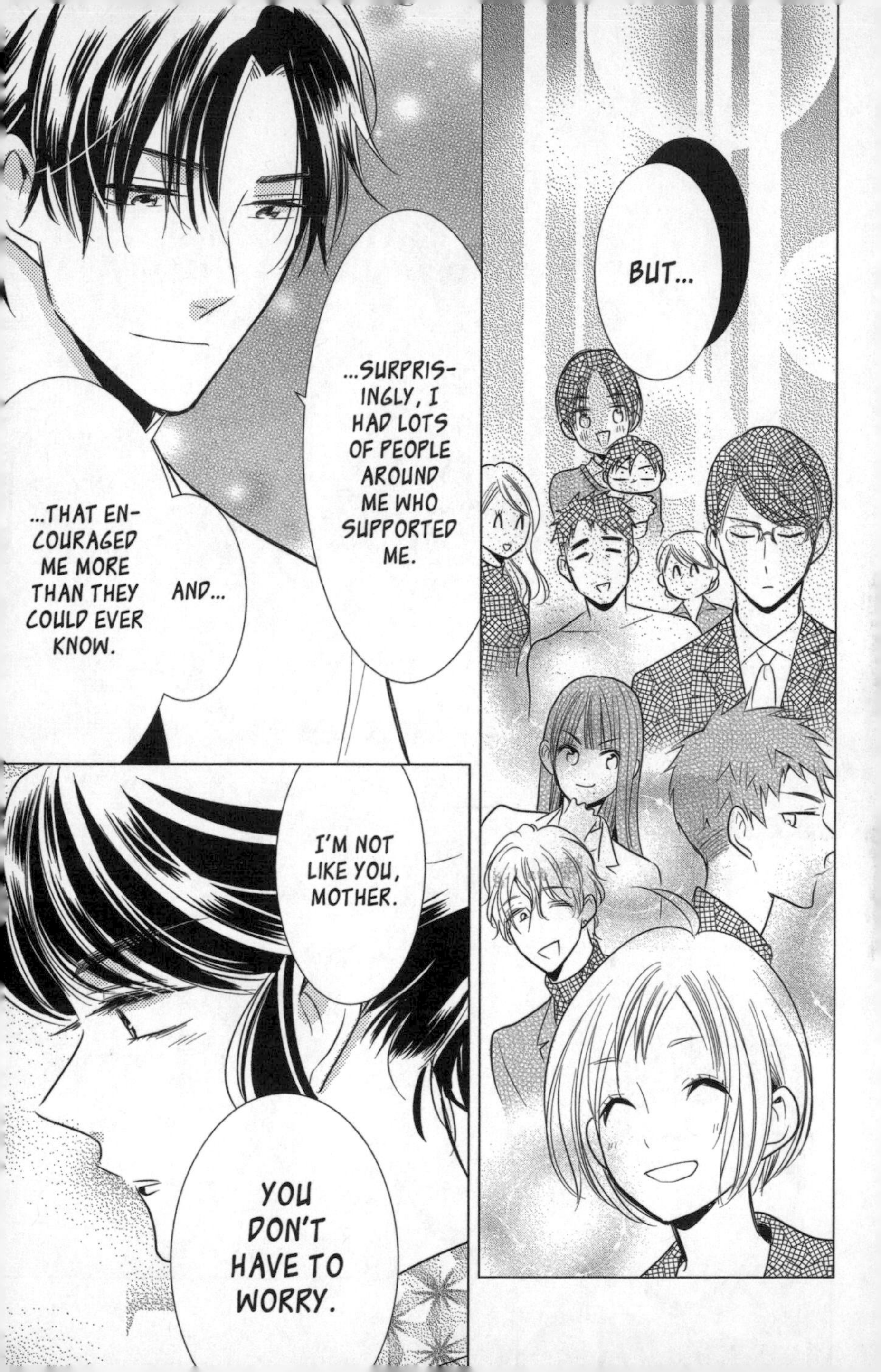
BUT...
...SURPRIS-INGLY, I HAD LOTS OF PEOPLE AROUND ME WHO SUPPORTED ME.
AND...
...THAT EN-COURAGED ME MORE THAN THEY COULD EVER KNOW.
I'M NOT LIKE YOU, MOTHER.
YOU DON'T HAVE TO WORRY.

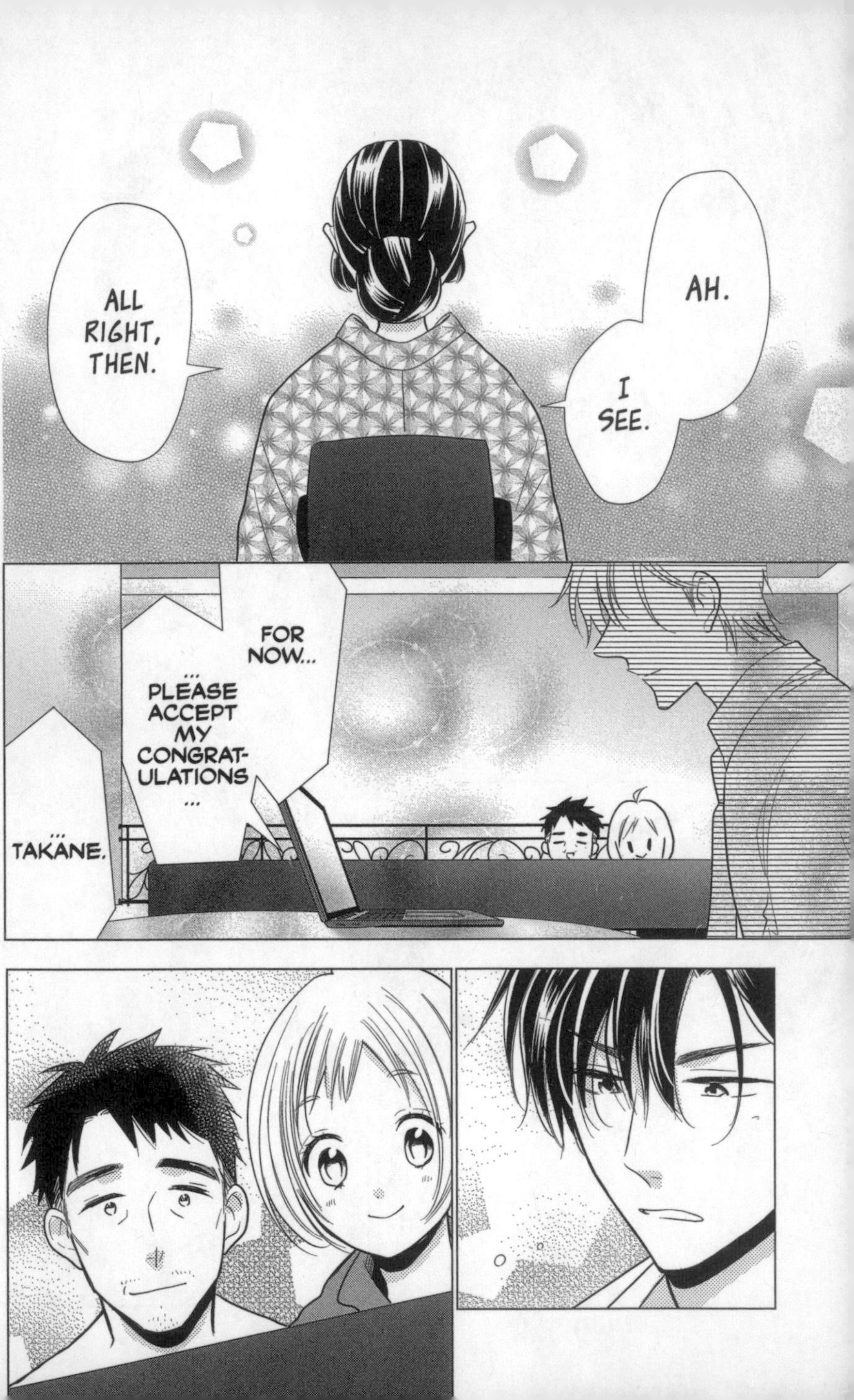
AH.
I SEE.
ALL RIGHT, THEN.
FOR NOW...
...PLEASE ACCEPT MY CONGRATULATIONS...
...TAKANE.

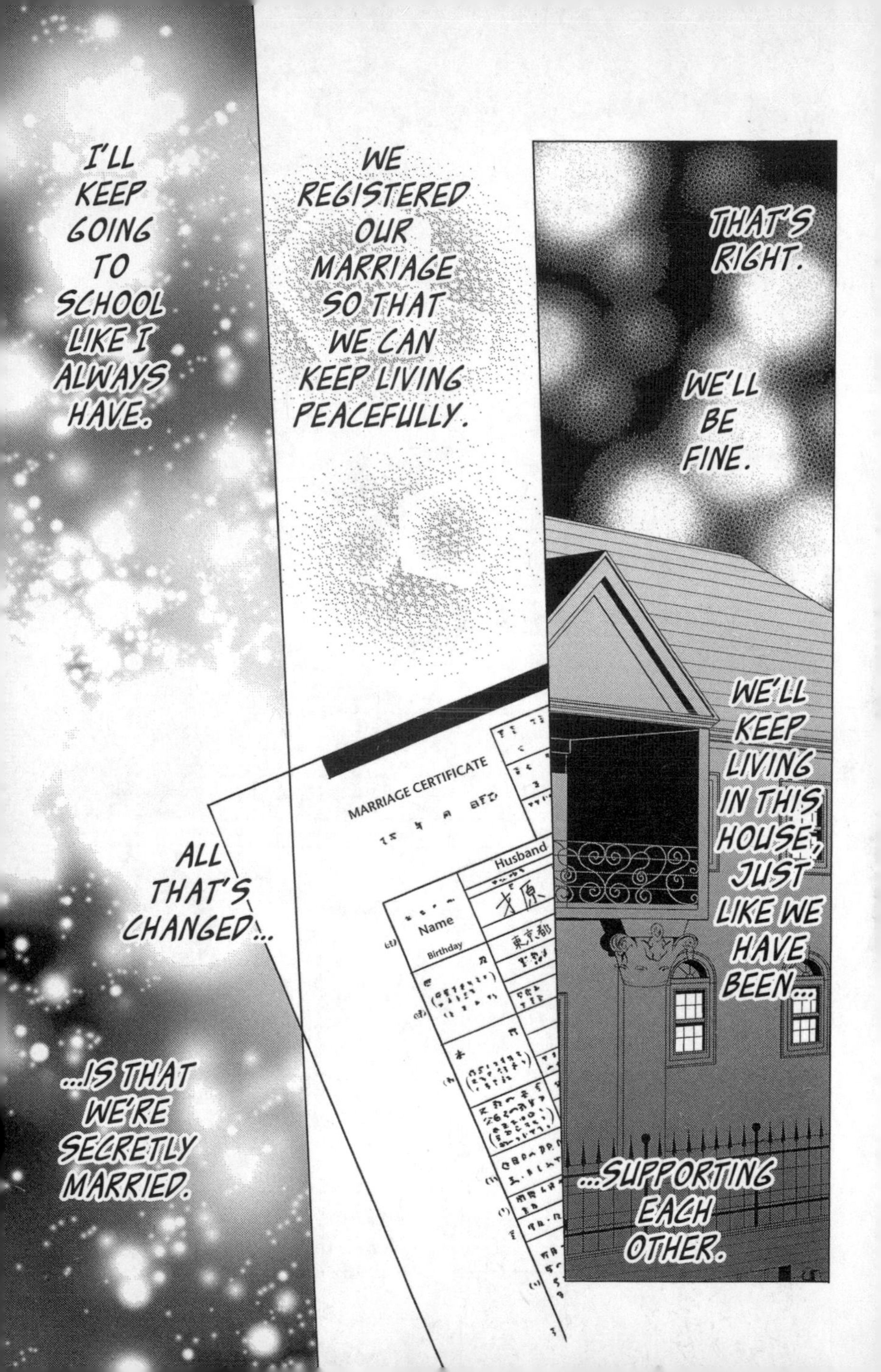
THAT'S RIGHT.
WE'LL BE FINE.
WE'LL KEEP LIVING IN THIS HOUSE, JUST LIKE WE HAVE BEEN...
...SUPPORTING EACH OTHER.
WE REGISTERED OUR MARRIAGE SO THAT WE CAN KEEP LIVING PEACEFULLY.
MARRIAGE CERTIFICATE
Husband
Name
Birthday
I'LL KEEP GOING TO SCHOOL LIKE I ALWAYS HAVE.
ALL THAT'S CHANGED...
...IS THAT WE'RE SECRETLY MARRIED.

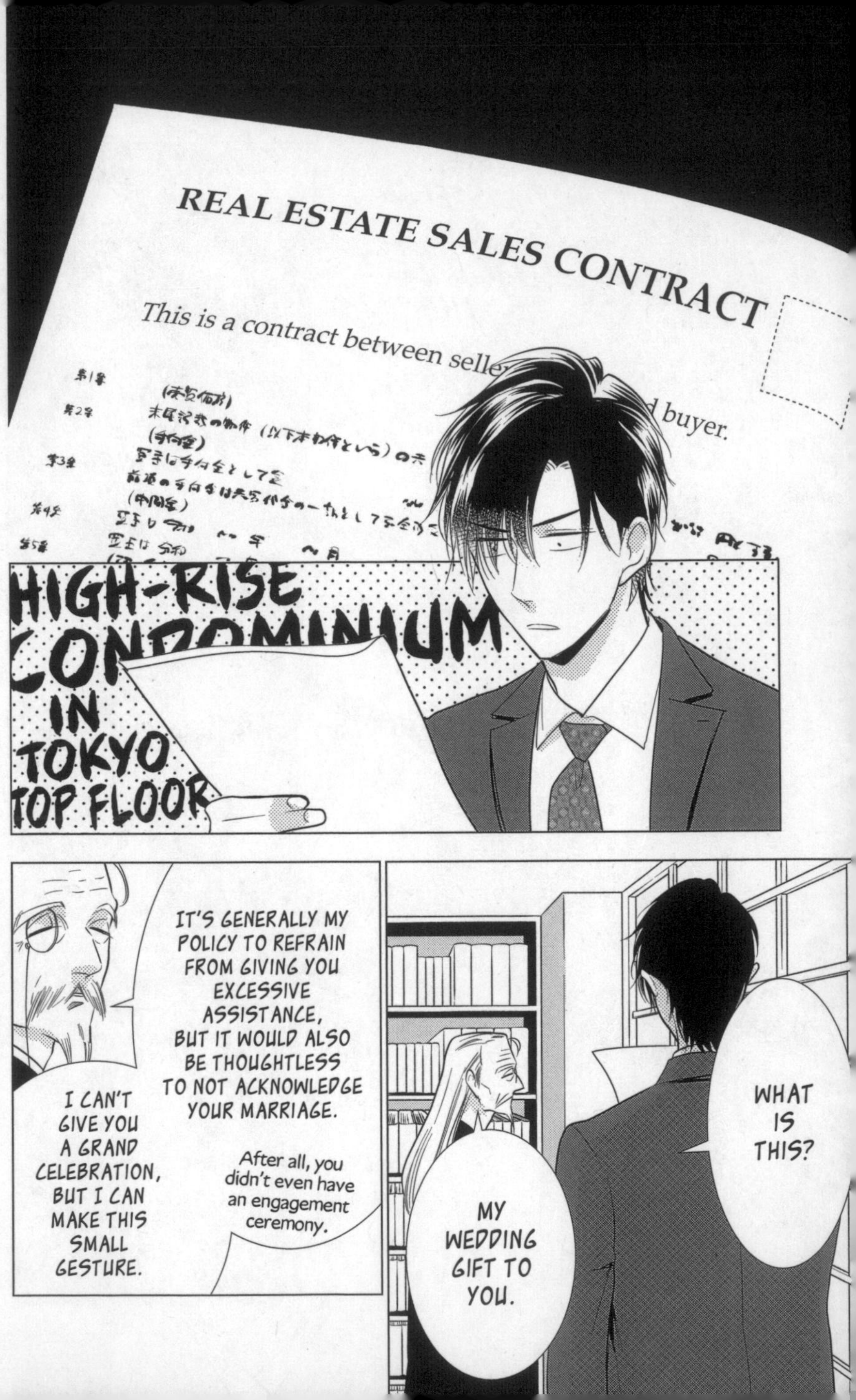
REAL ESTATE SALES CONTRACT
This is a contract between seller and buyer.
HIGH-RISE CONDOMINIUM IN TOKYO TOP FLOOR
WHAT IS THIS?
MY WEDDING GIFT TO YOU.
IT'S GENERALLY MY POLICY TO REFRAIN FROM GIVING YOU EXCESSIVE ASSISTANCE, BUT IT WOULD ALSO BE THOUGHTLESS TO NOT ACKNOWLEDGE YOUR MARRIAGE.
After all, you didn't even have an engagement ceremony.
I CAN'T GIVE YOU A GRAND CELEBRATION, BUT I CAN MAKE THIS SMALL GESTURE.

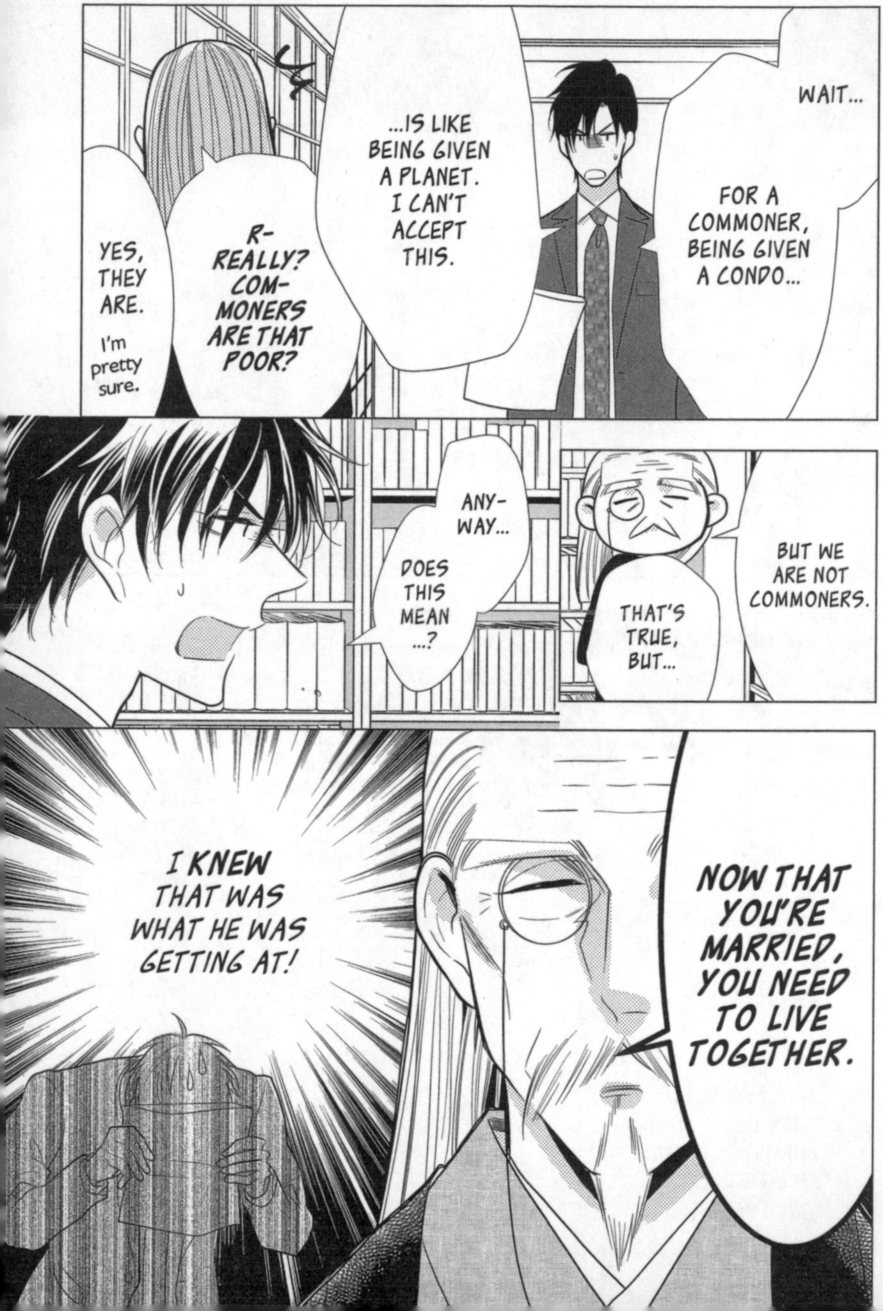
WAIT...
FOR A COMMONER, BEING GIVEN A CONDO...
...IS LIKE BEING GIVEN A PLANET. I CAN'T ACCEPT THIS.
R-REALLY? COM-MONERS ARE THAT POOR?
YES, THEY ARE.
I'm pretty sure.
BUT WE ARE NOT COMMONERS.
THAT'S TRUE, BUT...
ANY-WAY...
DOES THIS MEAN ...?
NOW THAT YOU'RE MARRIED, YOU NEED TO LIVE TOGETHER.
I KNEW THAT WAS WHAT HE WAS GETTING AT!

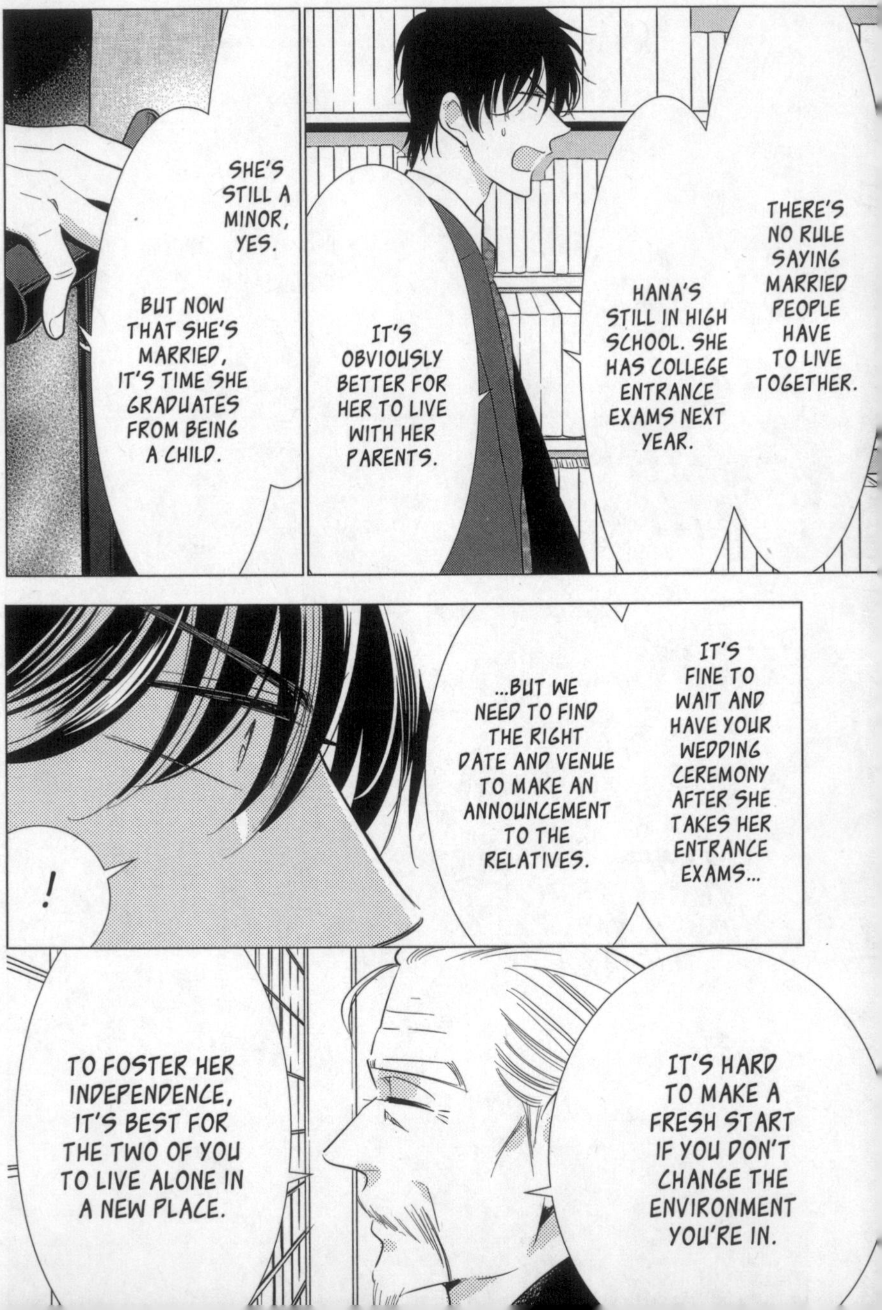
THERE'S NO RULE SAYING MARRIED PEOPLE HAVE TO LIVE TOGETHER.
HANA'S STILL IN HIGH SCHOOL. SHE HAS COLLEGE ENTRANCE EXAMS NEXT YEAR.
IT'S OBVIOUSLY BETTER FOR HER TO LIVE WITH HER PARENTS.
SHE'S STILL A MINOR, YES.
BUT NOW THAT SHE'S MARRIED, IT'S TIME SHE GRADUATES FROM BEING A CHILD.
IT'S FINE TO WAIT AND HAVE YOUR WEDDING CEREMONY AFTER SHE TAKES HER ENTRANCE EXAMS...
...BUT WE NEED TO FIND THE RIGHT DATE AND VENUE TO MAKE AN ANNOUNCEMENT TO THE RELATIVES.
!
IT'S HARD TO MAKE A FRESH START IF YOU DON'T CHANGE THE ENVIRONMENT YOU'RE IN.
TO FOSTER HER INDEPENDENCE, IT'S BEST FOR THE TWO OF YOU TO LIVE ALONE IN A NEW PLACE.

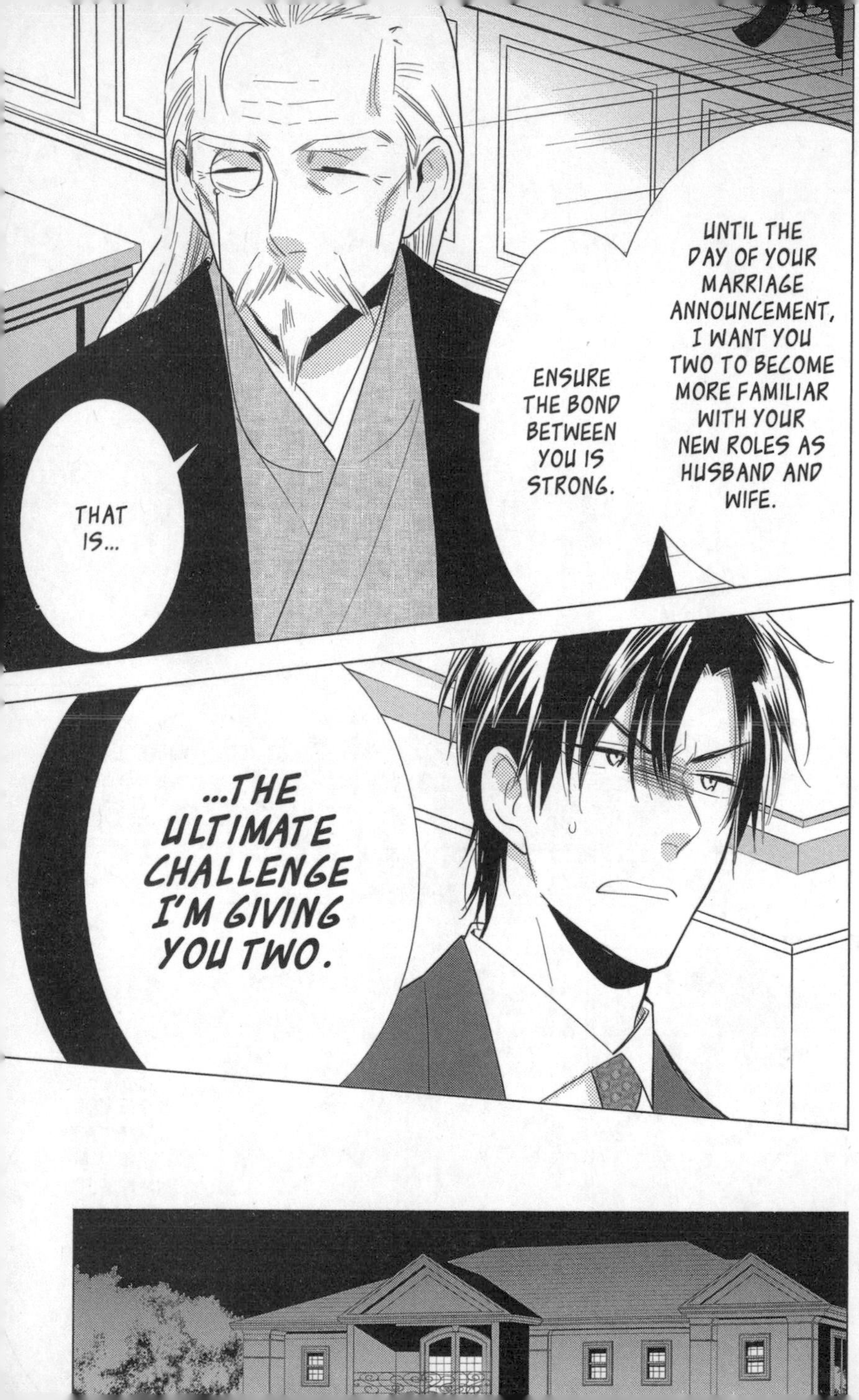
UNTIL THE DAY OF YOUR MARRIAGE ANNOUNCEMENT, I WANT YOU TWO TO BECOME MORE FAMILIAR WITH YOUR NEW ROLES AS HUSBAND AND WIFE.
ENSURE THE BOND BETWEEN YOU IS STRONG.
THAT IS...
...THE ULTIMATE CHALLENGE I'M GIVING YOU TWO.

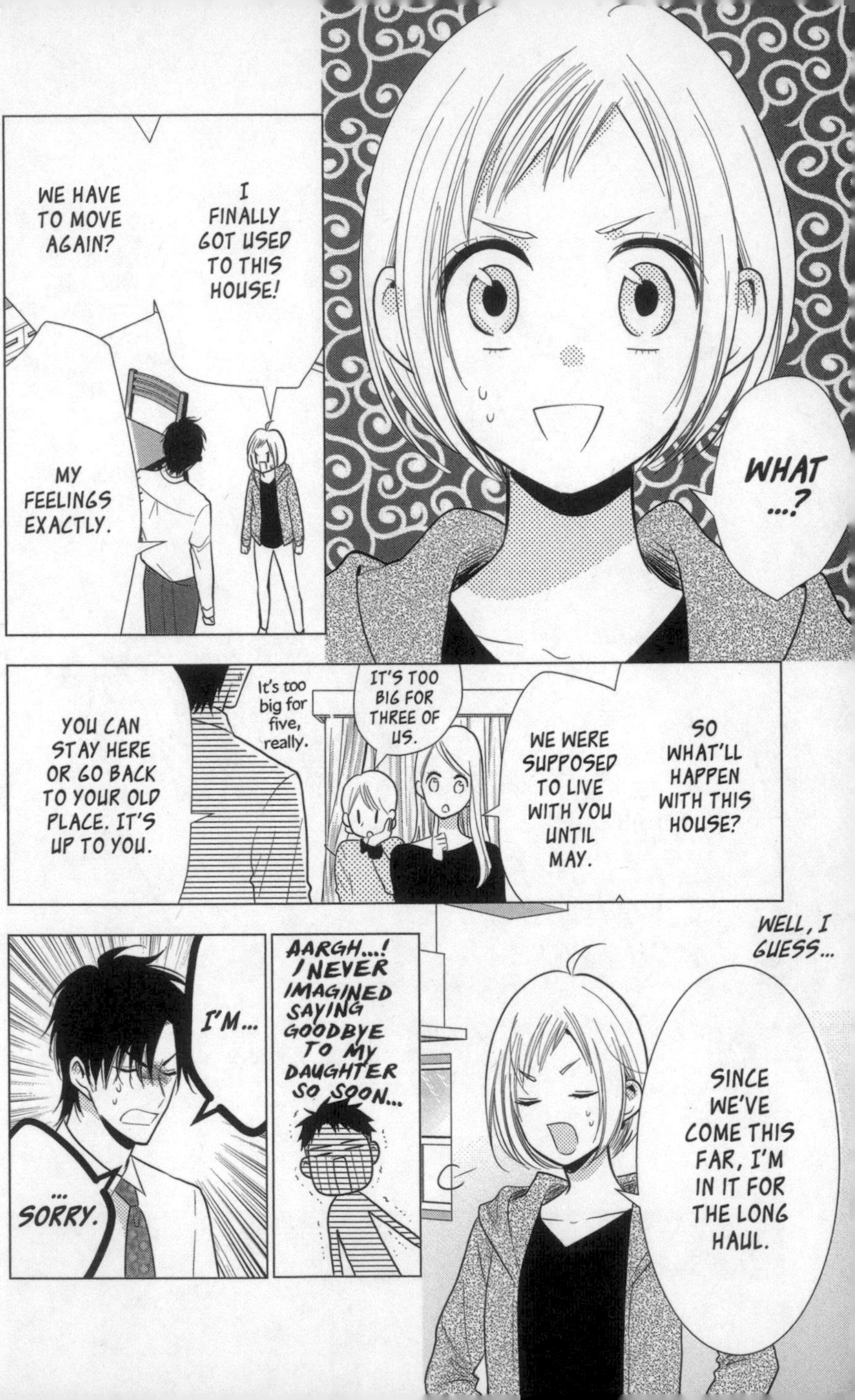
WHAT ...?
WE HAVE TO MOVE AGAIN?
I FINALLY GOT USED TO THIS HOUSE!
MY FEELINGS EXACTLY.
SO WHAT'LL HAPPEN WITH THIS HOUSE?
WE WERE SUPPOSED TO LIVE WITH YOU UNTIL MAY.
IT'S TOO BIG FOR THREE OF US.
It's too big for five, really.
YOU CAN STAY HERE OR GO BACK TO YOUR OLD PLACE. IT'S UP TO YOU.
WELL, I GUESS...
SINCE WE'VE COME THIS FAR, I'M IN IT FOR THE LONG HAUL.
AARGH...! I NEVER IMAGINED SAYING GOODBYE TO MY DAUGHTER SO SOON...
I'M...
... SORRY.

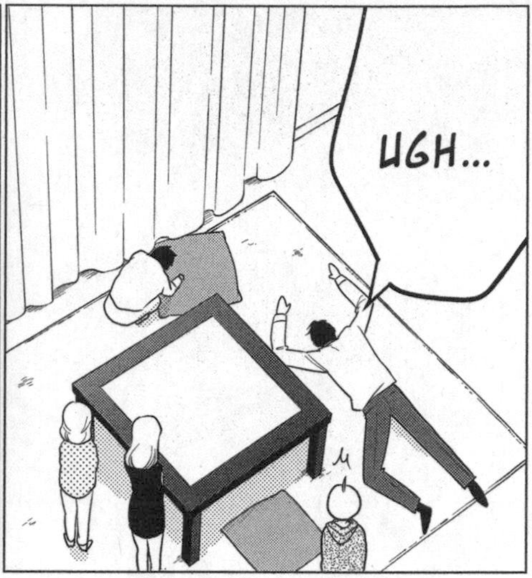
UGH...

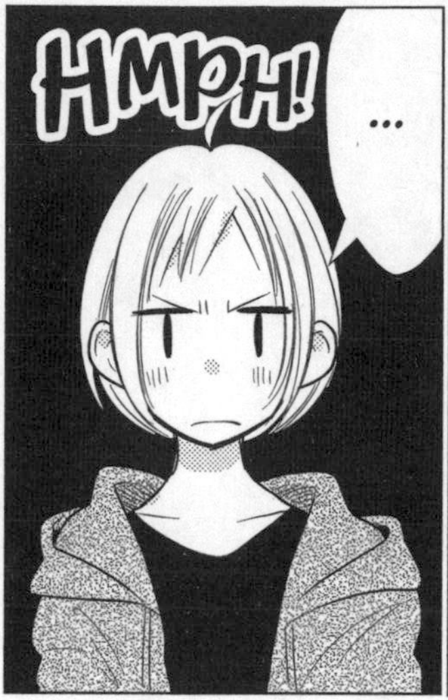
HMPH!
...

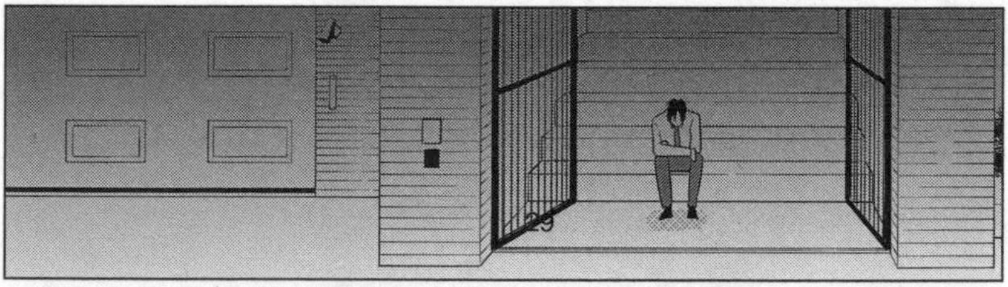
29

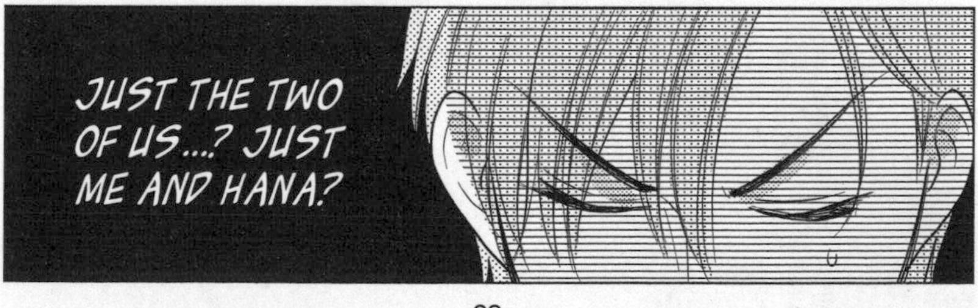
JUST THE TWO OF US...? JUST ME AND HANA?

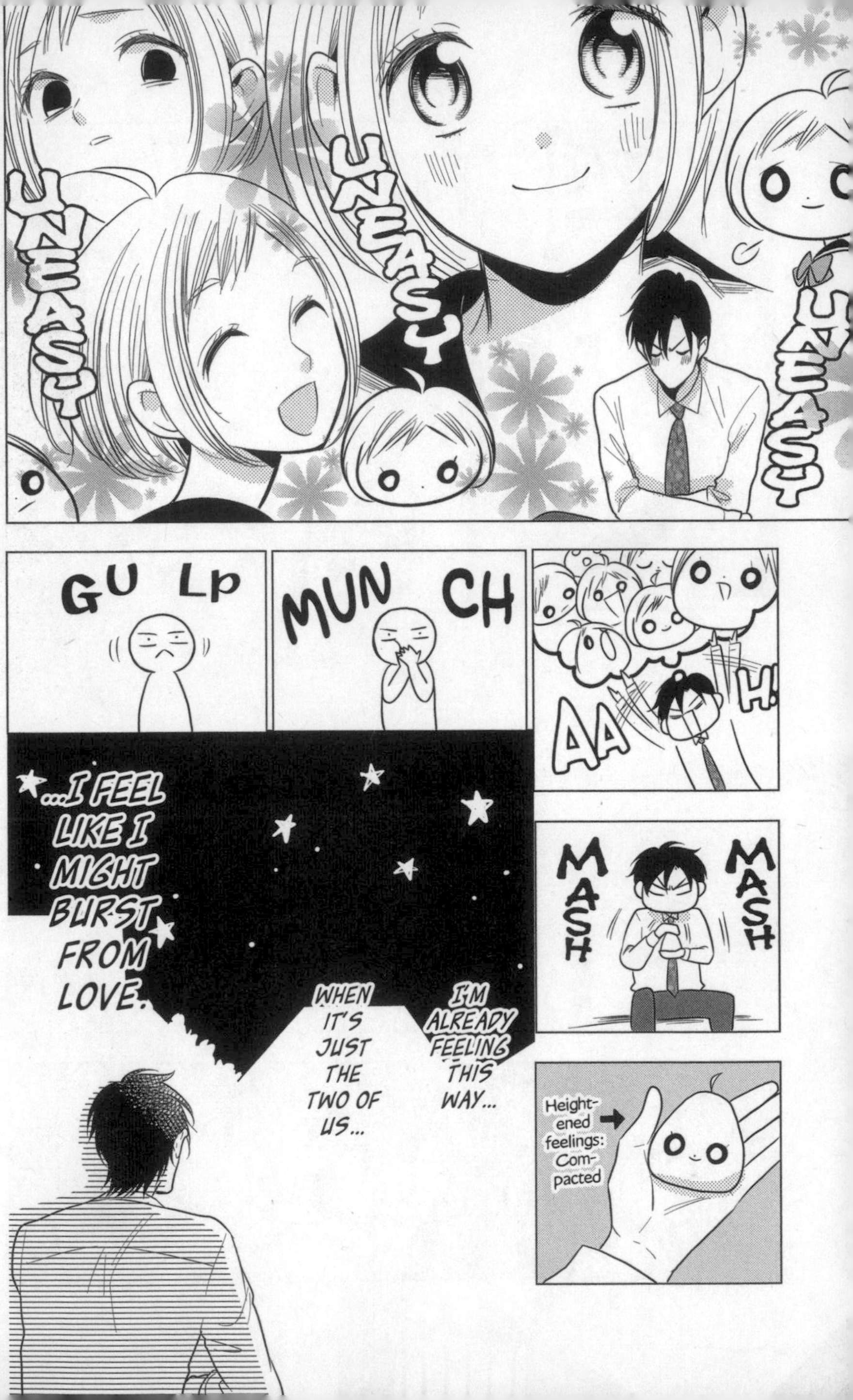
UNEASY
UNEASY
UNEASY
AA H!
MUN CH
GU Lp
MASH MASH
Height-ened feelings: Com-pacted
...I FEEL LIKE I MIGHT BURST FROM LOVE.
I'M ALREADY FEELING THIS WAY...
WHEN IT'S JUST THE TWO OF US...

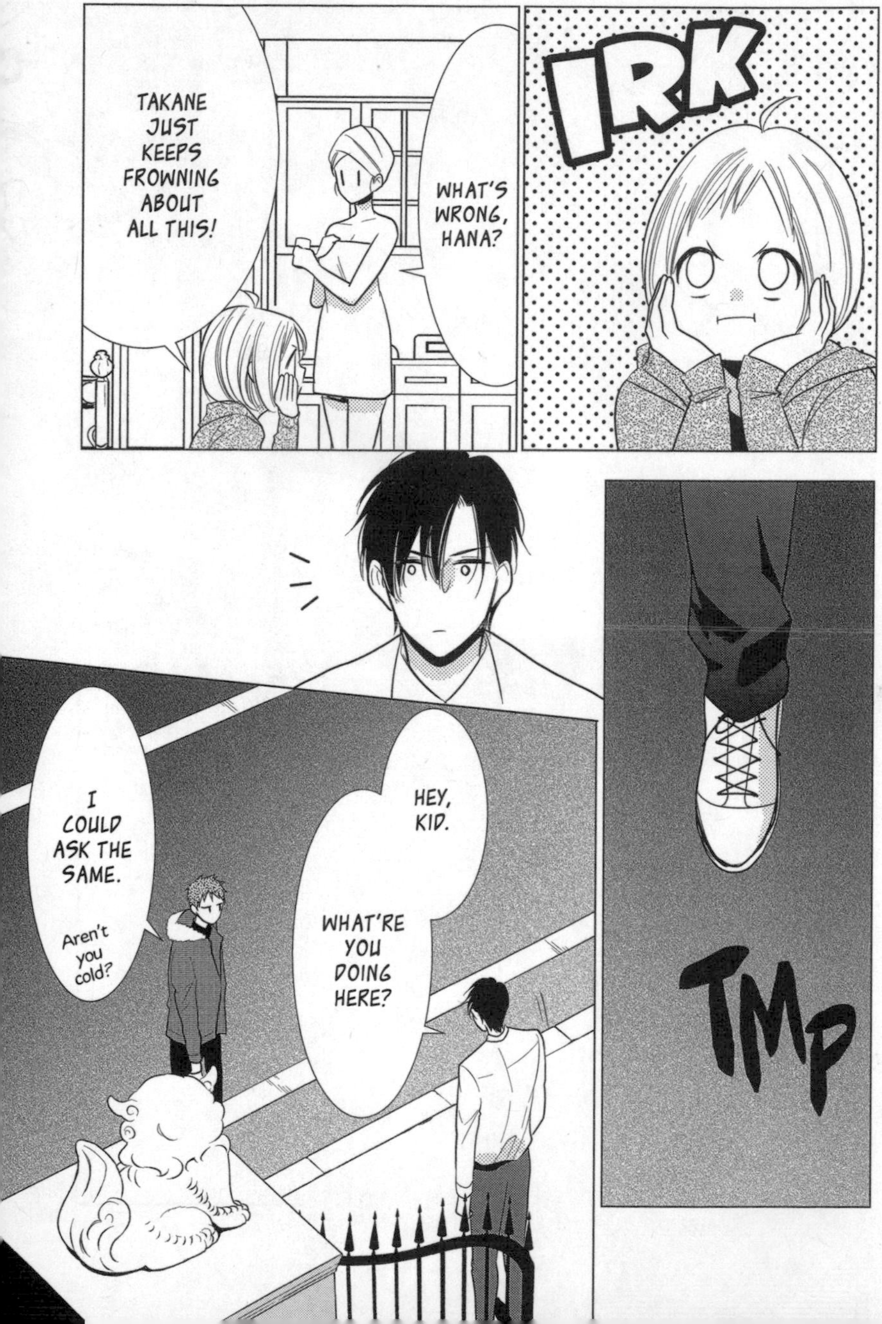
IRK
WHAT'S WRONG, HANA?
TAKANE JUST KEEPS FROWNING ABOUT ALL THIS!
TMP
HEY, KID.
WHAT'RE YOU DOING HERE?
I COULD ASK THE SAME.
Aren't you cold?

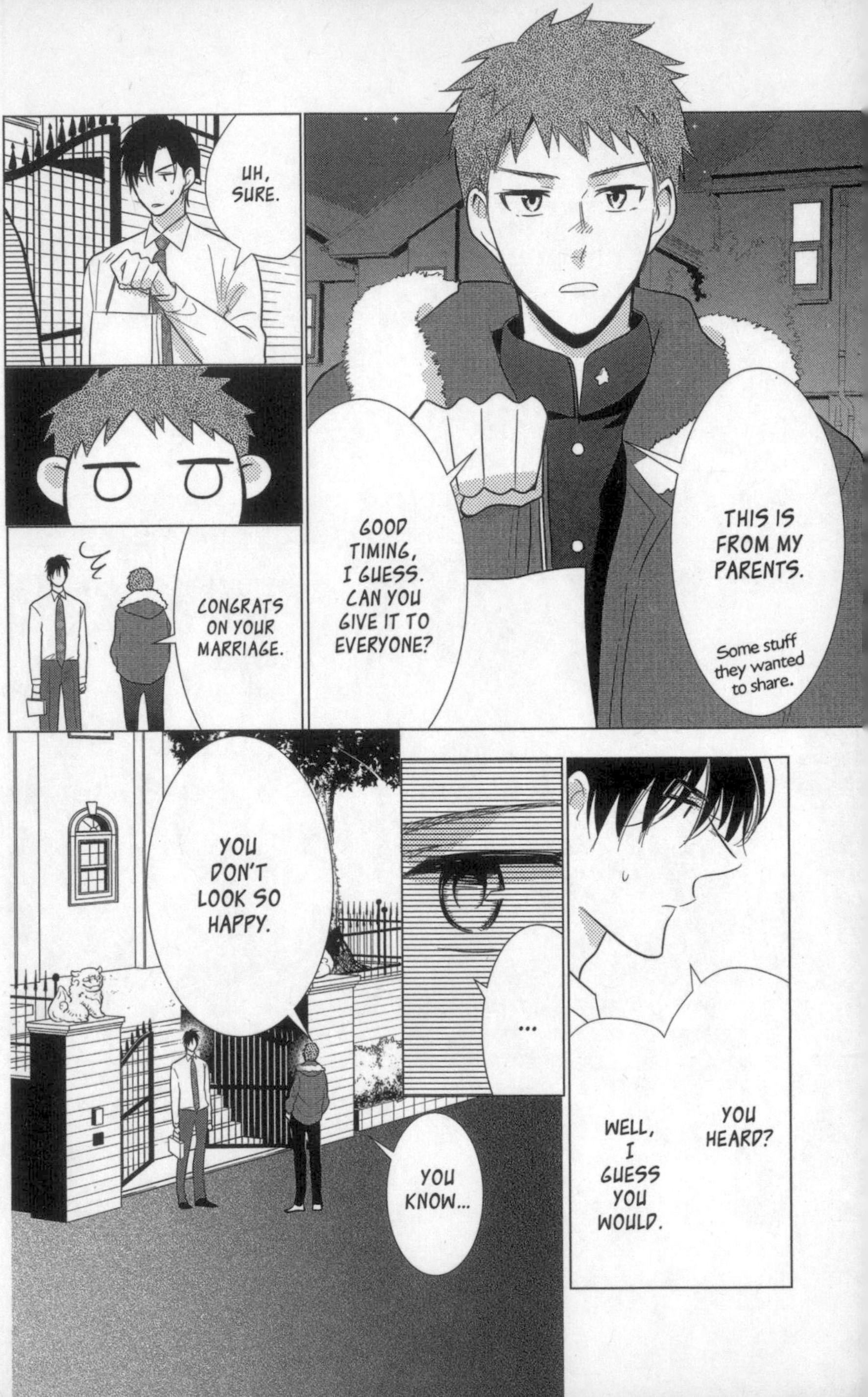
THIS IS FROM MY PARENTS.
Some stuff they wanted to share.
GOOD TIMING, I GUESS. CAN YOU GIVE IT TO EVERYONE?
UH, SURE.
CONGRATS ON YOUR MARRIAGE.
YOU HEARD?
WELL, I GUESS YOU WOULD.
...
YOU DON'T LOOK SO HAPPY.
YOU KNOW...

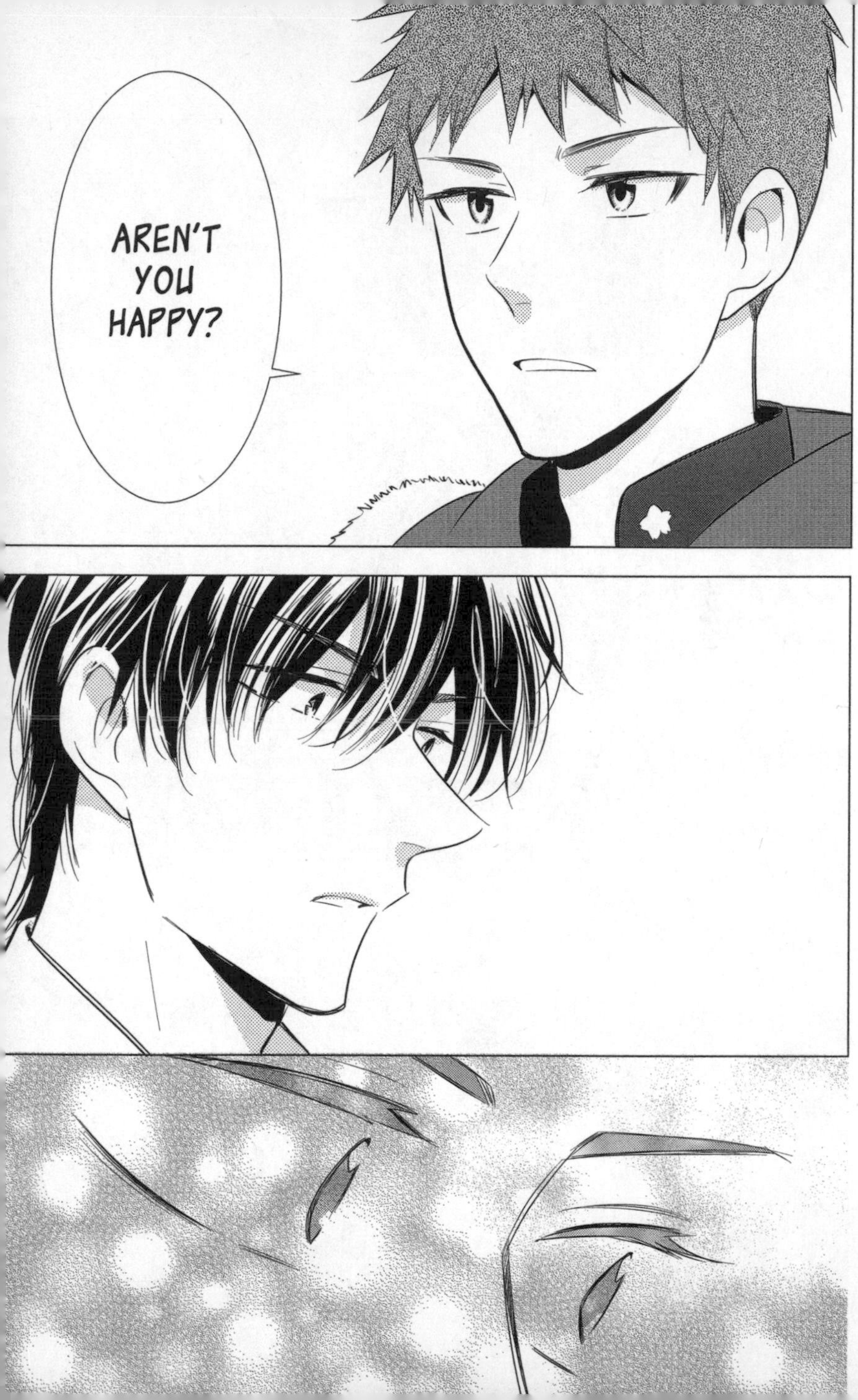
AREN'T YOU HAPPY?

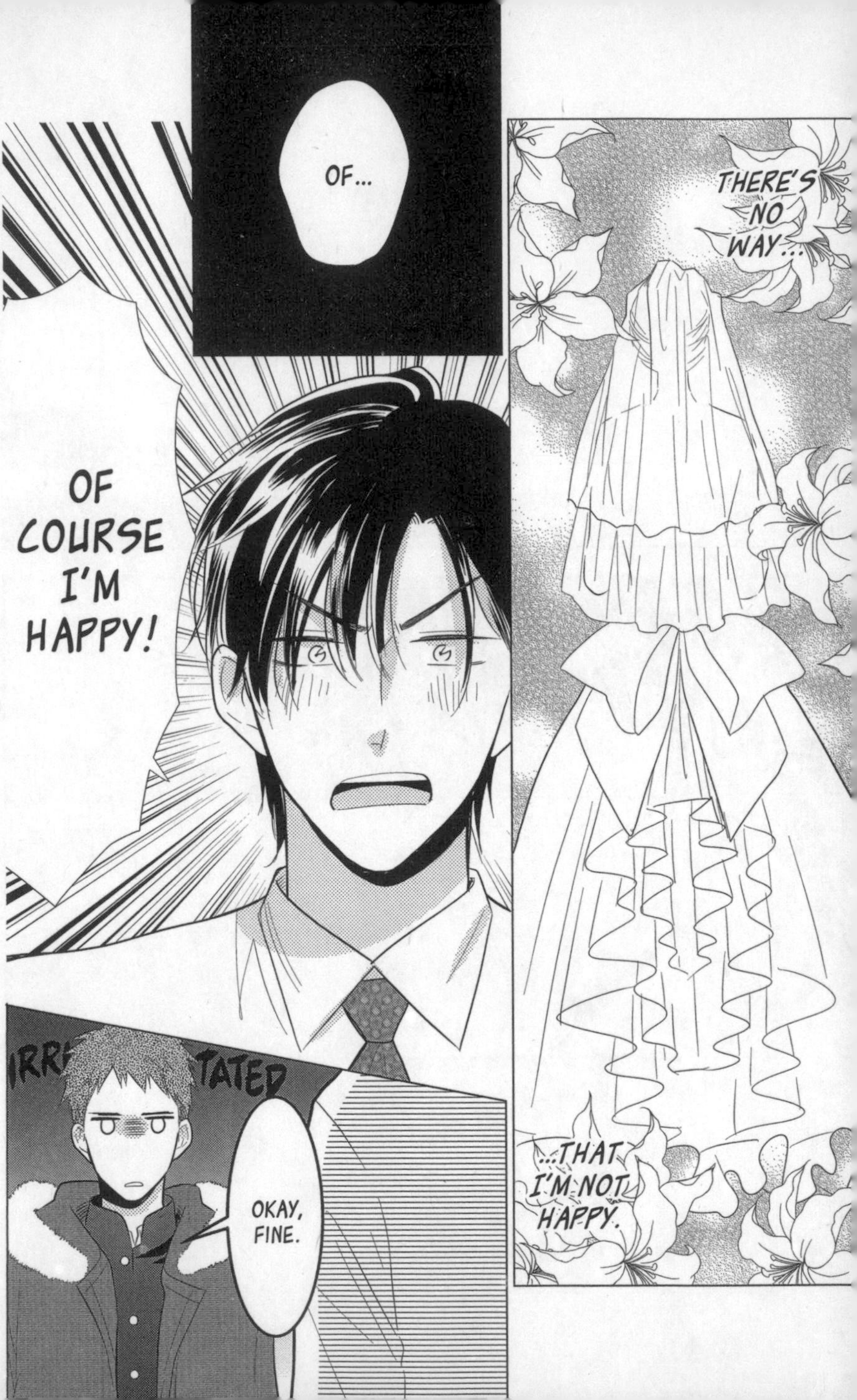
THERE'S NO WAY...
...THAT I'M NOT HAPPY.
OF...
OF COURSE I'M HAPPY!
OKAY, FINE.

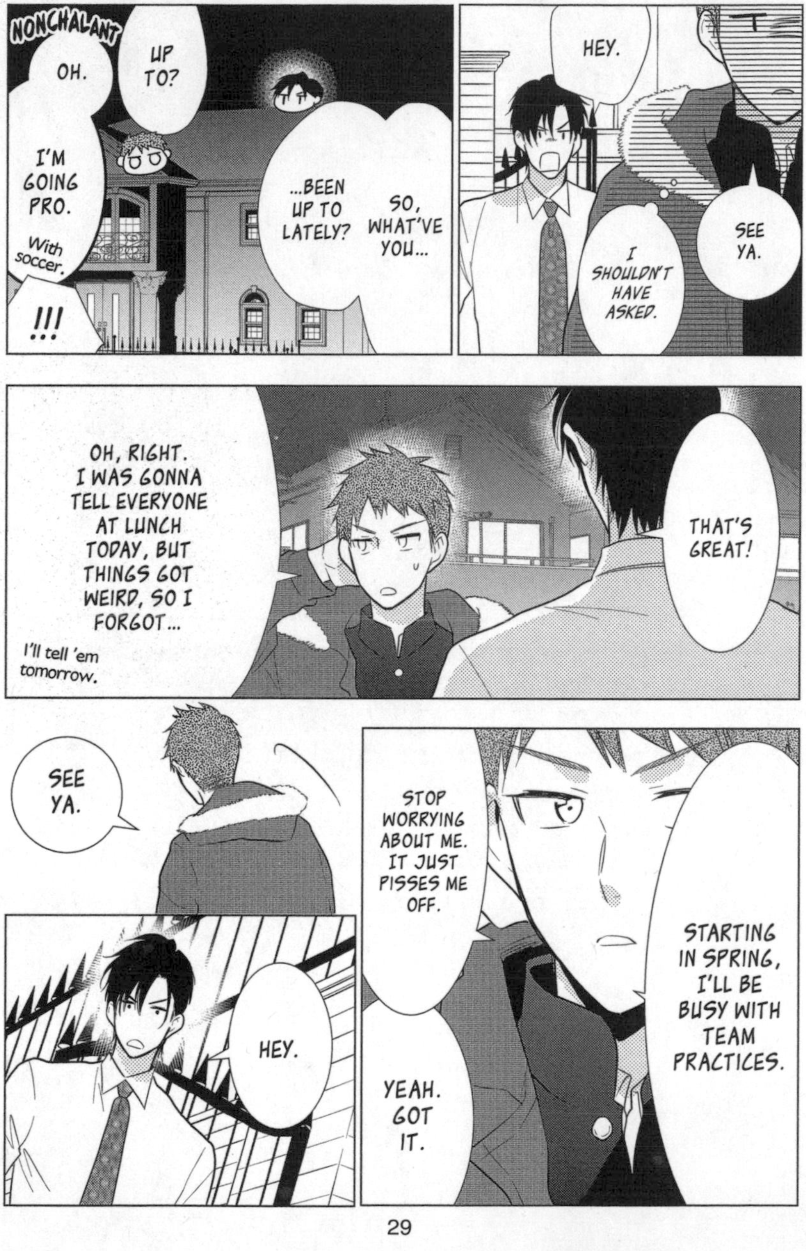
HEY.
SEE YA.
I SHOULDN'T HAVE ASKED.
SO, WHAT'VE YOU...
...BEEN UP TO LATELY?
UP TO?
NONCHALANT
OH.
I'M GOING PRO.
With soccer.
!!!
THAT'S GREAT!
OH, RIGHT. I WAS GONNA TELL EVERYONE AT LUNCH TODAY, BUT THINGS GOT WEIRD, SO I FORGOT...
I'll tell 'em tomorrow.
STARTING IN SPRING, I'LL BE BUSY WITH TEAM PRACTICES.
STOP WORRYING ABOUT ME. IT JUST PISSES ME OFF.
YEAH. GOT IT.
SEE YA.
HEY.

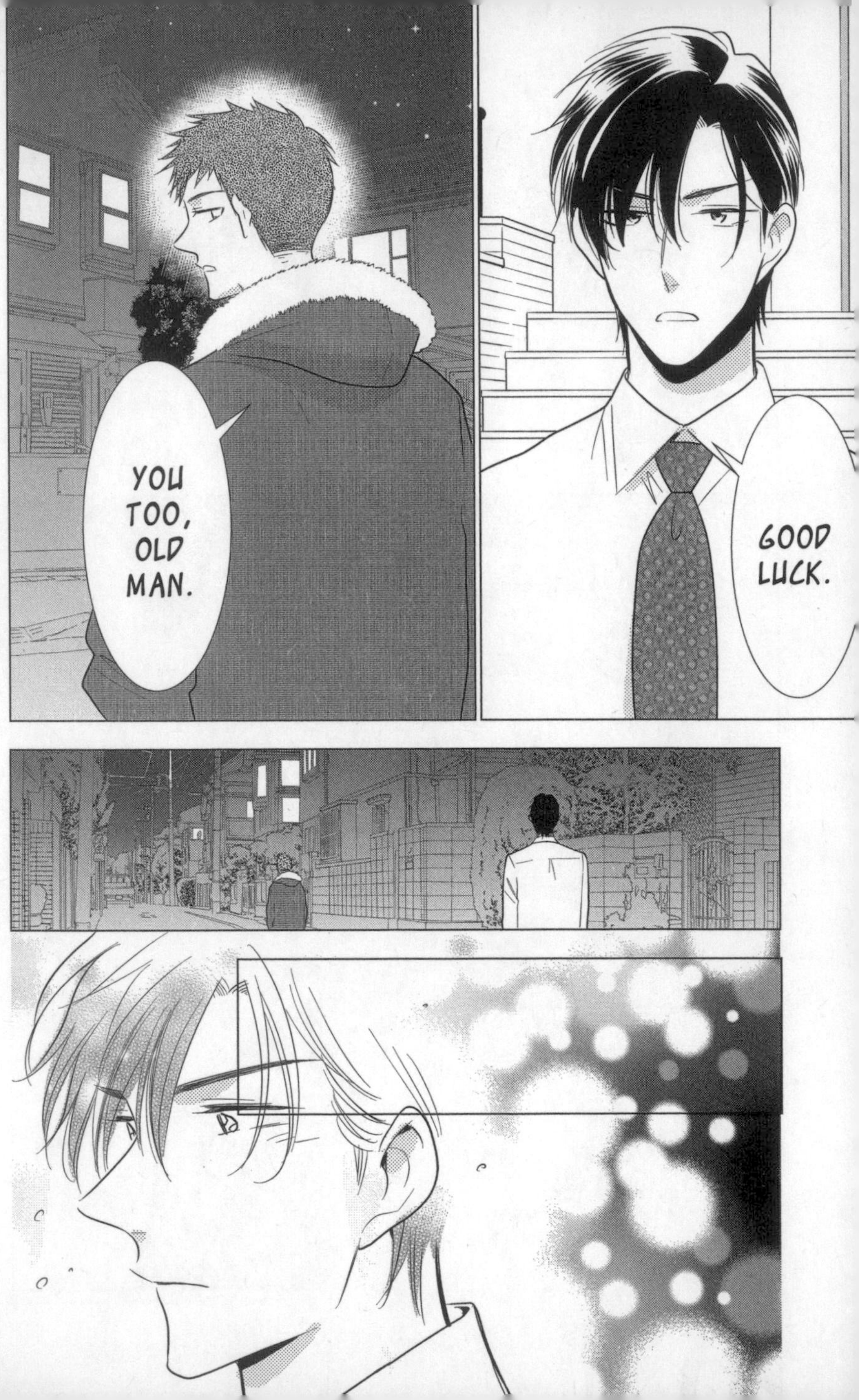
GOOD LUCK.
YOU TOO, OLD MAN.

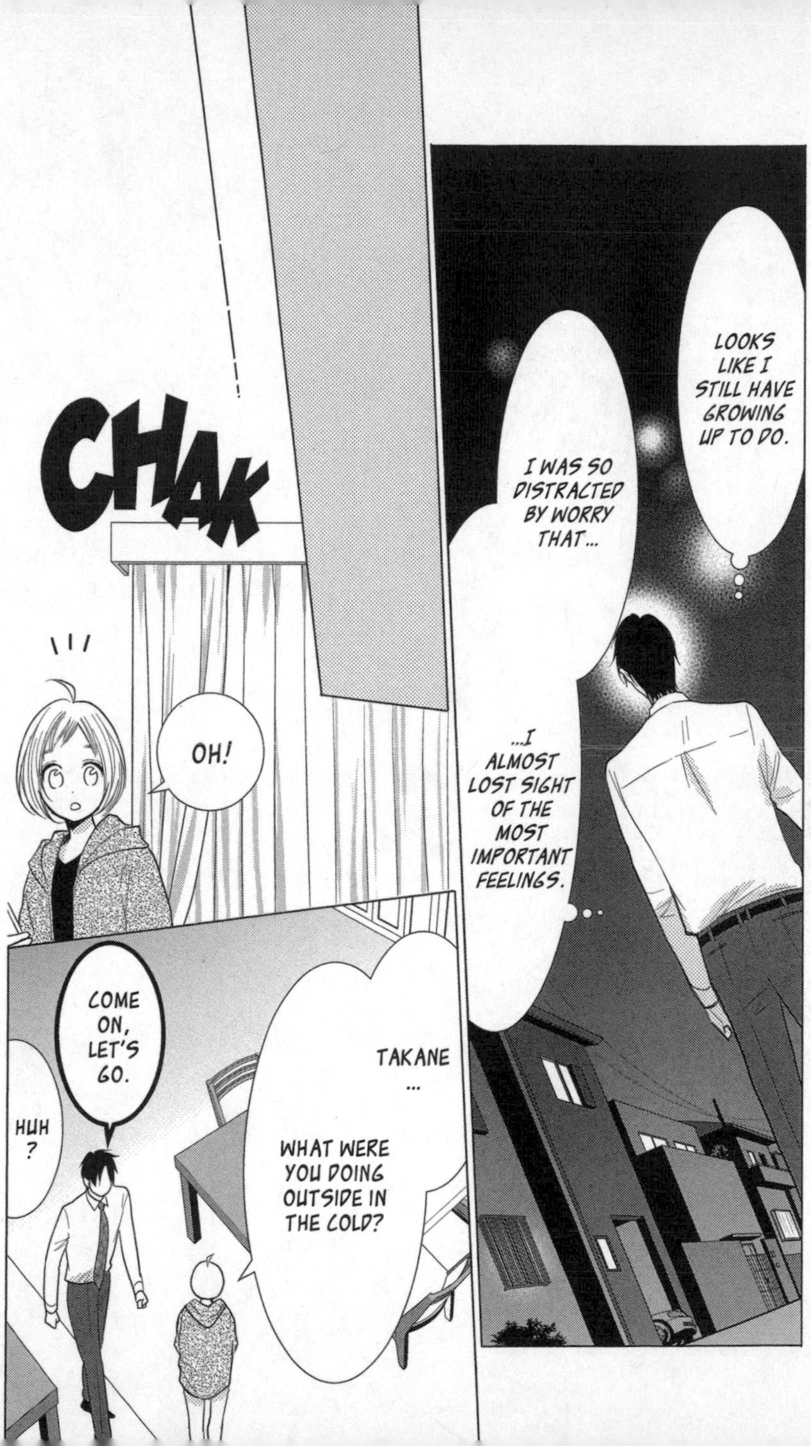
LOOKS LIKE I STILL HAVE GROWING UP TO DO.
I WAS SO DISTRACTED BY WORRY THAT...
...I ALMOST LOST SIGHT OF THE MOST IMPORTANT FEELINGS.
CHAK
OH!
TAKANE...
WHAT WERE YOU DOING OUTSIDE IN THE COLD?
COME ON, LET'S GO.
HUH?

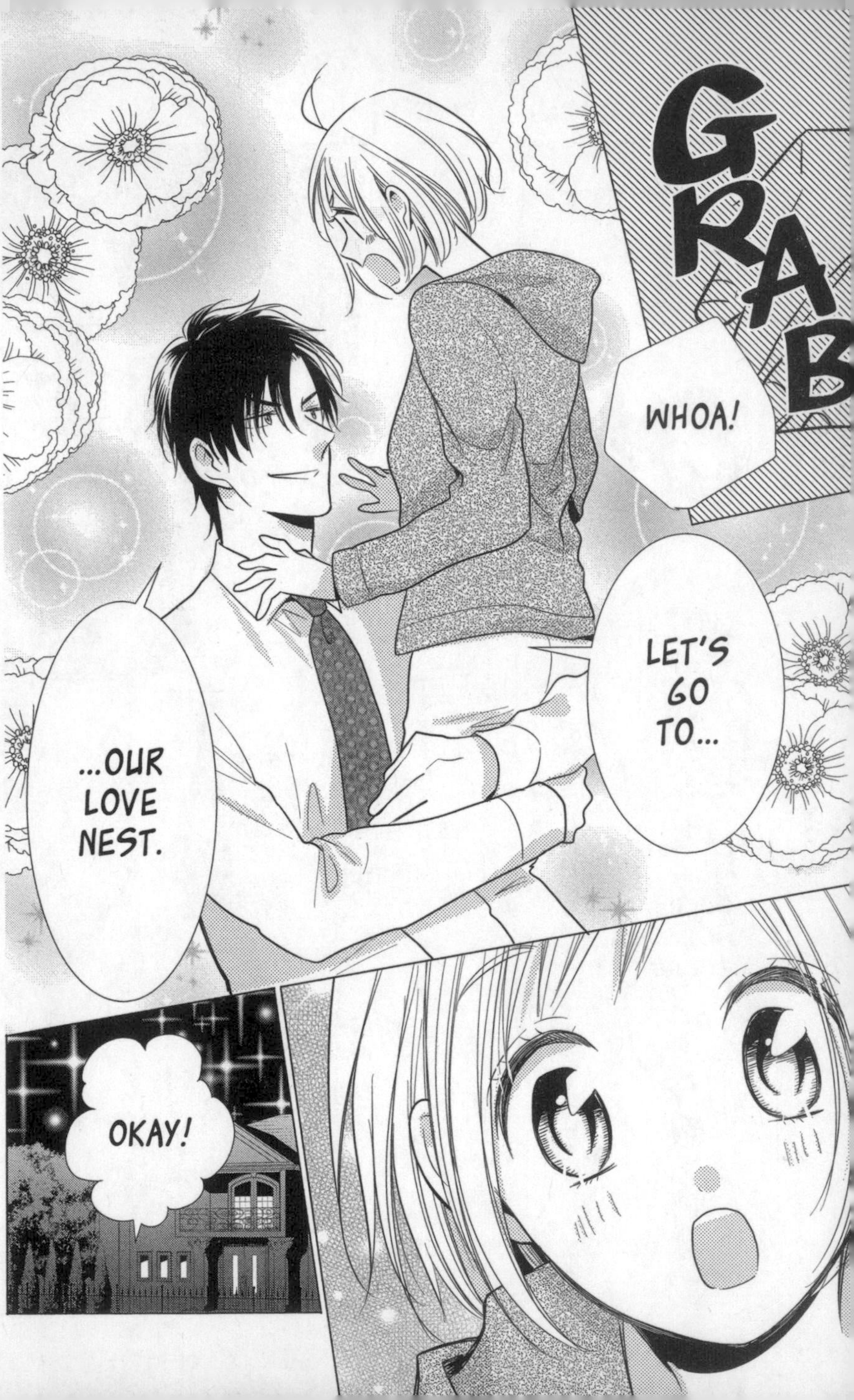
GRAB
WHOA!
LET'S GO TO...
...OUR LOVE NEST.
OKAY!

Chapter 97

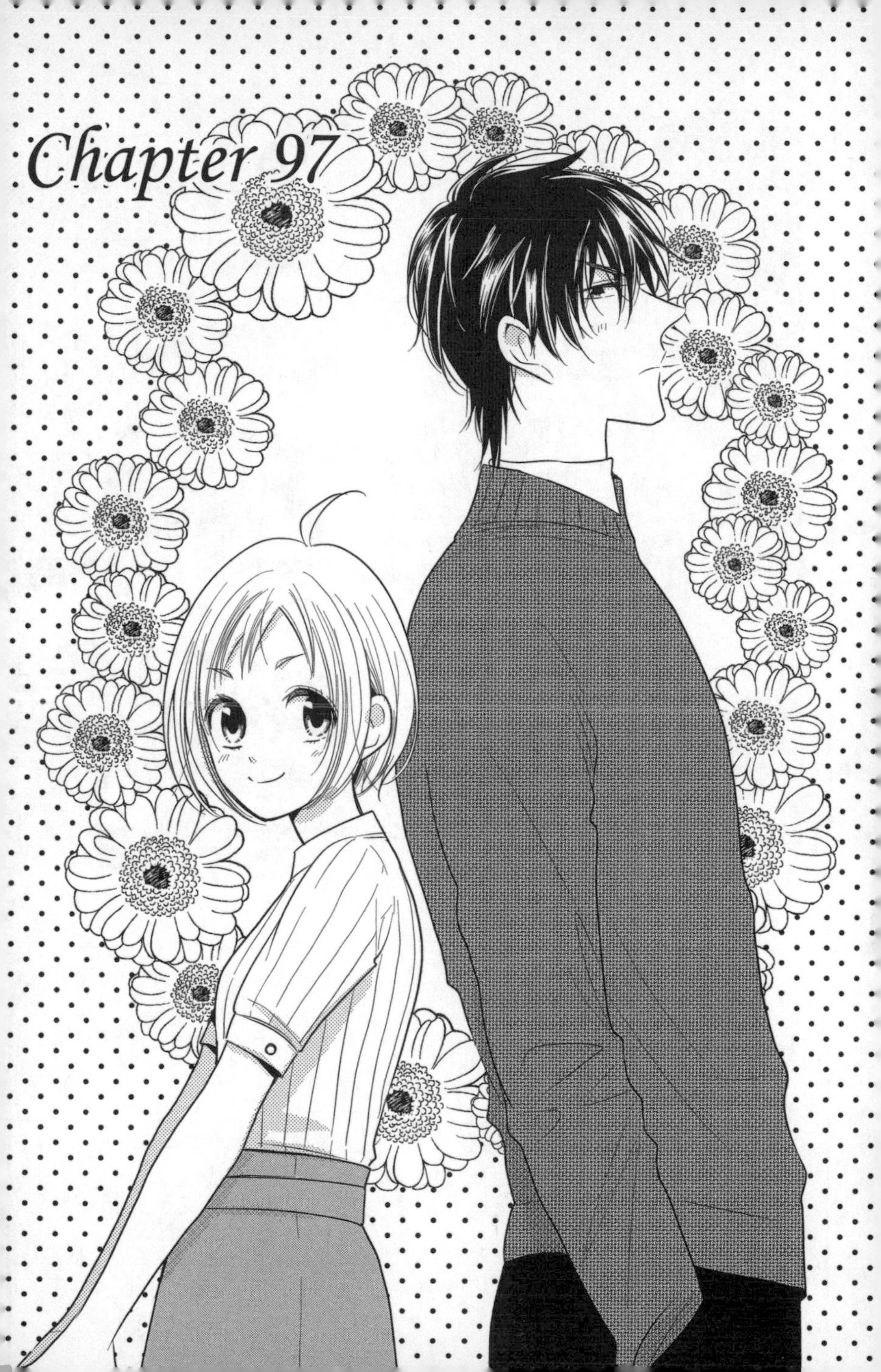

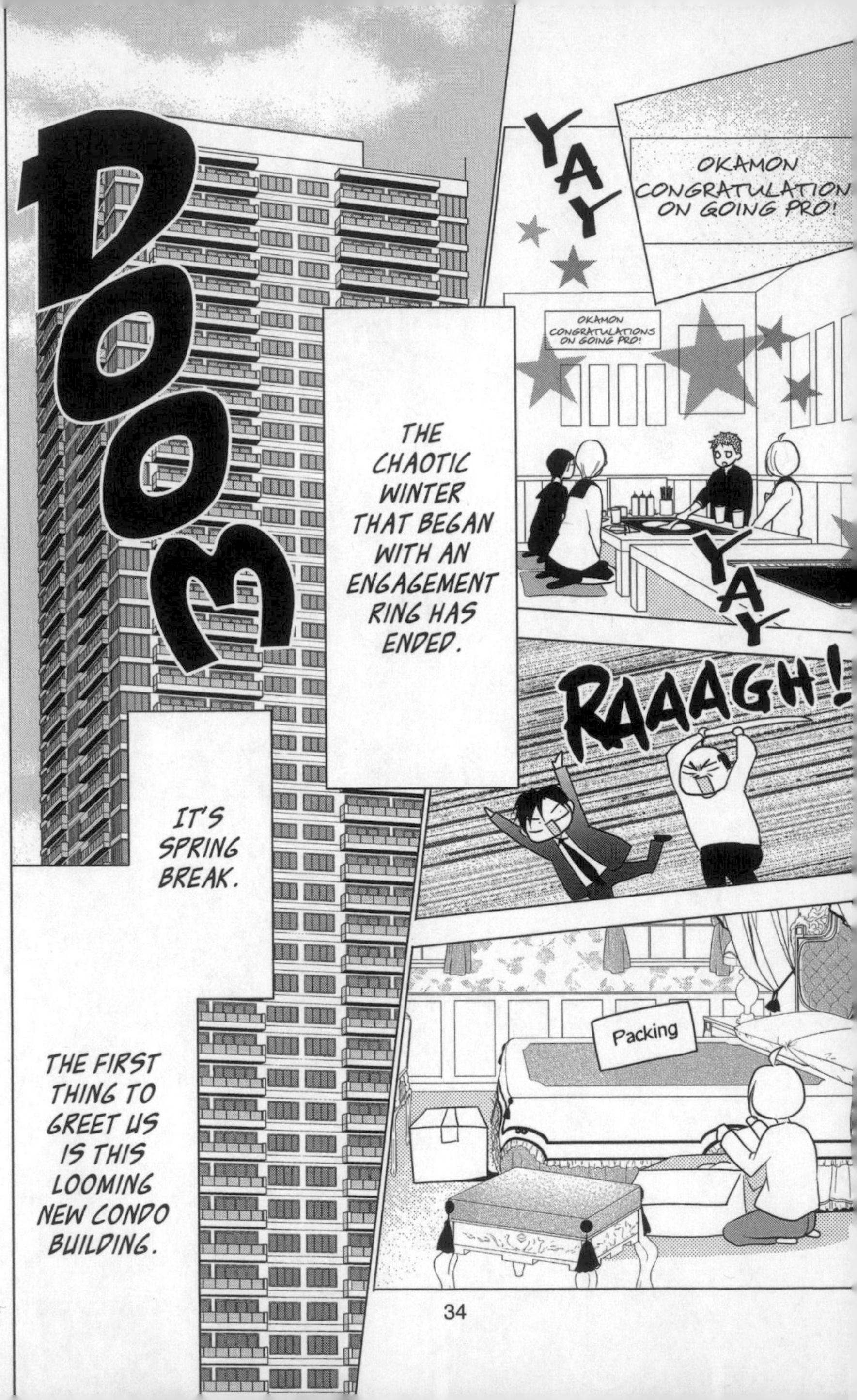
YAY
OKAMON CONGRATULATION ON GOING PRO!
OKAMON CONGRATULATIONS ON GOING PRO!
YAY
RAAAGH!
Packing
DOOM
THE CHAOTIC WINTER THAT BEGAN WITH AN ENGAGEMENT RING HAS ENDED.
IT'S SPRING BREAK.
THE FIRST THING TO GREET US IS THIS LOOMING NEW CONDO BUILDING.

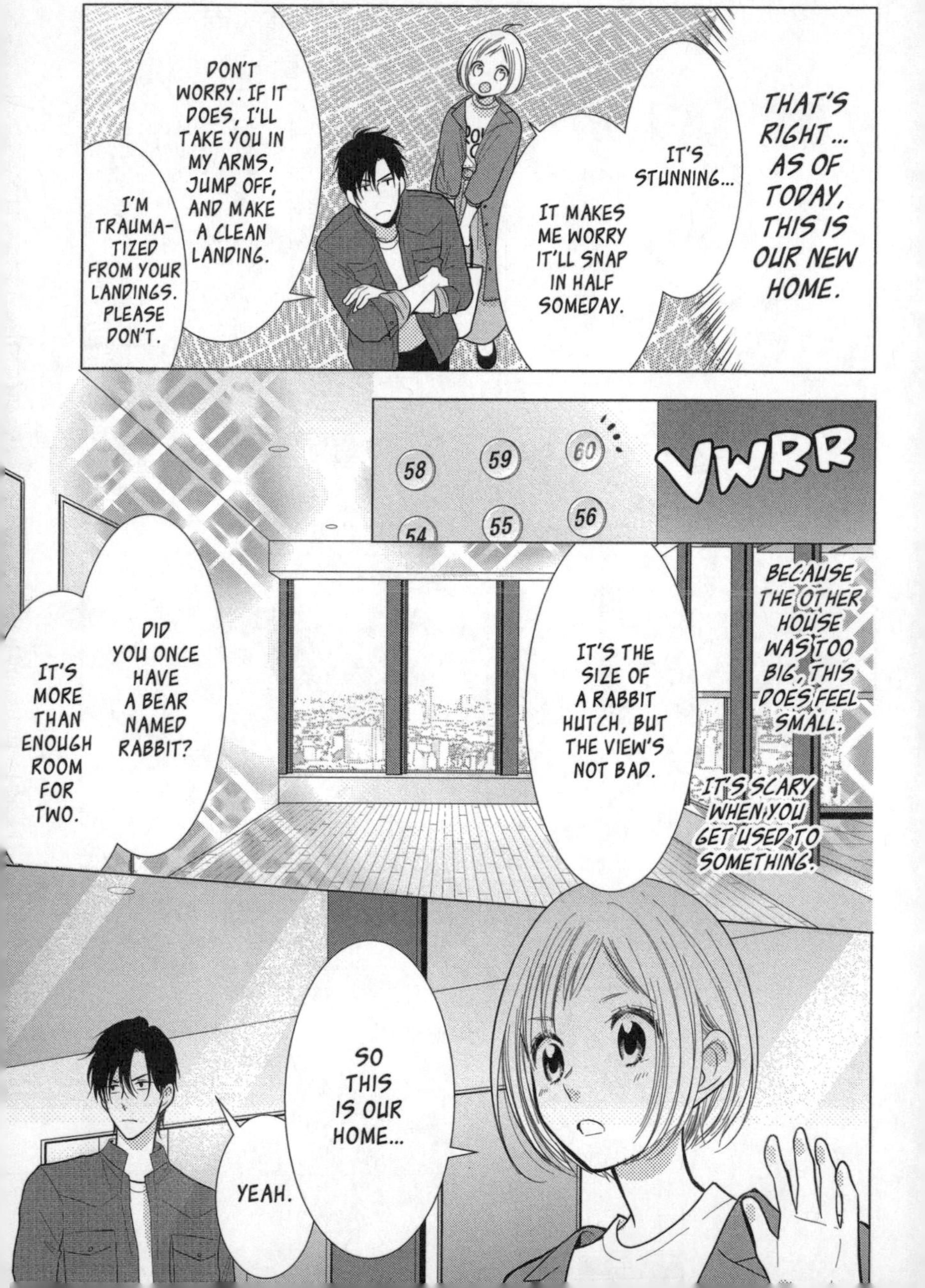
THAT'S RIGHT... AS OF TODAY, THIS IS OUR NEW HOME.
IT'S STUNNING...
IT MAKES ME WORRY IT'LL SNAP IN HALF SOMEDAY.
DON'T WORRY. IF IT DOES, I'LL TAKE YOU IN MY ARMS, JUMP OFF, AND MAKE A CLEAN LANDING.
I'M TRAUMATIZED FROM YOUR LANDINGS. PLEASE DON'T.
VWRR
58 59 60
54 55 56
BECAUSE THE OTHER HOUSE WAS TOO BIG, THIS DOES FEEL SMALL.
IT'S SCARY WHEN YOU GET USED TO SOMETHING.
IT'S THE SIZE OF A RABBIT HUTCH, BUT THE VIEW'S NOT BAD.
DID YOU ONCE HAVE A BEAR NAMED RABBIT?
IT'S MORE THAN ENOUGH ROOM FOR TWO.
SO THIS IS OUR HOME...
YEAH.

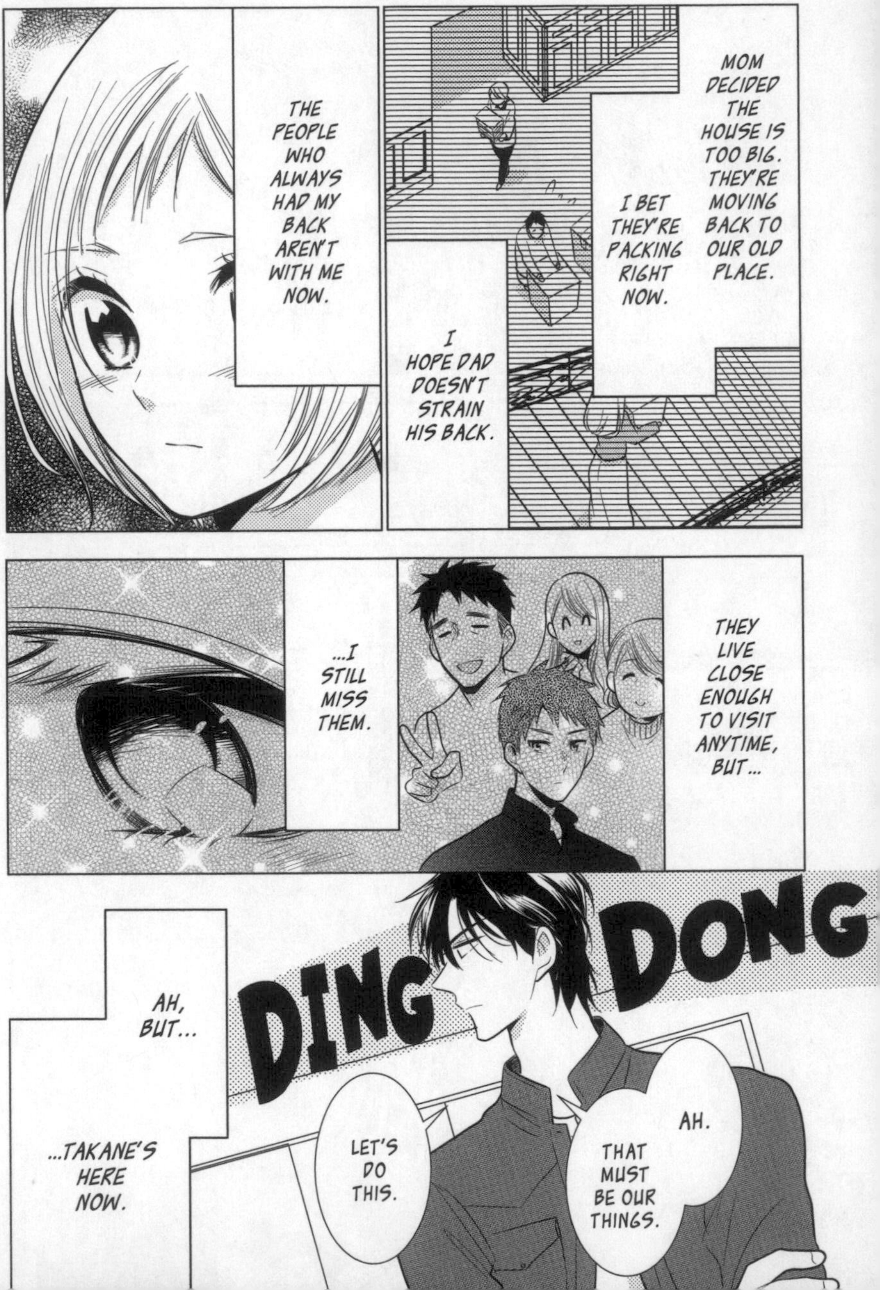
MOM DECIDED THE HOUSE IS TOO BIG. THEY'RE MOVING BACK TO OUR OLD PLACE.
I BET THEY'RE PACKING RIGHT NOW.
I HOPE DAD DOESN'T STRAIN HIS BACK.
THE PEOPLE WHO ALWAYS HAD MY BACK AREN'T WITH ME NOW.
THEY LIVE CLOSE ENOUGH TO VISIT ANYTIME, BUT...
...I STILL MISS THEM.
DING DONG
AH.
THAT MUST BE OUR THINGS.
LET'S DO THIS.
AH, BUT...
...TAKANE'S HERE NOW.

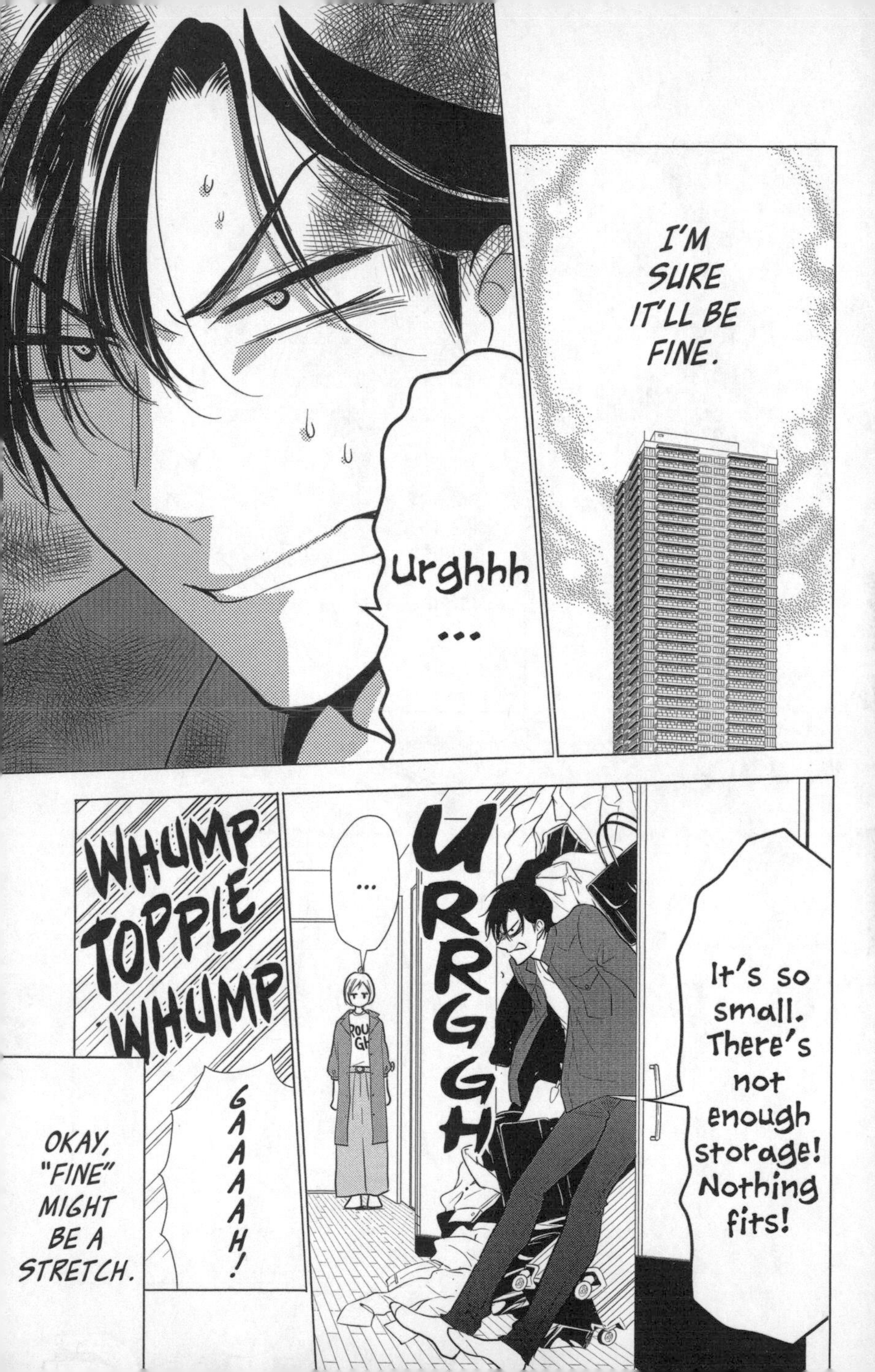
I'M SURE IT'LL BE FINE.
Urghhh ...
It's so small. There's not enough storage! Nothing fits!
URRGGH
...
WHUMP TOPPLE WHUMP
GAAAAAH!
OKAY, "FINE" MIGHT BE A STRETCH.

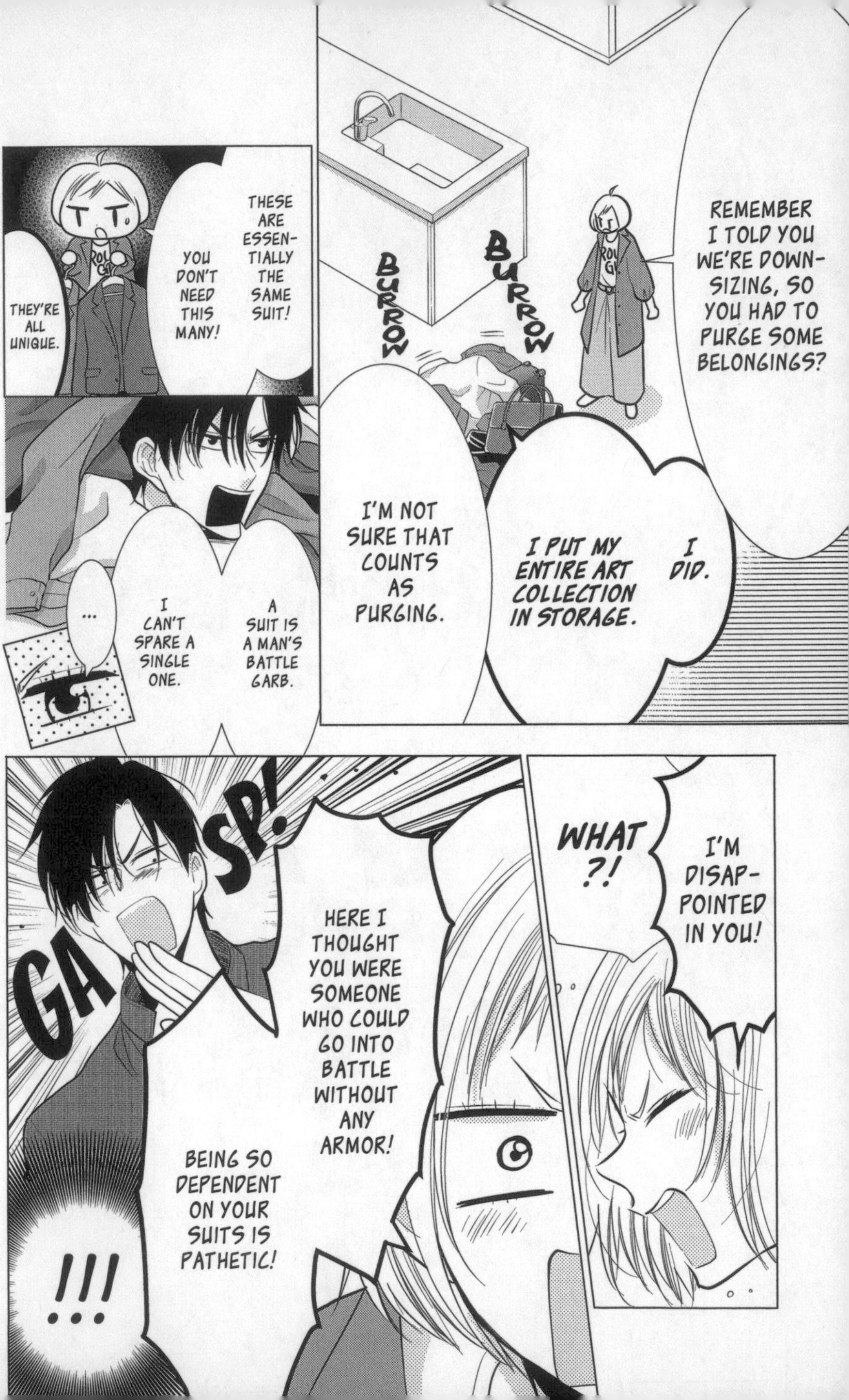
REMEMBER I TOLD YOU WE'RE DOWN-SIZING, SO YOU HAD TO PURGE SOME BELONGINGS?
BURROW
BURROW
I DID.
I PUT MY ENTIRE ART COLLECTION IN STORAGE.
I'M NOT SURE THAT COUNTS AS PURGING.
THESE ARE ESSEN-TIALLY THE SAME SUIT!
YOU DON'T NEED THIS MANY!
THEY'RE ALL UNIQUE.
A SUIT IS A MAN'S BATTLE GARB.
I CAN'T SPARE A SINGLE ONE.
...
I'M DISAP-POINTED IN YOU!
WHAT?!
HERE I THOUGHT YOU WERE SOMEONE WHO COULD GO INTO BATTLE WITHOUT ANY ARMOR!
BEING SO DEPENDENT ON YOUR SUITS IS PATHETIC!
GASP!
!!!

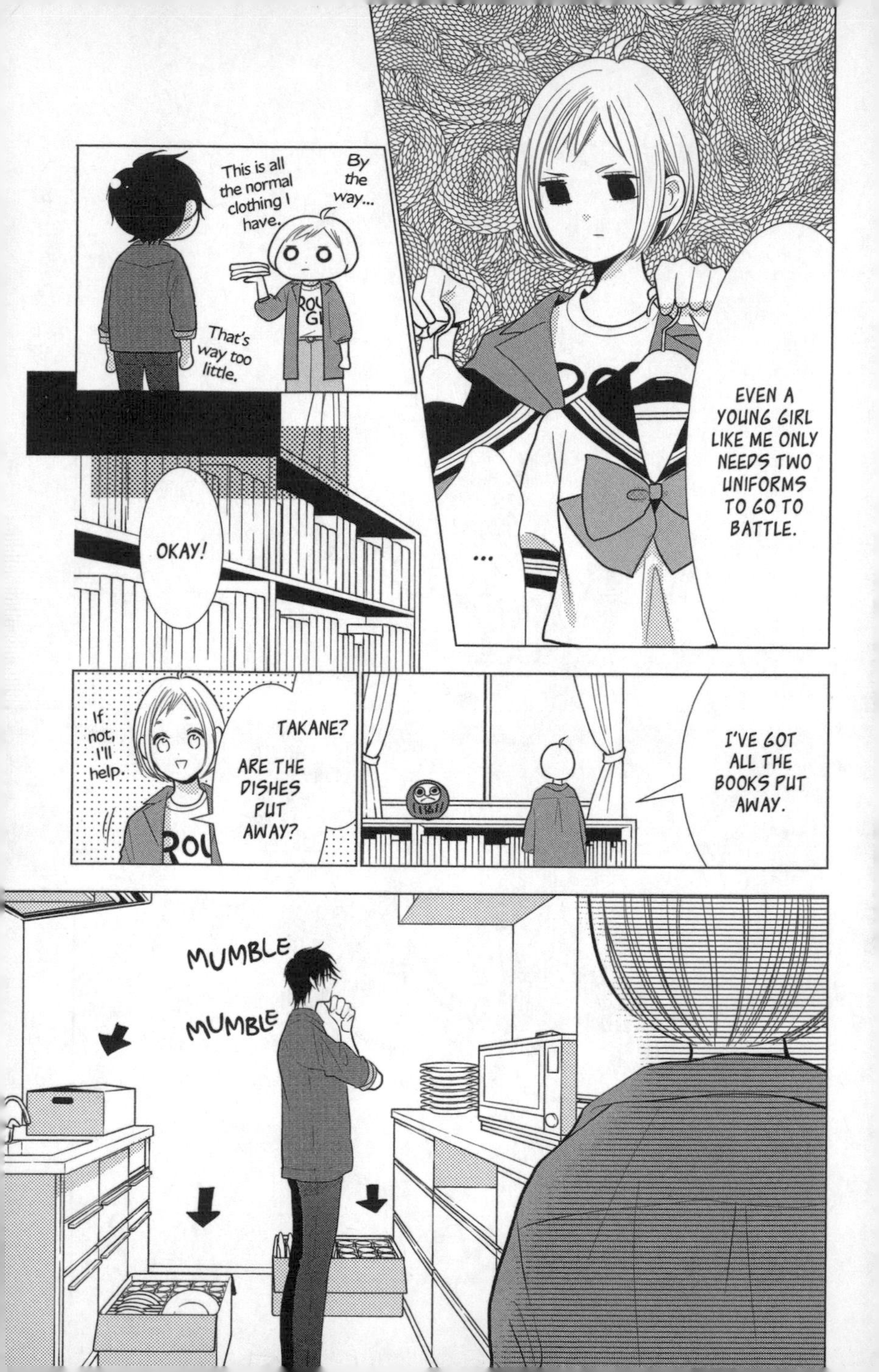
EVEN A YOUNG GIRL LIKE ME ONLY NEEDS TWO UNIFORMS TO GO TO BATTLE.
...
By the way...
This is all the normal clothing I have.
That's way too little.
OKAY!
I'VE GOT ALL THE BOOKS PUT AWAY.
TAKANE? ARE THE DISHES PUT AWAY?
If not, I'll help.
MUMBLE
MUMBLE

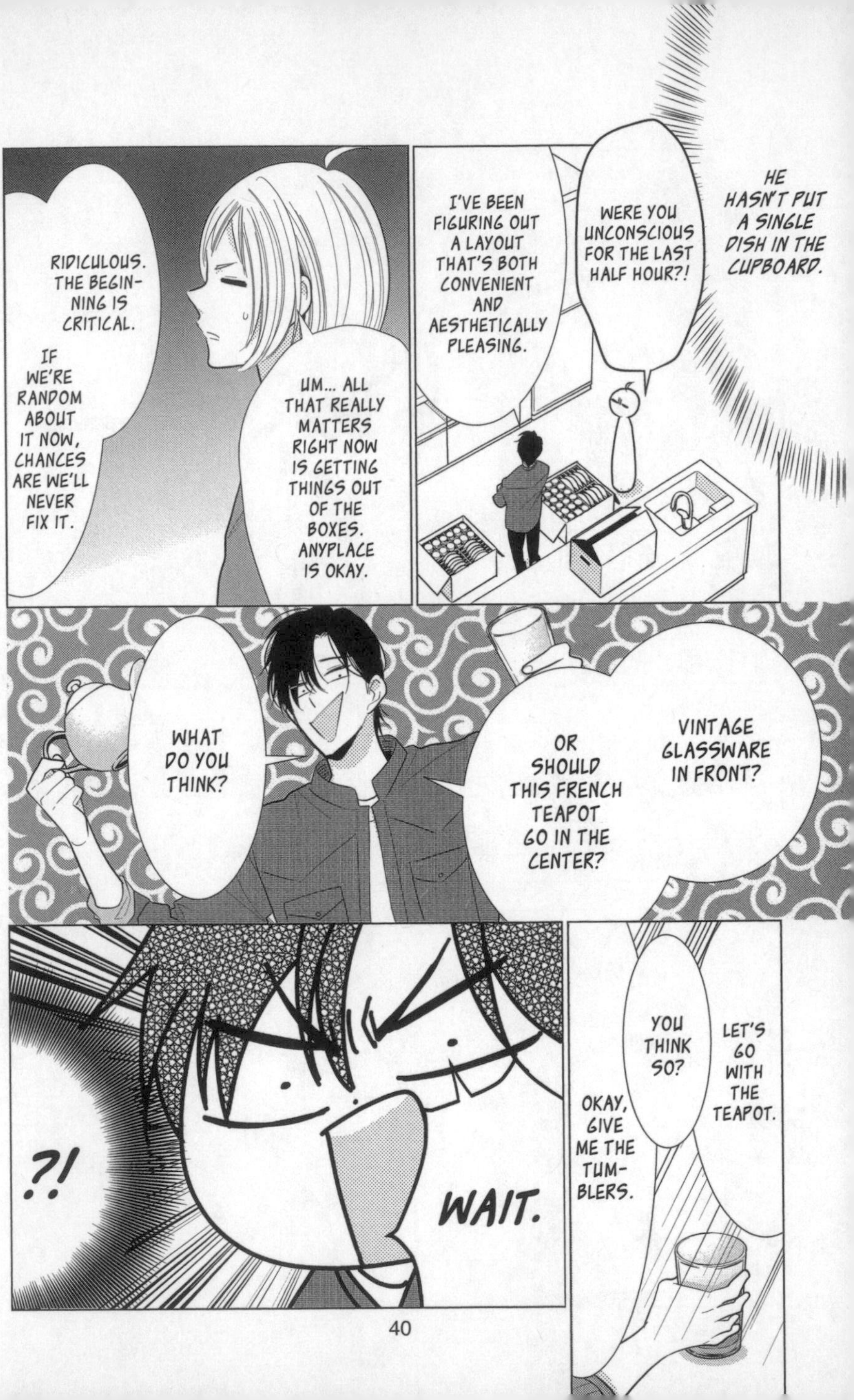
HE HASN'T PUT A SINGLE DISH IN THE CUPBOARD.
WERE YOU UNCONSCIOUS FOR THE LAST HALF HOUR?!
I'VE BEEN FIGURING OUT A LAYOUT THAT'S BOTH CONVENIENT AND AESTHETICALLY PLEASING.
UM... ALL THAT REALLY MATTERS RIGHT NOW IS GETTING THINGS OUT OF THE BOXES. ANYPLACE IS OKAY.
RIDICULOUS. THE BEGIN-NING IS CRITICAL.
IF WE'RE RANDOM ABOUT IT NOW, CHANCES ARE WE'LL NEVER FIX IT.
VINTAGE GLASSWARE IN FRONT?
OR SHOULD THIS FRENCH TEAPOT GO IN THE CENTER?
WHAT DO YOU THINK?
LET'S GO WITH THE TEAPOT.
YOU THINK SO?
OKAY, GIVE ME THE TUM-BLERS.
WAIT.
?!

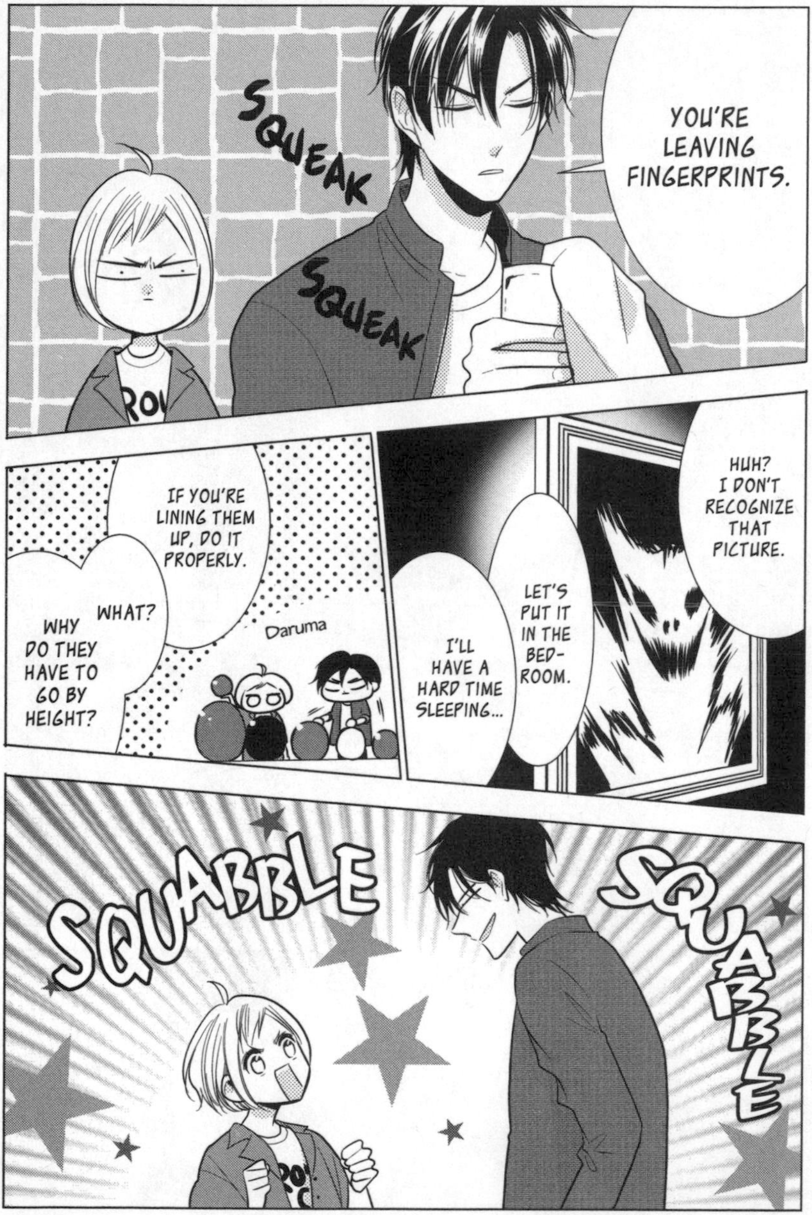
YOU'RE LEAVING FINGERPRINTS.
SQUEAK
SQUEAK
HUH? I DON'T RECOGNIZE THAT PICTURE.
LET'S PUT IT IN THE BED-ROOM.
I'LL HAVE A HARD TIME SLEEPING...
IF YOU'RE LINING THEM UP, DO IT PROPERLY.
WHAT?
WHY DO THEY HAVE TO GO BY HEIGHT?
Daruma
SQUABBLE
SQUABBLE

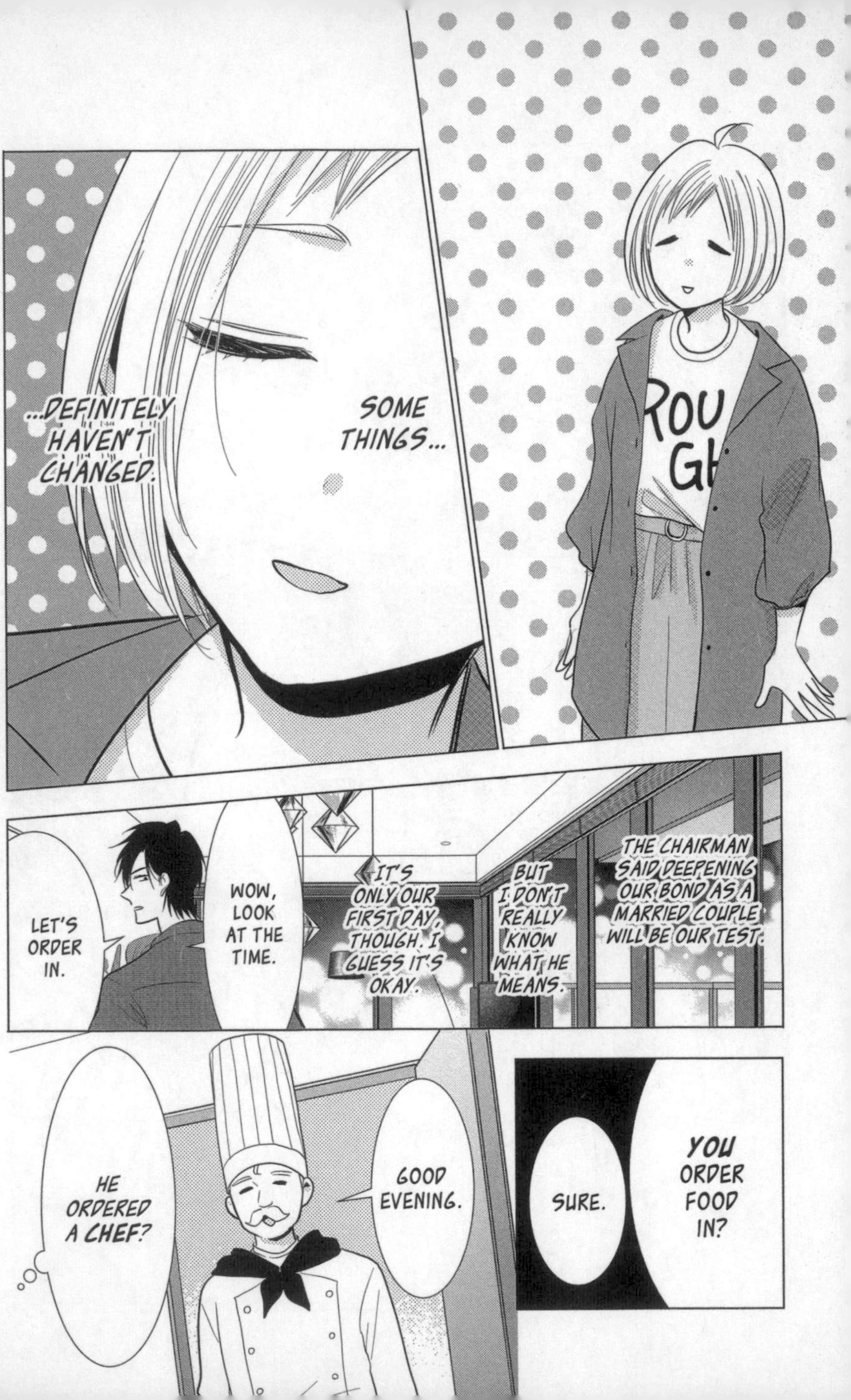
SOME THINGS...
...DEFINITELY HAVEN'T CHANGED.
THE CHAIRMAN SAID DEEPENING OUR BOND AS A MARRIED COUPLE WILL BE OUR TEST.
BUT I DON'T REALLY KNOW WHAT HE MEANS.
IT'S ONLY OUR FIRST DAY, THOUGH. I GUESS IT'S OKAY.
WOW, LOOK AT THE TIME.
LET'S ORDER IN.
YOU ORDER FOOD IN?
SURE.
GOOD EVENING.
HE ORDERED A CHEF?

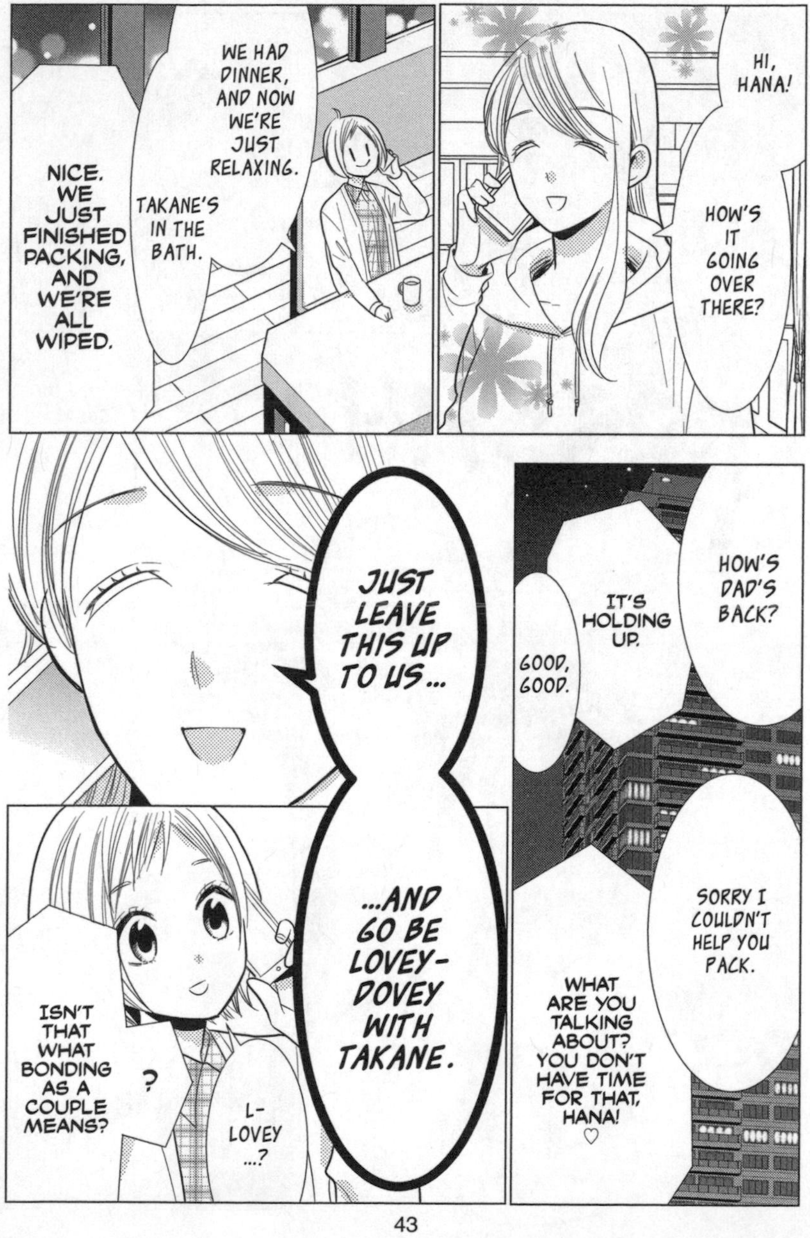
HI, HANA!
HOW'S IT GOING OVER THERE?
WE HAD DINNER, AND NOW WE'RE JUST RELAXING.
TAKANE'S IN THE BATH.
NICE. WE JUST FINISHED PACKING, AND WE'RE ALL WIPED.
HOW'S DAD'S BACK?
IT'S HOLDING UP.
GOOD, GOOD.
SORRY I COULDN'T HELP YOU PACK.
WHAT ARE YOU TALKING ABOUT? YOU DON'T HAVE TIME FOR THAT, HANA! ♡
JUST LEAVE THIS UP TO US...
...AND GO BE LOVEY-DOVEY WITH TAKANE.
L-LOVEY...?
?
ISN'T THAT WHAT BONDING AS A COUPLE MEANS?

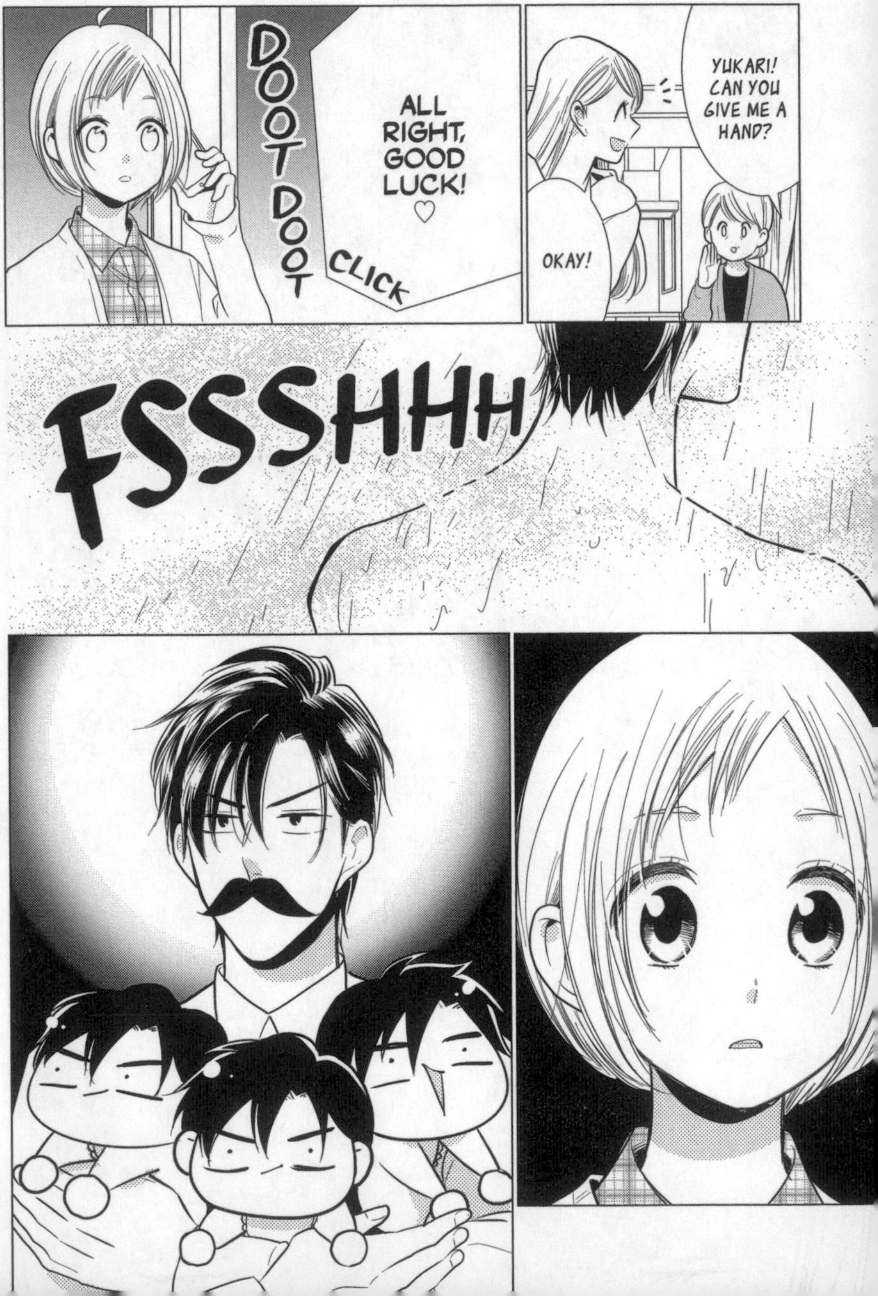
YUKARI! CAN YOU GIVE ME A HAND?
OKAY!
ALL RIGHT, GOOD LUCK! ♡
DOOT DOOT DOOT
CLICK
FSSSHHH

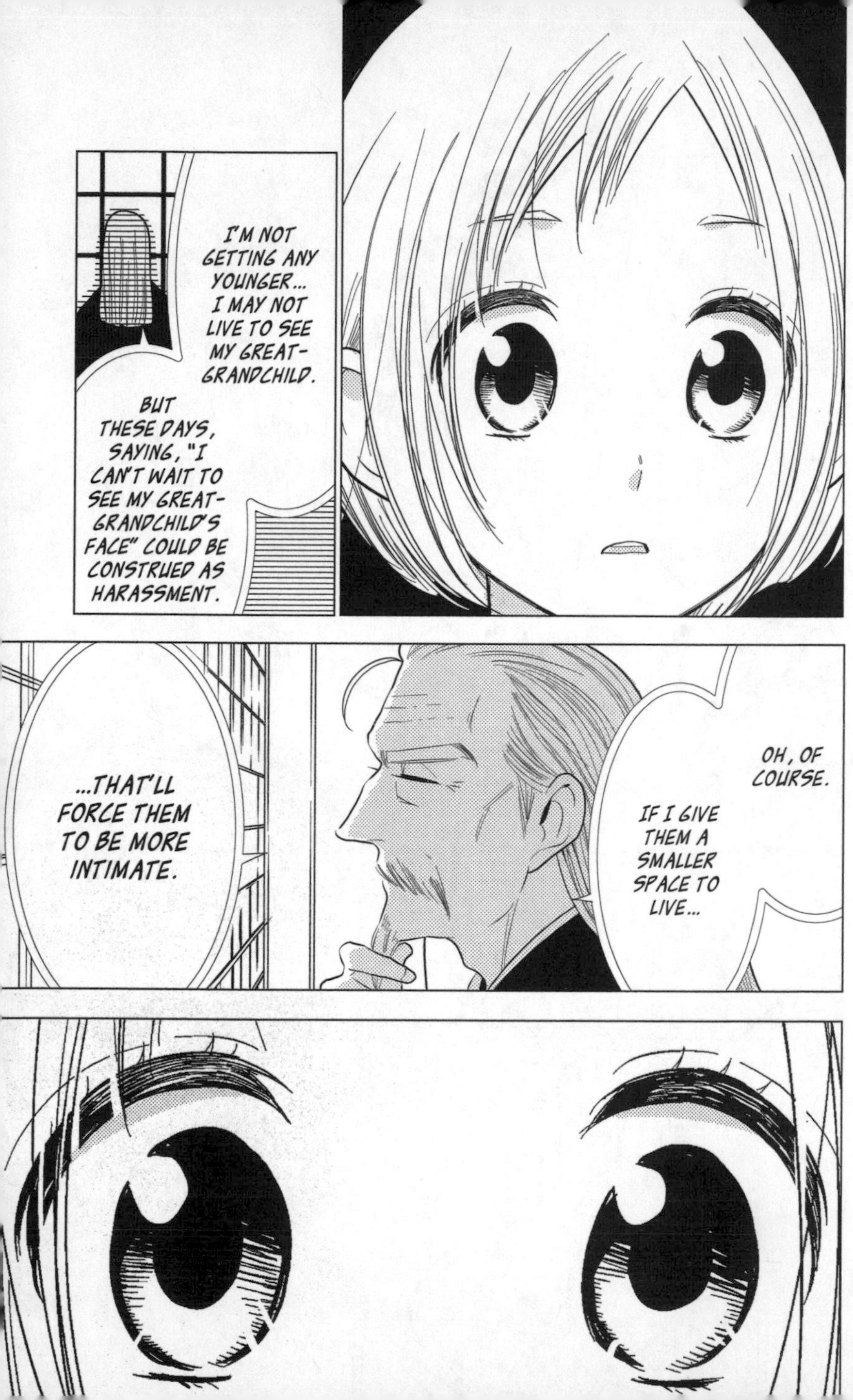
I'M NOT GETTING ANY YOUNGER... I MAY NOT LIVE TO SEE MY GREAT-GRANDCHILD.
BUT THESE DAYS, SAYING, "I CAN'T WAIT TO SEE MY GREAT-GRANDCHILD'S FACE" COULD BE CONSTRUED AS HARASSMENT.
OH, OF COURSE.
IF I GIVE THEM A SMALLER SPACE TO LIVE...
...THAT'LL FORCE THEM TO BE MORE INTIMATE.

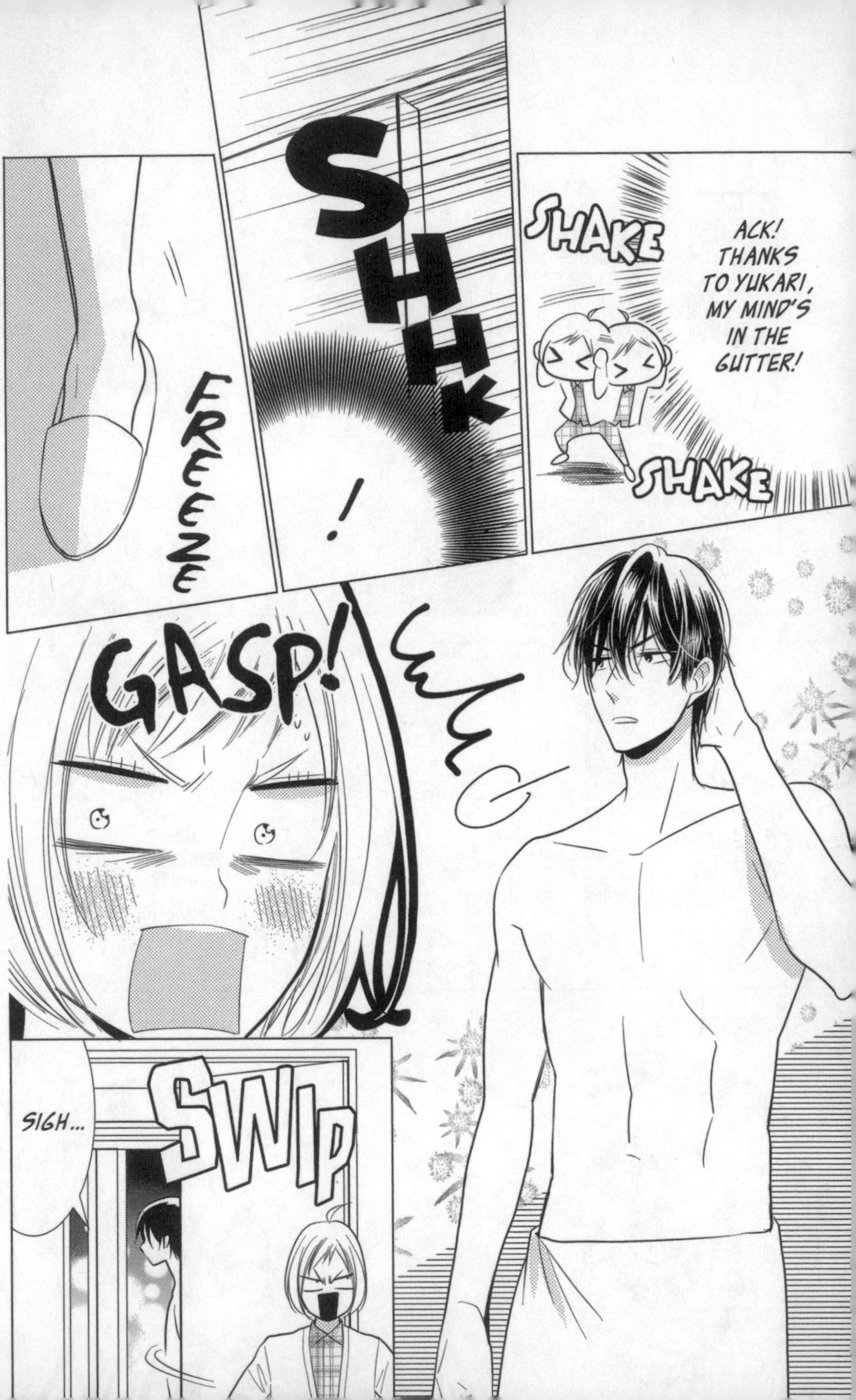
SHAKE
ACK! THANKS TO YUKARI, MY MIND'S IN THE GUTTER!
SHAKE
SHHK
!
FREEZE
GASP!
SWIP
SIGH...

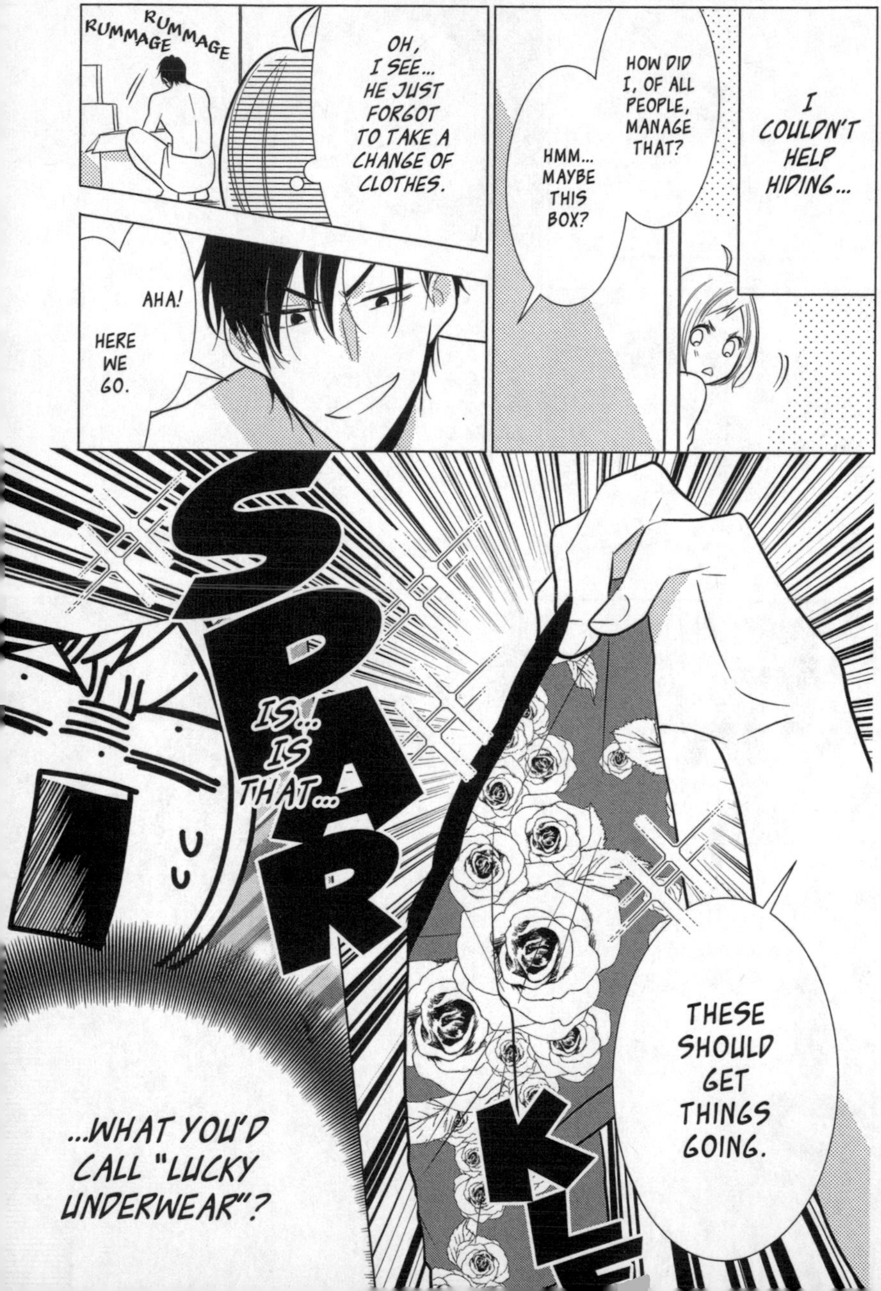
I COULDN'T HELP HIDING...
HOW DID I, OF ALL PEOPLE, MANAGE THAT?
HMM... MAYBE THIS BOX?
OH, I SEE... HE JUST FORGOT TO TAKE A CHANGE OF CLOTHES.
RUMMAGE RUMMAGE
AHA!
HERE WE GO.
THESE SHOULD GET THINGS GOING.
SPARKLE
IS... IS THAT...
...WHAT YOU'D CALL "LUCKY UNDERWEAR"?

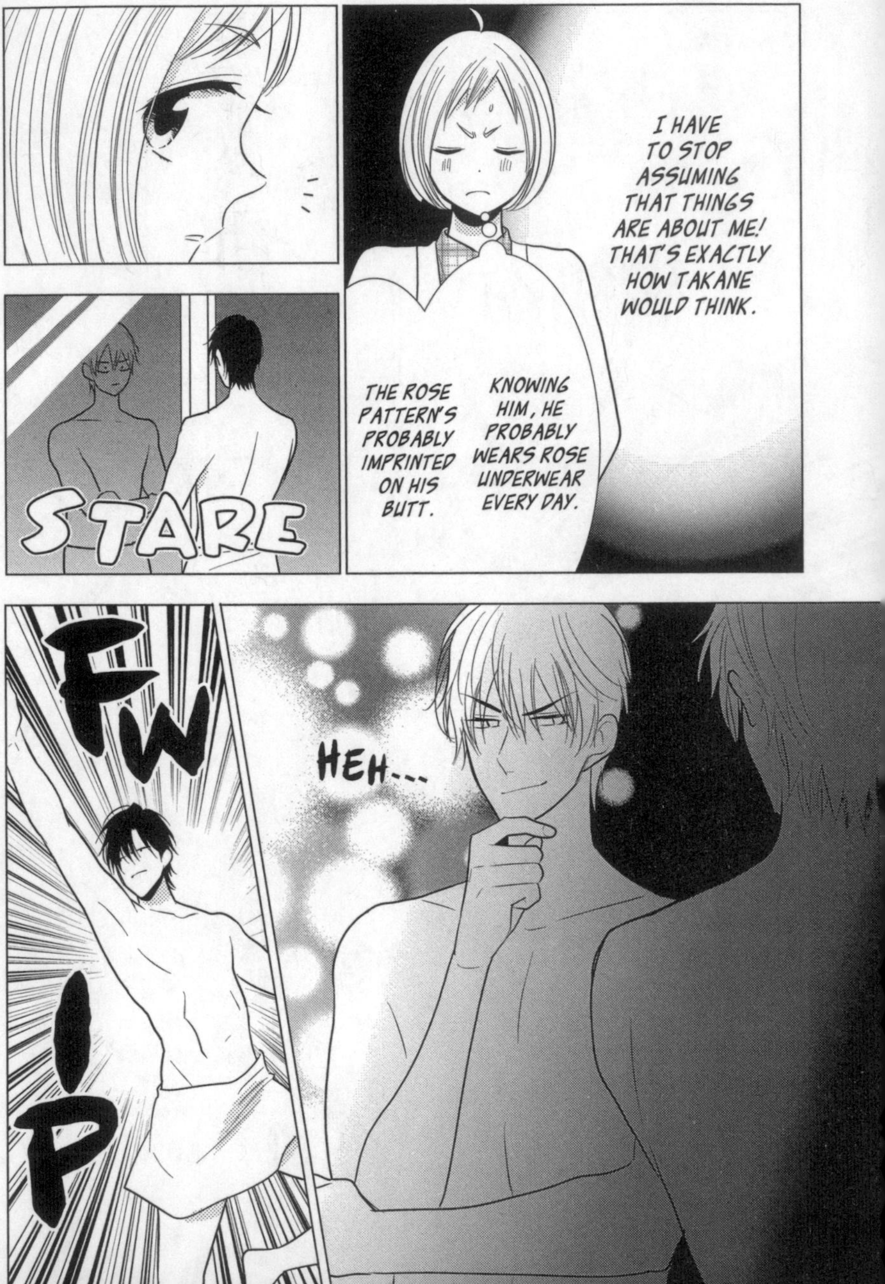
I HAVE TO STOP ASSUMING THAT THINGS ARE ABOUT ME! THAT'S EXACTLY HOW TAKANE WOULD THINK.
KNOWING HIM, HE PROBABLY WEARS ROSE UNDERWEAR EVERY DAY.
THE ROSE PATTERN'S PROBABLY IMPRINTED ON HIS BUTT.
STARE
HEH...
FWIP

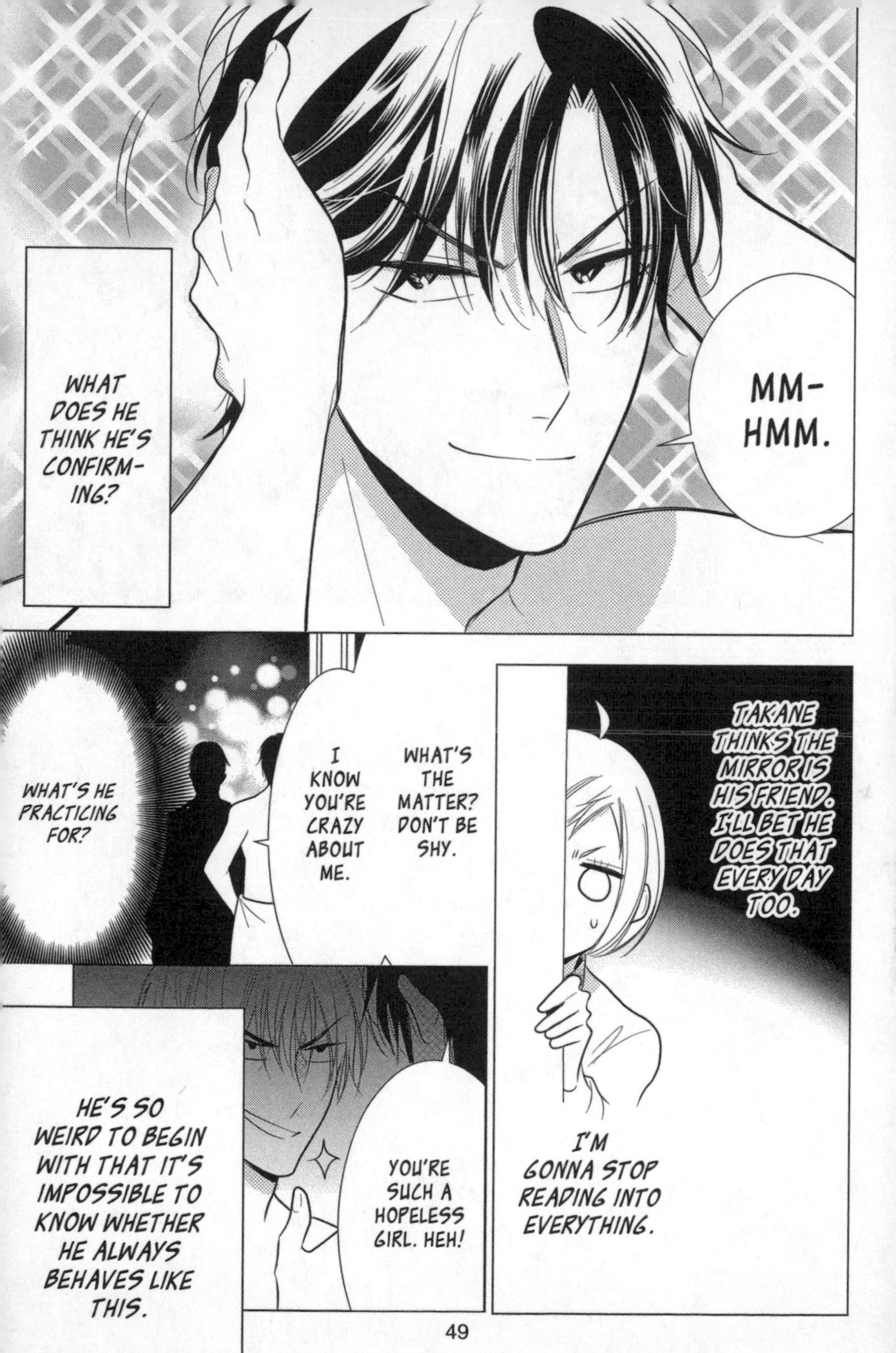
MM-HMM.
WHAT DOES HE THINK HE'S CONFIRMING?
TAKANE THINKS THE MIRROR IS HIS FRIEND. I'LL BET HE DOES THAT EVERY DAY TOO.
I'M GONNA STOP READING INTO EVERYTHING.
WHAT'S THE MATTER? DON'T BE SHY.
I KNOW YOU'RE CRAZY ABOUT ME.
WHAT'S HE PRACTICING FOR?
YOU'RE SUCH A HOPELESS GIRL. HEH!
HE'S SO WEIRD TO BEGIN WITH THAT IT'S IMPOSSIBLE TO KNOW WHETHER HE ALWAYS BEHAVES LIKE THIS.

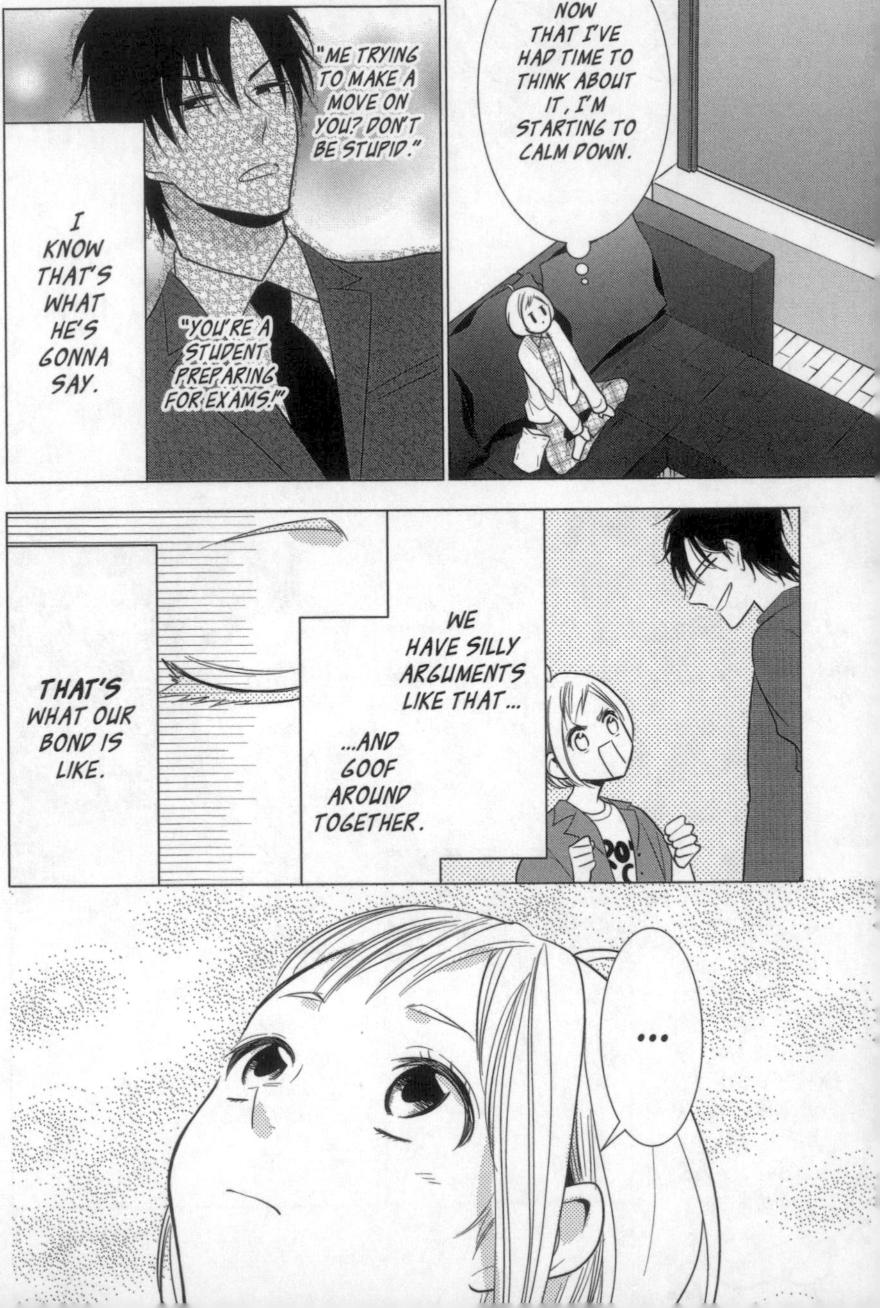
NOW THAT I'VE HAD TIME TO THINK ABOUT IT, I'M STARTING TO CALM DOWN.
"ME TRYING TO MAKE A MOVE ON YOU? DON'T BE STUPID."
"YOU'RE A STUDENT PREPARING FOR EXAMS!"
I KNOW THAT'S WHAT HE'S GONNA SAY.
WE HAVE SILLY ARGUMENTS LIKE THAT...
...AND GOOF AROUND TOGETHER.
THAT'S WHAT OUR BOND IS LIKE.
...

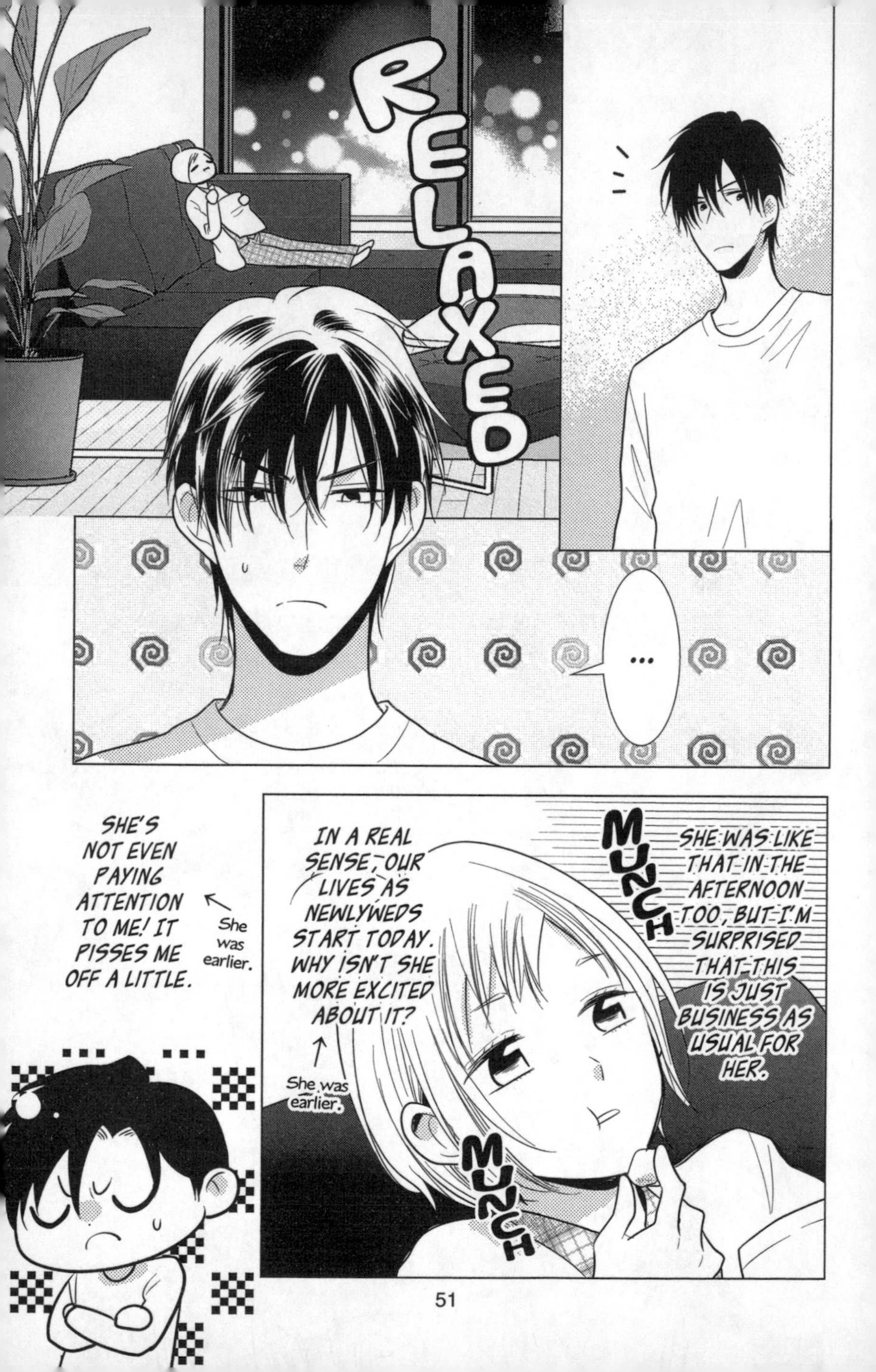
RELAXED
...
MUNCH
SHE WAS LIKE THAT IN THE AFTERNOON TOO, BUT I'M SURPRISED THAT THIS IS JUST BUSINESS AS USUAL FOR HER.
IN A REAL SENSE, OUR LIVES AS NEWLYWEDS START TODAY. WHY ISN'T SHE MORE EXCITED ABOUT IT?
She was earlier.
MUNCH
SHE'S NOT EVEN PAYING ATTENTION TO ME! IT PISSES ME OFF A LITTLE.
She was earlier.

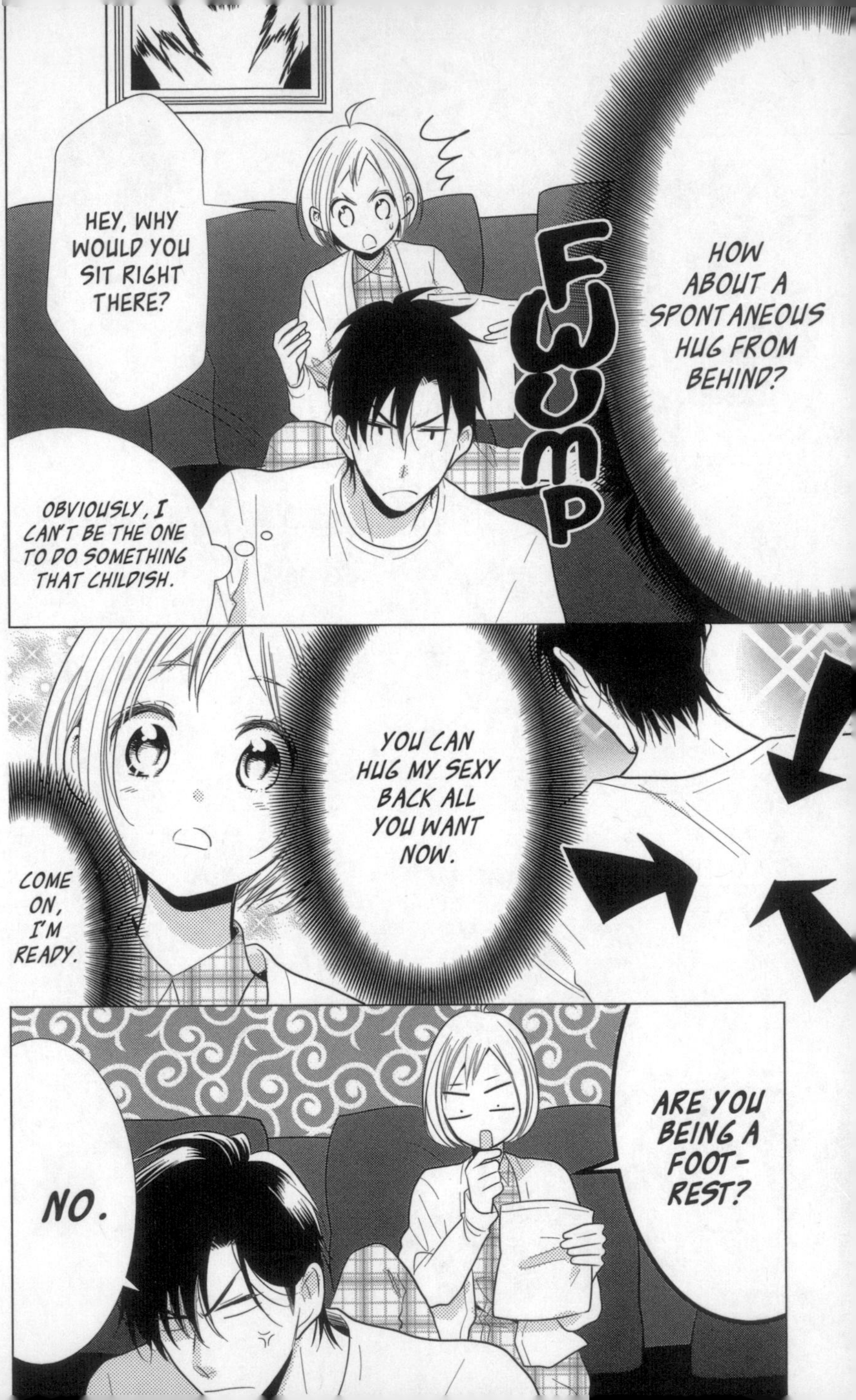
HOW ABOUT A SPONTANEOUS HUG FROM BEHIND?
FWUMP
HEY, WHY WOULD YOU SIT RIGHT THERE?
OBVIOUSLY, I CAN'T BE THE ONE TO DO SOMETHING THAT CHILDISH.
YOU CAN HUG MY SEXY BACK ALL YOU WANT NOW.
COME ON, I'M READY.
ARE YOU BEING A FOOT-REST?
NO.

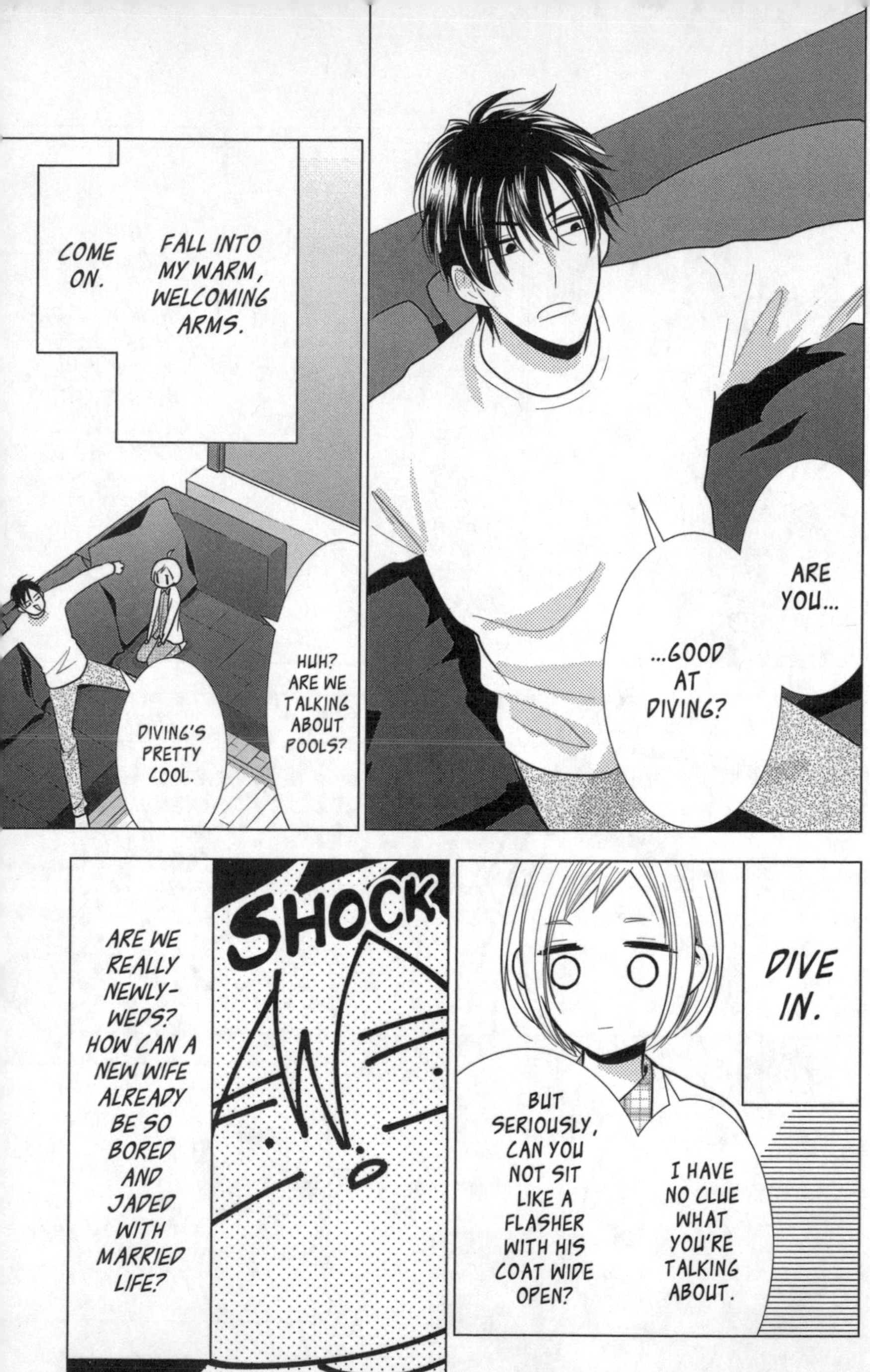
ARE YOU...
...GOOD AT DIVING?
COME ON.
FALL INTO MY WARM, WELCOMING ARMS.
HUH? ARE WE TALKING ABOUT POOLS?
DIVING'S PRETTY COOL.
DIVE IN.
I HAVE NO CLUE WHAT YOU'RE TALKING ABOUT.
BUT SERIOUSLY, CAN YOU NOT SIT LIKE A FLASHER WITH HIS COAT WIDE OPEN?
SHOCK
ARE WE REALLY NEWLY-WEDS? HOW CAN A NEW WIFE ALREADY BE SO BORED AND JADED WITH MARRIED LIFE?

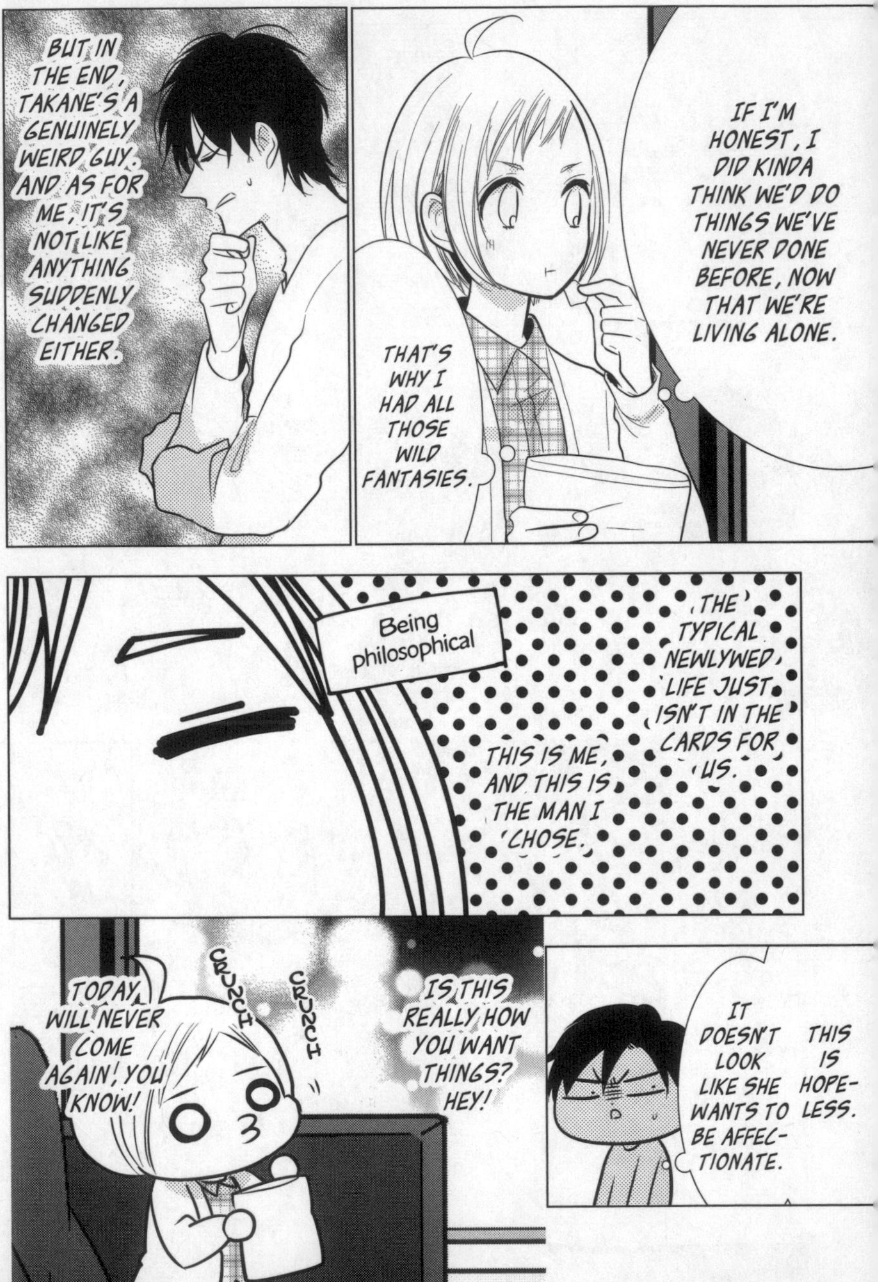
IF I'M HONEST, I DID KINDA THINK WE'D DO THINGS WE'VE NEVER DONE BEFORE, NOW THAT WE'RE LIVING ALONE.
THAT'S WHY I HAD ALL THOSE WILD FANTASIES.
BUT IN THE END, TAKANE'S A GENUINELY WEIRD GUY. AND AS FOR ME, IT'S NOT LIKE ANYTHING SUDDENLY CHANGED EITHER.
THE TYPICAL NEWLYWED LIFE JUST ISN'T IN THE CARDS FOR US.
THIS IS ME, AND THIS IS THE MAN I CHOSE.
Being philosophical
THIS IS HOPE-LESS.
IT DOESN'T LOOK LIKE SHE WANTS TO BE AFFEC-TIONATE.
IS THIS REALLY HOW YOU WANT THINGS? HEY!
CRUNCH
CRUNCH
TODAY WILL NEVER COME AGAIN, YOU KNOW!

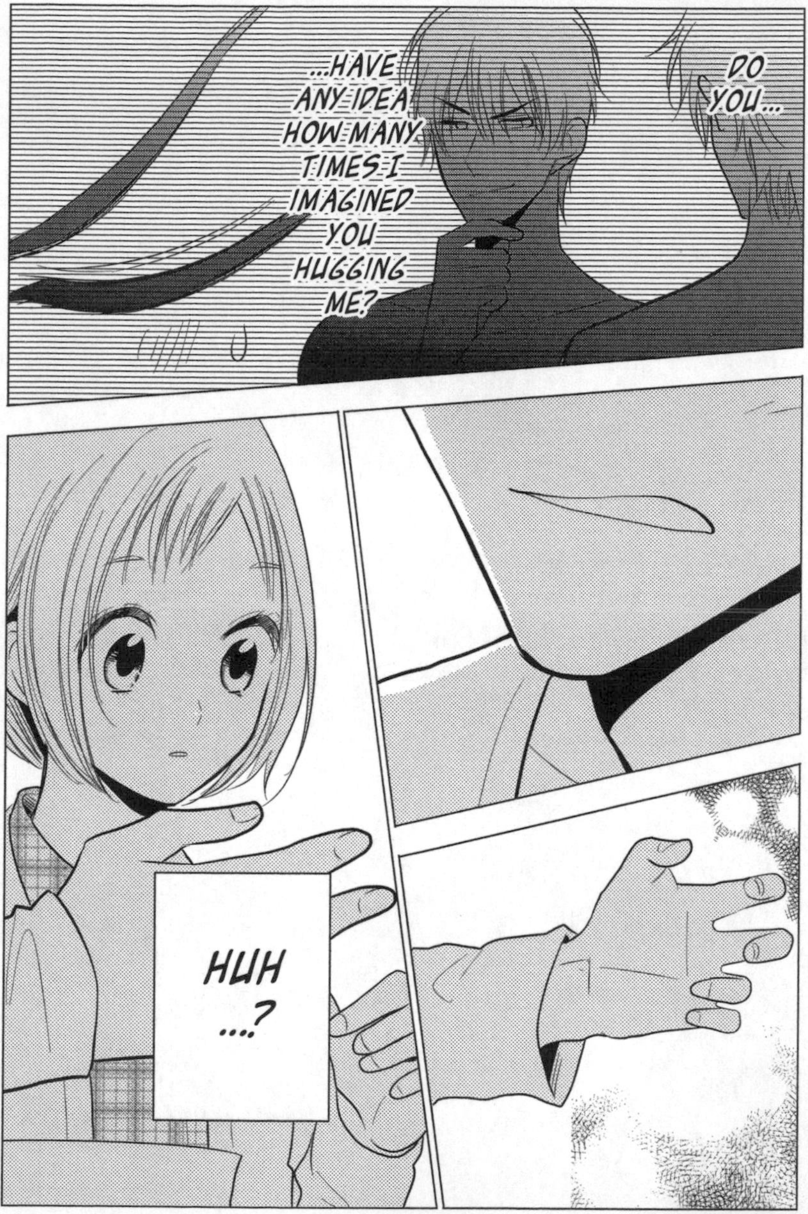
DO YOU...
...HAVE ANY IDEA HOW MANY TIMES I IMAGINED YOU HUGGING ME?
HUH ...?

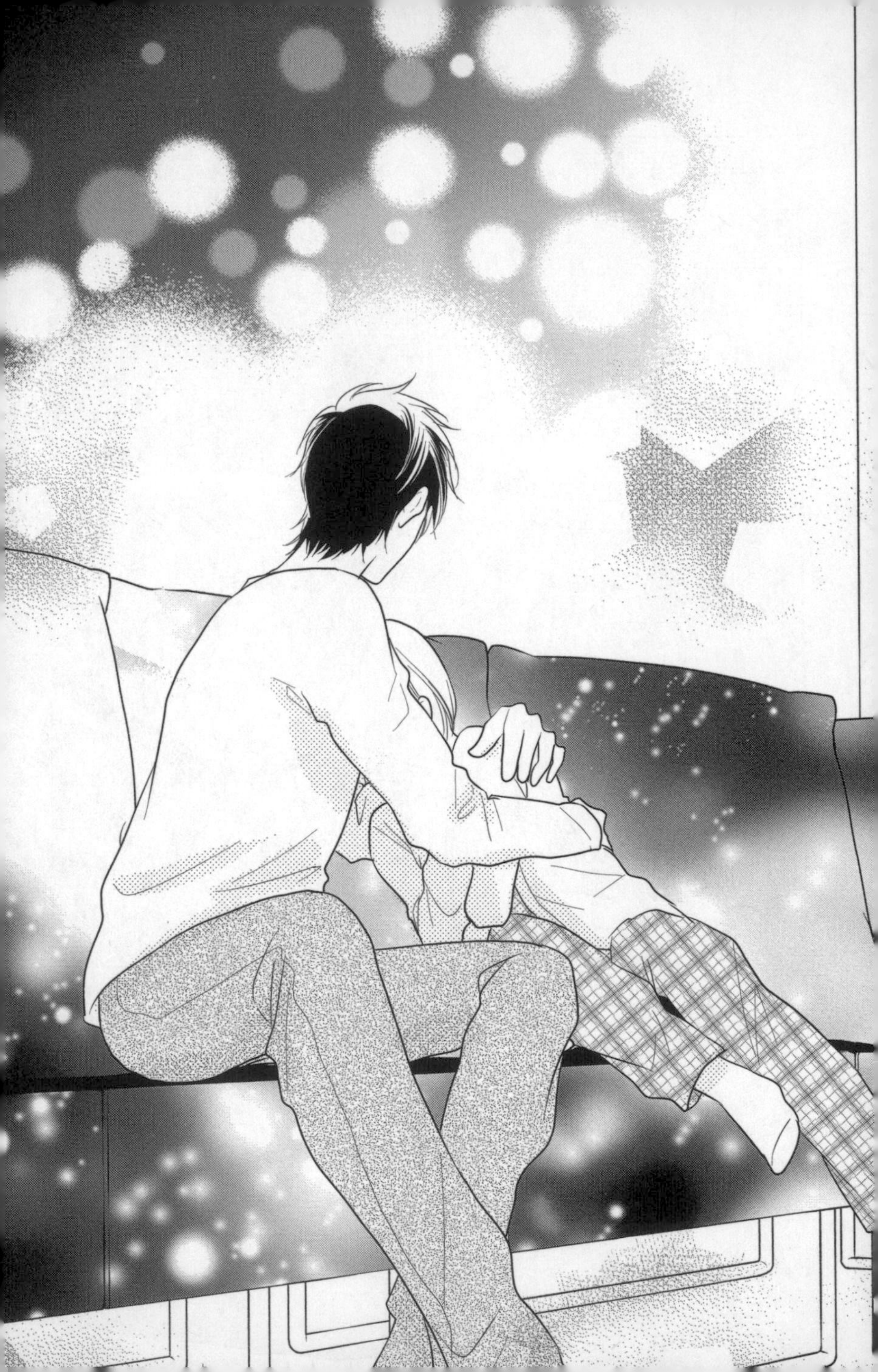

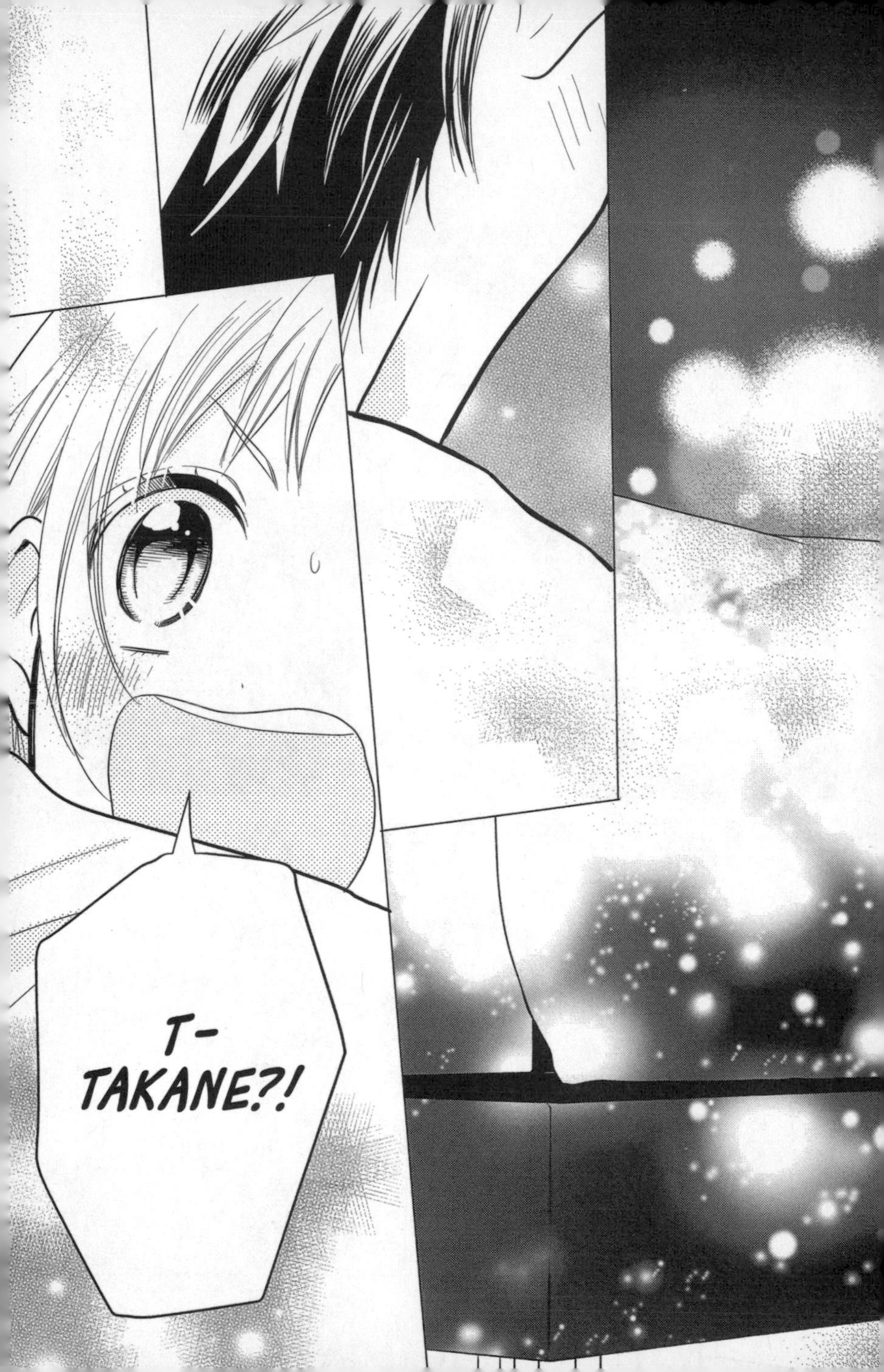
T-TAKANE?!

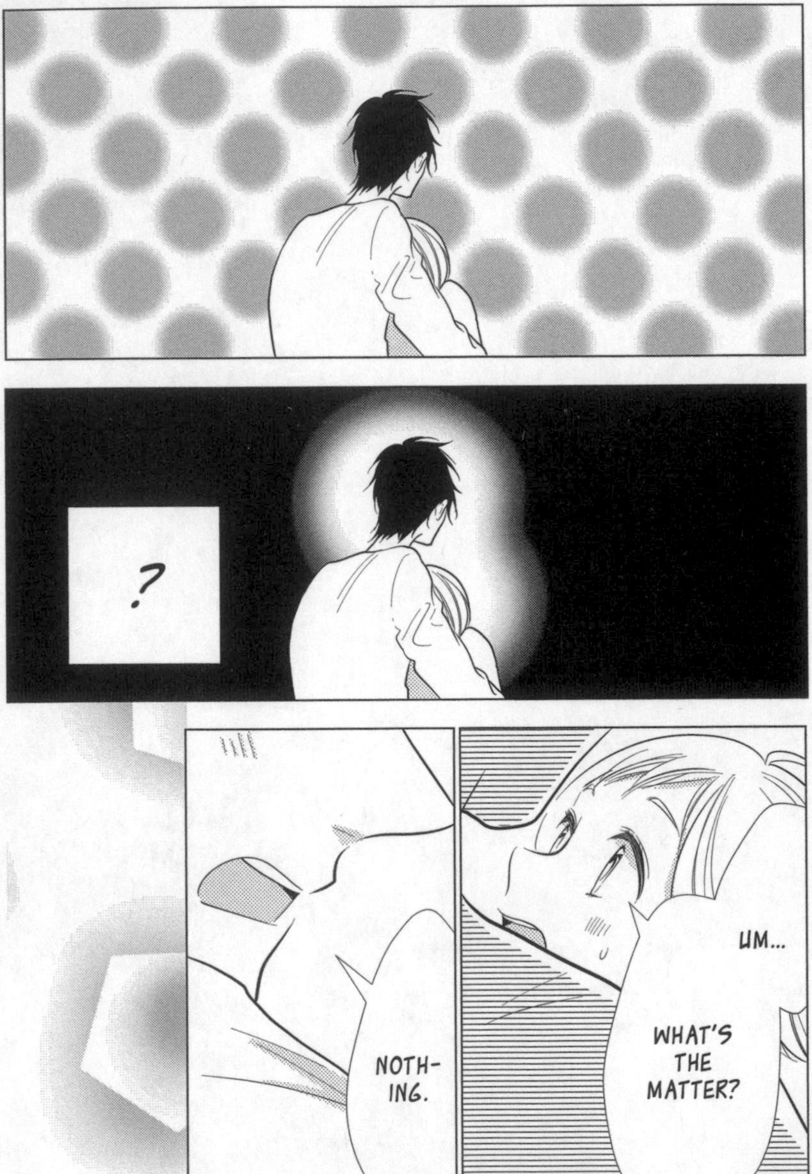
?
UM...
WHAT'S THE MATTER?
NOTH-ING.

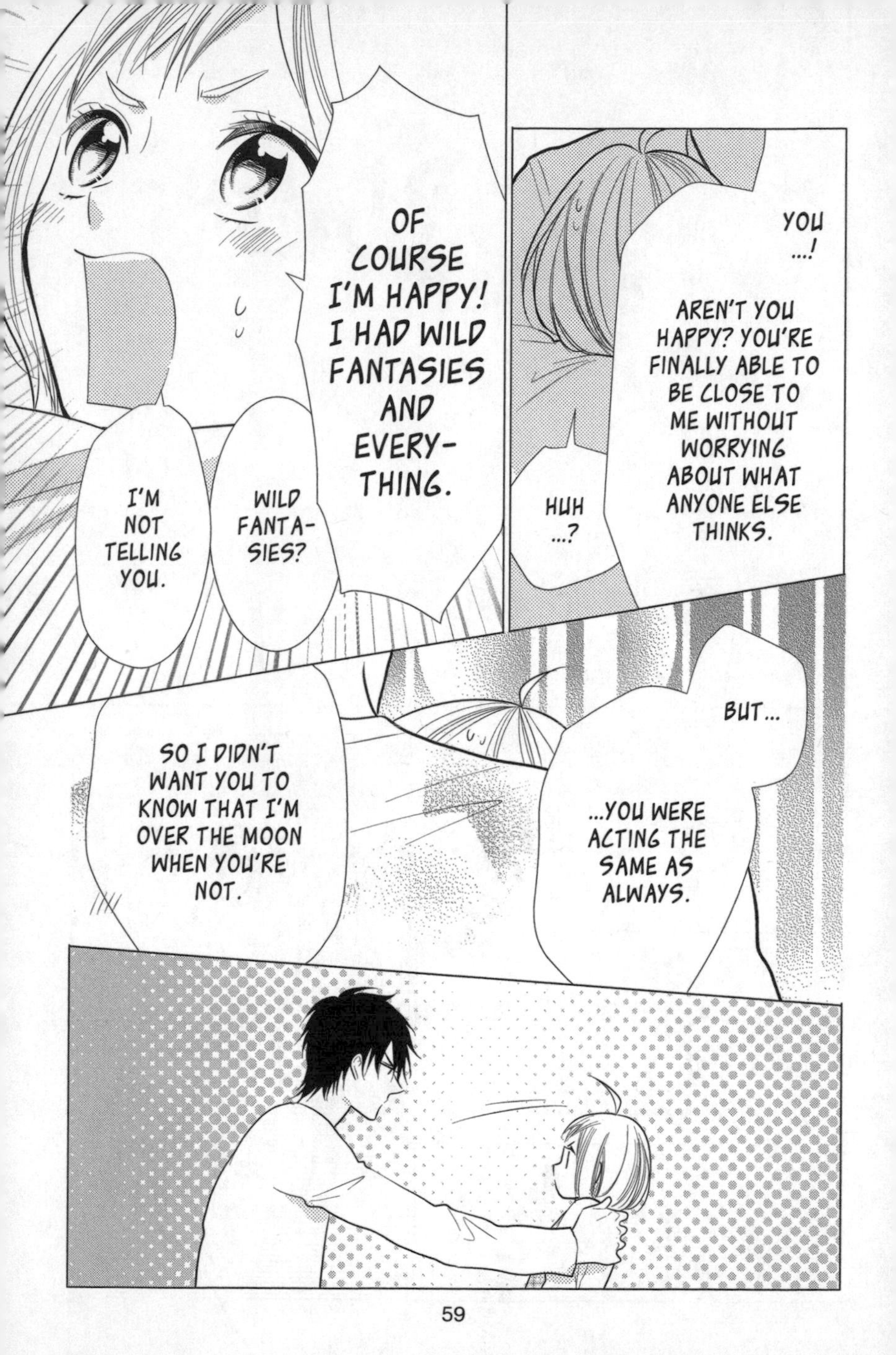
YOU ...!
AREN'T YOU HAPPY? YOU'RE FINALLY ABLE TO BE CLOSE TO ME WITHOUT WORRYING ABOUT WHAT ANYONE ELSE THINKS.
HUH ...?
OF COURSE I'M HAPPY! I HAD WILD FANTASIES AND EVERY-THING.
WILD FANTA-SIES?
I'M NOT TELLING YOU.
BUT...
...YOU WERE ACTING THE SAME AS ALWAYS.
SO I DIDN'T WANT YOU TO KNOW THAT I'M OVER THE MOON WHEN YOU'RE NOT.

BLUSH

INCH...

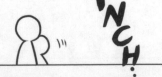
INCH...

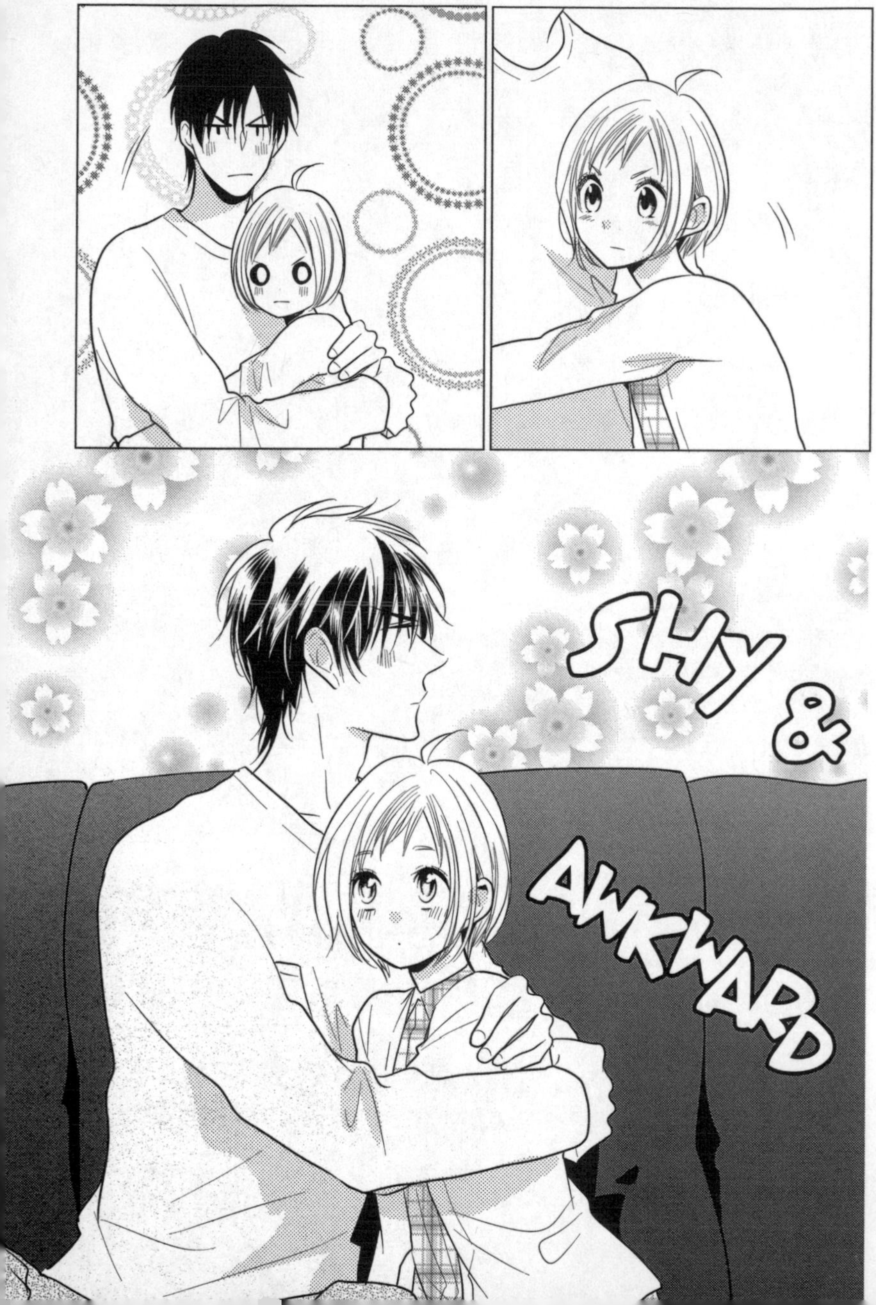
SHY & AWKWARD

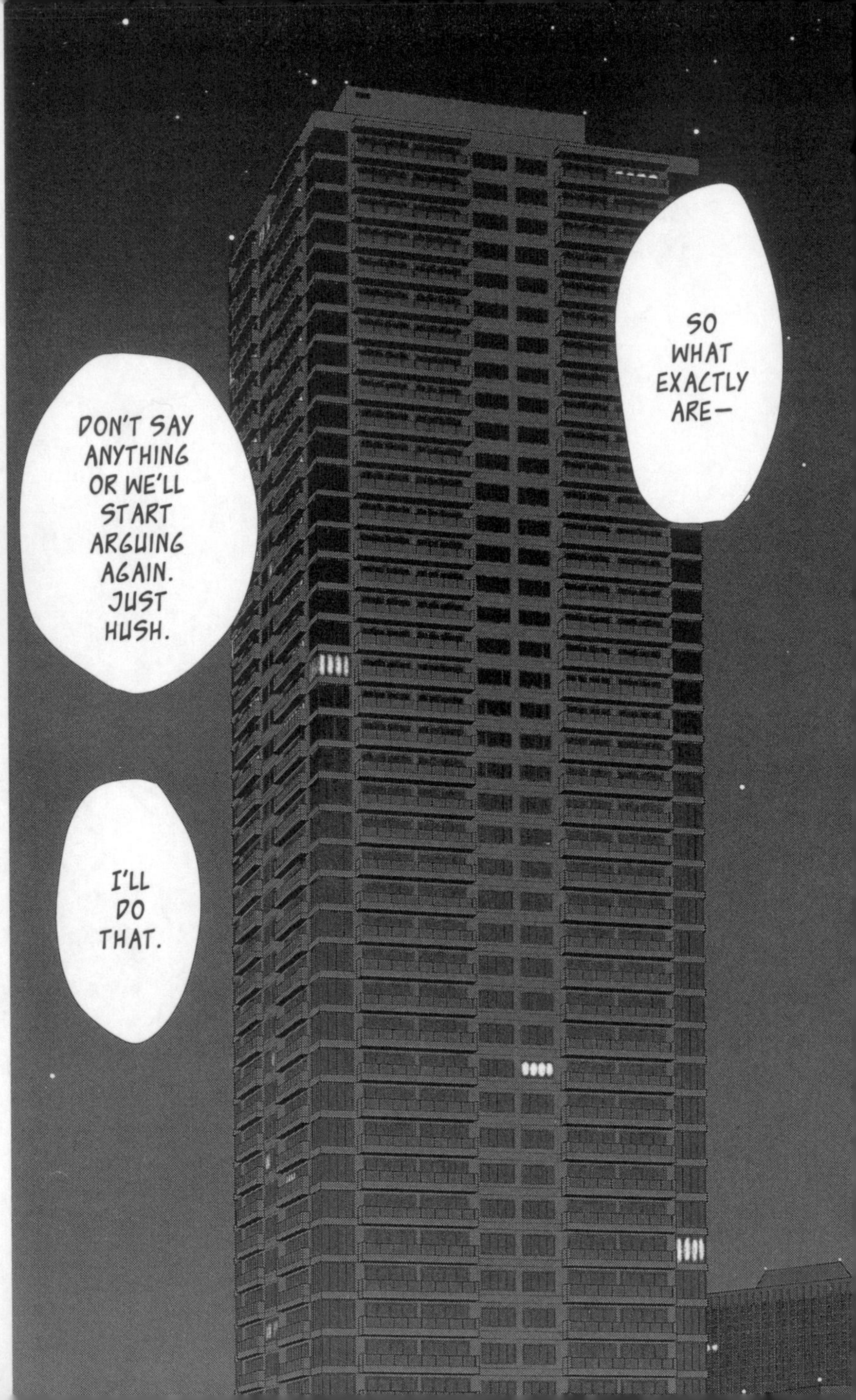
SO WHAT EXACTLY ARE—
DON'T SAY ANYTHING OR WE'LL START ARGUING AGAIN. JUST HUSH.
I'LL DO THAT.

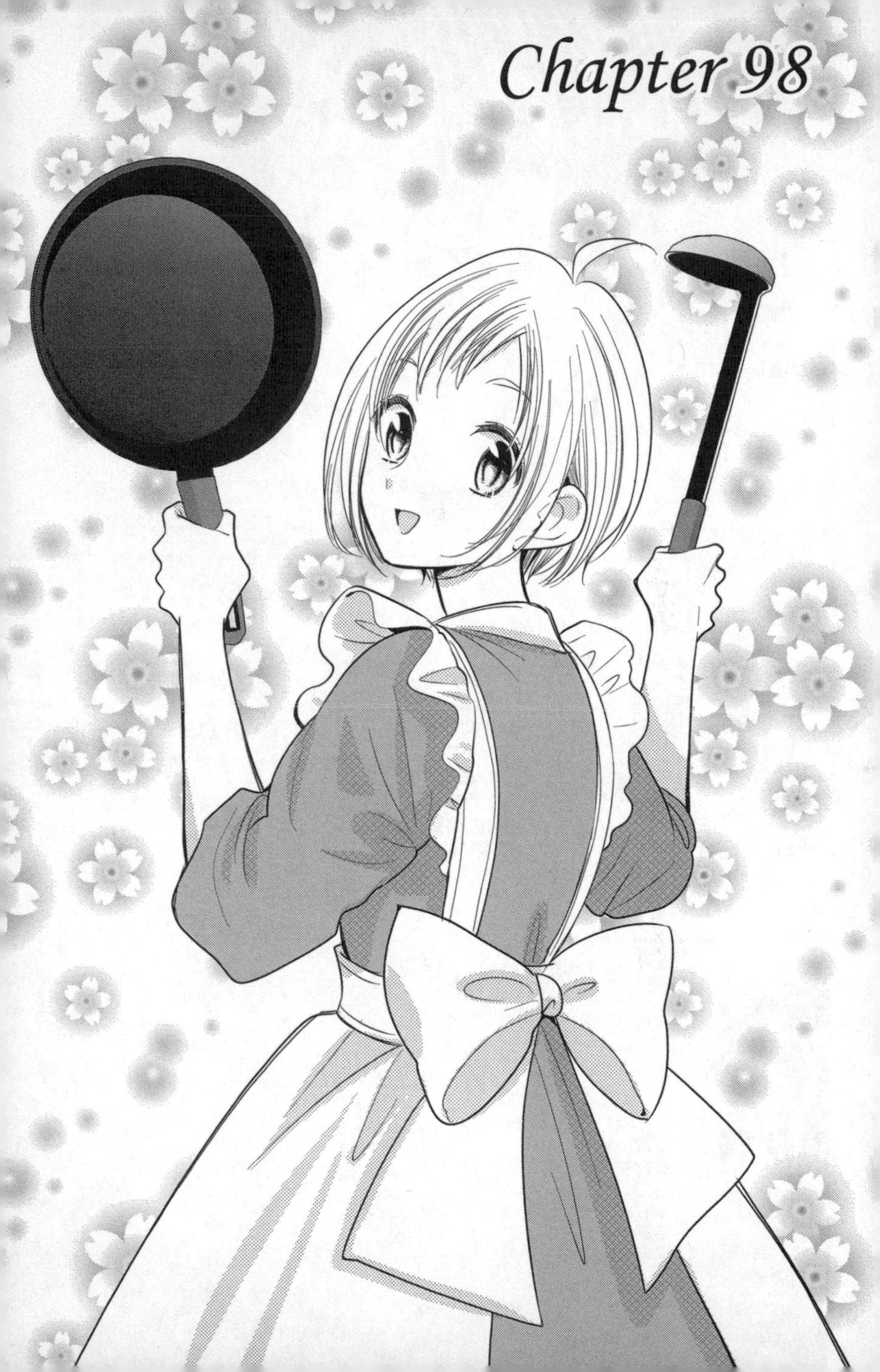
Chapter 98

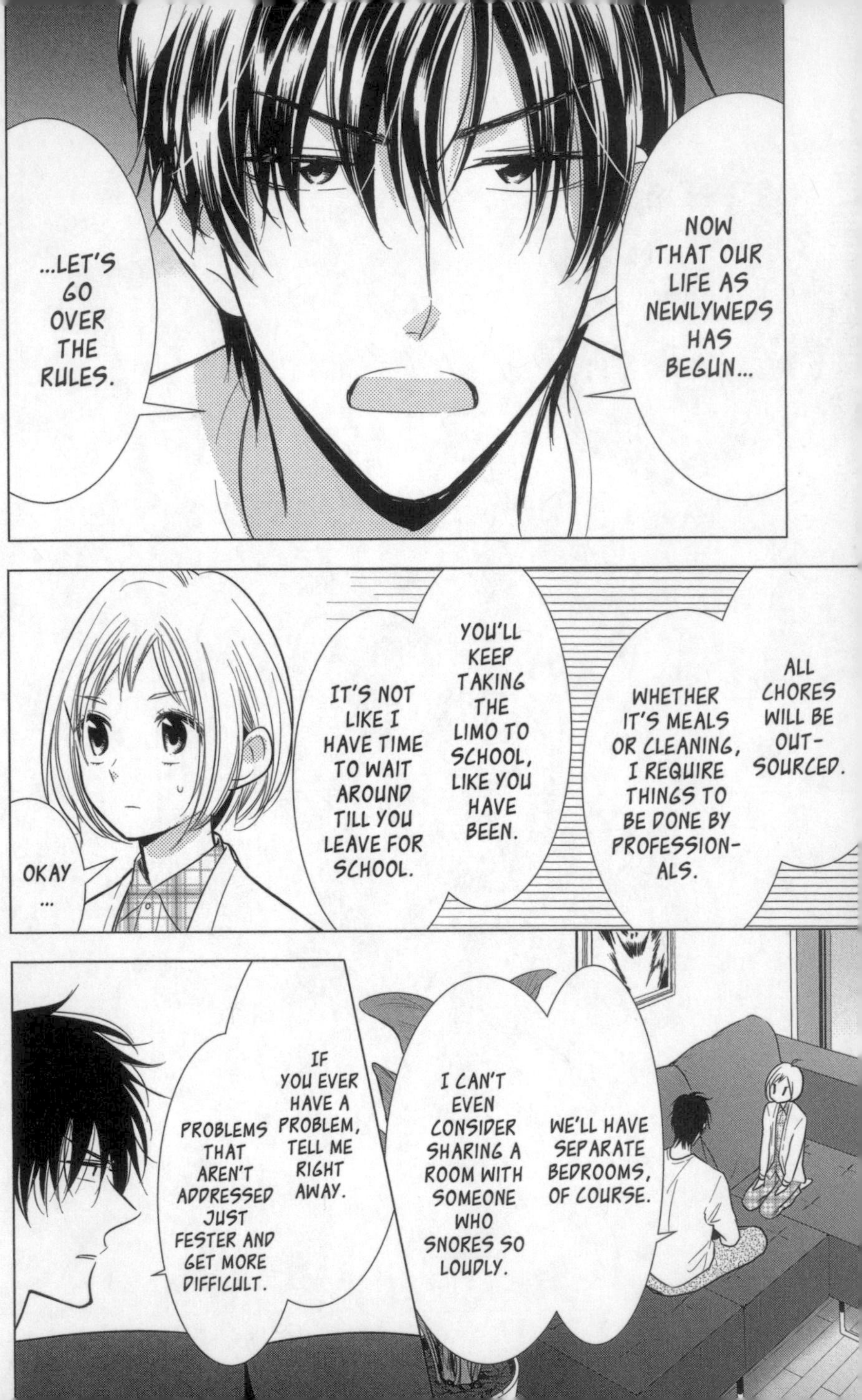
NOW THAT OUR LIFE AS NEWLYWEDS HAS BEGUN...
...LET'S GO OVER THE RULES.
ALL CHORES WILL BE OUT-SOURCED.
WHETHER IT'S MEALS OR CLEANING, I REQUIRE THINGS TO BE DONE BY PROFESSION-ALS.
YOU'LL KEEP TAKING THE LIMO TO SCHOOL, LIKE YOU HAVE BEEN.
IT'S NOT LIKE I HAVE TIME TO WAIT AROUND TILL YOU LEAVE FOR SCHOOL.
OKAY...
WE'LL HAVE SEPARATE BEDROOMS, OF COURSE.
I CAN'T EVEN CONSIDER SHARING A ROOM WITH SOMEONE WHO SNORES SO LOUDLY.
IF YOU EVER HAVE A PROBLEM, TELL ME RIGHT AWAY.
PROBLEMS THAT AREN'T ADDRESSED JUST FESTER AND GET MORE DIFFICULT.

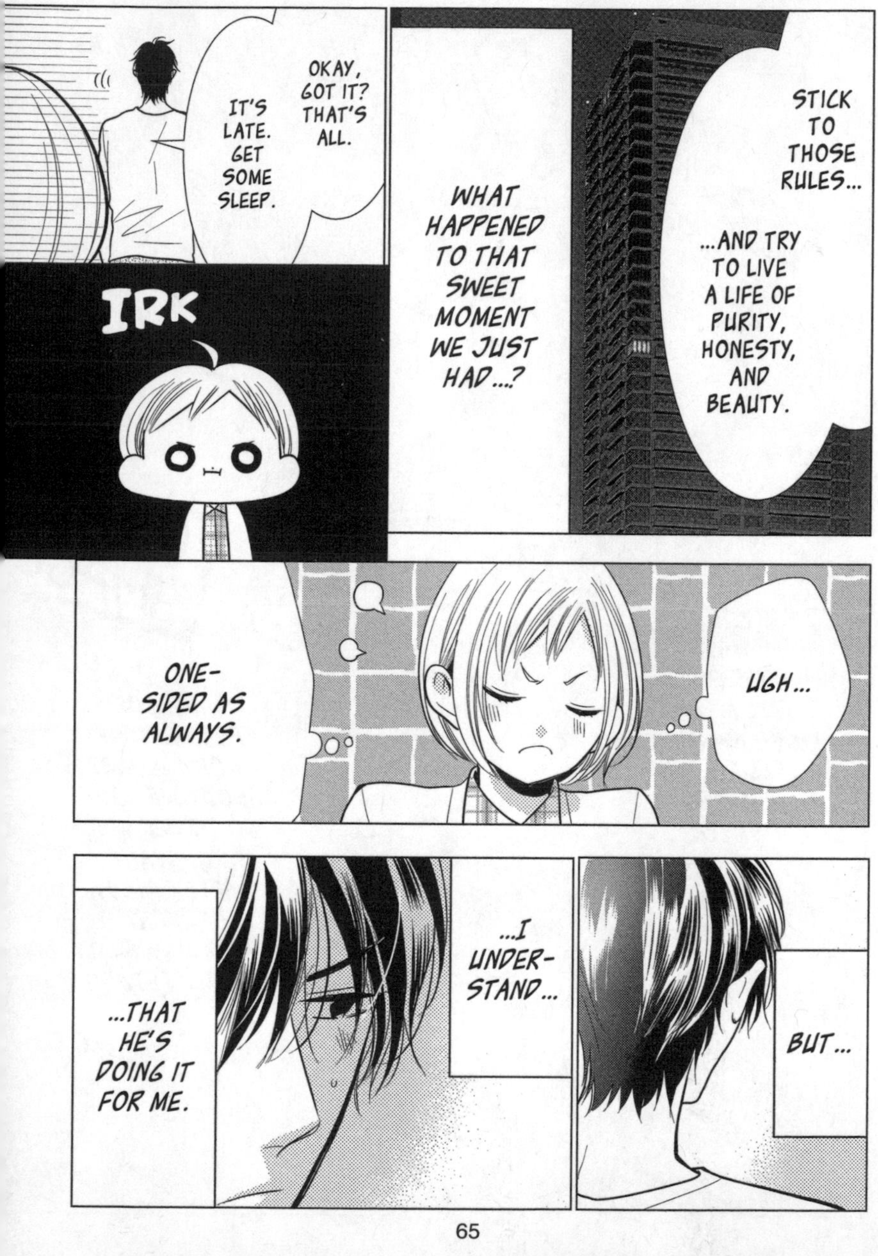
STICK TO THOSE RULES...
...AND TRY TO LIVE A LIFE OF PURITY, HONESTY, AND BEAUTY.
OKAY, GOT IT? THAT'S ALL.
IT'S LATE. GET SOME SLEEP.
IRK
WHAT HAPPENED TO THAT SWEET MOMENT WE JUST HAD...?
UGH...
ONE-SIDED AS ALWAYS.
BUT...
...I UNDER-STAND...
...THAT HE'S DOING IT FOR ME.

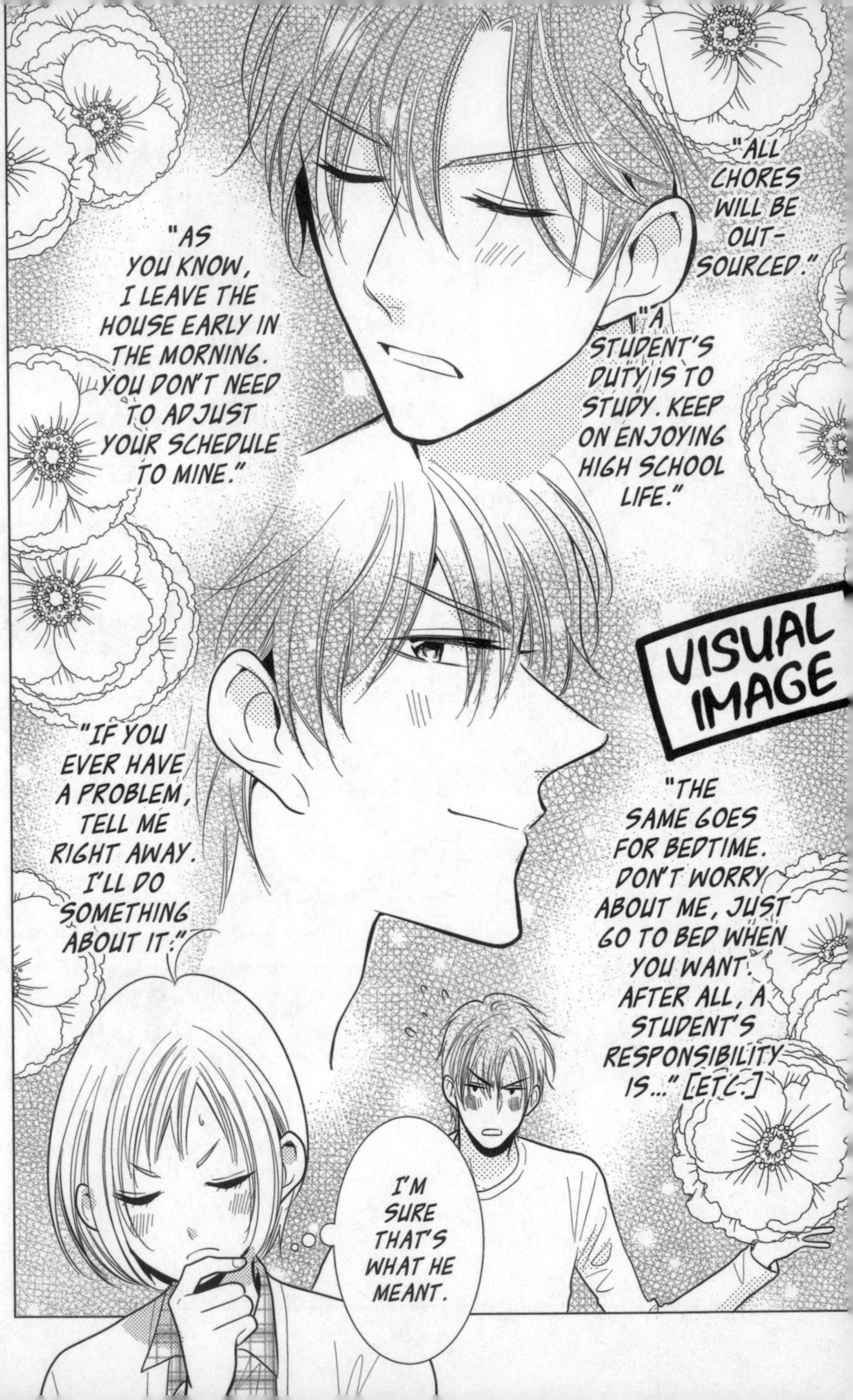
"ALL CHORES WILL BE OUT-SOURCED."
"AS YOU KNOW, I LEAVE THE HOUSE EARLY IN THE MORNING. YOU DON'T NEED TO ADJUST YOUR SCHEDULE TO MINE."
"A STUDENT'S DUTY IS TO STUDY. KEEP ON ENJOYING HIGH SCHOOL LIFE."
VISUAL IMAGE
"THE SAME GOES FOR BEDTIME. DON'T WORRY ABOUT ME, JUST GO TO BED WHEN YOU WANT. AFTER ALL, A STUDENT'S RESPONSIBILITY IS..." [ETC.]
"IF YOU EVER HAVE A PROBLEM, TELL ME RIGHT AWAY. I'LL DO SOMETHING ABOUT IT."
I'M SURE THAT'S WHAT HE MEANT.

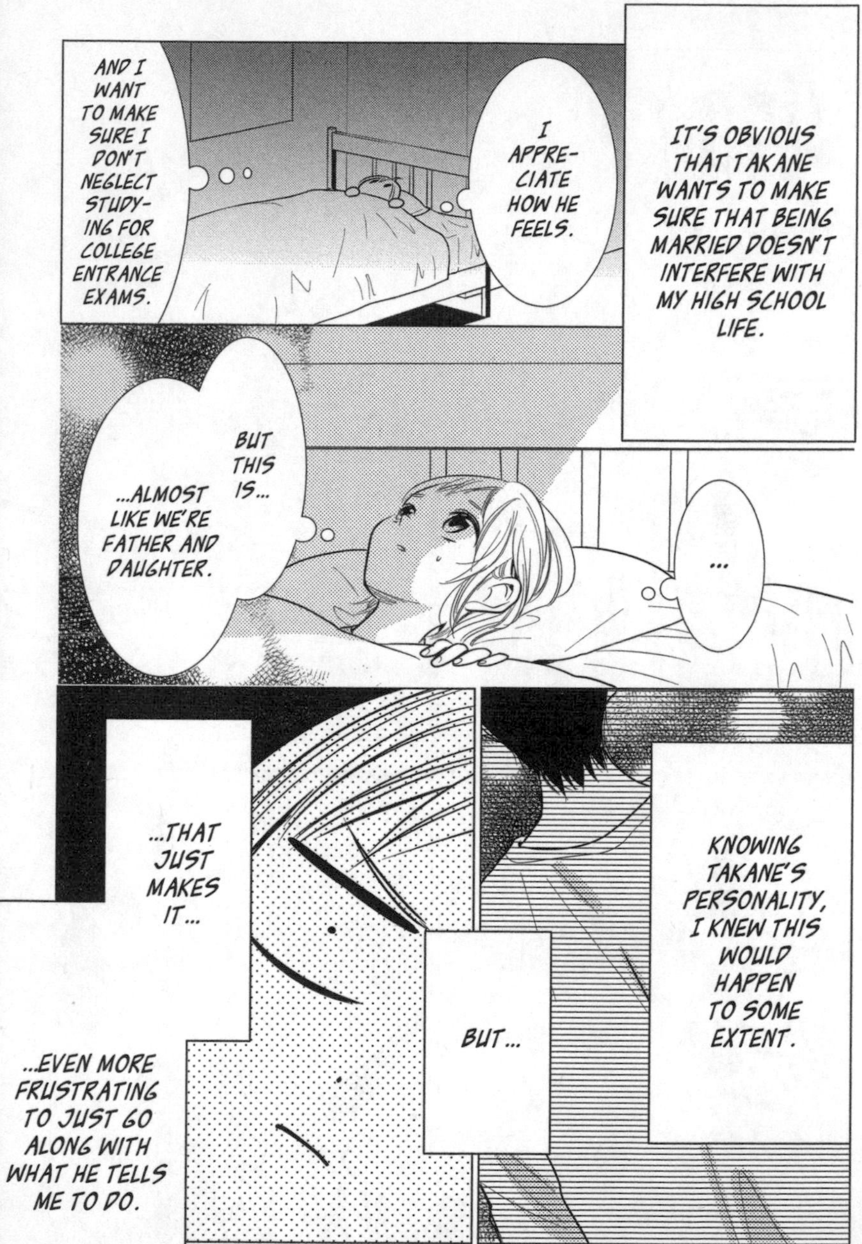
IT'S OBVIOUS THAT TAKANE WANTS TO MAKE SURE THAT BEING MARRIED DOESN'T INTERFERE WITH MY HIGH SCHOOL LIFE.
I APPRECIATE HOW HE FEELS.
AND I WANT TO MAKE SURE I DON'T NEGLECT STUDYING FOR COLLEGE ENTRANCE EXAMS.
...
BUT THIS IS...
...ALMOST LIKE WE'RE FATHER AND DAUGHTER.
KNOWING TAKANE'S PERSONALITY, I KNEW THIS WOULD HAPPEN TO SOME EXTENT.
BUT...
...THAT JUST MAKES IT...
...EVEN MORE FRUSTRATING TO JUST GO ALONG WITH WHAT HE TELLS ME TO DO.

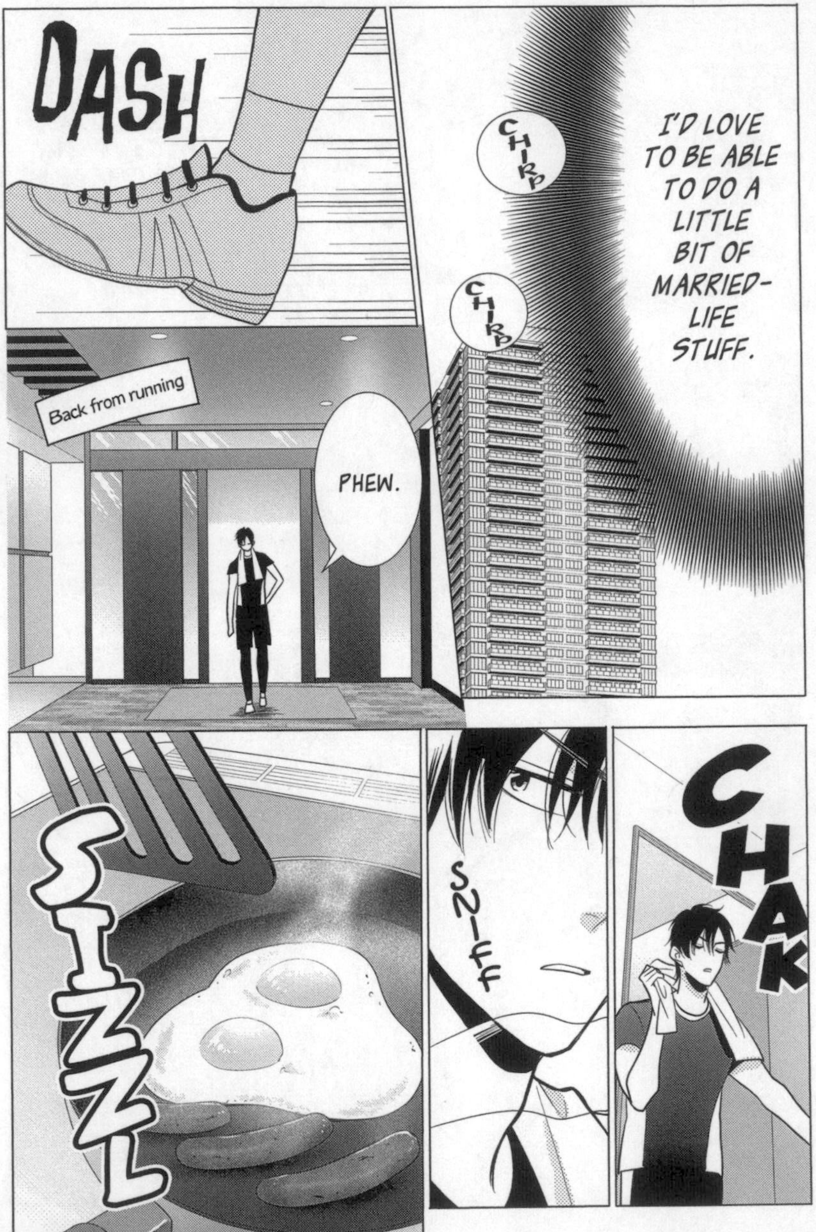
I'D LOVE TO BE ABLE TO DO A LITTLE BIT OF MARRIED-LIFE STUFF.
CHIRP
CHIRP
DASH
Back from running
PHEW.
CHAK
SNIFF
SIZZL

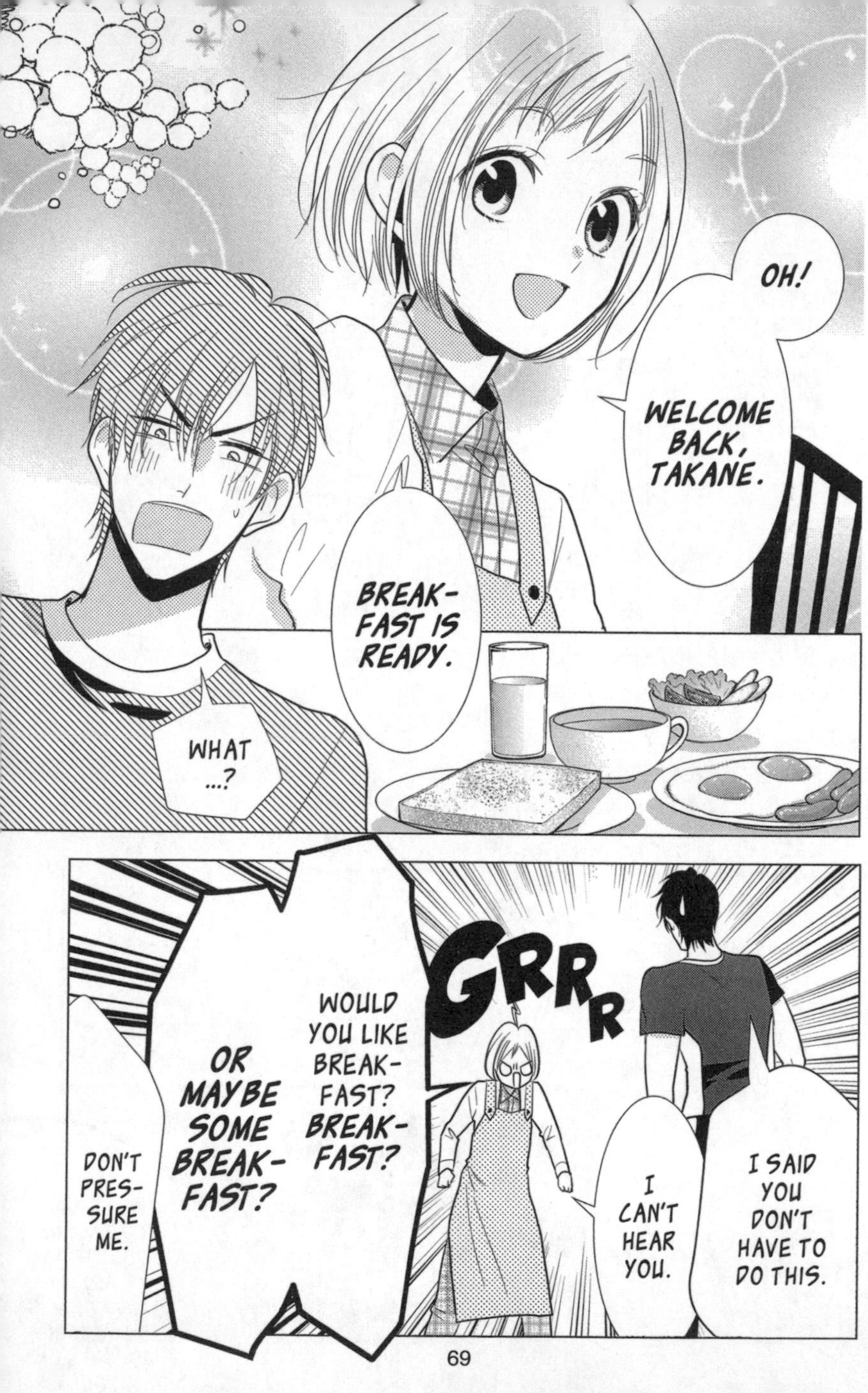
OH!
WELCOME BACK, TAKANE.
BREAK-FAST IS READY.
WHAT ...?
I SAID YOU DON'T HAVE TO DO THIS.
I CAN'T HEAR YOU.
GRRR
WOULD YOU LIKE BREAK-FAST? BREAK-FAST?
OR MAYBE SOME BREAK-FAST?
DON'T PRES-SURE ME.

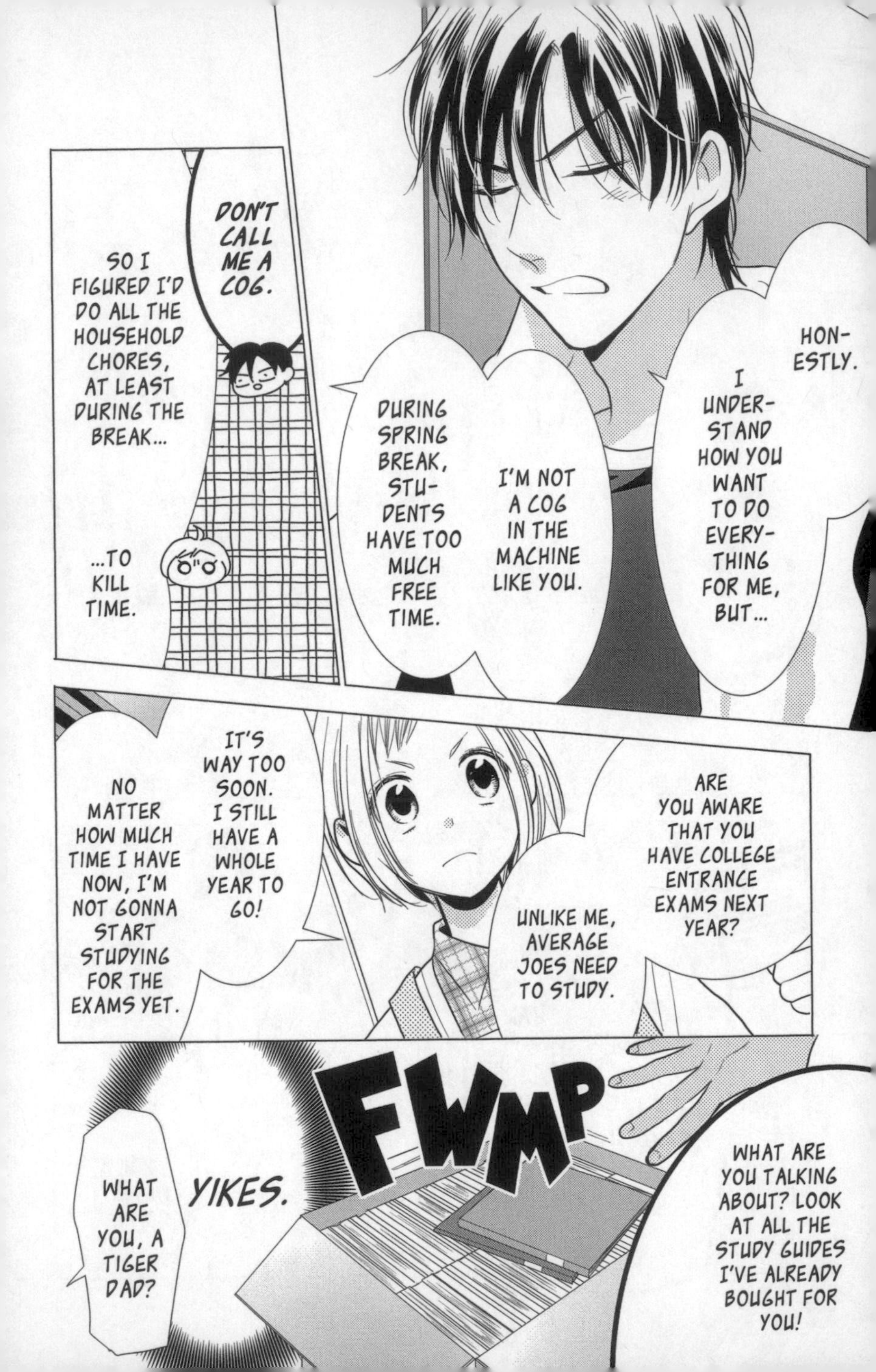
HON-ESTLY.
I UNDER-STAND HOW YOU WANT TO DO EVERY-THING FOR ME, BUT...
I'M NOT A COG IN THE MACHINE LIKE YOU.
DURING SPRING BREAK, STU-DENTS HAVE TOO MUCH FREE TIME.
DON'T CALL ME A COG.
SO I FIGURED I'D DO ALL THE HOUSEHOLD CHORES, AT LEAST DURING THE BREAK...
...TO KILL TIME.
ARE YOU AWARE THAT YOU HAVE COLLEGE ENTRANCE EXAMS NEXT YEAR?
UNLIKE ME, AVERAGE JOES NEED TO STUDY.
IT'S WAY TOO SOON. I STILL HAVE A WHOLE YEAR TO GO!
NO MATTER HOW MUCH TIME I HAVE NOW, I'M NOT GONNA START STUDYING FOR THE EXAMS YET.
FWMP
WHAT ARE YOU TALKING ABOUT? LOOK AT ALL THE STUDY GUIDES I'VE ALREADY BOUGHT FOR YOU!
YIKES.
WHAT ARE YOU, A TIGER DAD?

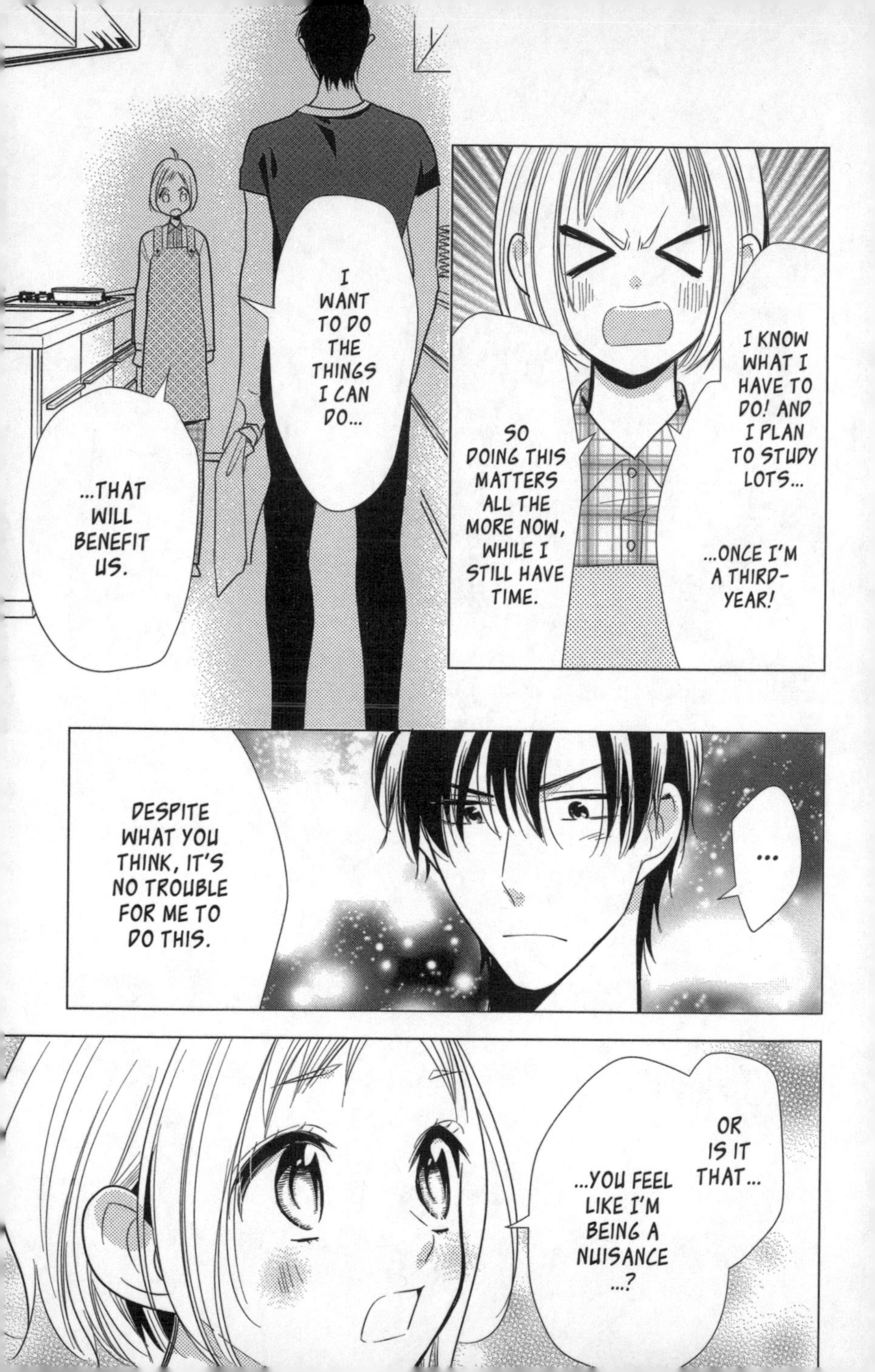
I KNOW WHAT I HAVE TO DO! AND I PLAN TO STUDY LOTS...
...ONCE I'M A THIRD-YEAR!
SO DOING THIS MATTERS ALL THE MORE NOW, WHILE I STILL HAVE TIME.
I WANT TO DO THE THINGS I CAN DO...
...THAT WILL BENEFIT US.
...
DESPITE WHAT YOU THINK, IT'S NO TROUBLE FOR ME TO DO THIS.
OR IS IT THAT...
...YOU FEEL LIKE I'M BEING A NUISANCE ...?

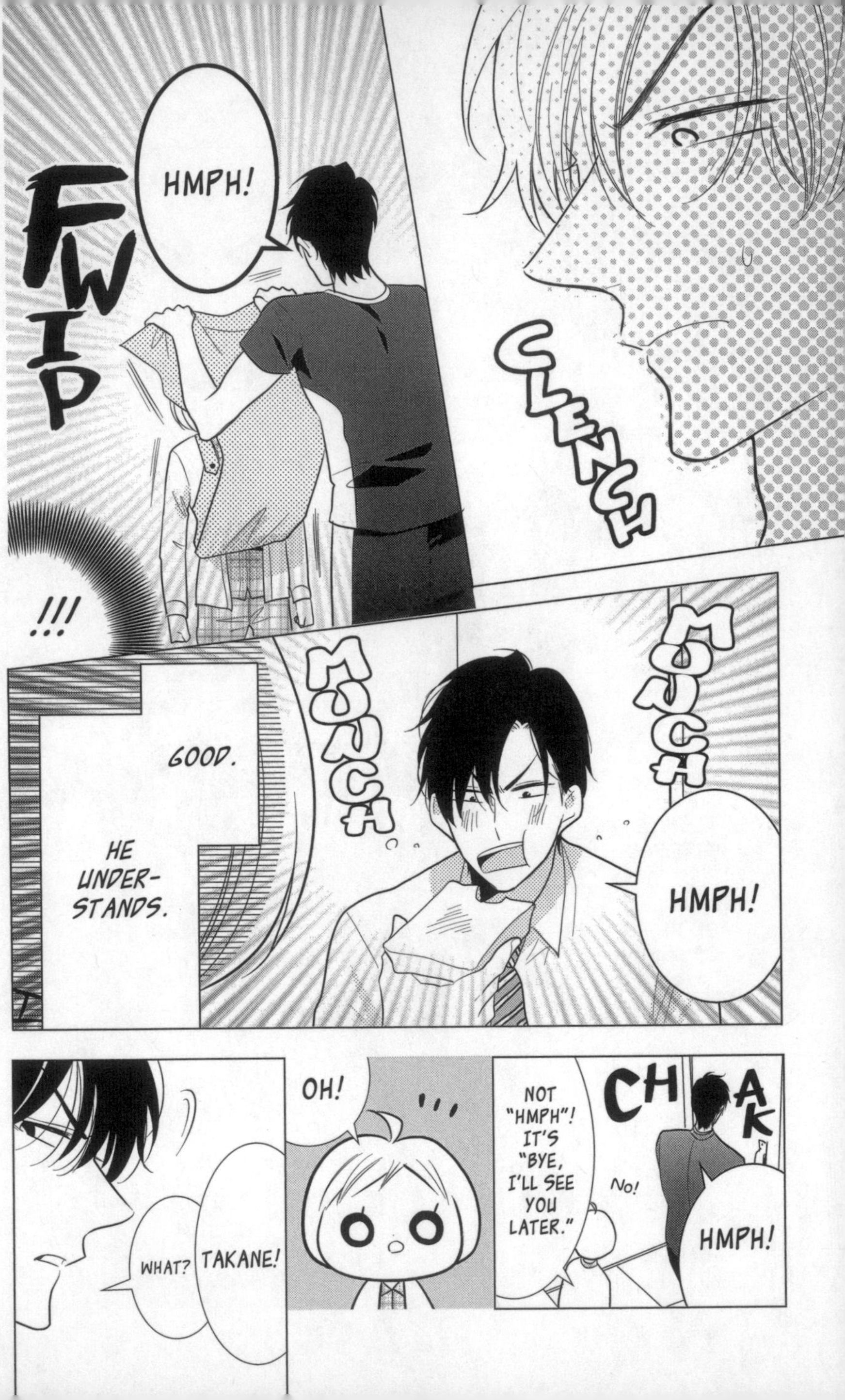
CLENCH
HMPH!
FWIP
!!!
MUNCH
HMPH!
MUNCH
GOOD.
HE UNDER-STANDS.
CHAK
NOT "HMPH"! IT'S "BYE, I'LL SEE YOU LATER."
No!
HMPH!
OH!
TAKANE!
WHAT?

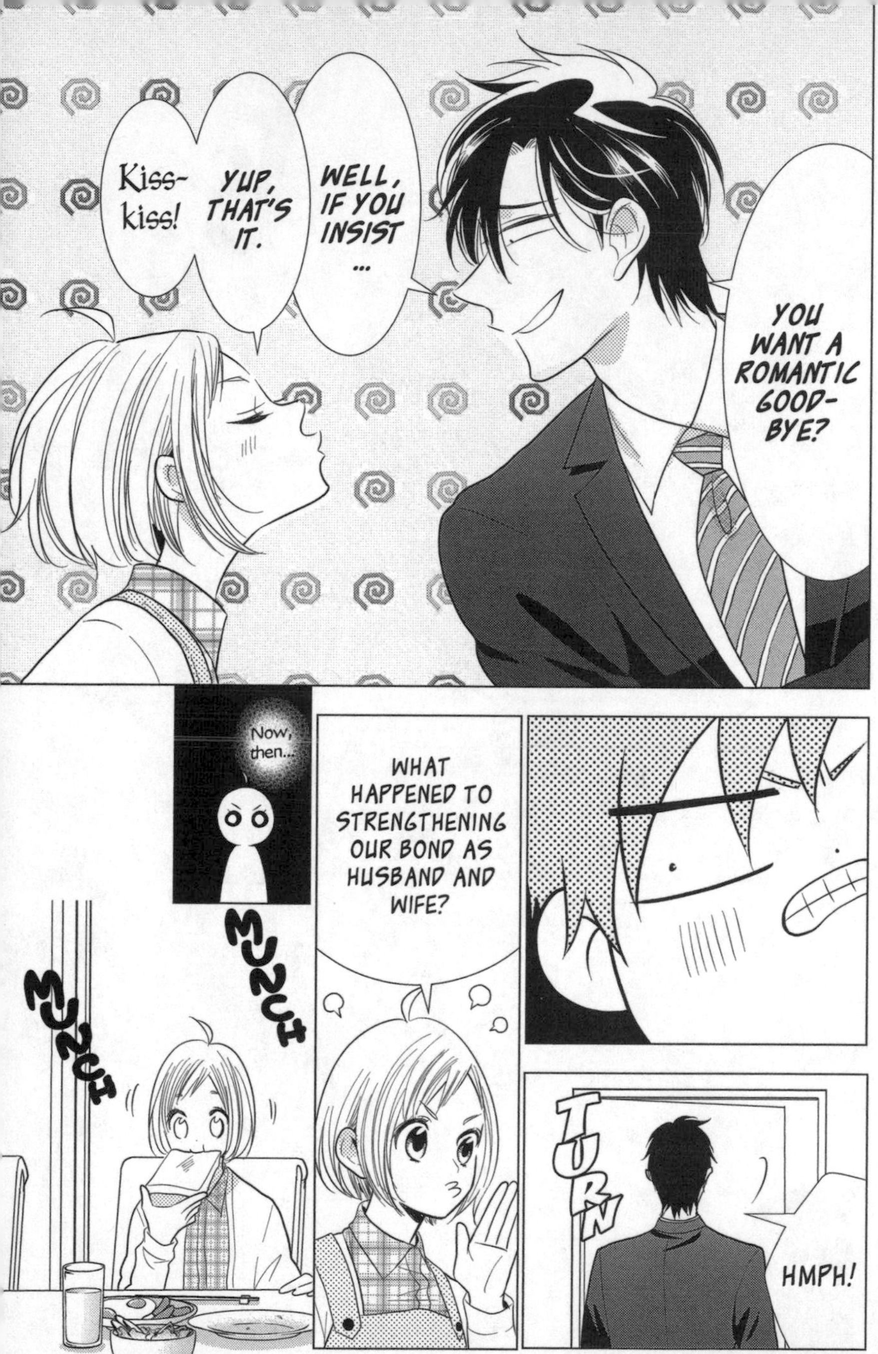
YOU WANT A ROMANTIC GOOD-BYE?
WELL, IF YOU INSIST ...
YUP, THAT'S IT.
Kiss-kiss!
TURN
HMPH!
WHAT HAPPENED TO STRENGTHENING OUR BOND AS HUSBAND AND WIFE?
Now, then...
MUNCH
MUNCH

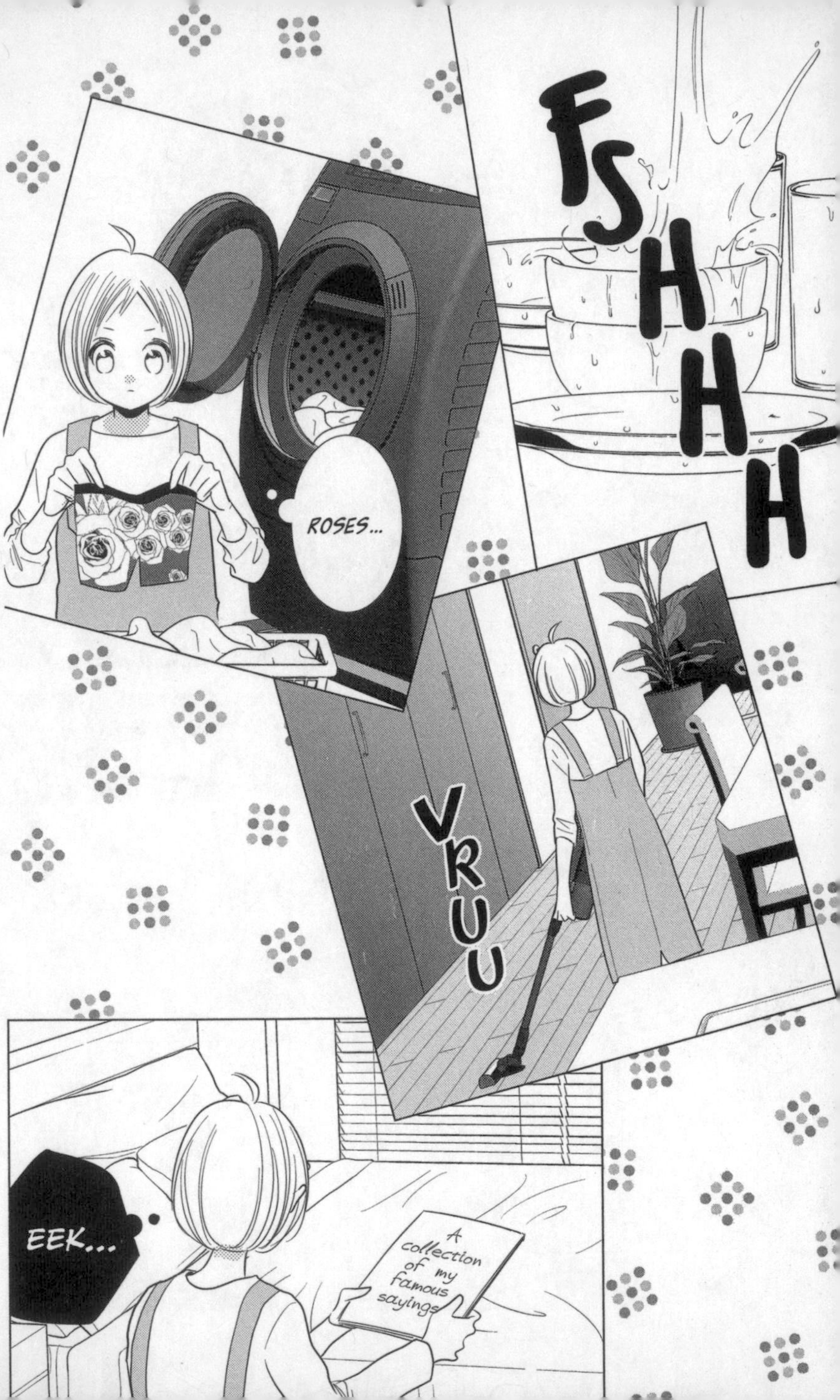
FSHHHH
ROSES...
VRUU
EEK...
A collection of my famous sayings

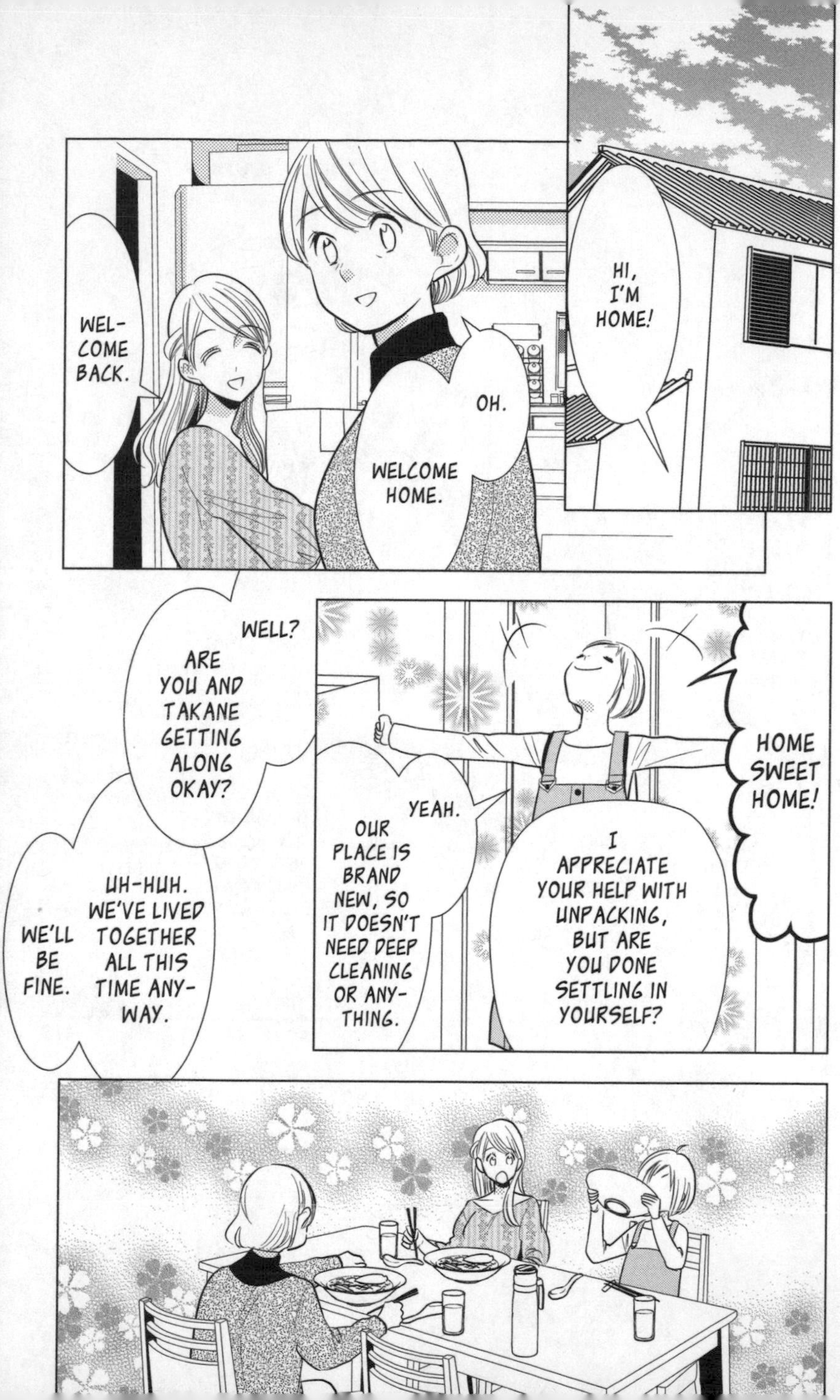
HI, I'M HOME!
OH.
WELCOME HOME.
WEL-COME BACK.
HOME SWEET HOME!
I APPRECIATE YOUR HELP WITH UNPACKING, BUT ARE YOU DONE SETTLING IN YOURSELF?
YEAH.
OUR PLACE IS BRAND NEW, SO IT DOESN'T NEED DEEP CLEANING OR ANY-THING.
WELL?
ARE YOU AND TAKANE GETTING ALONG OKAY?
UH-HUH. WE'VE LIVED TOGETHER ALL THIS TIME ANY-WAY.
WE'LL BE FINE.

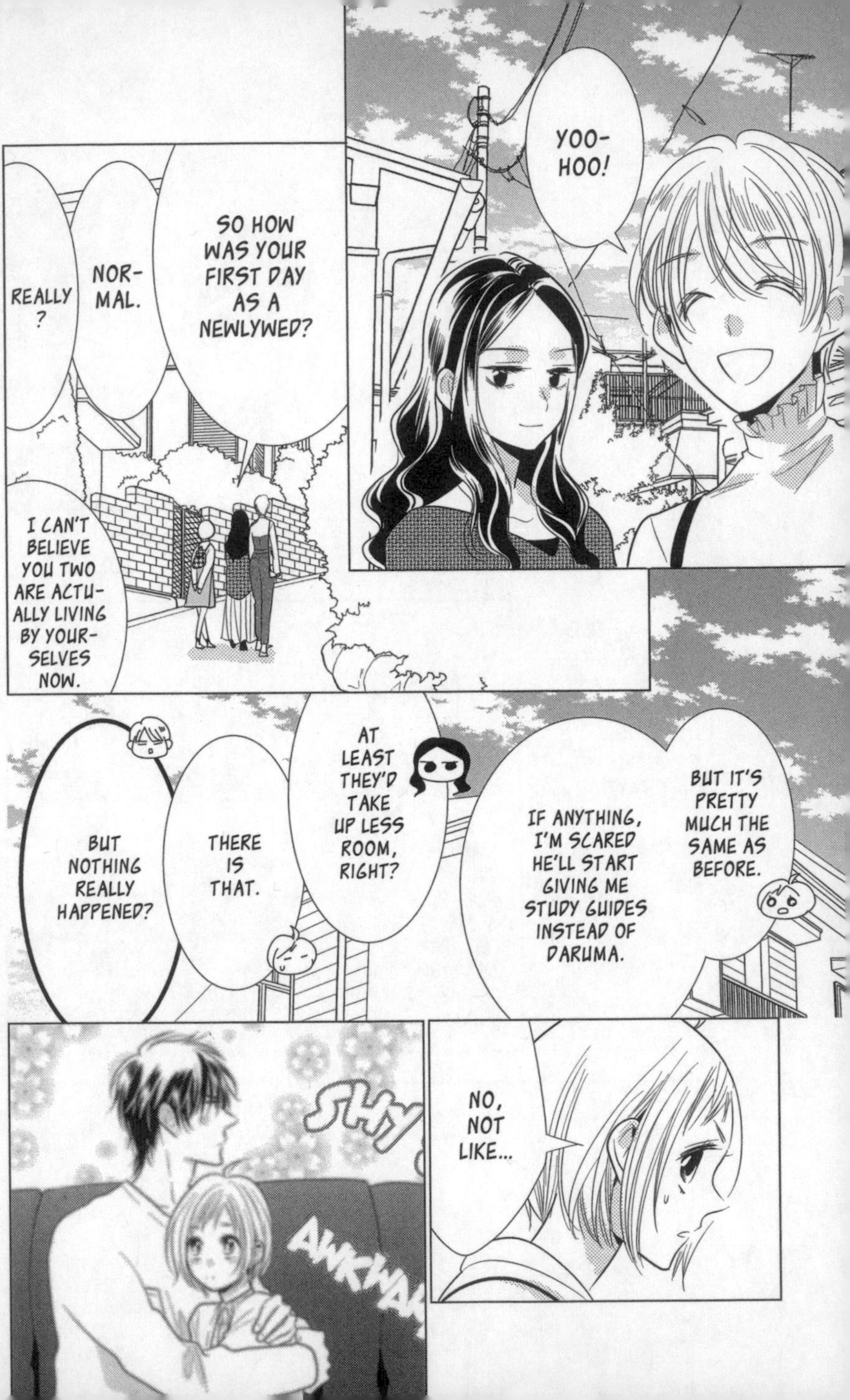
YOO-HOO!
SO HOW WAS YOUR FIRST DAY AS A NEWLYWED?
NOR-MAL.
REALLY?
I CAN'T BELIEVE YOU TWO ARE ACTUALLY LIVING BY YOURSELVES NOW.
BUT IT'S PRETTY MUCH THE SAME AS BEFORE.
IF ANYTHING, I'M SCARED HE'LL START GIVING ME STUDY GUIDES INSTEAD OF DARUMA.
AT LEAST THEY'D TAKE UP LESS ROOM, RIGHT?
THERE IS THAT.
BUT NOTHING REALLY HAPPENED?
NO, NOT LIKE...
SHY
AWKWA

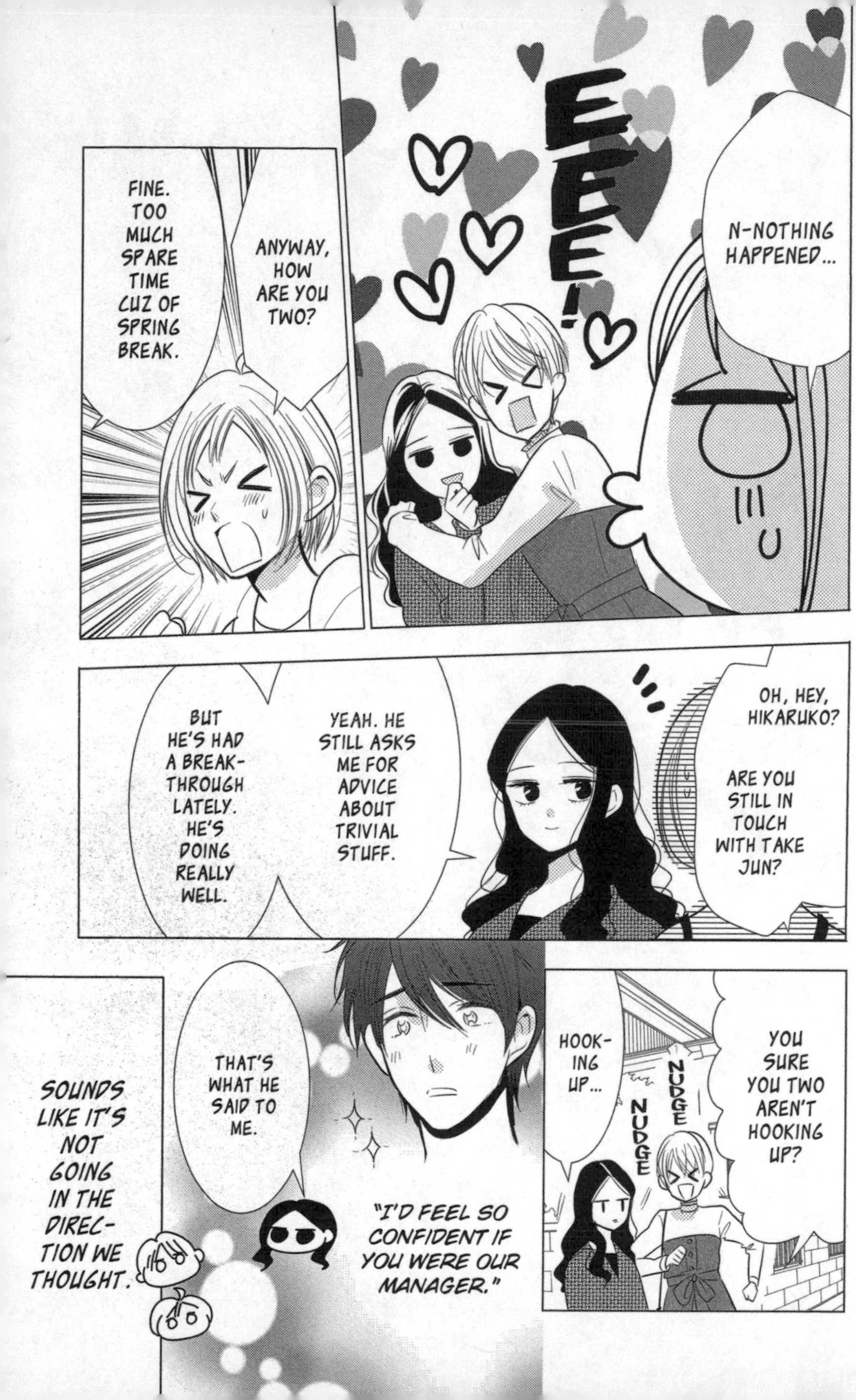
N-NOTHING HAPPENED...
EEEE!
ANYWAY, HOW ARE YOU TWO?
FINE. TOO MUCH SPARE TIME CUZ OF SPRING BREAK.
OH, HEY, HIKARUKO?
ARE YOU STILL IN TOUCH WITH TAKE JUN?
YEAH. HE STILL ASKS ME FOR ADVICE ABOUT TRIVIAL STUFF.
BUT HE'S HAD A BREAK-THROUGH LATELY. HE'S DOING REALLY WELL.
YOU SURE YOU TWO AREN'T HOOKING UP?
NUDGE
NUDGE
HOOKING UP...
THAT'S WHAT HE SAID TO ME.
"I'D FEEL SO CONFIDENT IF YOU WERE OUR MANAGER."
SOUNDS LIKE IT'S NOT GOING IN THE DIRECTION WE THOUGHT.

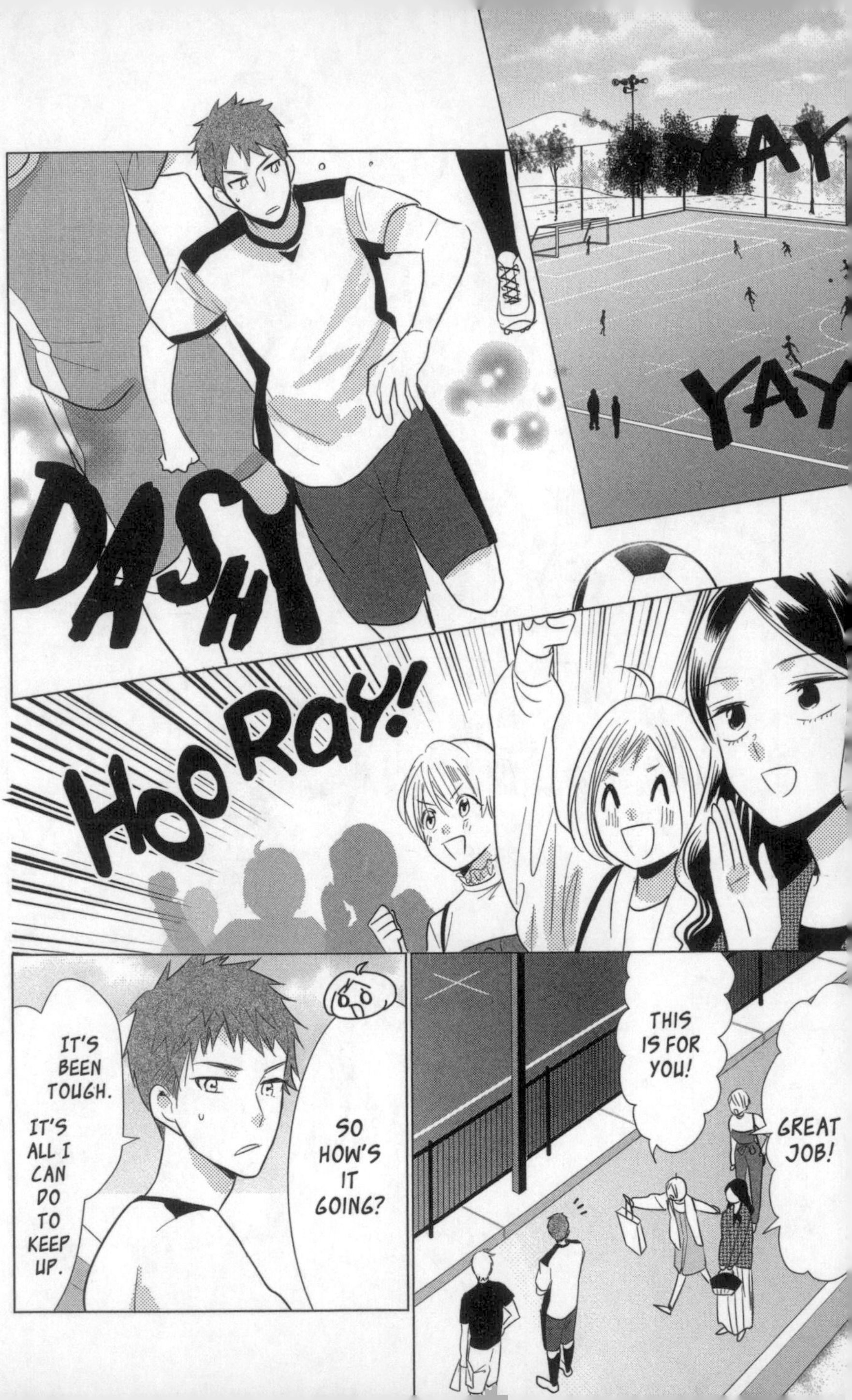
YAY
YAY
DASH
HOORAY!
THIS IS FOR YOU!
GREAT JOB!
SO HOW'S IT GOING?
IT'S BEEN TOUGH.
IT'S ALL I CAN DO TO KEEP UP.

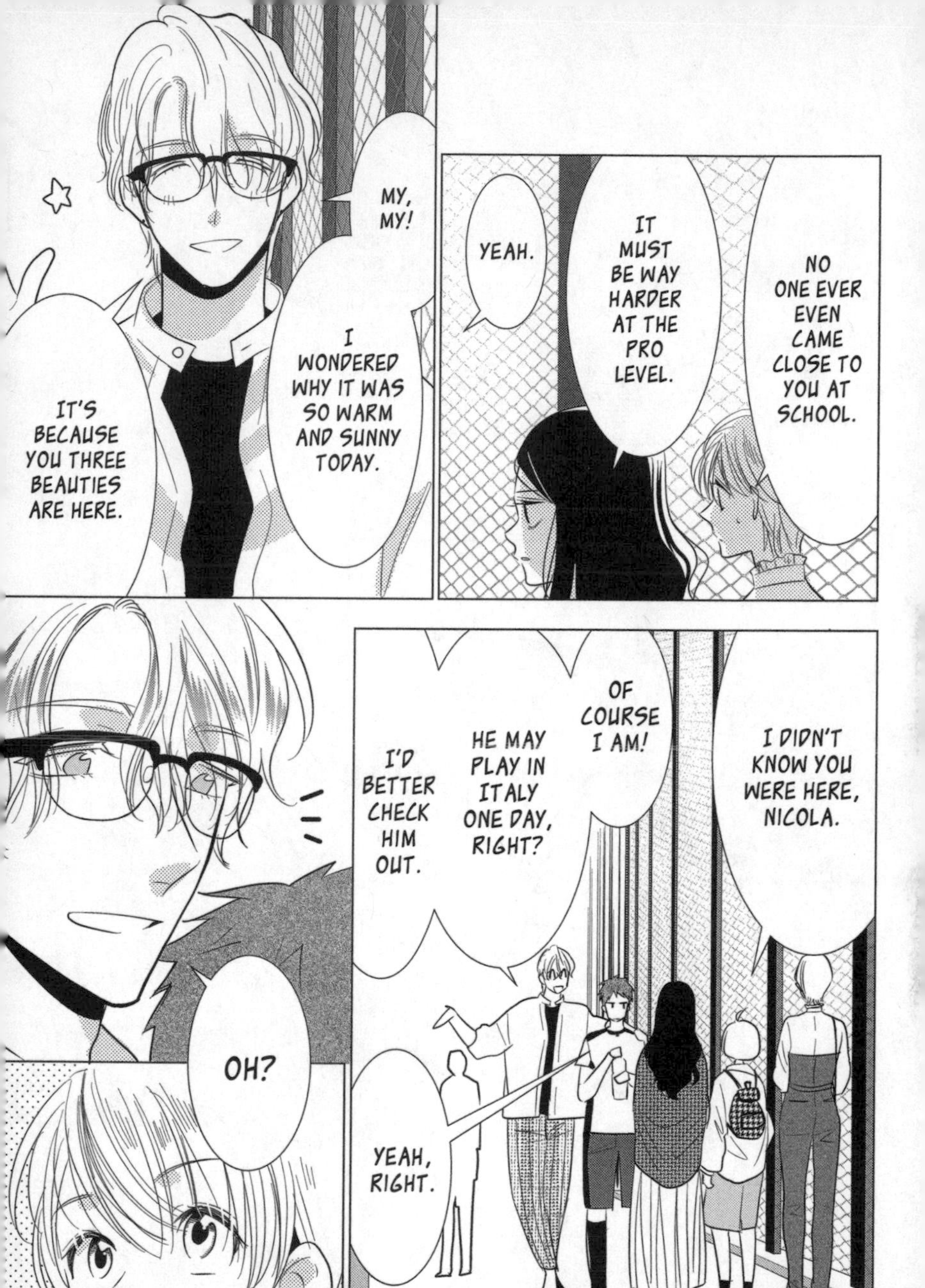
NO ONE EVER EVEN CAME CLOSE TO YOU AT SCHOOL.
IT MUST BE WAY HARDER AT THE PRO LEVEL.
YEAH.
MY, MY!
I WONDERED WHY IT WAS SO WARM AND SUNNY TODAY.
IT'S BECAUSE YOU THREE BEAUTIES ARE HERE.
I DIDN'T KNOW YOU WERE HERE, NICOLA.
OF COURSE I AM!
HE MAY PLAY IN ITALY ONE DAY, RIGHT?
I'D BETTER CHECK HIM OUT.
YEAH, RIGHT.
OH?

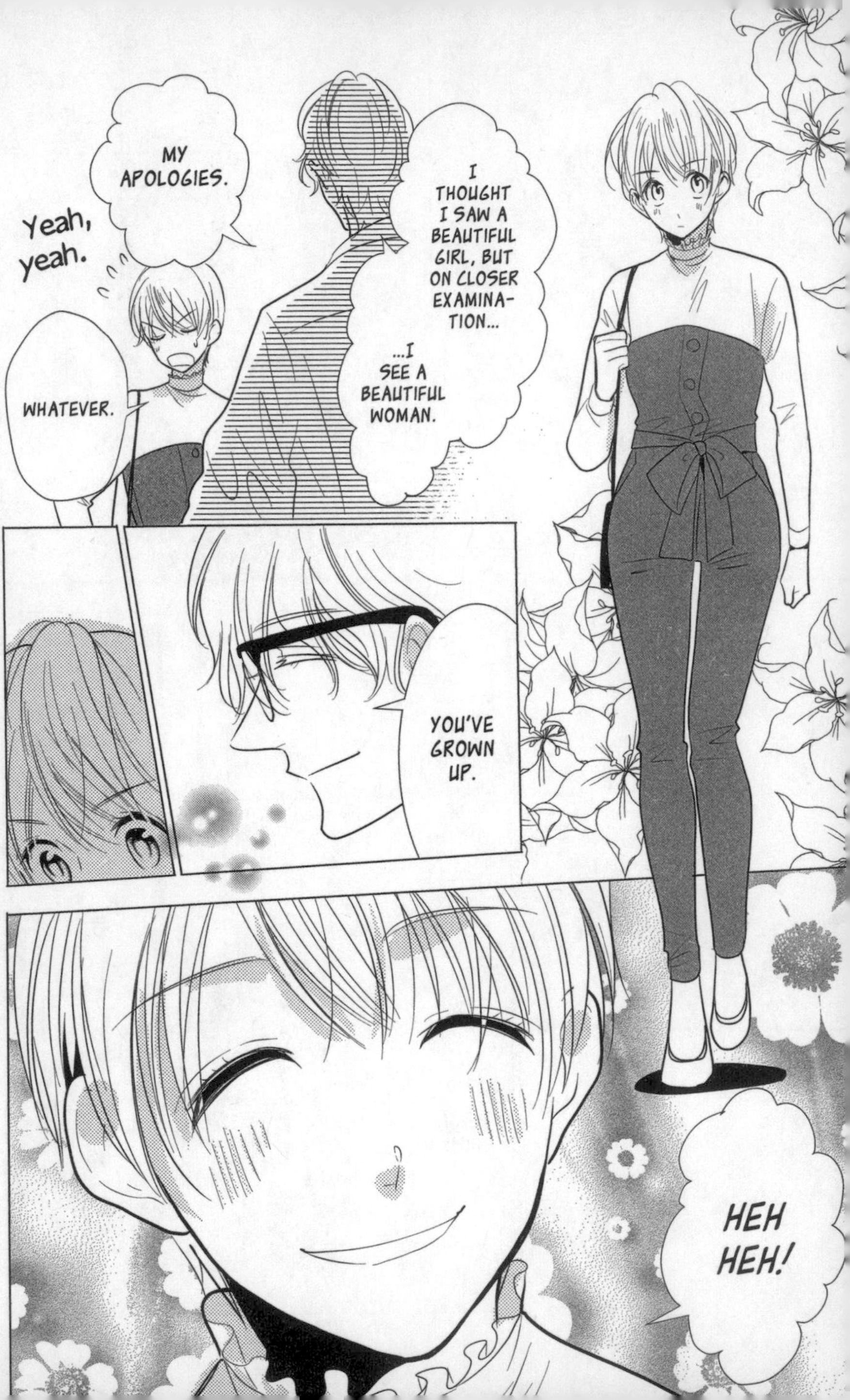
I THOUGHT I SAW A BEAUTIFUL GIRL, BUT ON CLOSER EXAMINATION...
...I SEE A BEAUTIFUL WOMAN.
MY APOLOGIES.
Yeah, yeah.
WHATEVER.
YOU'VE GROWN UP.
HEH HEH!

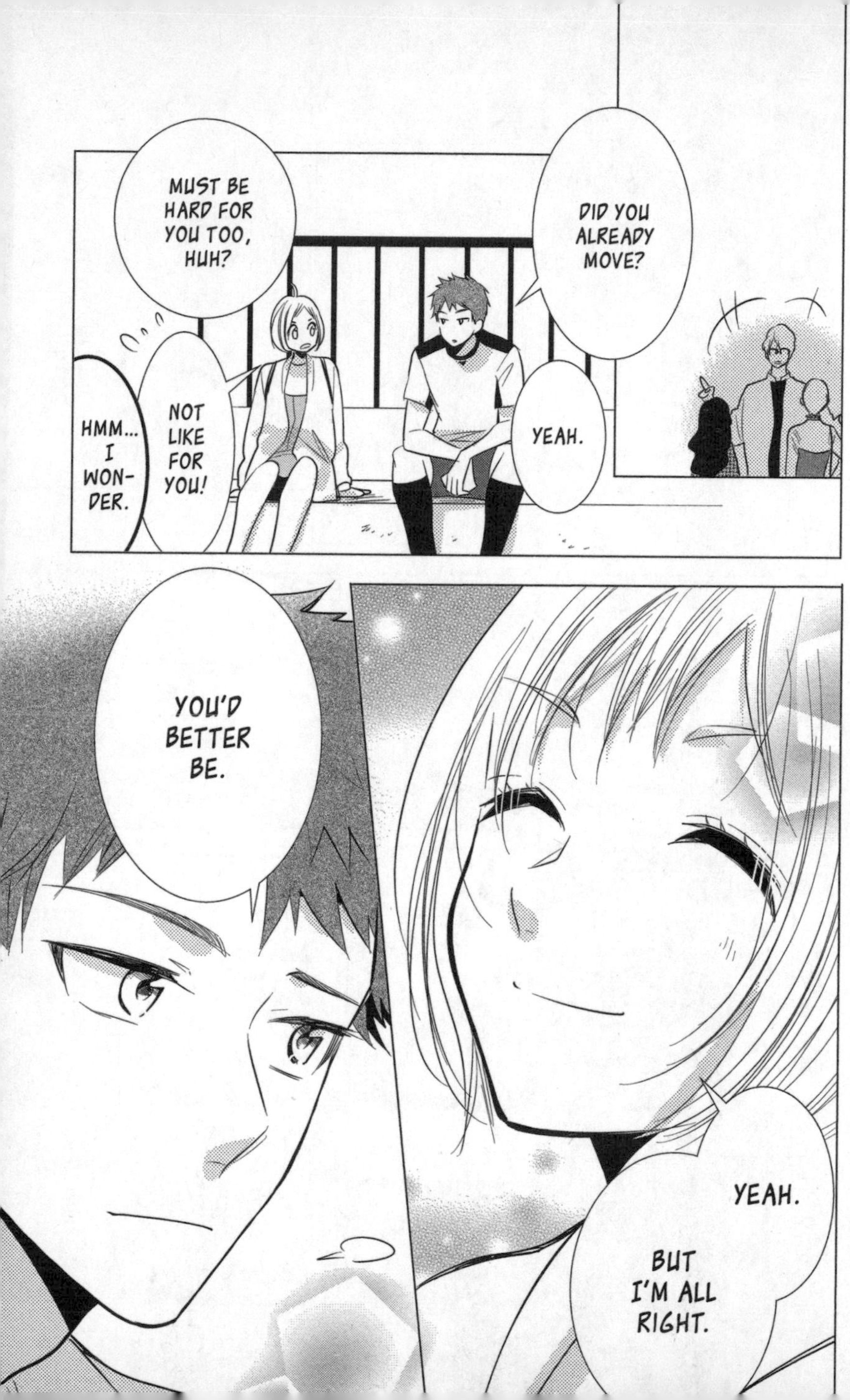
DID YOU ALREADY MOVE?
YEAH.
MUST BE HARD FOR YOU TOO, HUH?
NOT LIKE FOR YOU!
HMM... I WON-DER.
YEAH.
BUT I'M ALL RIGHT.
YOU'D BETTER BE.

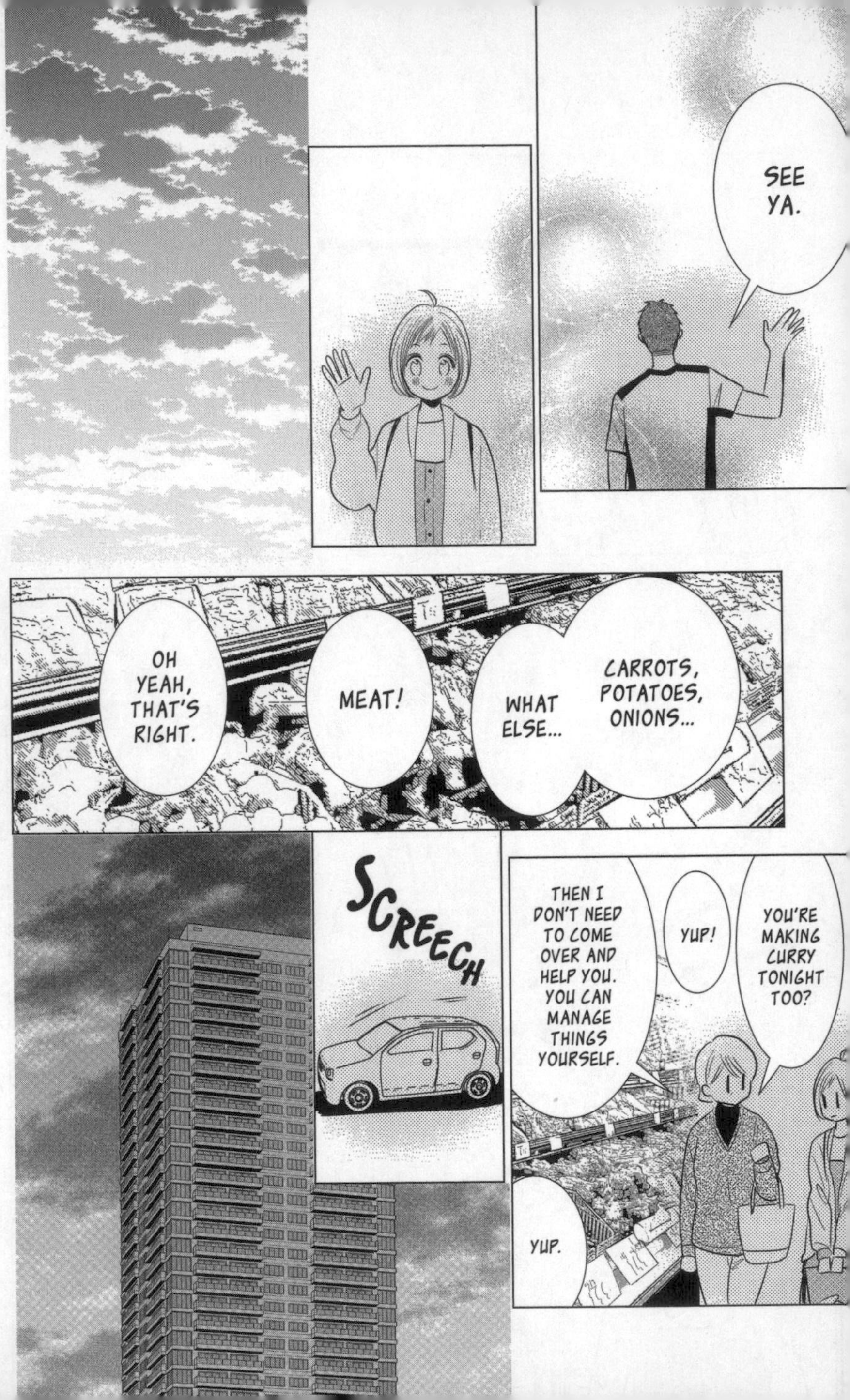
SEE YA.
CARROTS, POTATOES, ONIONS...
WHAT ELSE...
MEAT!
OH YEAH, THAT'S RIGHT.
YOU'RE MAKING CURRY TONIGHT TOO?
YUP!
THEN I DON'T NEED TO COME OVER AND HELP YOU. YOU CAN MANAGE THINGS YOURSELF.
YUP.
SCREECH

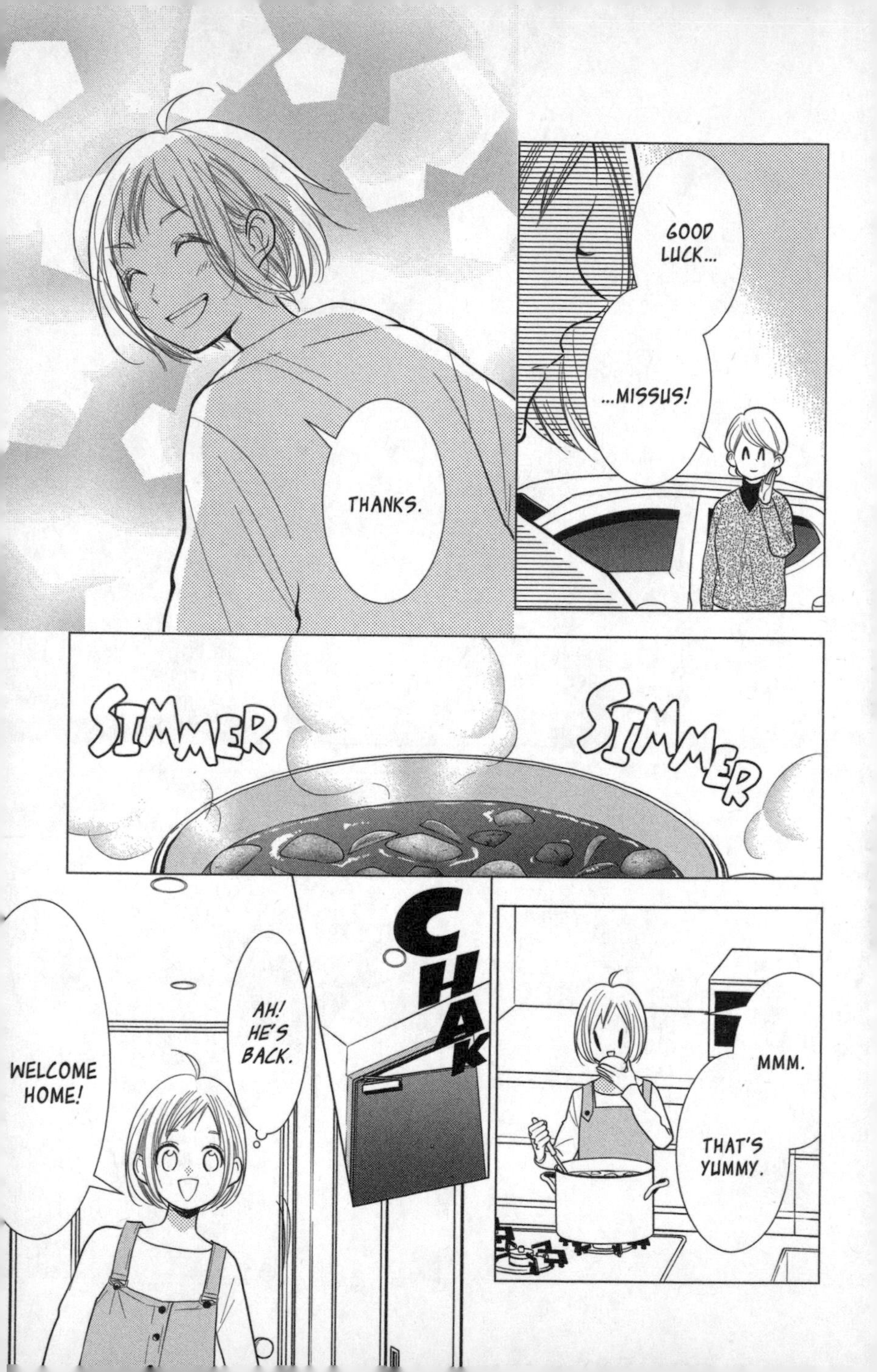
GOOD LUCK...
...MISSUS!
THANKS.
SIMMER
SIMMER
MMM.
THAT'S YUMMY.
CHAK
AH! HE'S BACK.
WELCOME HOME!

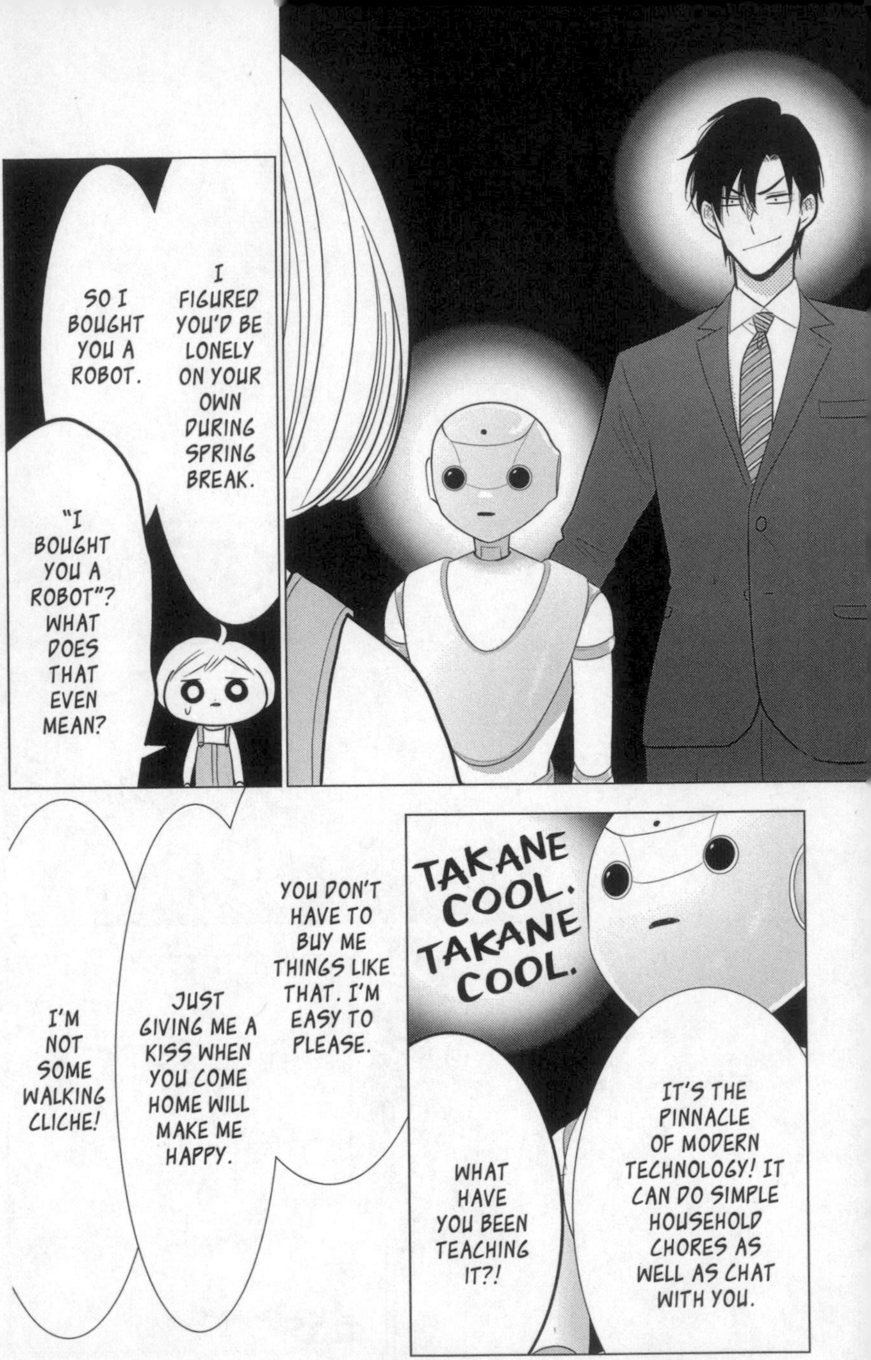
I FIGURED YOU'D BE LONELY ON YOUR OWN DURING SPRING BREAK.
SO I BOUGHT YOU A ROBOT.
"I BOUGHT YOU A ROBOT"? WHAT DOES THAT EVEN MEAN?
TAKANE COOL. TAKANE COOL.
IT'S THE PINNACLE OF MODERN TECHNOLOGY! IT CAN DO SIMPLE HOUSEHOLD CHORES AS WELL AS CHAT WITH YOU.
WHAT HAVE YOU BEEN TEACHING IT?!
YOU DON'T HAVE TO BUY ME THINGS LIKE THAT. I'M EASY TO PLEASE.
JUST GIVING ME A KISS WHEN YOU COME HOME WILL MAKE ME HAPPY.
I'M NOT SOME WALKING CLICHE!

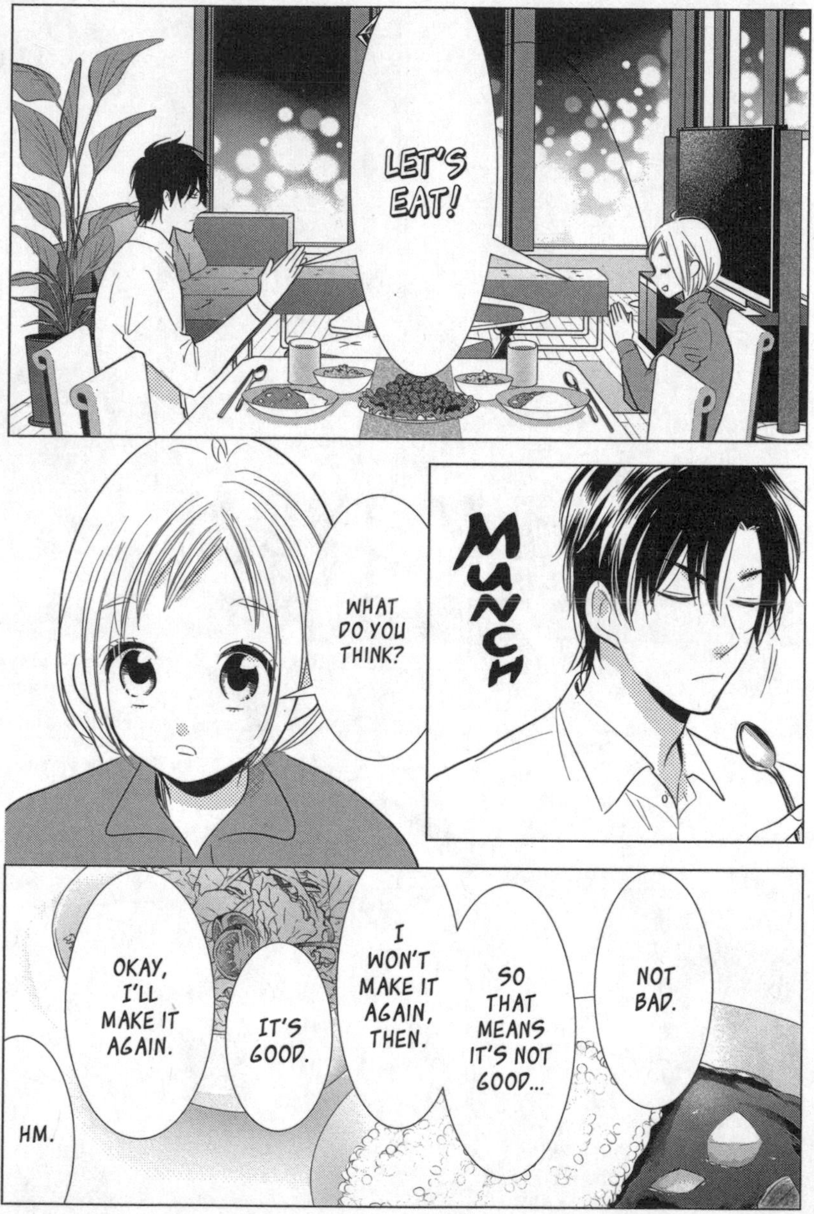
LET'S EAT!
MUNCH
WHAT DO YOU THINK?
NOT BAD.
SO THAT MEANS IT'S NOT GOOD...
I WON'T MAKE IT AGAIN, THEN.
IT'S GOOD.
OKAY, I'LL MAKE IT AGAIN.
HM.

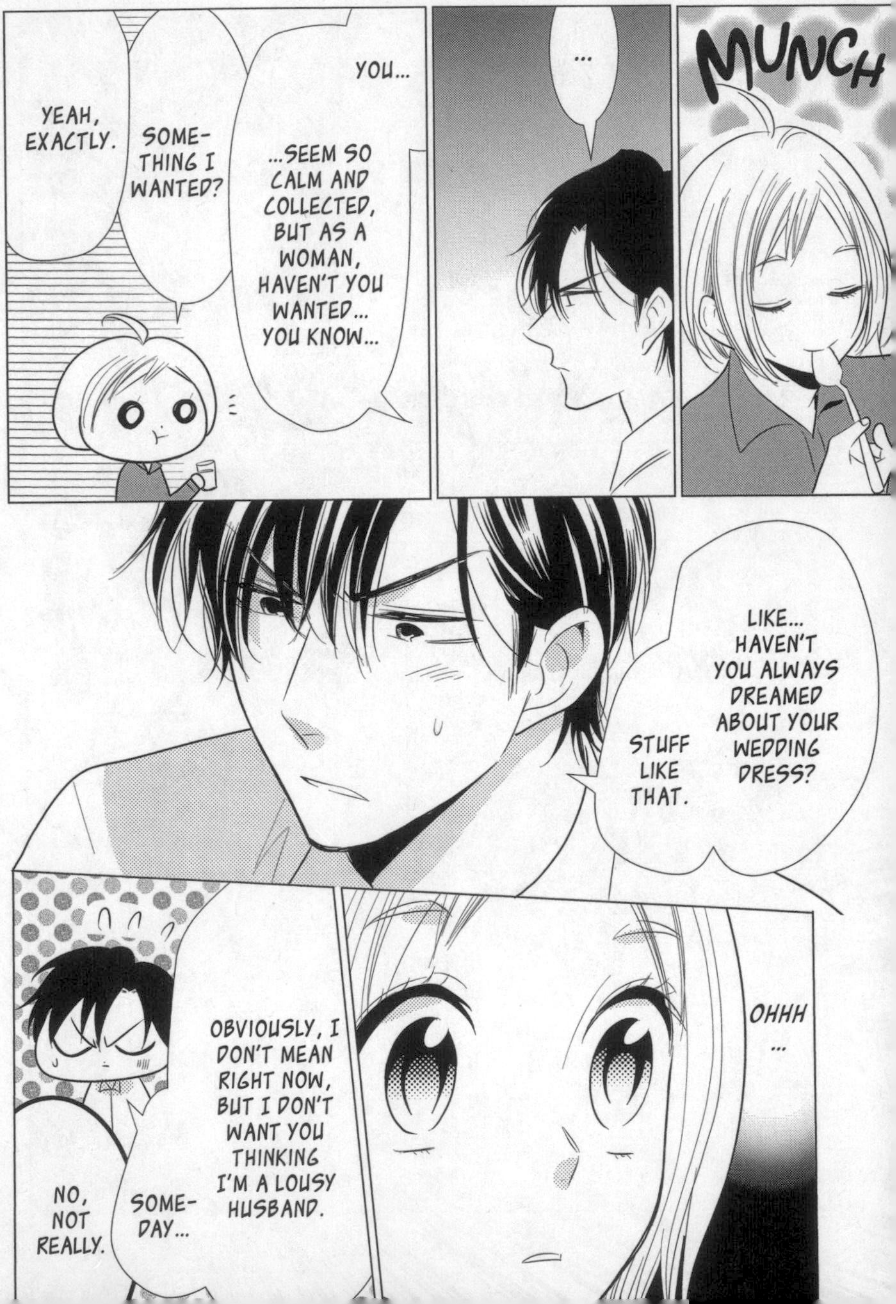
MUNCH
...
YOU...
...SEEM SO CALM AND COLLECTED, BUT AS A WOMAN, HAVEN'T YOU WANTED... YOU KNOW...
SOME-THING I WANTED?
YEAH, EXACTLY.
LIKE... HAVEN'T YOU ALWAYS DREAMED ABOUT YOUR WEDDING DRESS?
STUFF LIKE THAT.
OHHH ...
OBVIOUSLY, I DON'T MEAN RIGHT NOW, BUT I DON'T WANT YOU THINKING I'M A LOUSY HUSBAND.
SOME-DAY...
NO, NOT REALLY.

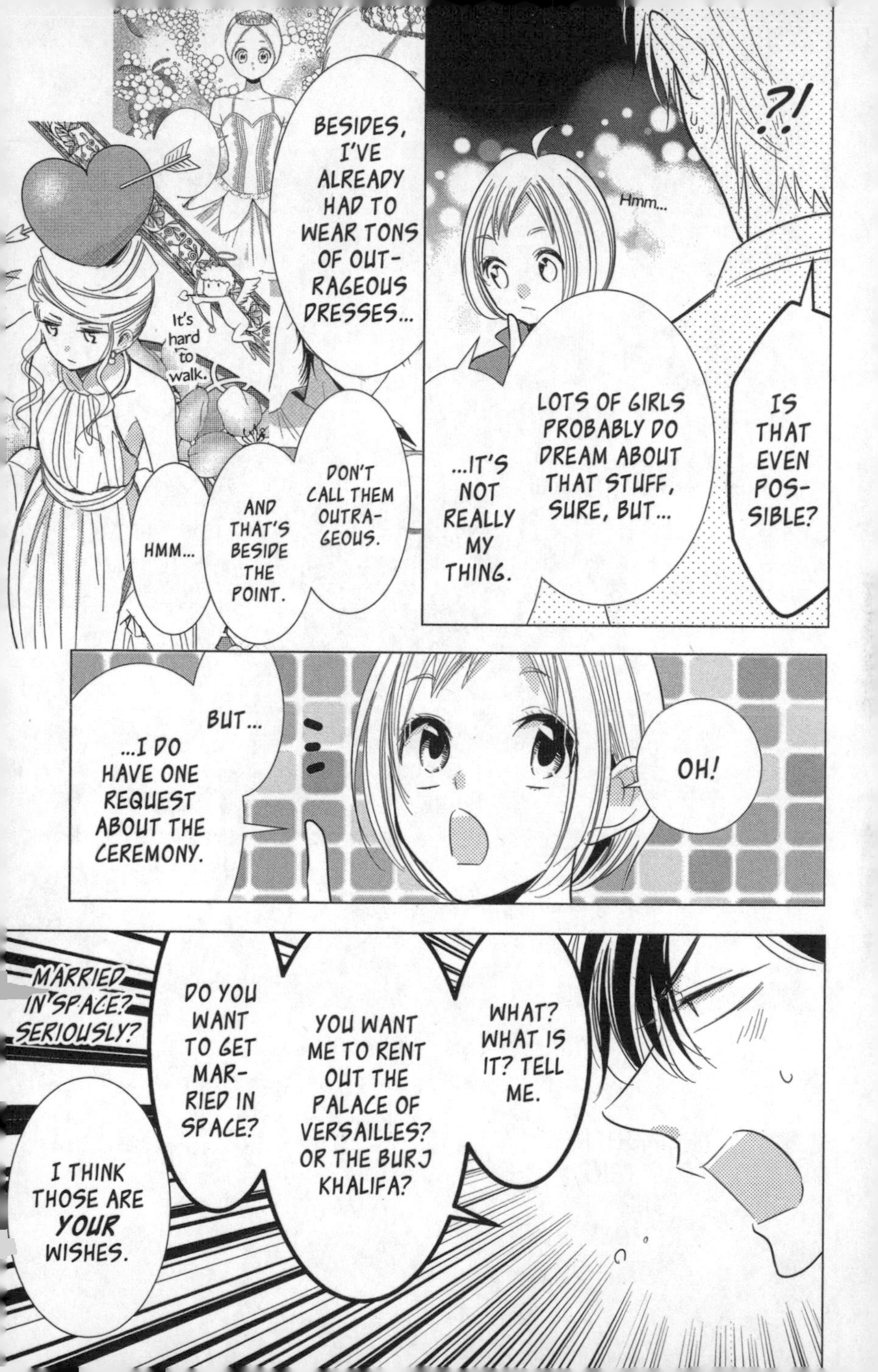
?!
Hmm...
IS THAT EVEN POSSIBLE?
LOTS OF GIRLS PROBABLY DO DREAM ABOUT THAT STUFF, SURE, BUT...
...IT'S NOT REALLY MY THING.
BESIDES, I'VE ALREADY HAD TO WEAR TONS OF OUTRAGEOUS DRESSES...
It's hard to walk.
DON'T CALL THEM OUTRAGEOUS.
AND THAT'S BESIDE THE POINT.
HMM...
OH!
BUT...
...I DO HAVE ONE REQUEST ABOUT THE CEREMONY.
WHAT? WHAT IS IT? TELL ME.
YOU WANT ME TO RENT OUT THE PALACE OF VERSAILLES? OR THE BURJ KHALIFA?
DO YOU WANT TO GET MARRIED IN SPACE?
MARRIED IN SPACE? SERIOUSLY?
I THINK THOSE ARE YOUR WISHES.

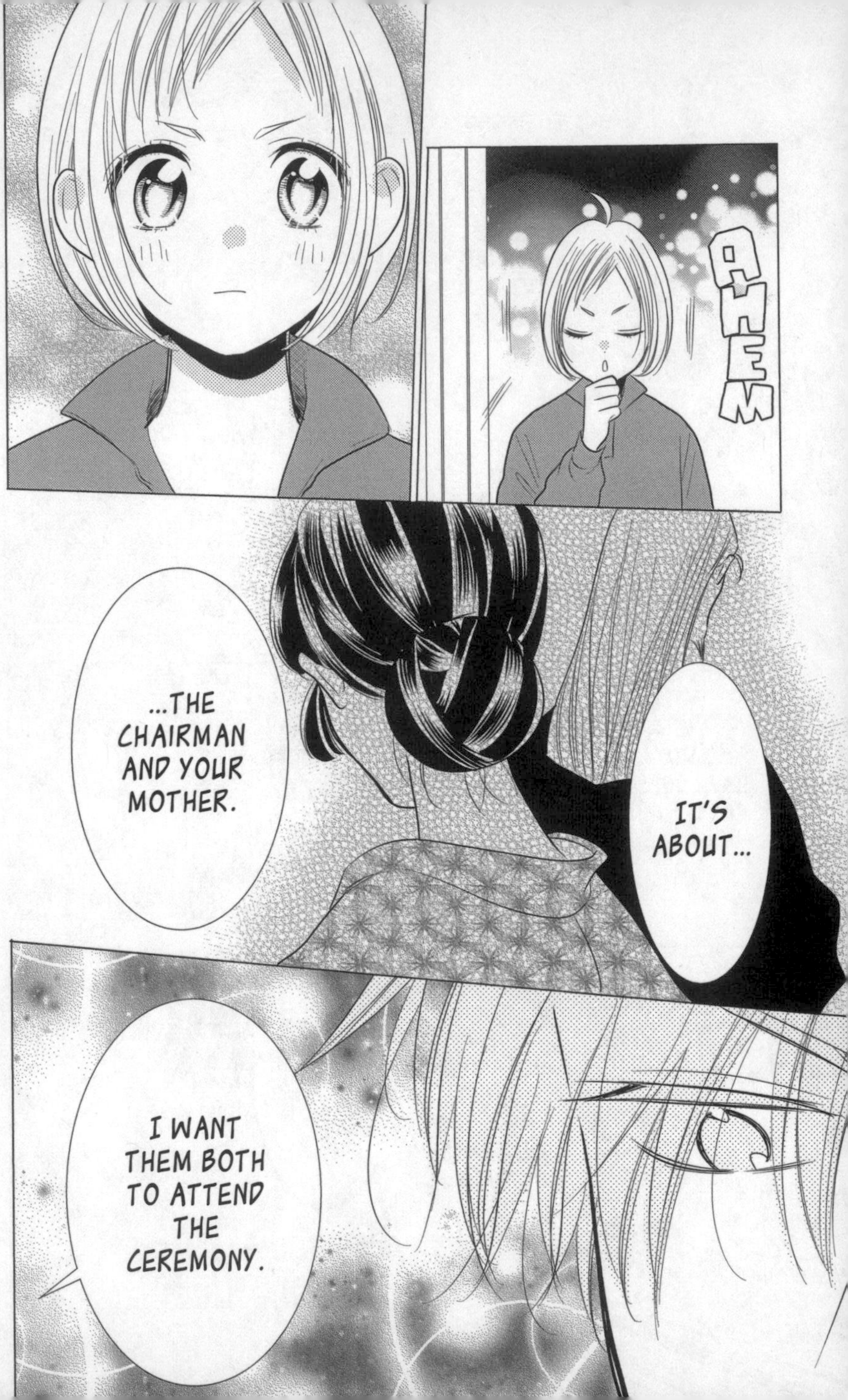
AHEM
IT'S ABOUT...
...THE CHAIRMAN AND YOUR MOTHER.
I WANT THEM BOTH TO ATTEND THE CEREMONY.

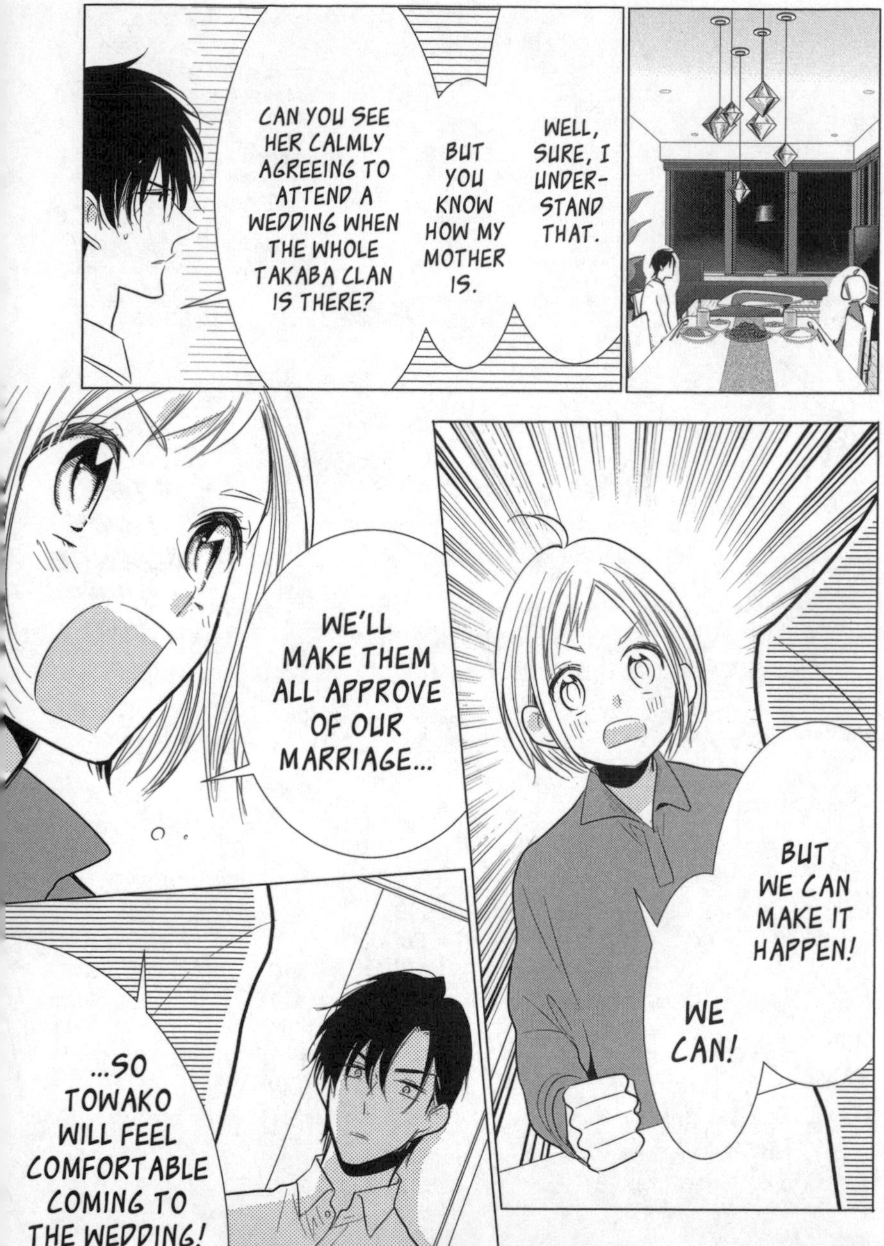
WELL, SURE, I UNDER-STAND THAT.
BUT YOU KNOW HOW MY MOTHER IS.
CAN YOU SEE HER CALMLY AGREEING TO ATTEND A WEDDING WHEN THE WHOLE TAKABA CLAN IS THERE?
BUT WE CAN MAKE IT HAPPEN!
WE CAN!
WE'LL MAKE THEM ALL APPROVE OF OUR MARRIAGE...
...SO TOWAKO WILL FEEL COMFORTABLE COMING TO THE WEDDING!

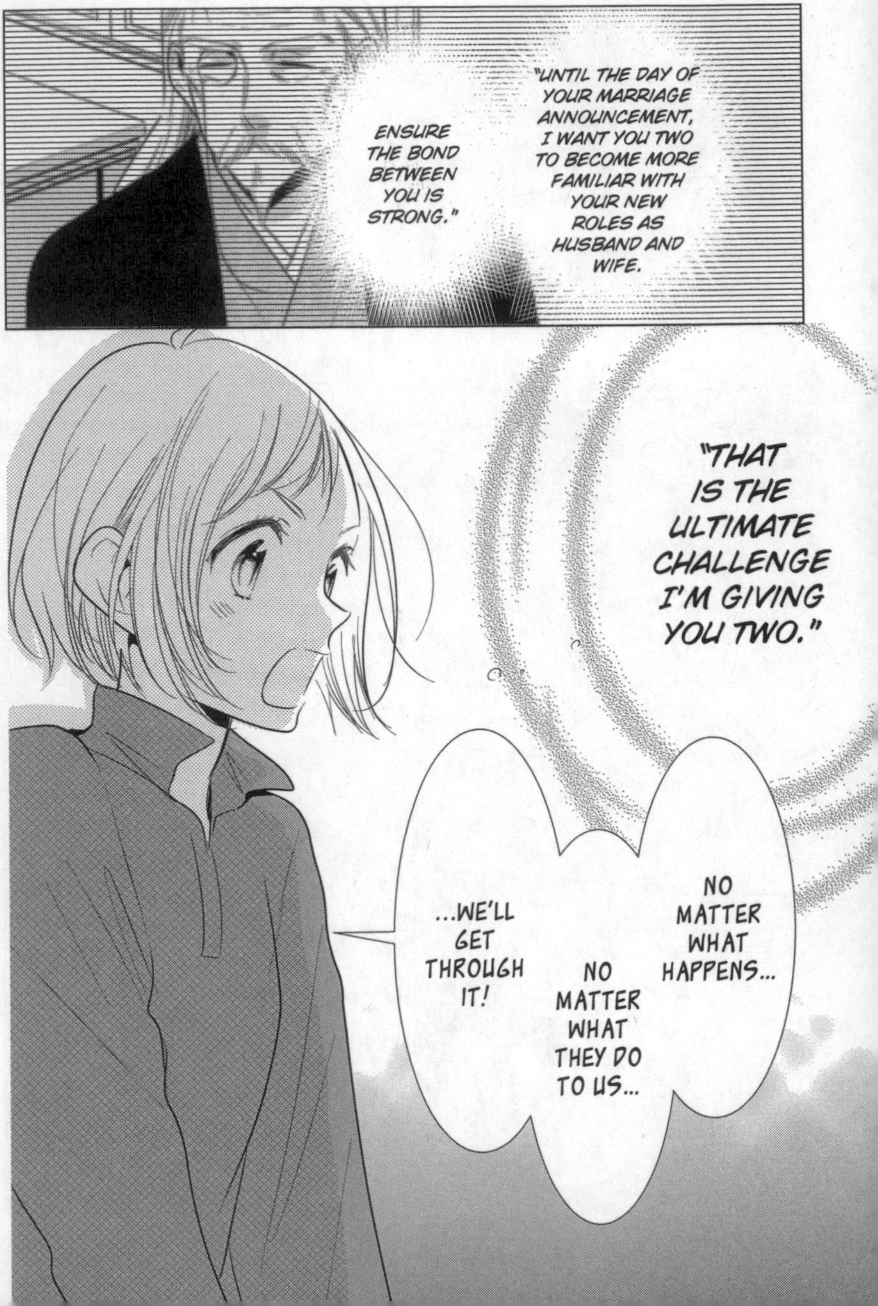
"UNTIL THE DAY OF YOUR MARRIAGE ANNOUNCEMENT, I WANT YOU TWO TO BECOME MORE FAMILIAR WITH YOUR NEW ROLES AS HUSBAND AND WIFE.
ENSURE THE BOND BETWEEN YOU IS STRONG."
"THAT IS THE ULTIMATE CHALLENGE I'M GIVING YOU TWO."
NO MATTER WHAT HAPPENS...
NO MATTER WHAT THEY DO TO US...
...WE'LL GET THROUGH IT!

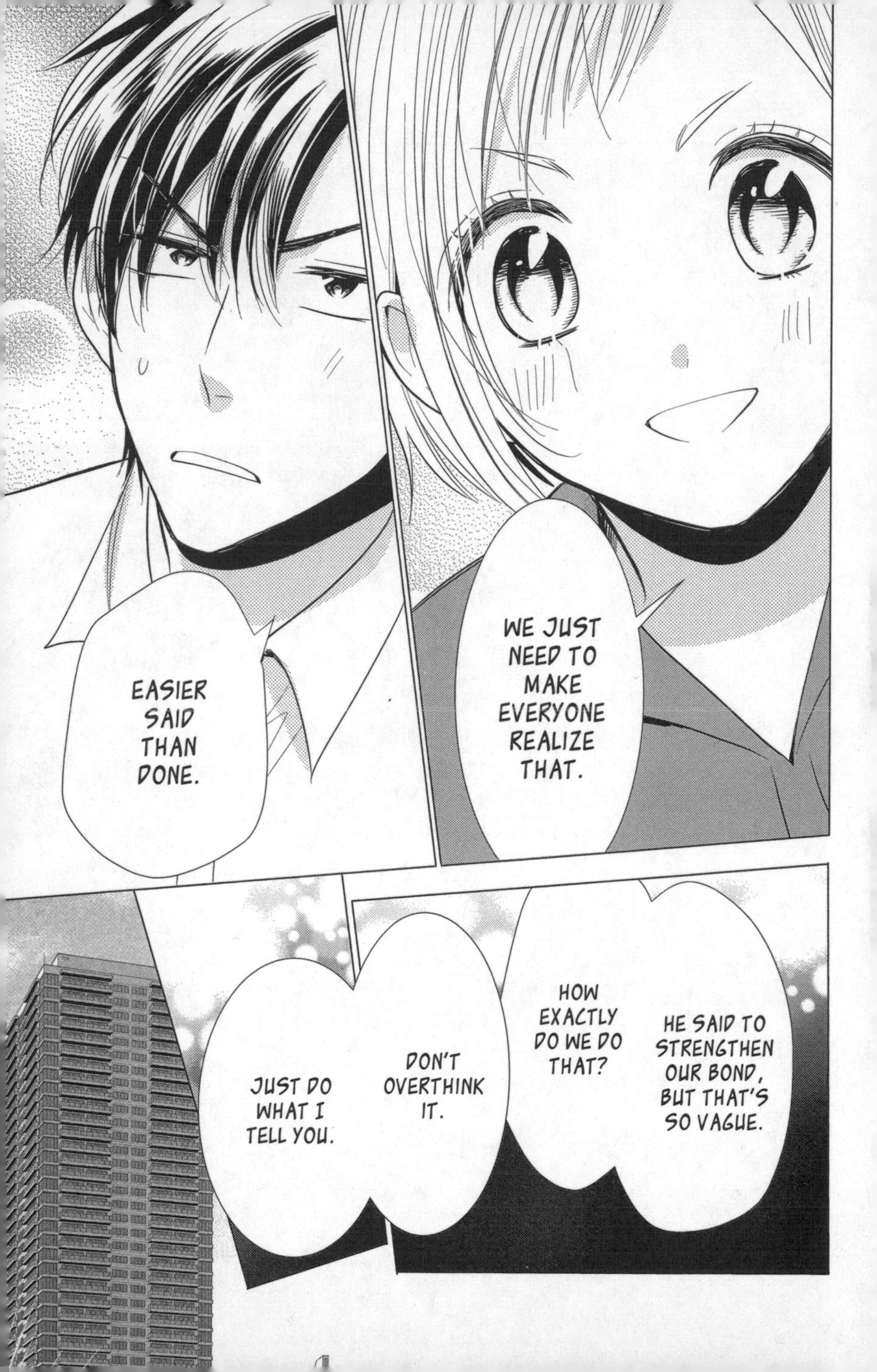
WE JUST NEED TO MAKE EVERYONE REALIZE THAT.
EASIER SAID THAN DONE.
HE SAID TO STRENGTHEN OUR BOND, BUT THAT'S SO VAGUE.
HOW EXACTLY DO WE DO THAT?
DON'T OVERTHINK IT.
JUST DO WHAT I TELL YOU.

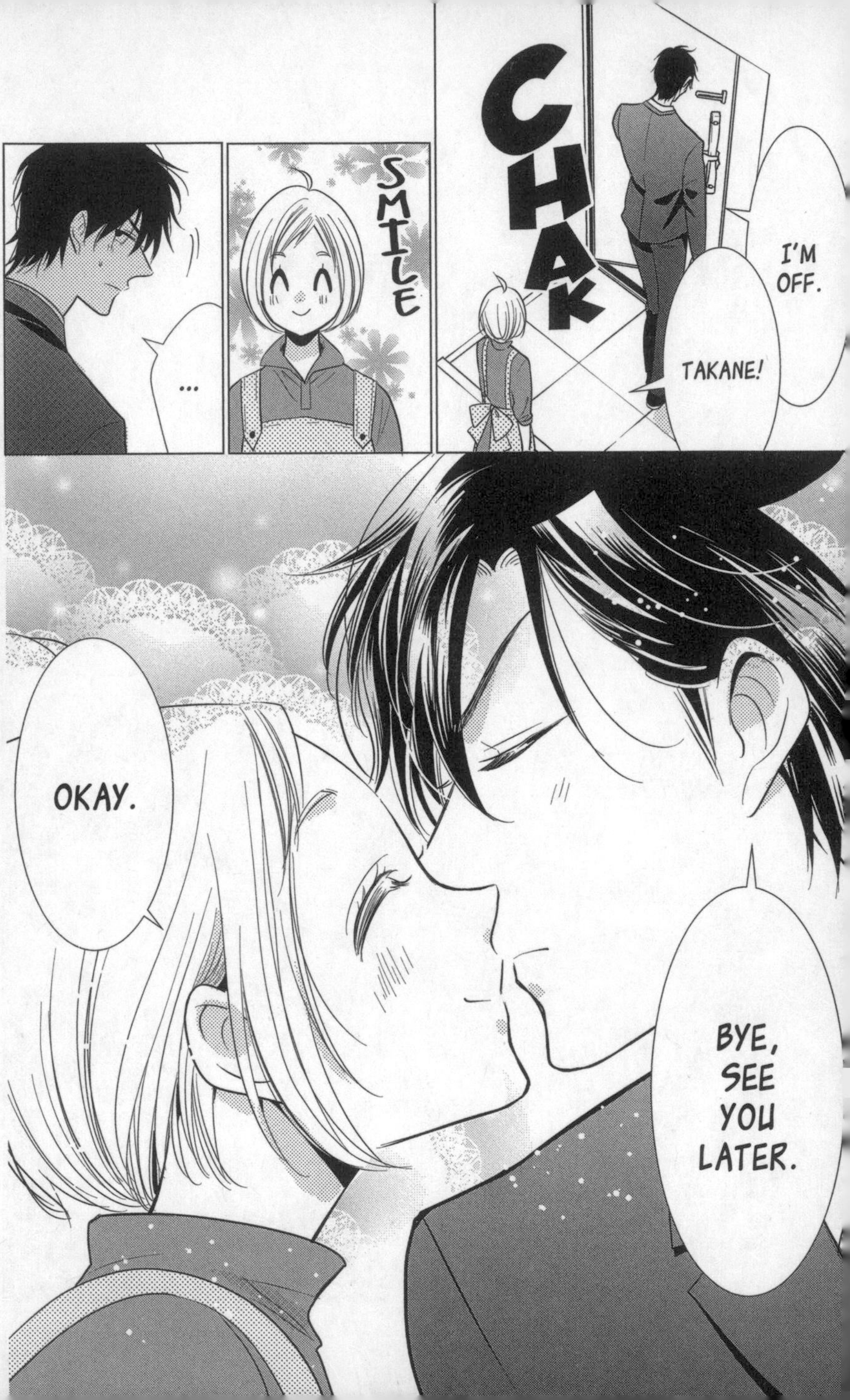
I'M OFF.
CHAK
TAKANE!
SMILE
...
BYE, SEE YOU LATER.
OKAY.

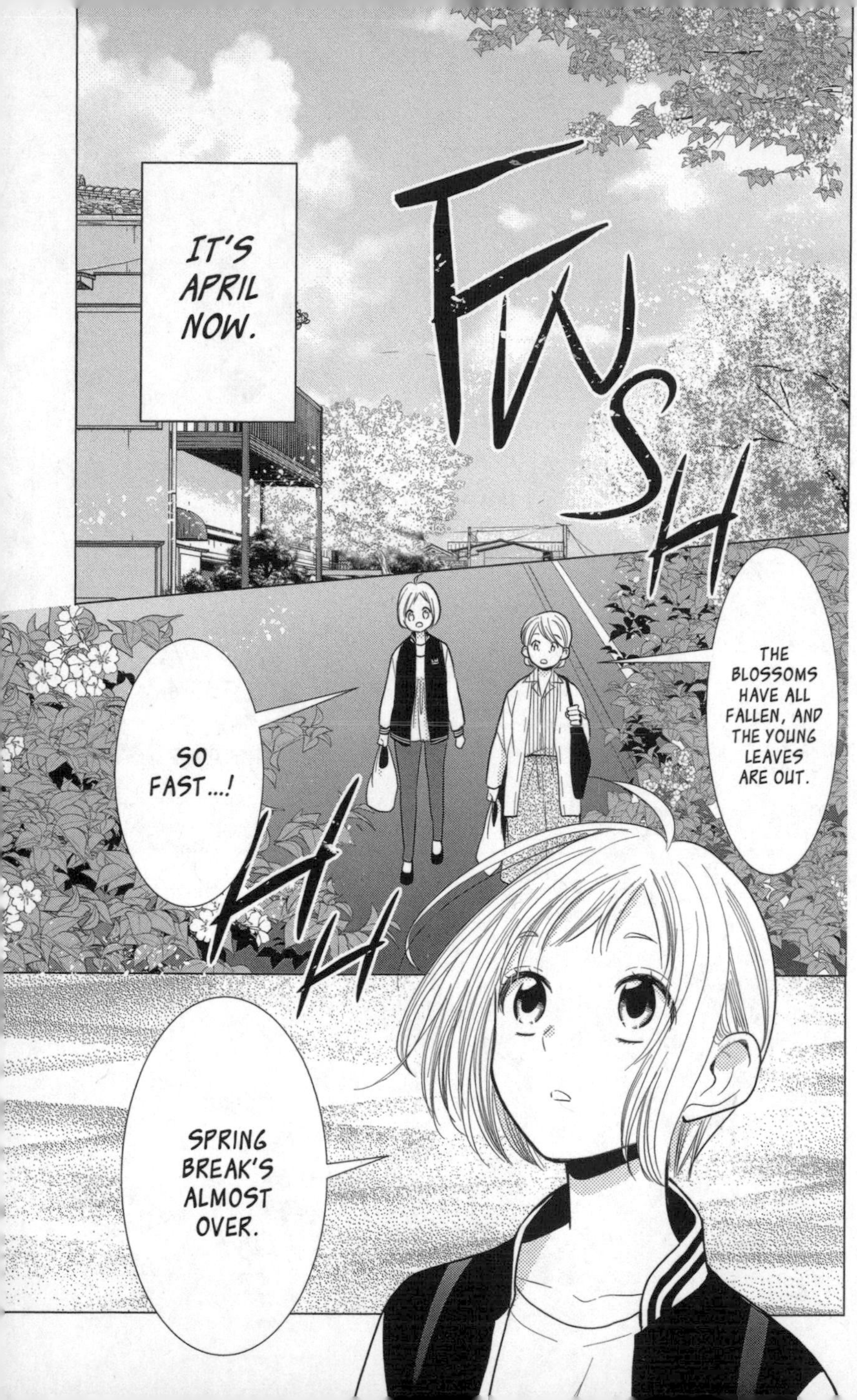
FWSH
IT'S APRIL NOW.
THE BLOSSOMS HAVE ALL FALLEN, AND THE YOUNG LEAVES ARE OUT.
SO FAST...!
HH
SPRING BREAK'S ALMOST OVER.

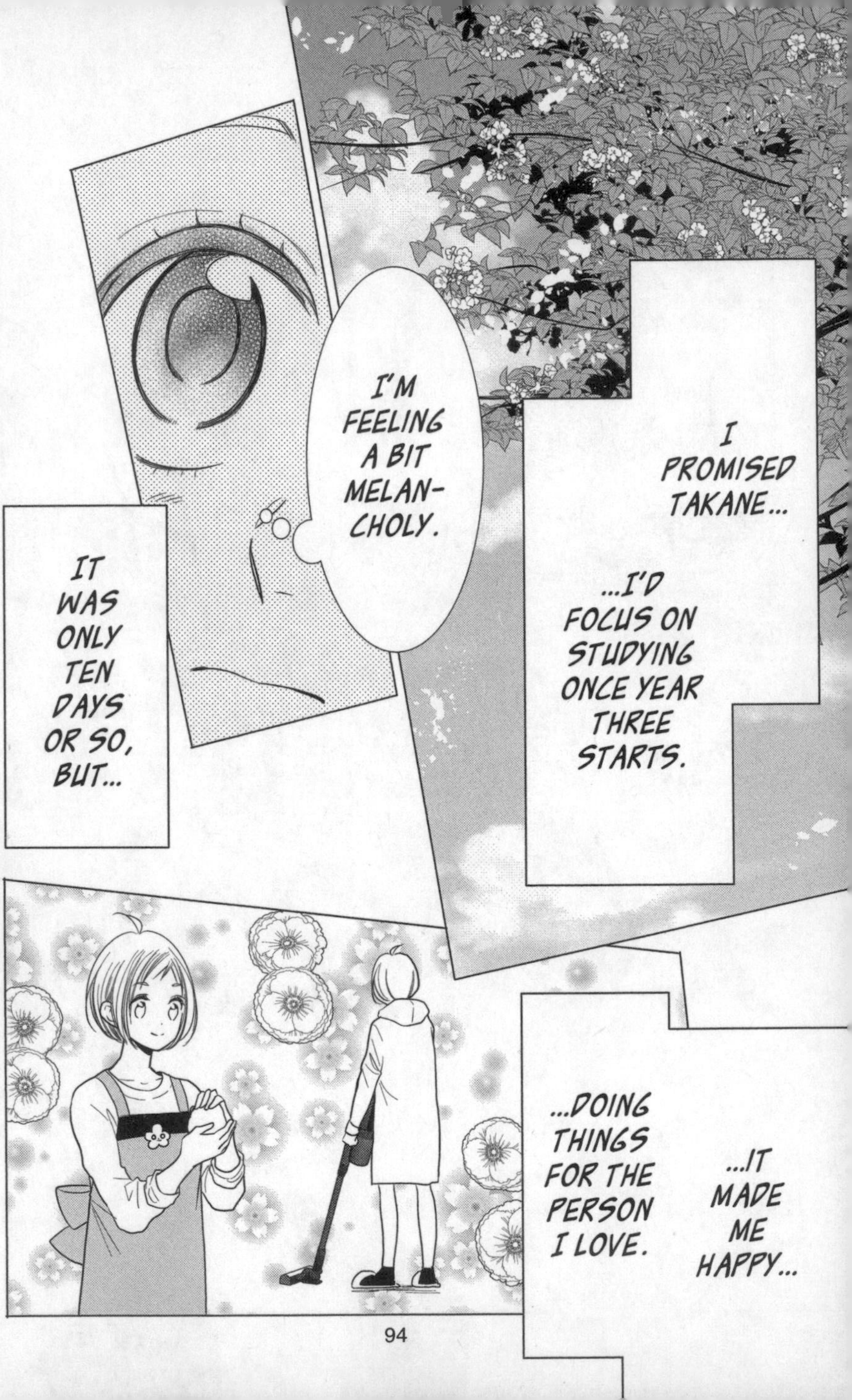
I PROMISED TAKANE...
...I'D FOCUS ON STUDYING ONCE YEAR THREE STARTS.
I'M FEELING A BIT MELAN-CHOLY.
IT WAS ONLY TEN DAYS OR SO, BUT...
...IT MADE ME HAPPY...
...DOING THINGS FOR THE PERSON I LOVE.

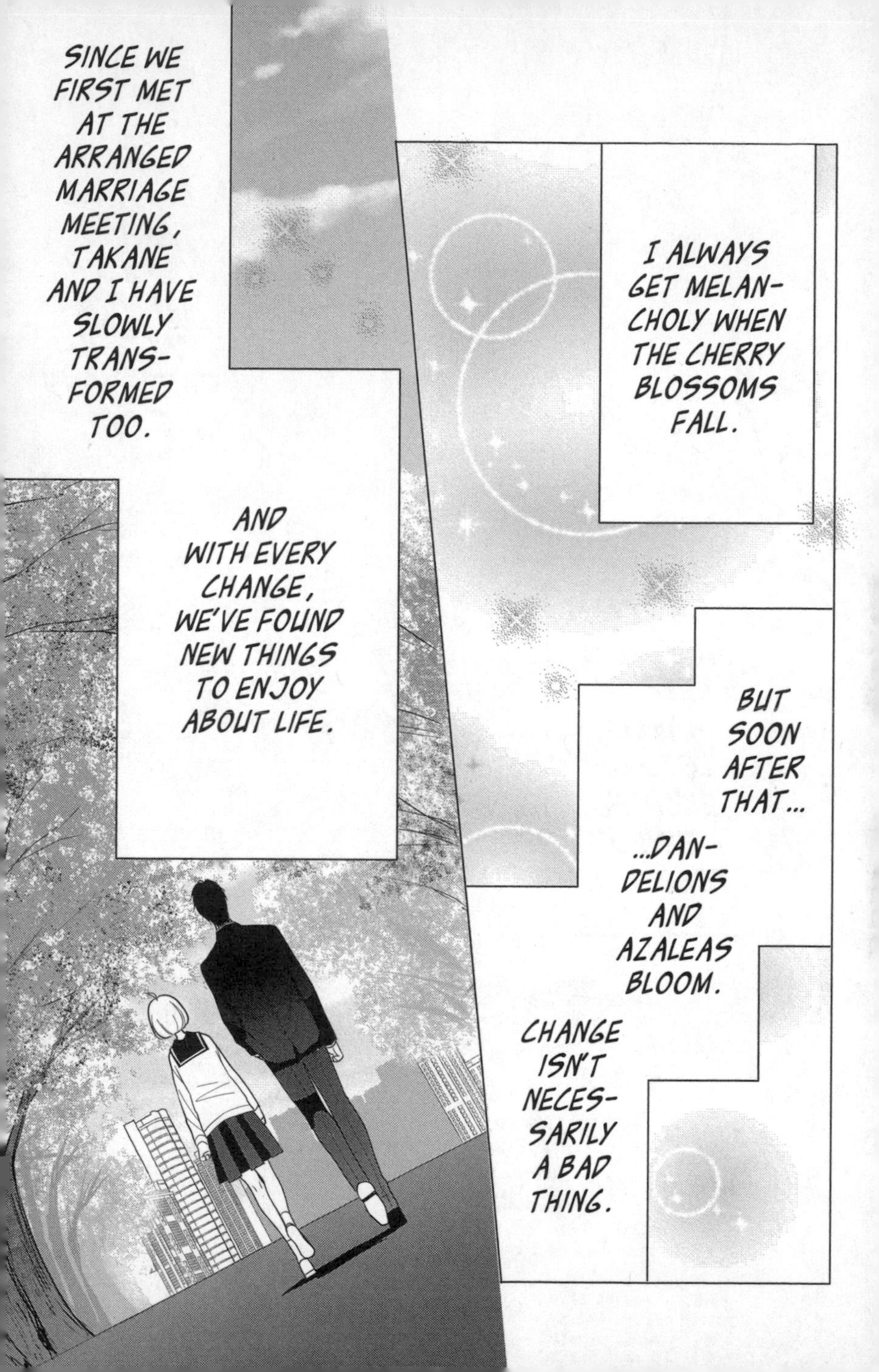
I ALWAYS GET MELAN-CHOLY WHEN THE CHERRY BLOSSOMS FALL.
BUT SOON AFTER THAT...
...DAN-DELIONS AND AZALEAS BLOOM.
CHANGE ISN'T NECES-SARILY A BAD THING.
SINCE WE FIRST MET AT THE ARRANGED MARRIAGE MEETING, TAKANE AND I HAVE SLOWLY TRANS-FORMED TOO.
AND WITH EVERY CHANGE, WE'VE FOUND NEW THINGS TO ENJOY ABOUT LIFE.

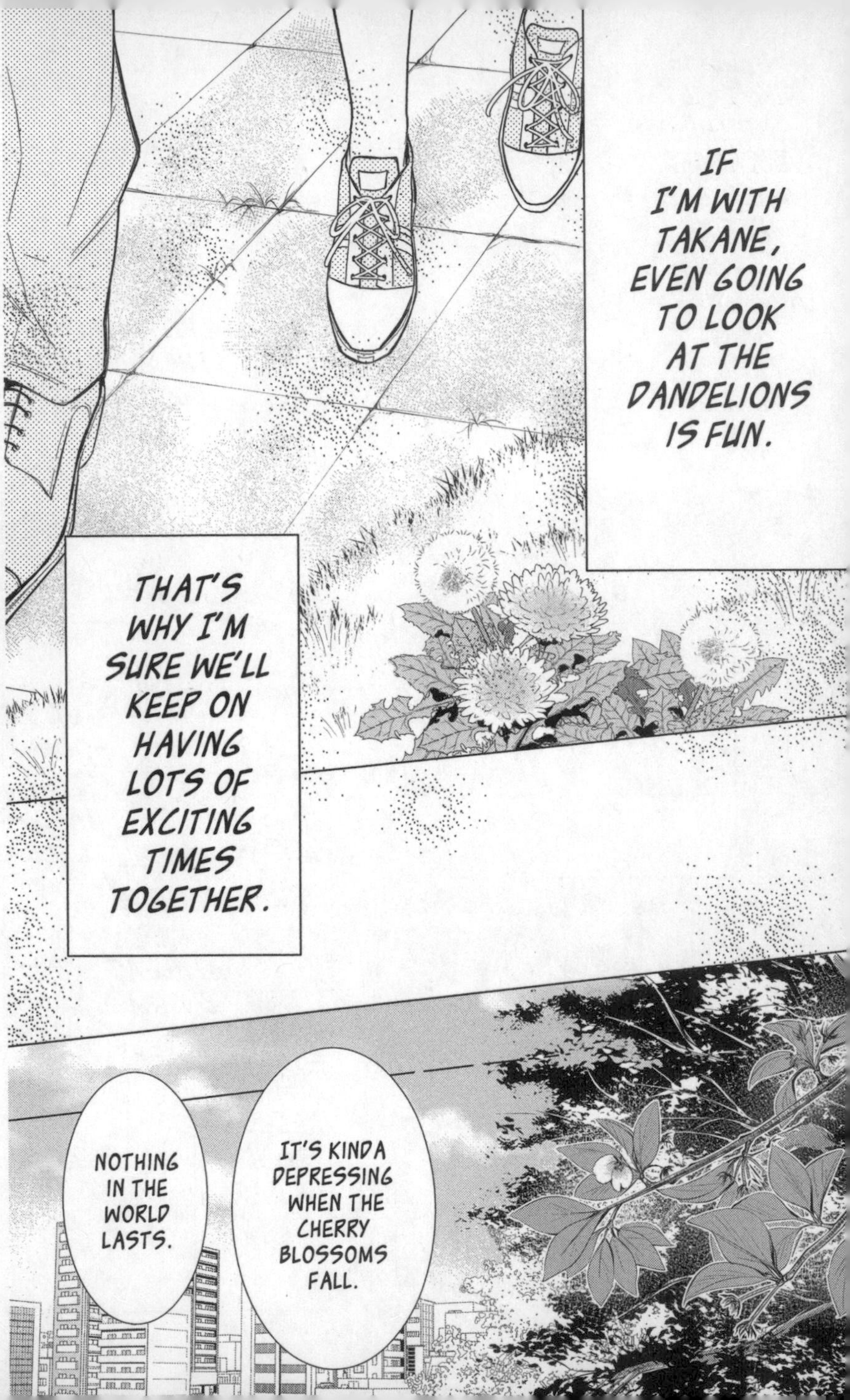
IF I'M WITH TAKANE, EVEN GOING TO LOOK AT THE DANDELIONS IS FUN.
THAT'S WHY I'M SURE WE'LL KEEP ON HAVING LOTS OF EXCITING TIMES TOGETHER.
IT'S KINDA DEPRESSING WHEN THE CHERRY BLOSSOMS FALL.
NOTHING IN THE WORLD LASTS.

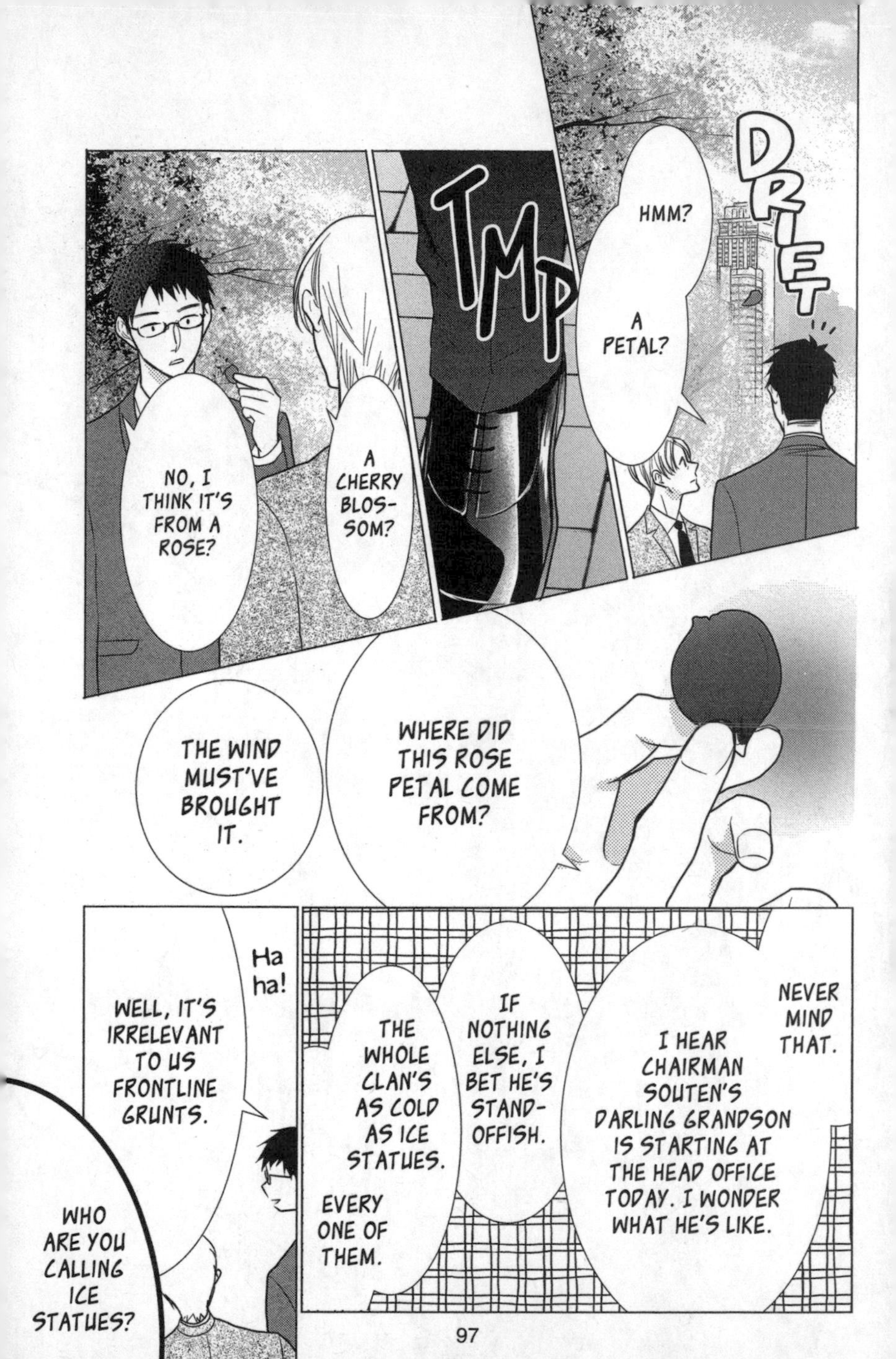
DRIFT
HMM?
A PETAL?
TMP
A CHERRY BLOS-SOM?
NO, I THINK IT'S FROM A ROSE?
WHERE DID THIS ROSE PETAL COME FROM?
THE WIND MUST'VE BROUGHT IT.
NEVER MIND THAT.
I HEAR CHAIRMAN SOUTEN'S DARLING GRANDSON IS STARTING AT THE HEAD OFFICE TODAY. I WONDER WHAT HE'S LIKE.
IF NOTHING ELSE, I BET HE'S STAND-OFFISH.
THE WHOLE CLAN'S AS COLD AS ICE STATUES.
EVERY ONE OF THEM.
Ha ha!
WELL, IT'S IRRELEVANT TO US FRONTLINE GRUNTS.
WHO ARE YOU CALLING ICE STATUES?

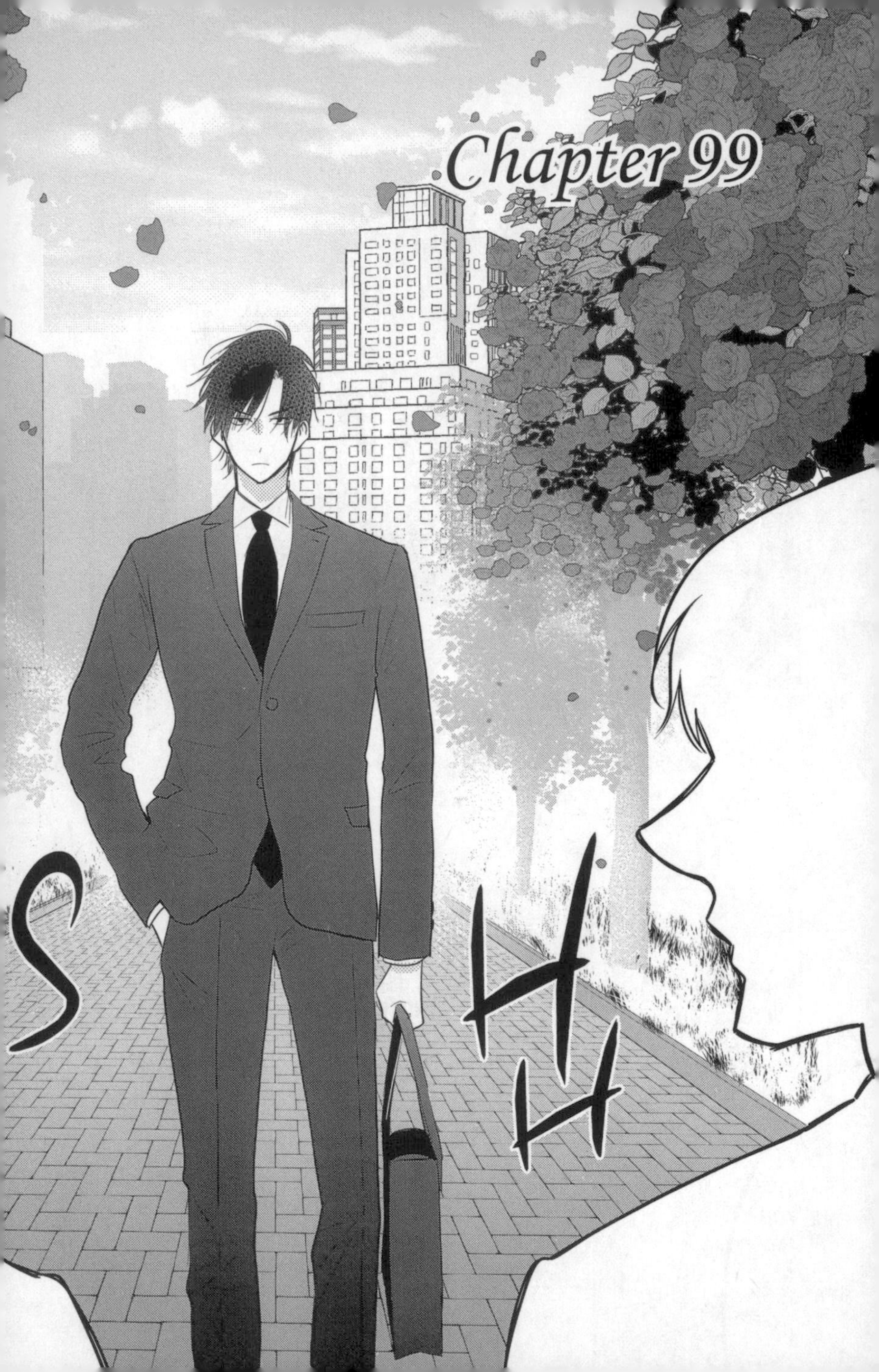
Chapter 99
SHH

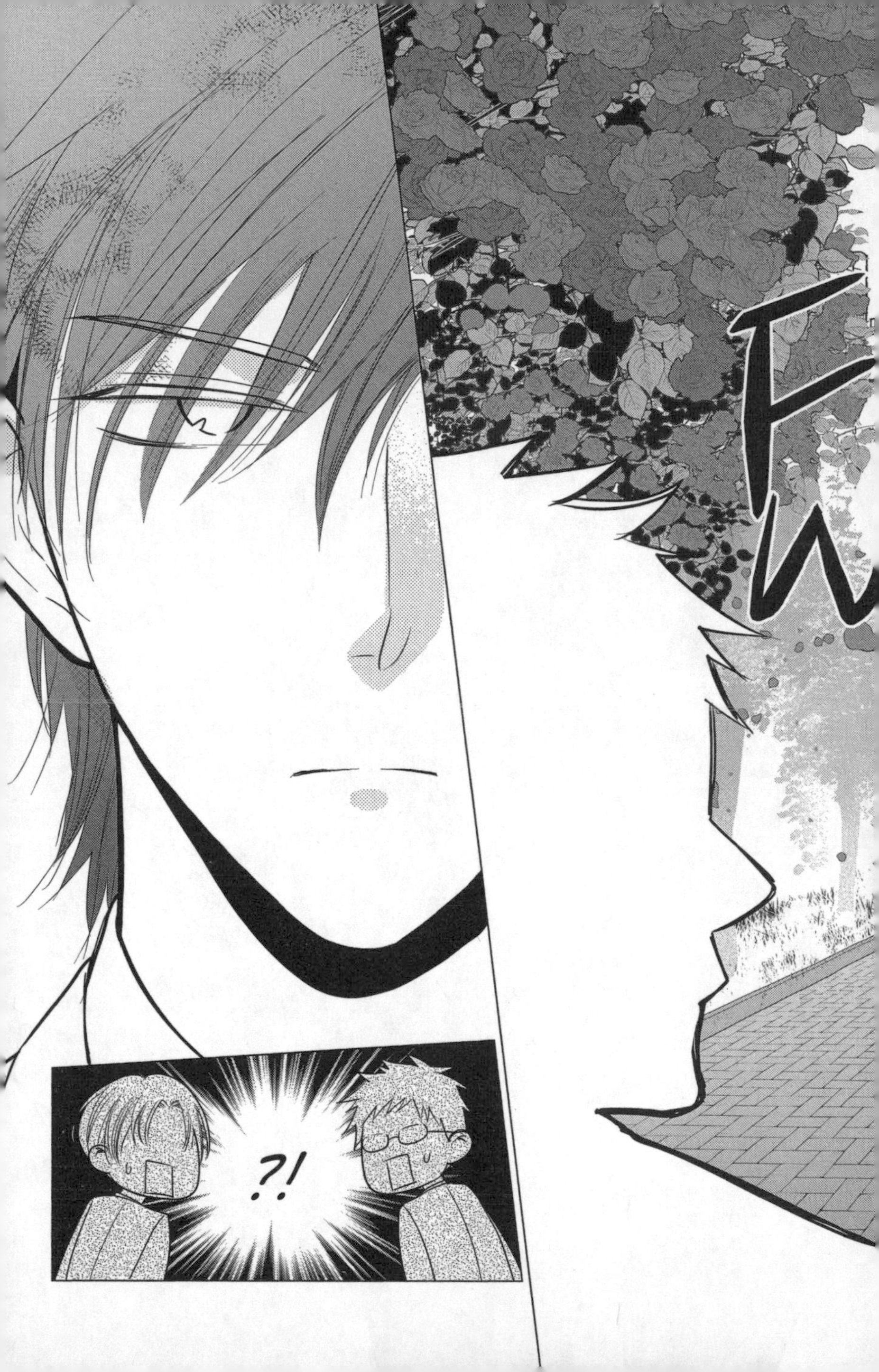
FW
?!

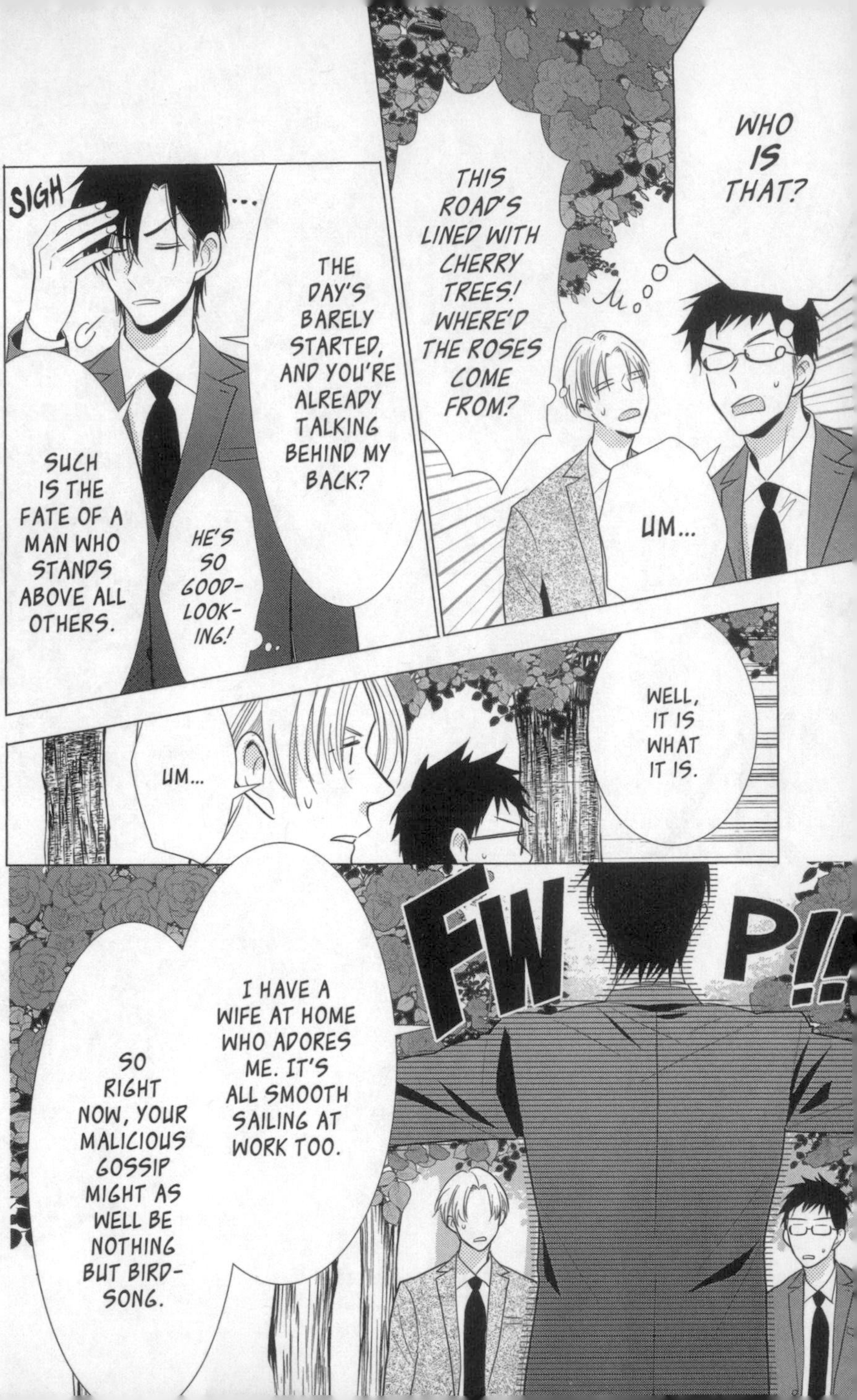
WHO IS THAT?
THIS ROAD'S LINED WITH CHERRY TREES! WHERE'D THE ROSES COME FROM?
UM...
SIGH
...
THE DAY'S BARELY STARTED, AND YOU'RE ALREADY TALKING BEHIND MY BACK?
HE'S SO GOOD-LOOKING!
SUCH IS THE FATE OF A MAN WHO STANDS ABOVE ALL OTHERS.
WELL, IT IS WHAT IT IS.
UM...
FWP!!
I HAVE A WIFE AT HOME WHO ADORES ME. IT'S ALL SMOOTH SAILING AT WORK TOO.
SO RIGHT NOW, YOUR MALICIOUS GOSSIP MIGHT AS WELL BE NOTHING BUT BIRD-SONG.

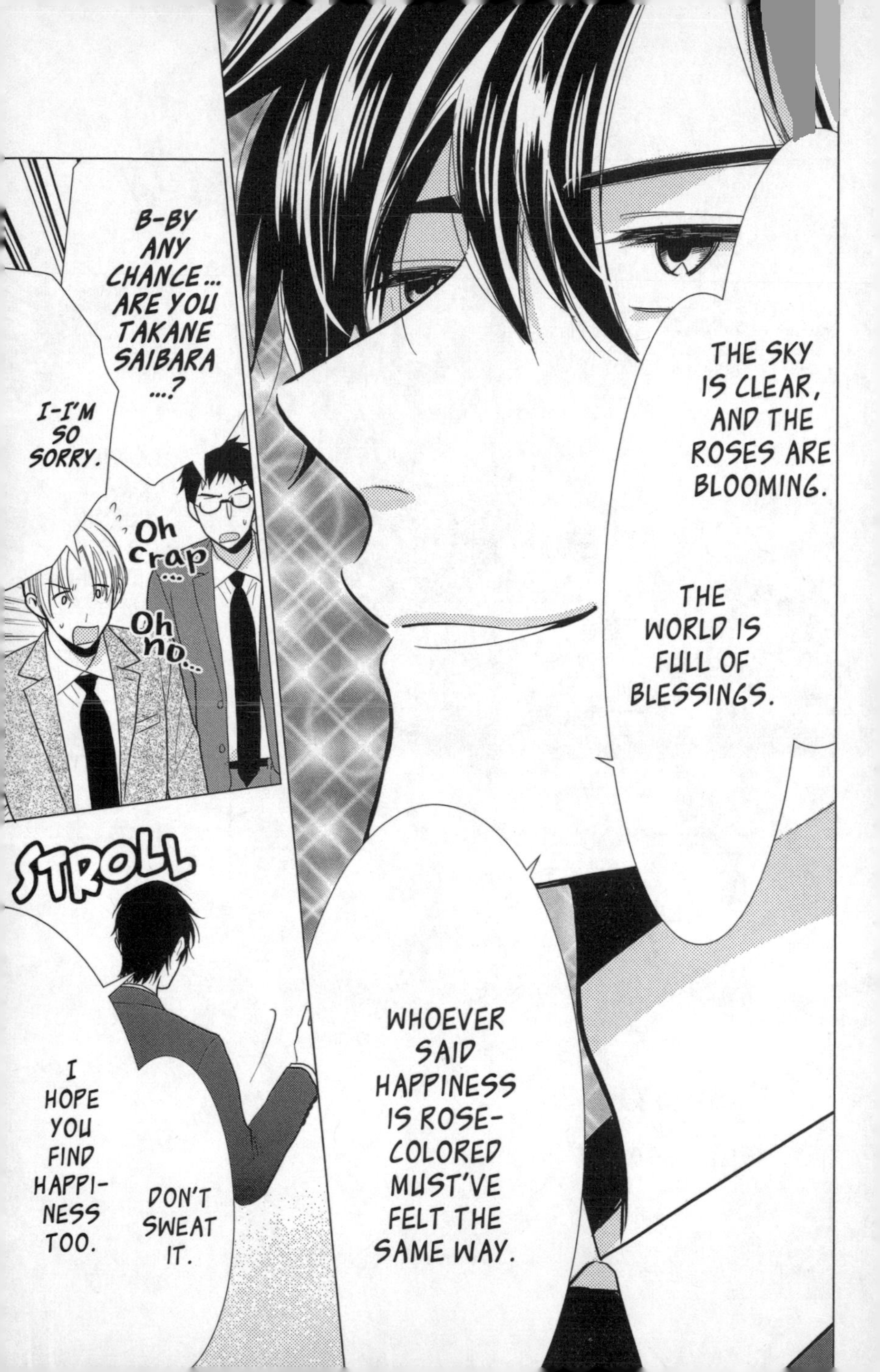
THE SKY IS CLEAR, AND THE ROSES ARE BLOOMING.
THE WORLD IS FULL OF BLESSINGS.
WHOEVER SAID HAPPINESS IS ROSE-COLORED MUST'VE FELT THE SAME WAY.
B-BY ANY CHANCE... ARE YOU TAKANE SAIBARA ...?
I-I'M SO SORRY.
Oh crap...
Oh no...
STROLL
DON'T SWEAT IT.
I HOPE YOU FIND HAPPI-NESS TOO.

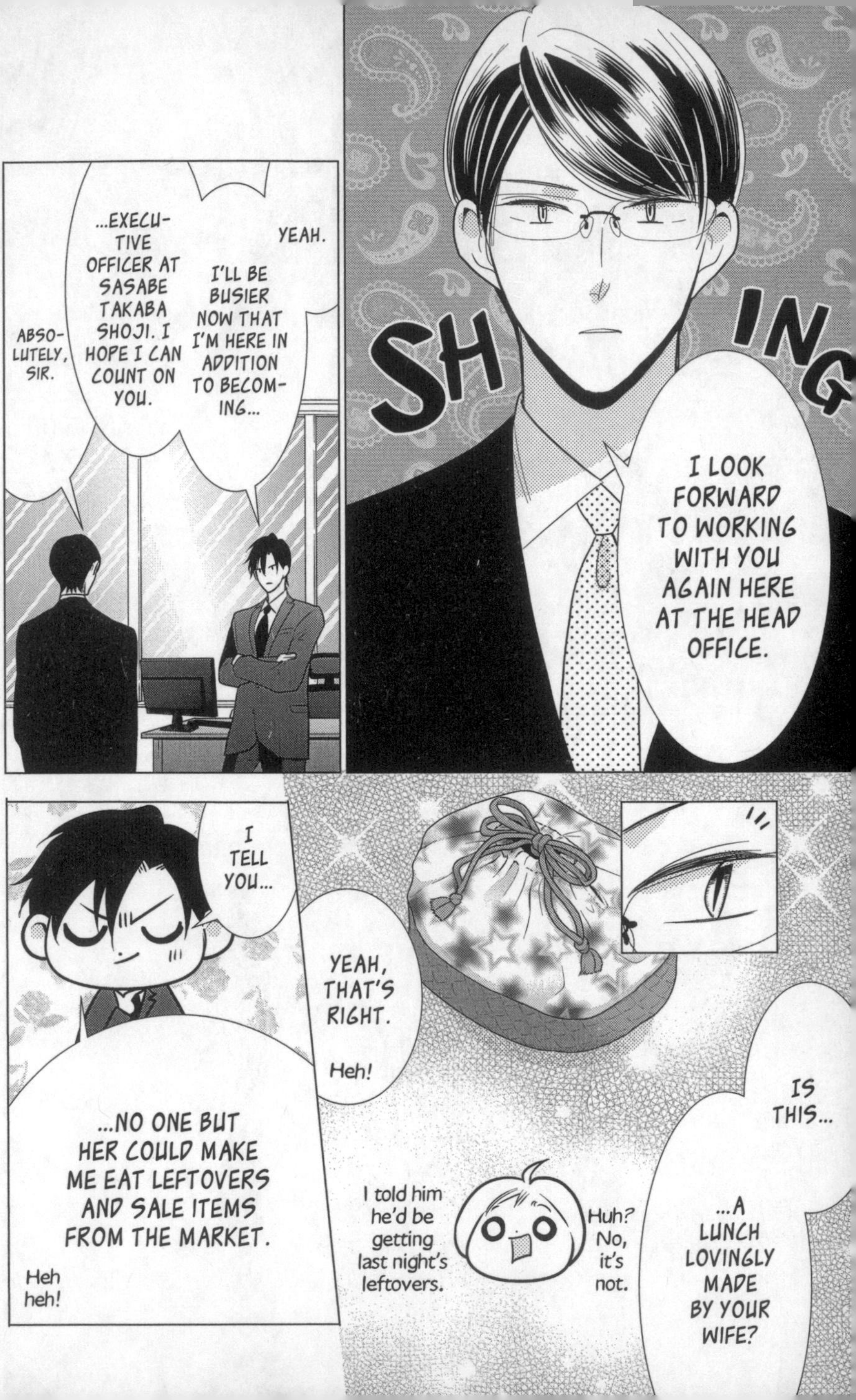
SHING
I LOOK FORWARD TO WORKING WITH YOU AGAIN HERE AT THE HEAD OFFICE.
YEAH.
I'LL BE BUSIER NOW THAT I'M HERE IN ADDITION TO BECOMING...
...EXECUTIVE OFFICER AT SASABE TAKABA SHOJI. I HOPE I CAN COUNT ON YOU.
ABSOLUTELY, SIR.
IS THIS...
...A LUNCH LOVINGLY MADE BY YOUR WIFE?
Huh? No, it's not.
I told him he'd be getting last night's leftovers.
YEAH, THAT'S RIGHT.
Heh!
I TELL YOU...
...NO ONE BUT HER COULD MAKE ME EAT LEFTOVERS AND SALE ITEMS FROM THE MARKET.
Heh heh!

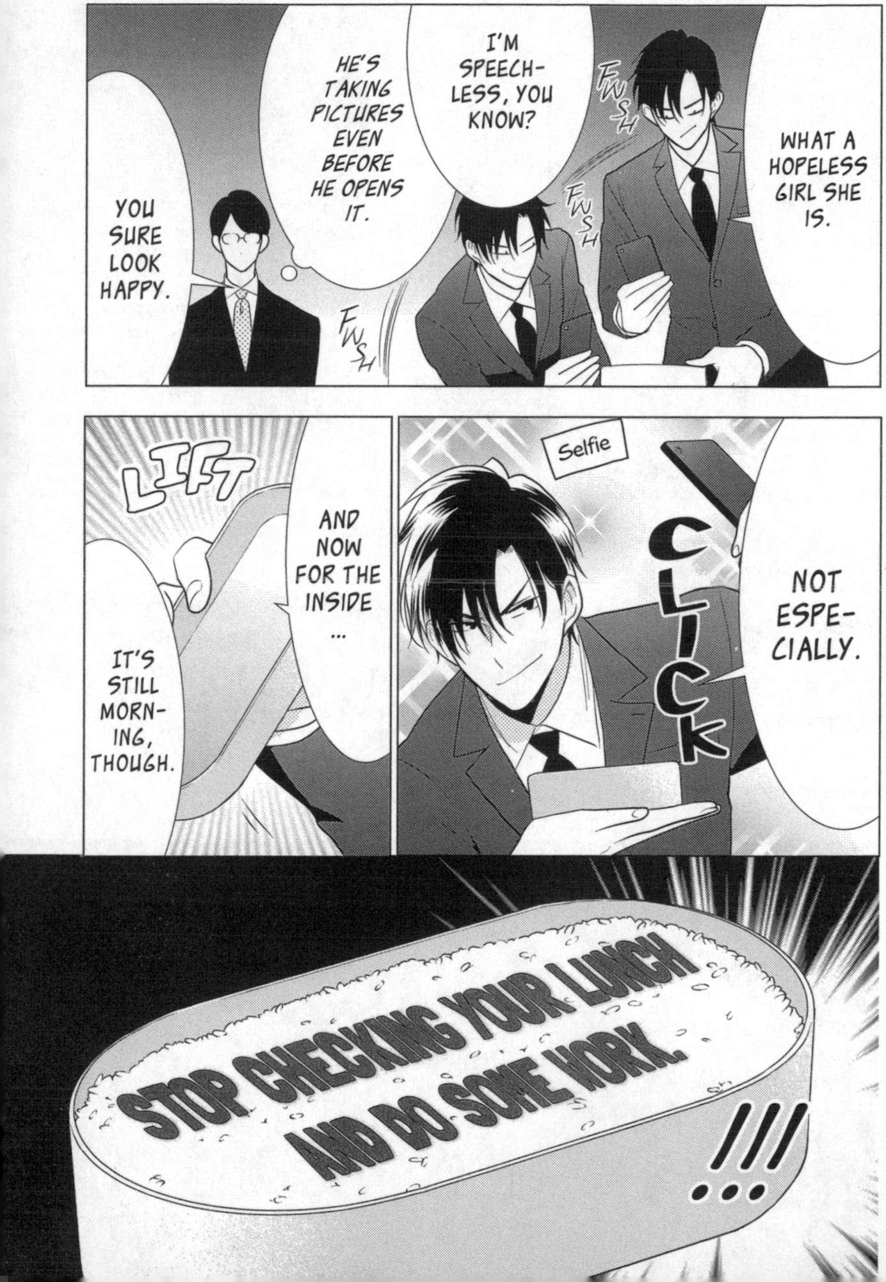
WHAT A HOPELESS GIRL SHE IS.
FWSH
FWSH
I'M SPEECH-LESS, YOU KNOW?
HE'S TAKING PICTURES EVEN BEFORE HE OPENS IT.
FWSH
YOU SURE LOOK HAPPY.
Selfie
NOT ESPE-CIALLY.
CLICK
AND NOW FOR THE INSIDE ...
LIFT
IT'S STILL MORNING, THOUGH.
STOP CHECKING YOUR LUNCH AND DO SOME WORK.
!!!

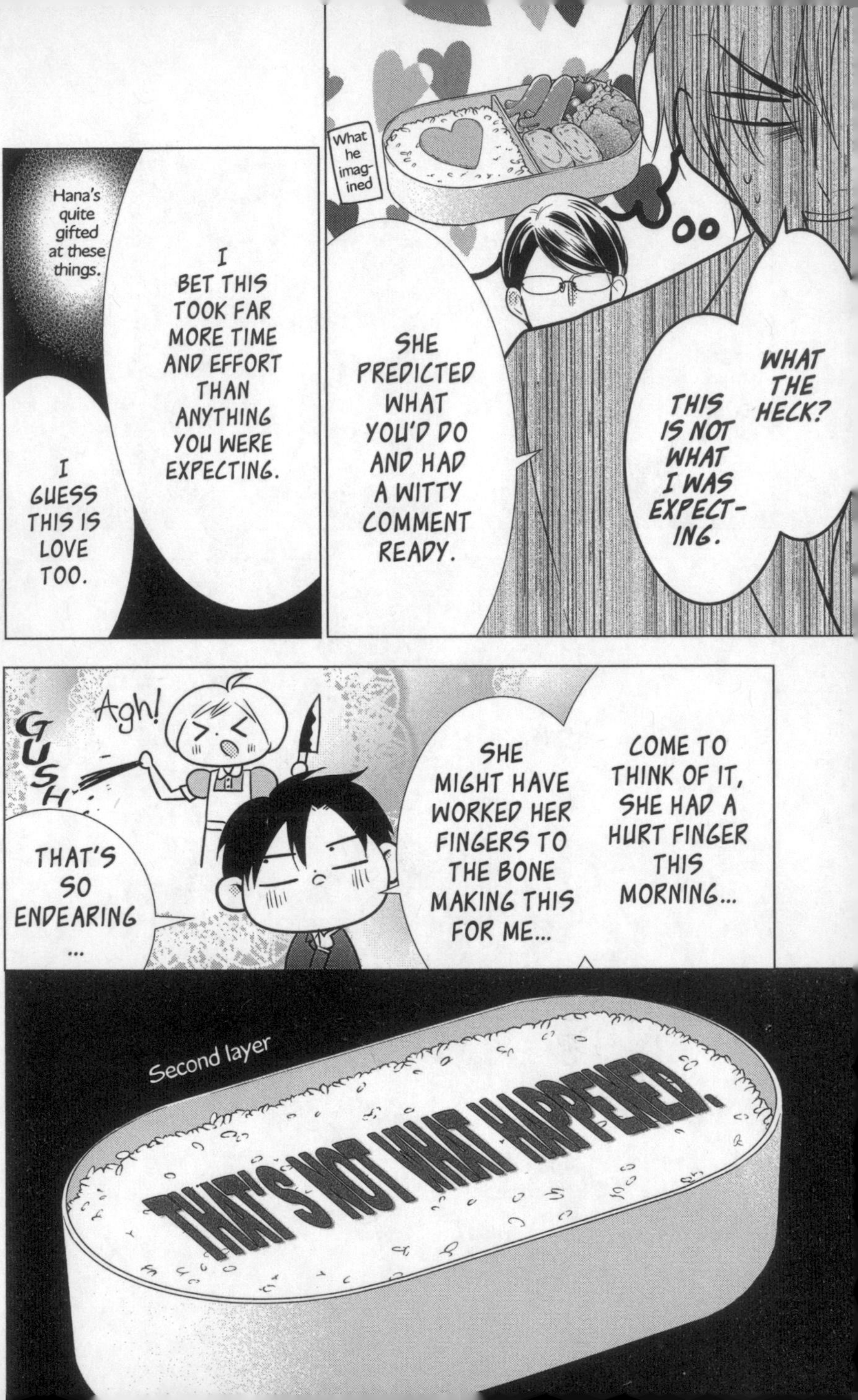
WHAT THE HECK?
THIS IS NOT WHAT I WAS EXPECTING.
OO
What he imagined
SHE PREDICTED WHAT YOU'D DO AND HAD A WITTY COMMENT READY.
I BET THIS TOOK FAR MORE TIME AND EFFORT THAN ANYTHING YOU WERE EXPECTING.
Hana's quite gifted at these things.
I GUESS THIS IS LOVE TOO.
COME TO THINK OF IT, SHE HAD A HURT FINGER THIS MORNING...
SHE MIGHT HAVE WORKED HER FINGERS TO THE BONE MAKING THIS FOR ME...
Agh!
GUSH
THAT'S SO ENDEARING...
Second layer
THAT'S NOT WHAT HAPPENED.

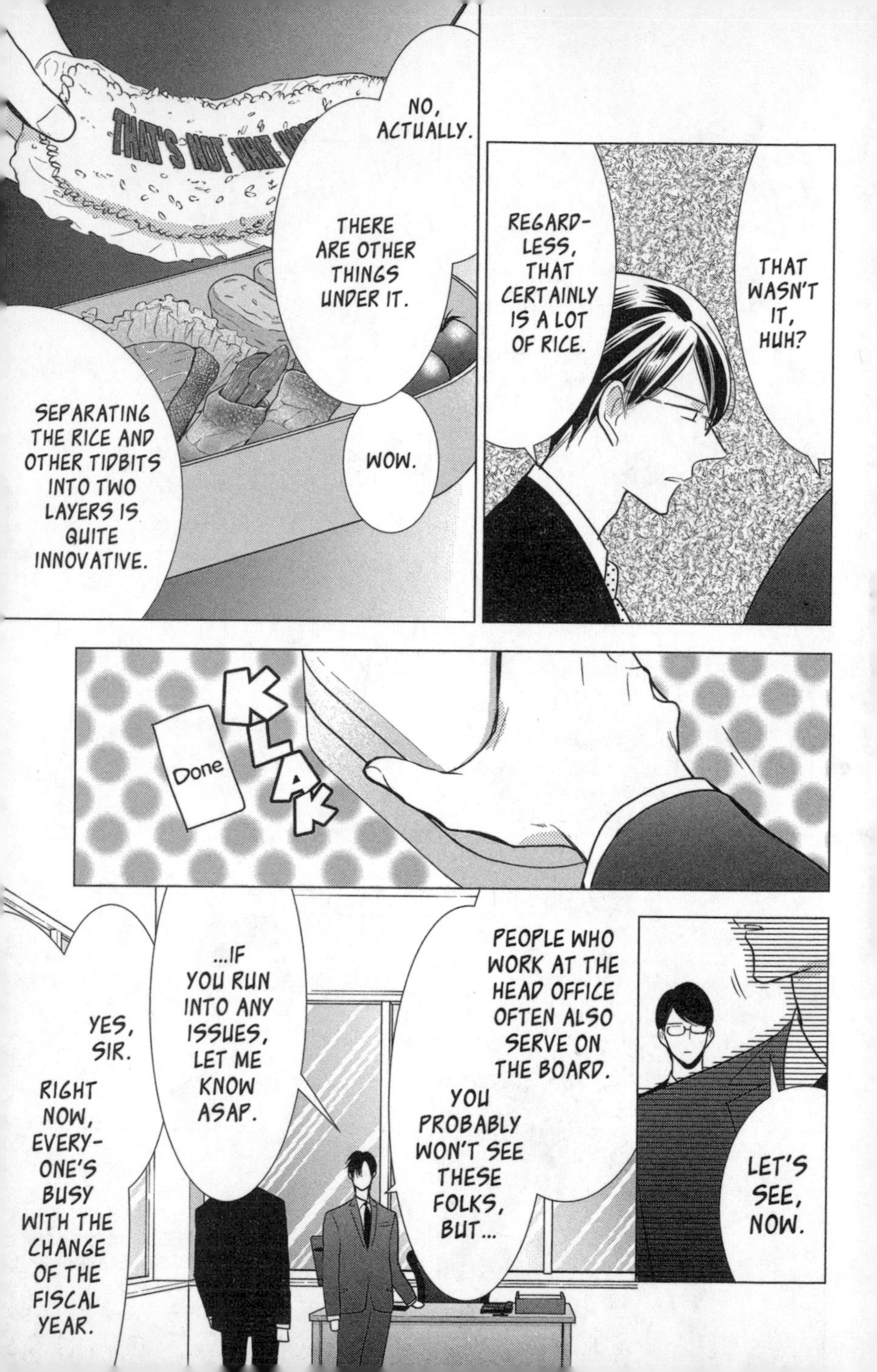
THAT WASN'T IT, HUH?
REGARDLESS, THAT CERTAINLY IS A LOT OF RICE.
NO, ACTUALLY.
THERE ARE OTHER THINGS UNDER IT.
WOW.
SEPARATING THE RICE AND OTHER TIDBITS INTO TWO LAYERS IS QUITE INNOVATIVE.
KLAK
Done
LET'S SEE, NOW.
PEOPLE WHO WORK AT THE HEAD OFFICE OFTEN ALSO SERVE ON THE BOARD.
YOU PROBABLY WON'T SEE THESE FOLKS, BUT...
...IF YOU RUN INTO ANY ISSUES, LET ME KNOW ASAP.
YES, SIR.
RIGHT NOW, EVERYONE'S BUSY WITH THE CHANGE OF THE FISCAL YEAR.

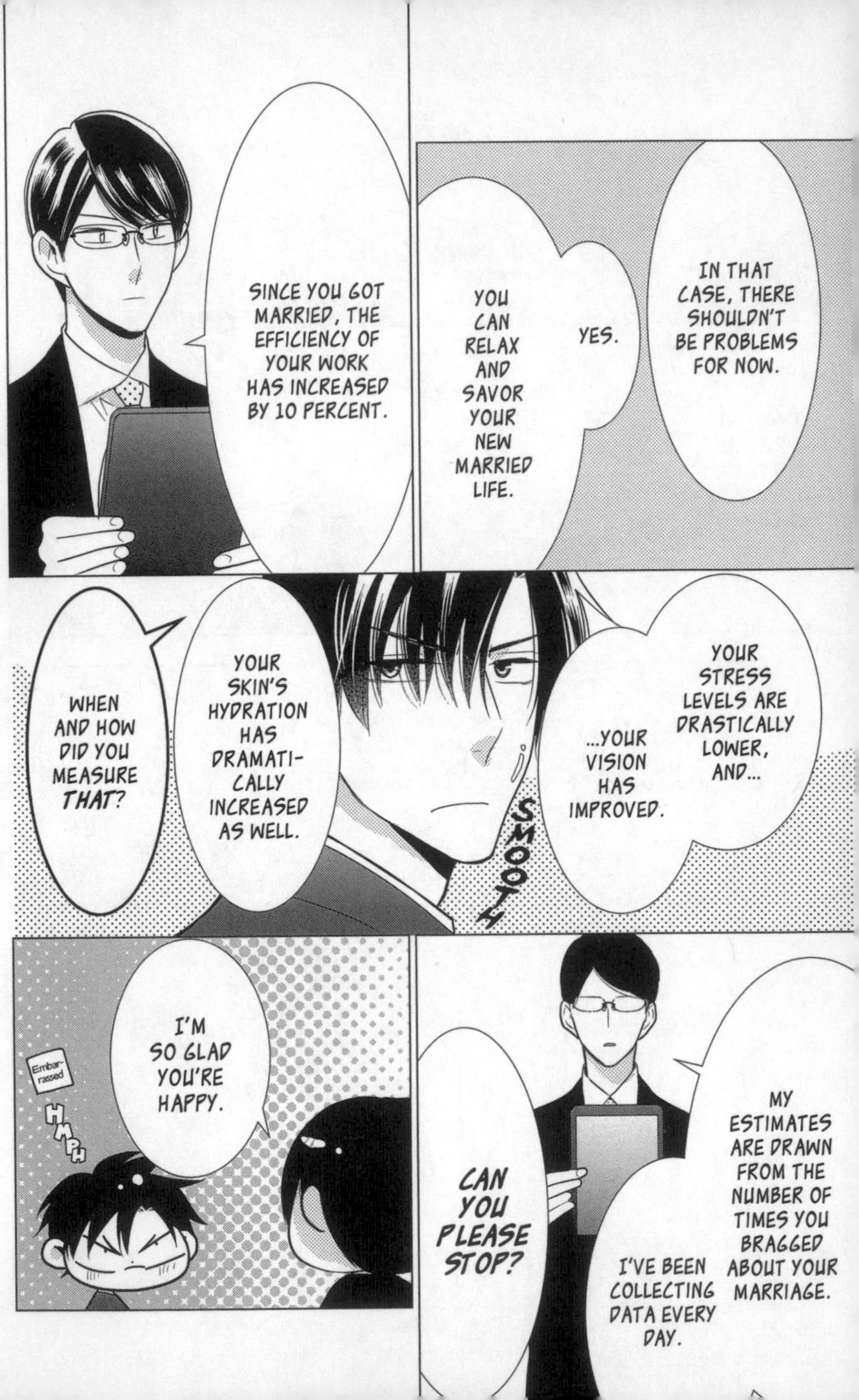
IN THAT CASE, THERE SHOULDN'T BE PROBLEMS FOR NOW.
YES.
YOU CAN RELAX AND SAVOR YOUR NEW MARRIED LIFE.
SINCE YOU GOT MARRIED, THE EFFICIENCY OF YOUR WORK HAS INCREASED BY 10 PERCENT.
YOUR STRESS LEVELS ARE DRASTICALLY LOWER, AND...
...YOUR VISION HAS IMPROVED.
SMOOTH
YOUR SKIN'S HYDRATION HAS DRAMATI-CALLY INCREASED AS WELL.
WHEN AND HOW DID YOU MEASURE THAT?
MY ESTIMATES ARE DRAWN FROM THE NUMBER OF TIMES YOU BRAGGED ABOUT YOUR MARRIAGE.
I'VE BEEN COLLECTING DATA EVERY DAY.
CAN YOU PLEASE STOP?
I'M SO GLAD YOU'RE HAPPY.
Embar-rassed
HMPH

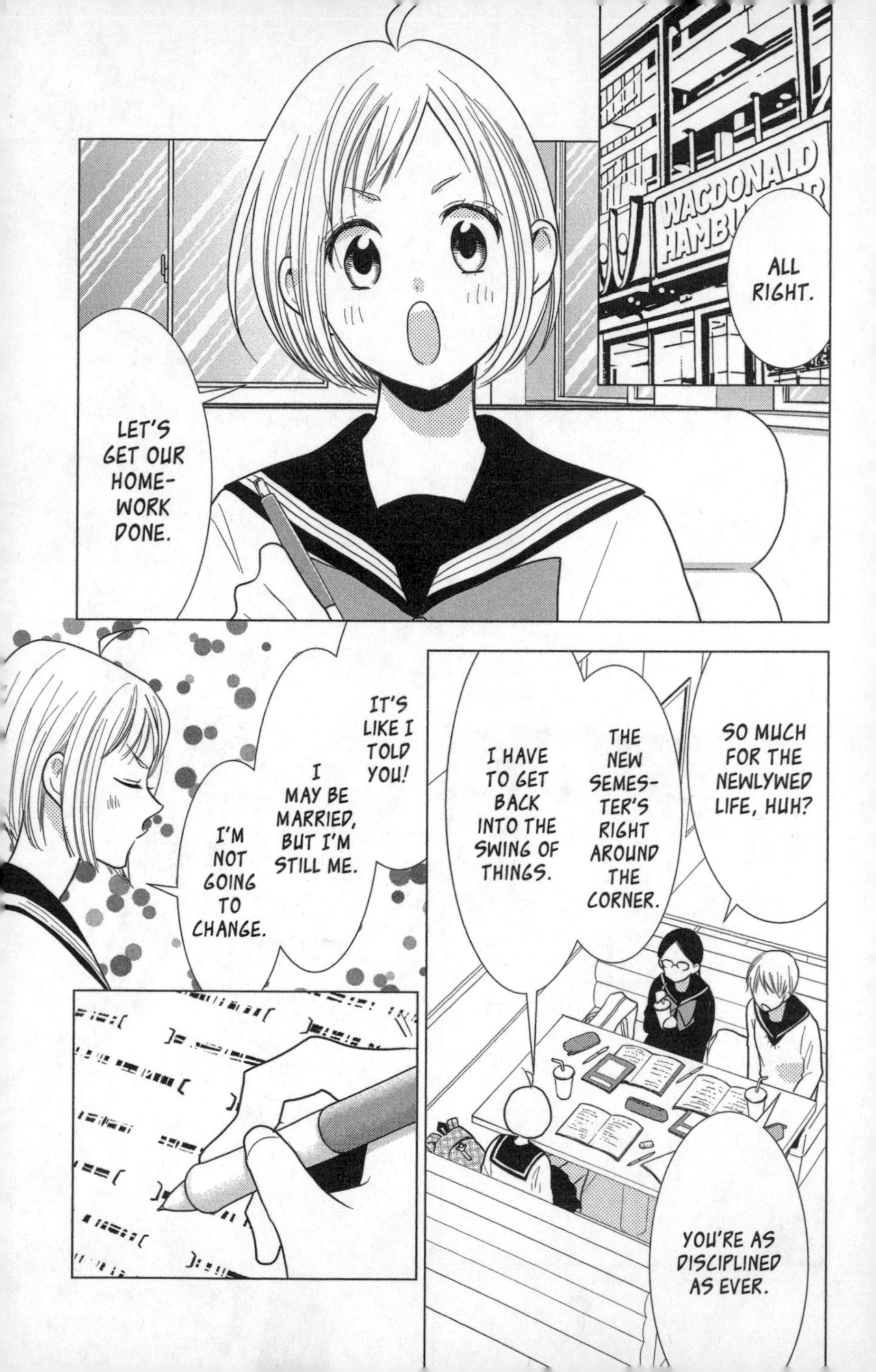
WACDONALD
HAMBU
ALL RIGHT.
LET'S GET OUR HOME-WORK DONE.
SO MUCH FOR THE NEWLYWED LIFE, HUH?
THE NEW SEMES-TER'S RIGHT AROUND THE CORNER.
I HAVE TO GET BACK INTO THE SWING OF THINGS.
YOU'RE AS DISCIPLINED AS EVER.
IT'S LIKE I TOLD YOU!
I MAY BE MARRIED, BUT I'M STILL ME.
I'M NOT GOING TO CHANGE.

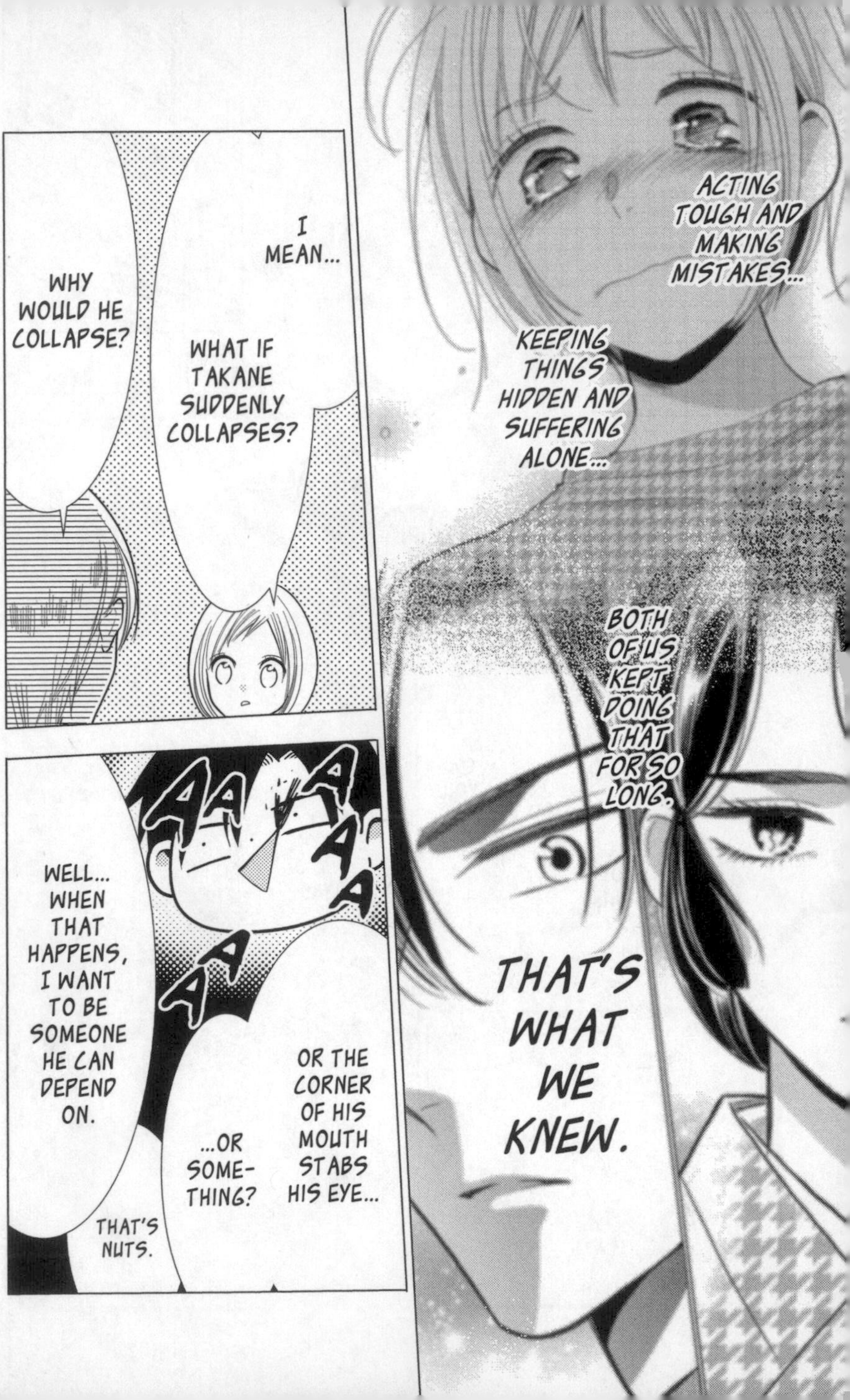
ACTING TOUGH AND MAKING MISTAKES...
KEEPING THINGS HIDDEN AND SUFFERING ALONE...
BOTH OF US KEPT DOING THAT FOR SO LONG.
THAT'S WHAT WE KNEW.
I MEAN...
WHAT IF TAKANE SUDDENLY COLLAPSES?
WHY WOULD HE COLLAPSE?
AAAAAAAA
OR THE CORNER OF HIS MOUTH STABS HIS EYE...
...OR SOMETHING?
THAT'S NUTS.
WELL... WHEN THAT HAPPENS, I WANT TO BE SOMEONE HE CAN DEPEND ON.

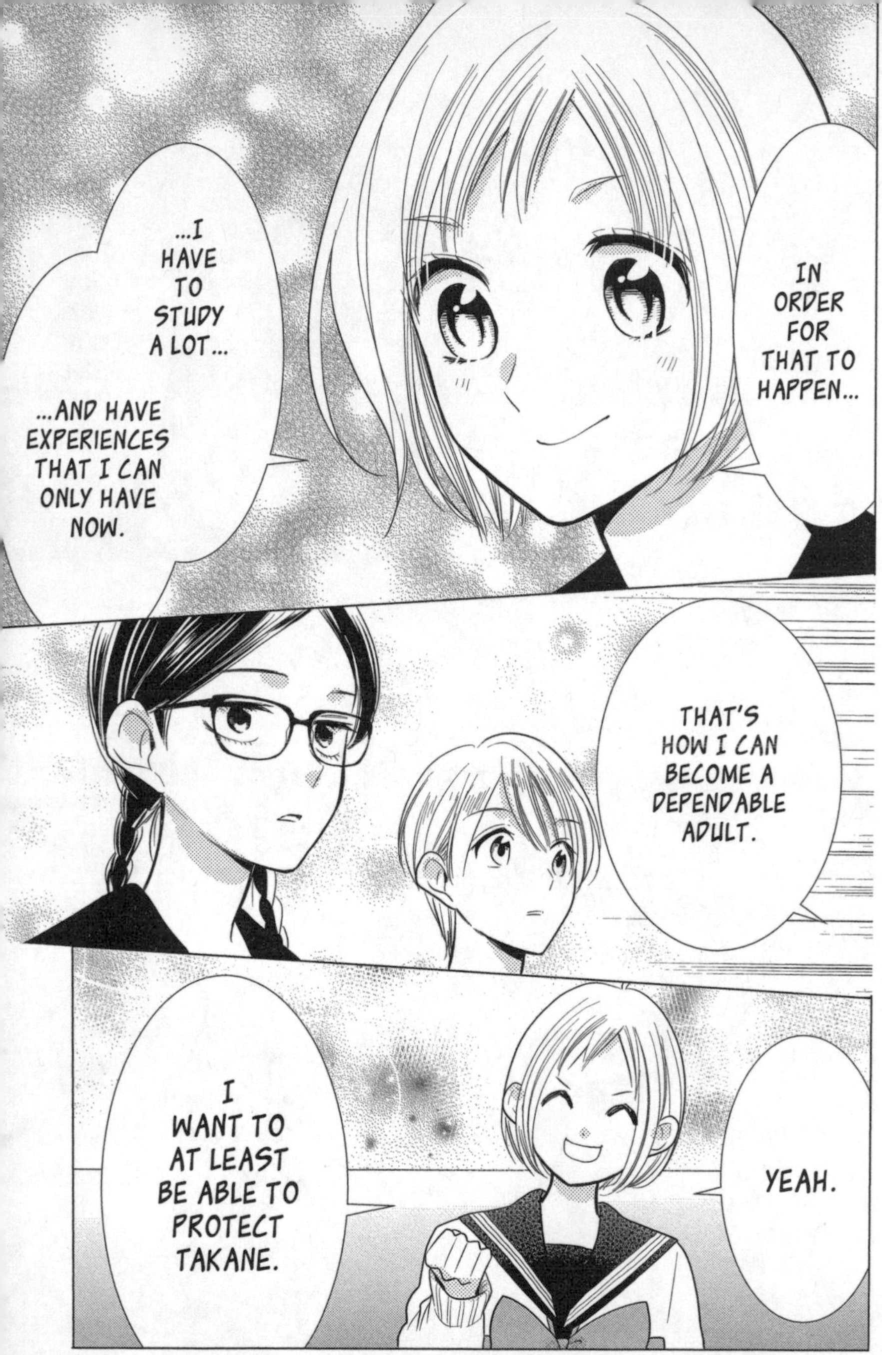
IN ORDER FOR THAT TO HAPPEN...
...I HAVE TO STUDY A LOT...
...AND HAVE EXPERIENCES THAT I CAN ONLY HAVE NOW.
THAT'S HOW I CAN BECOME A DEPENDABLE ADULT.
YEAH.
I WANT TO AT LEAST BE ABLE TO PROTECT TAKANE.

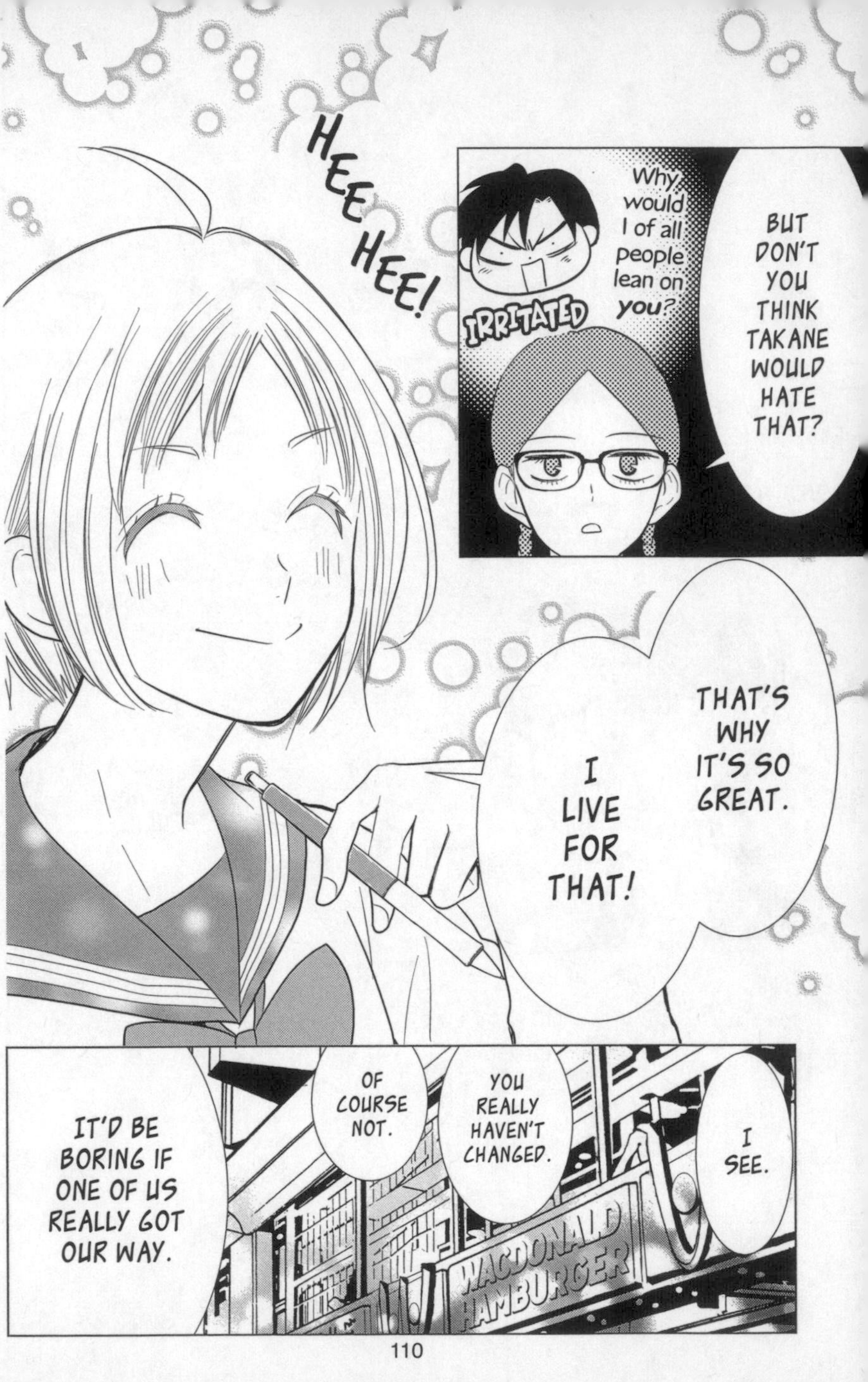
BUT DON'T YOU THINK TAKANE WOULD HATE THAT?
Why would I of all people lean on *you*?
IRRITATED
HEE HEE HEE!
THAT'S WHY IT'S SO GREAT.
I LIVE FOR THAT!
I SEE.
YOU REALLY HAVEN'T CHANGED.
OF COURSE NOT.
IT'D BE BORING IF ONE OF US REALLY GOT OUR WAY.
WACDONALD HAMBURGER

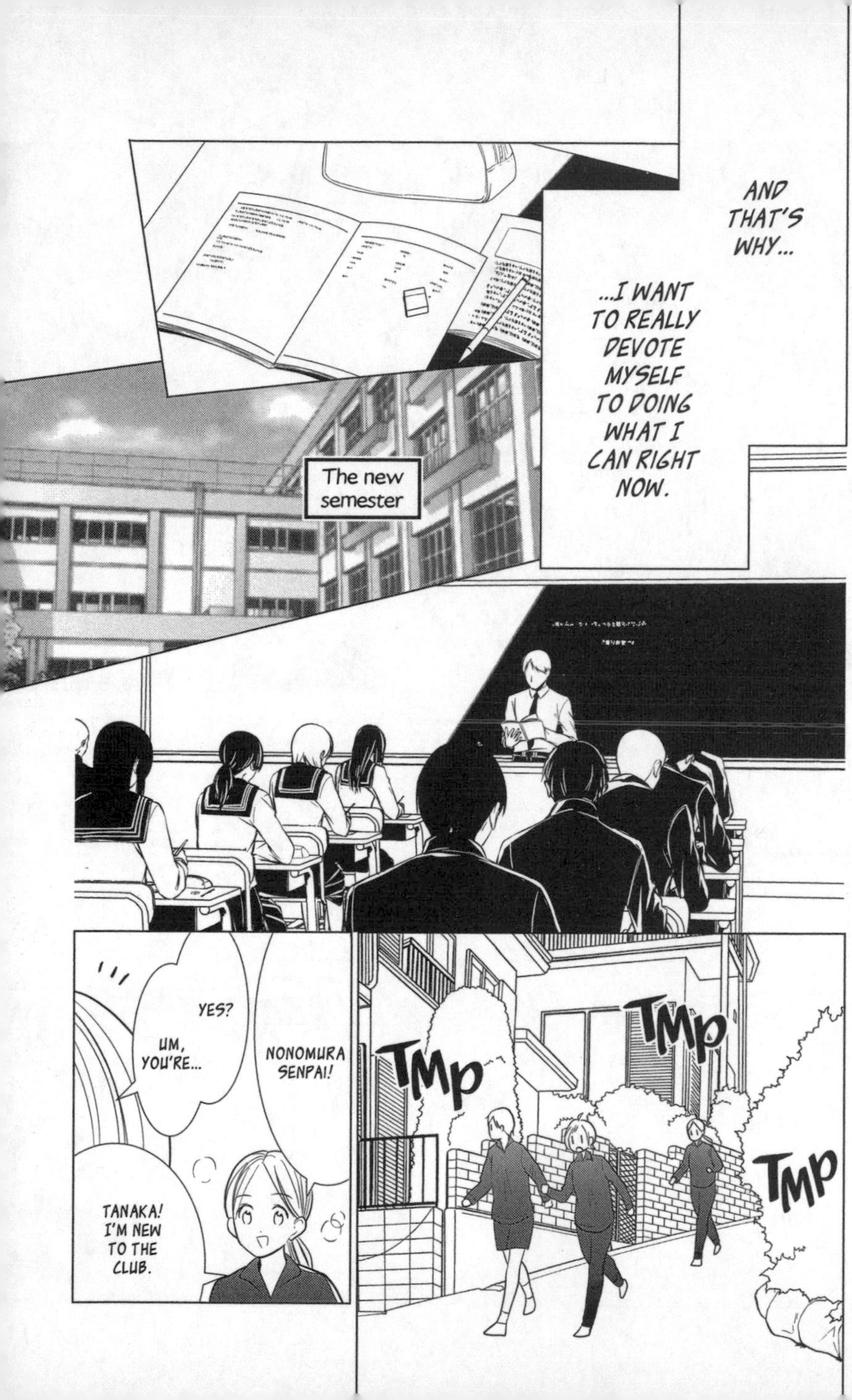
AND THAT'S WHY...
...I WANT TO REALLY DEVOTE MYSELF TO DOING WHAT I CAN RIGHT NOW.
The new semester
TMP
TMP
TMP
NONOMURA SENPAI!
YES?
UM, YOU'RE...
TANAKA! I'M NEW TO THE CLUB.

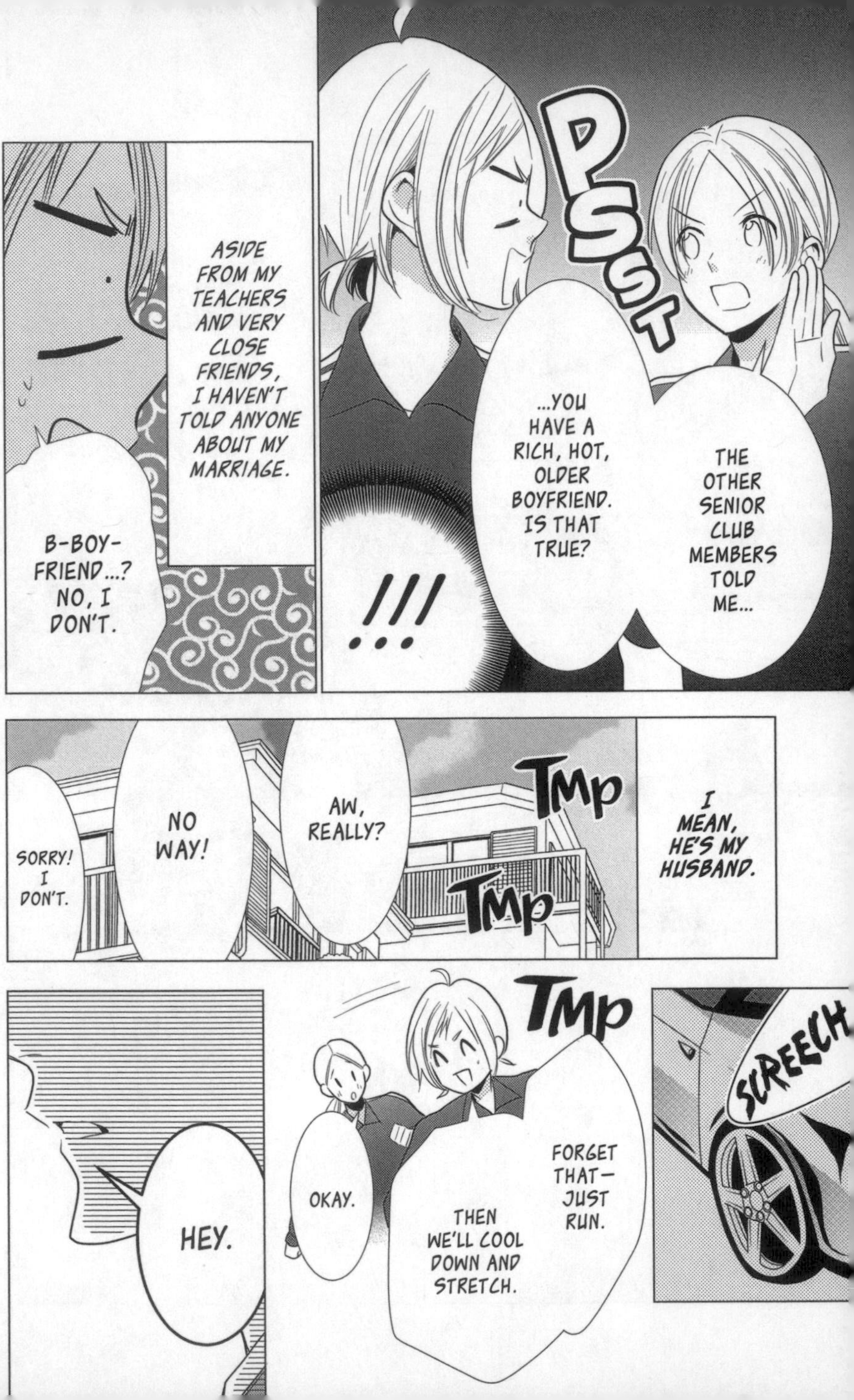
PSST
THE OTHER SENIOR CLUB MEMBERS TOLD ME...
...YOU HAVE A RICH, HOT, OLDER BOYFRIEND. IS THAT TRUE?
!!!
ASIDE FROM MY TEACHERS AND VERY CLOSE FRIENDS, I HAVEN'T TOLD ANYONE ABOUT MY MARRIAGE.
B-BOY-FRIEND...? NO, I DON'T.
I MEAN, HE'S MY HUSBAND.
TMP
TMP
AW, REALLY?
NO WAY!
SORRY! I DON'T.
SCREECH
TMP
FORGET THAT—JUST RUN.
THEN WE'LL COOL DOWN AND STRETCH.
OKAY.
HEY.

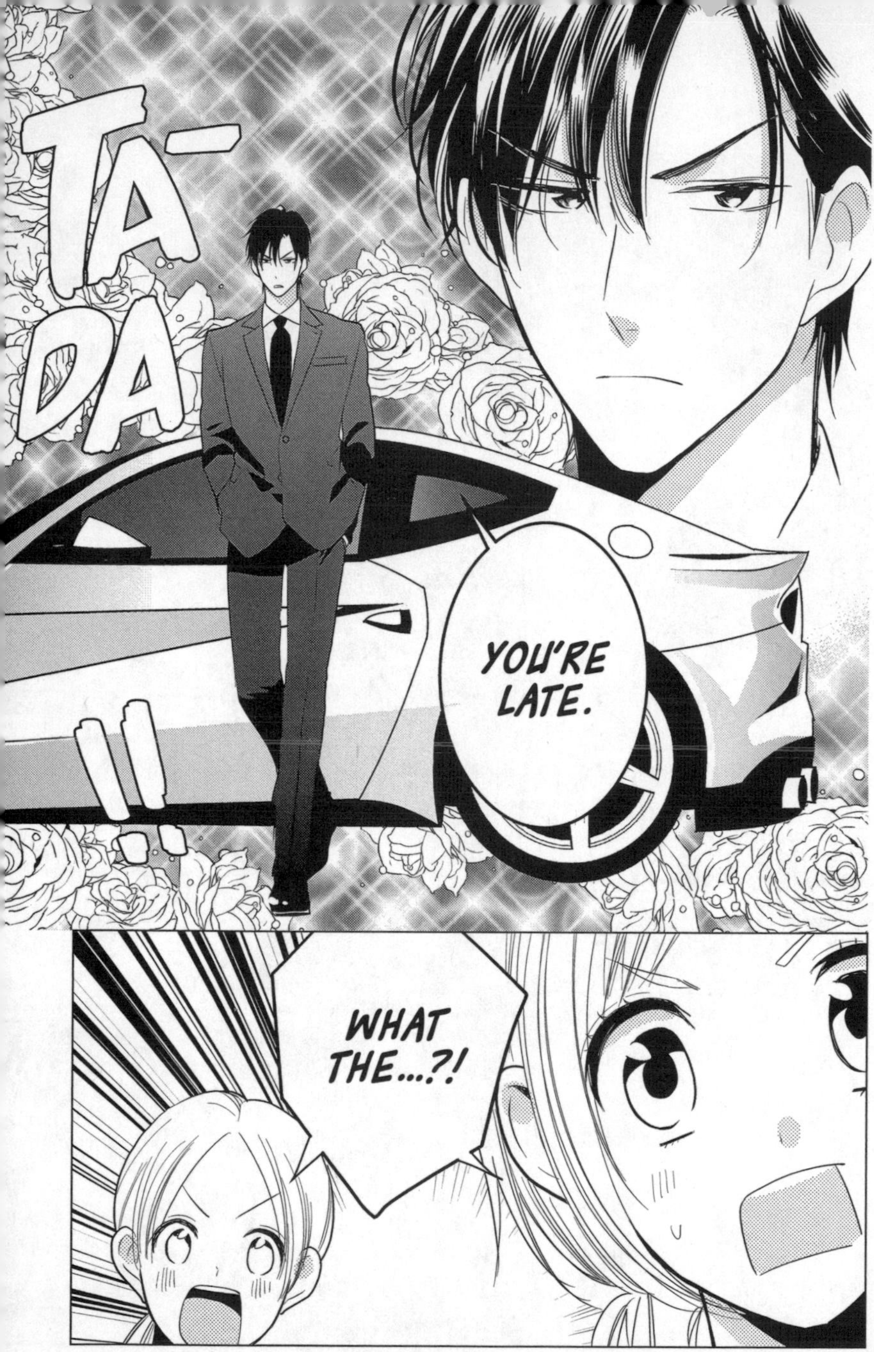
TA-DA
YOU'RE LATE.
!!
WHAT THE...?!

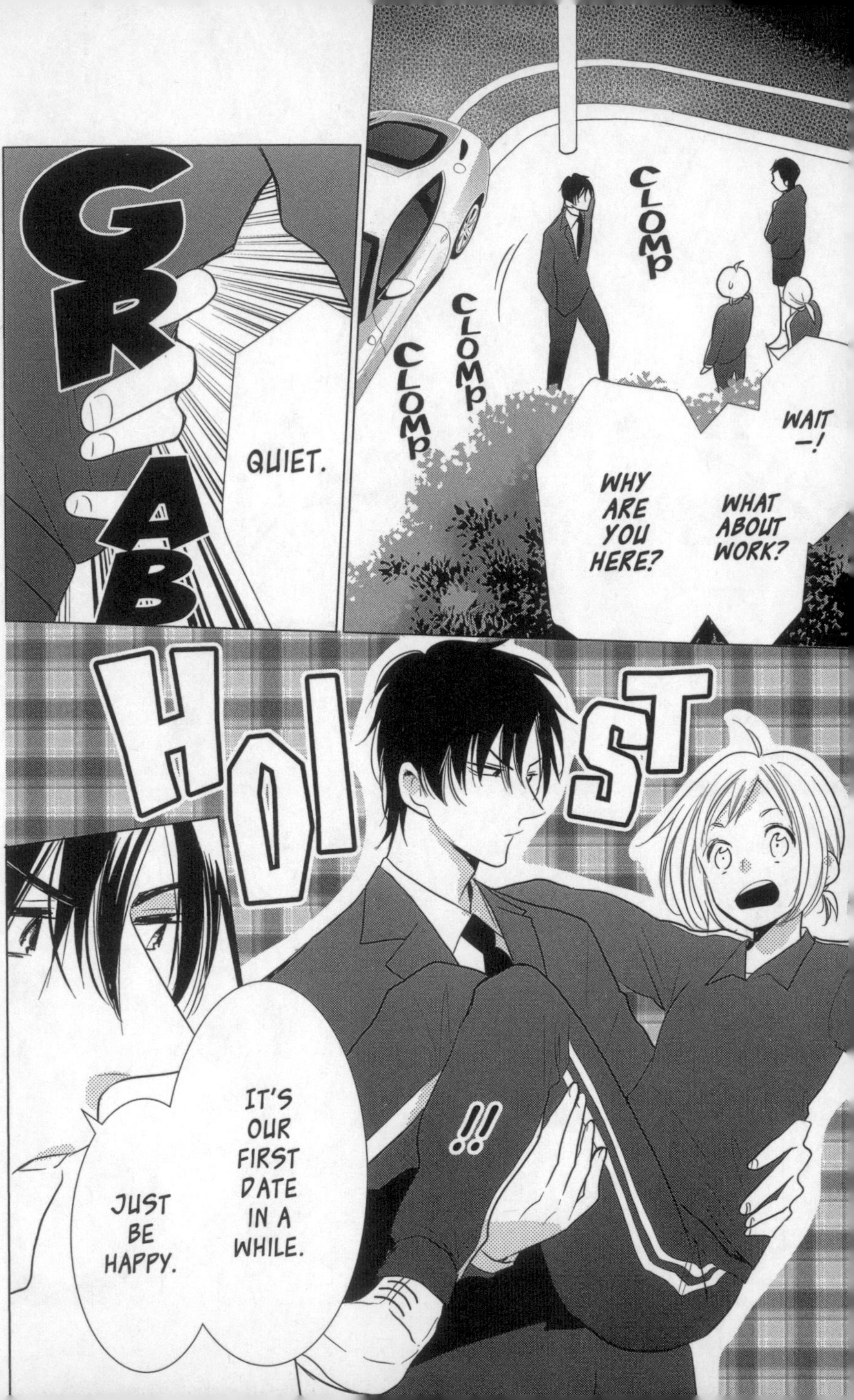
CLOMP
CLOMP
CLOMP
WAIT—!
WHAT ABOUT WORK?
WHY ARE YOU HERE?
GRAB
QUIET.
HOIST
!!
IT'S OUR FIRST DATE IN A WHILE.
JUST BE HAPPY.

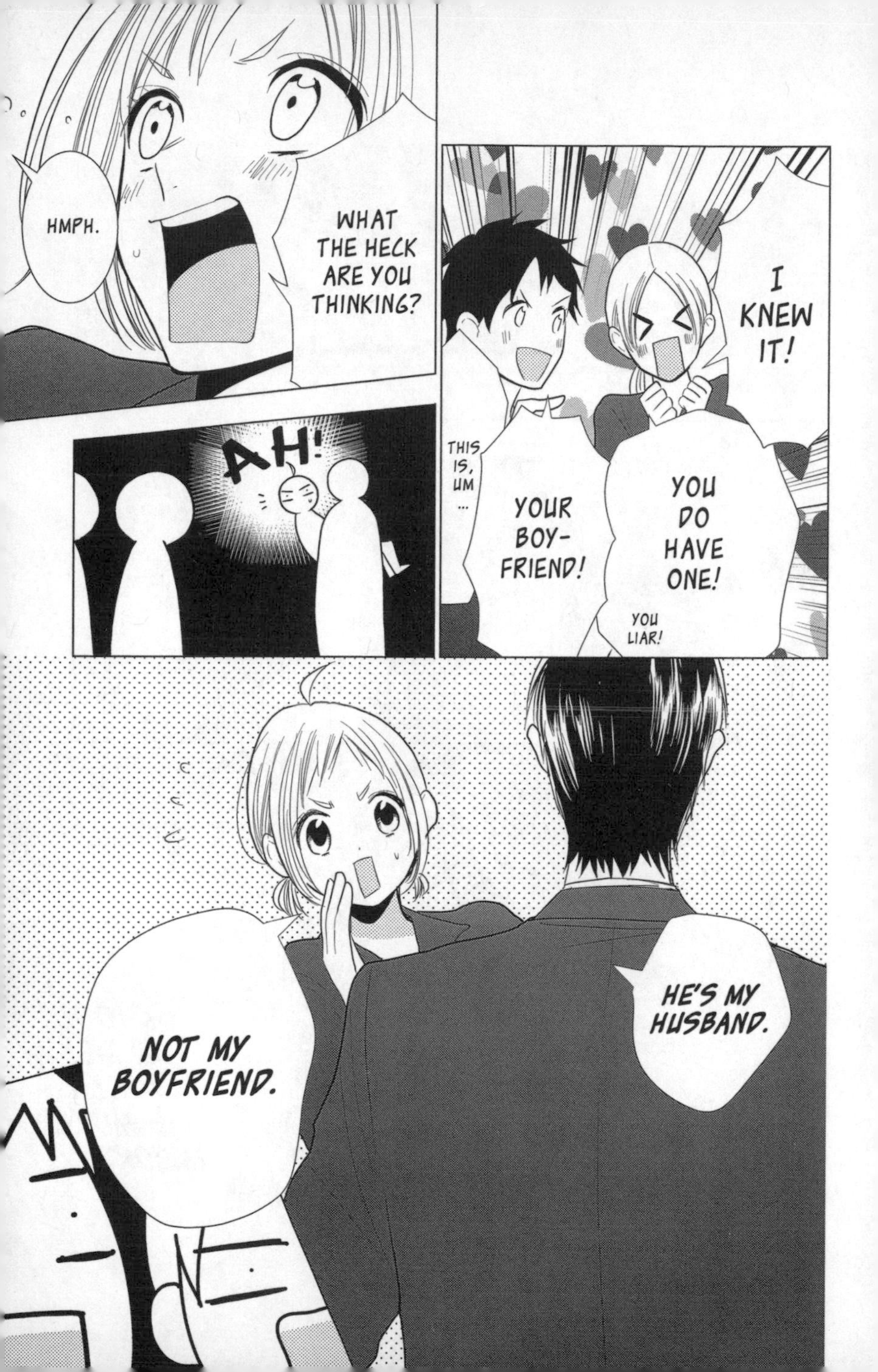
I KNEW IT!
YOU DO HAVE ONE!
YOU LIAR!
THIS IS, UM ...
YOUR BOY-FRIEND!
WHAT THE HECK ARE YOU THINKING?
HMPH.
AH!
HE'S MY HUSBAND.
NOT MY BOYFRIEND.

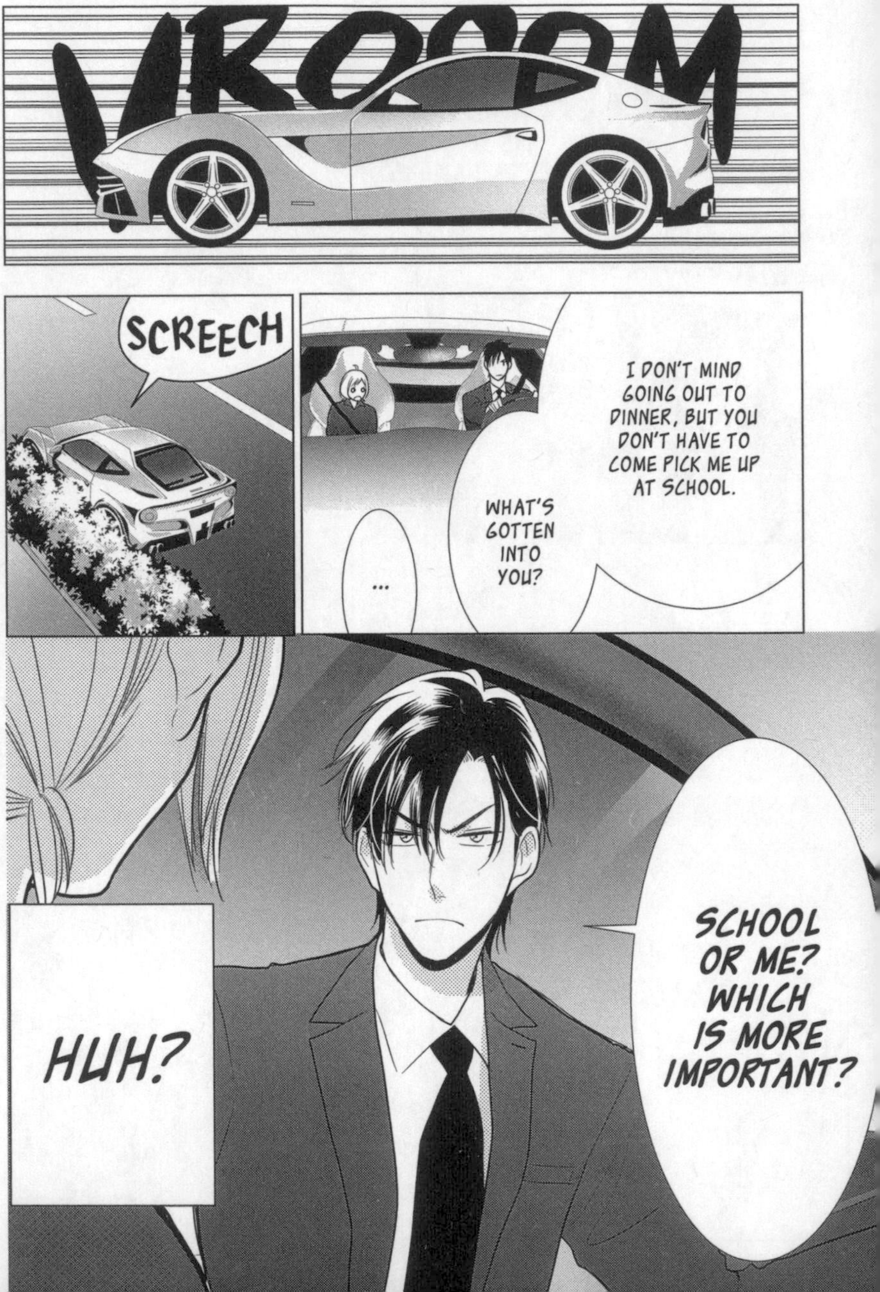
VROOOM
I DON'T MIND GOING OUT TO DINNER, BUT YOU DON'T HAVE TO COME PICK ME UP AT SCHOOL.
WHAT'S GOTTEN INTO YOU?
...
SCREECH
SCHOOL OR ME? WHICH IS MORE IMPORTANT?
HUH?

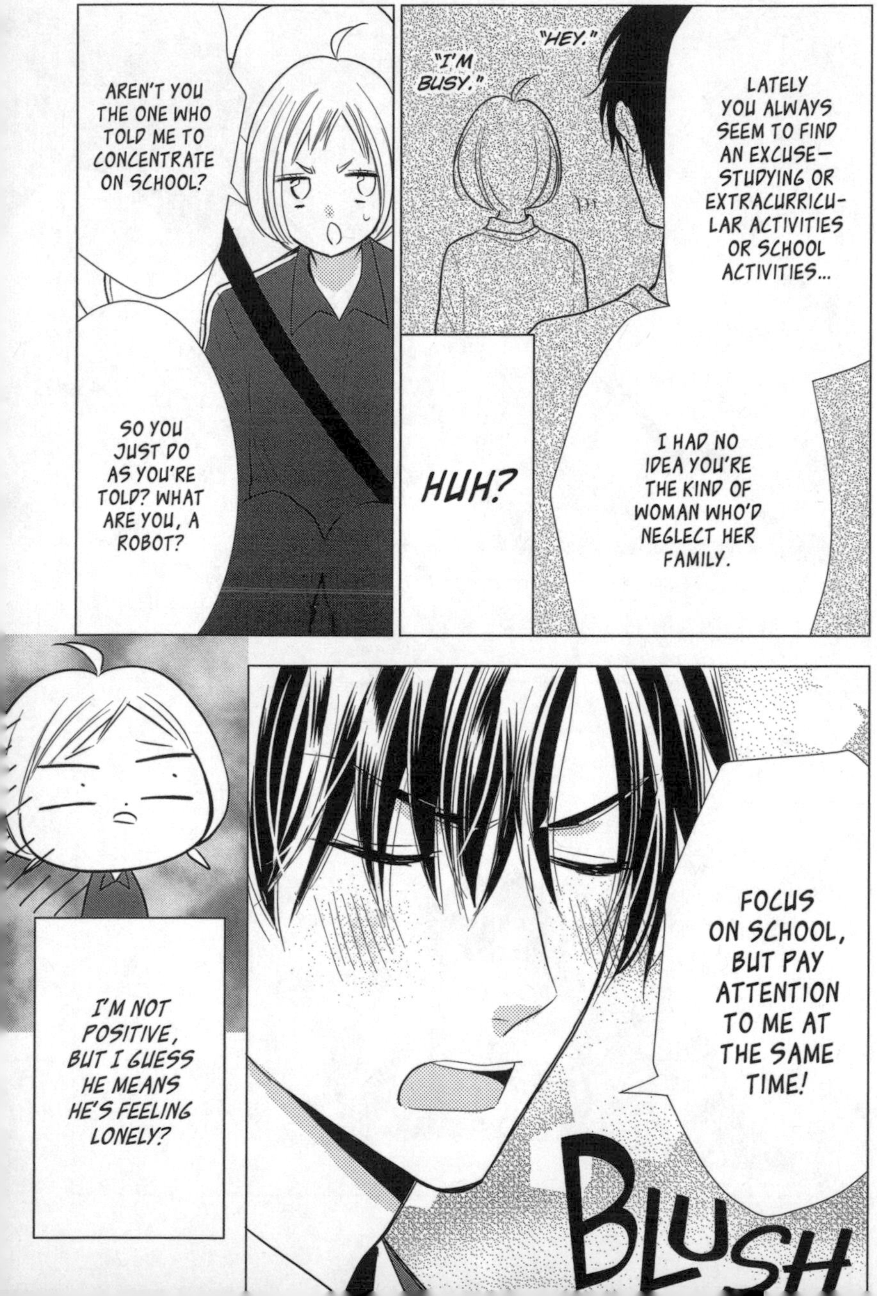

"HEY."
"I'M BUSY."
LATELY YOU ALWAYS SEEM TO FIND AN EXCUSE—STUDYING OR EXTRACURRICU-LAR ACTIVITIES OR SCHOOL ACTIVITIES...
I HAD NO IDEA YOU'RE THE KIND OF WOMAN WHO'D NEGLECT HER FAMILY.
HUH?
AREN'T YOU THE ONE WHO TOLD ME TO CONCENTRATE ON SCHOOL?
SO YOU JUST DO AS YOU'RE TOLD? WHAT ARE YOU, A ROBOT?
FOCUS ON SCHOOL, BUT PAY ATTENTION TO ME AT THE SAME TIME!
BLUSH
I'M NOT POSITIVE, BUT I GUESS HE MEANS HE'S FEELING LONELY?

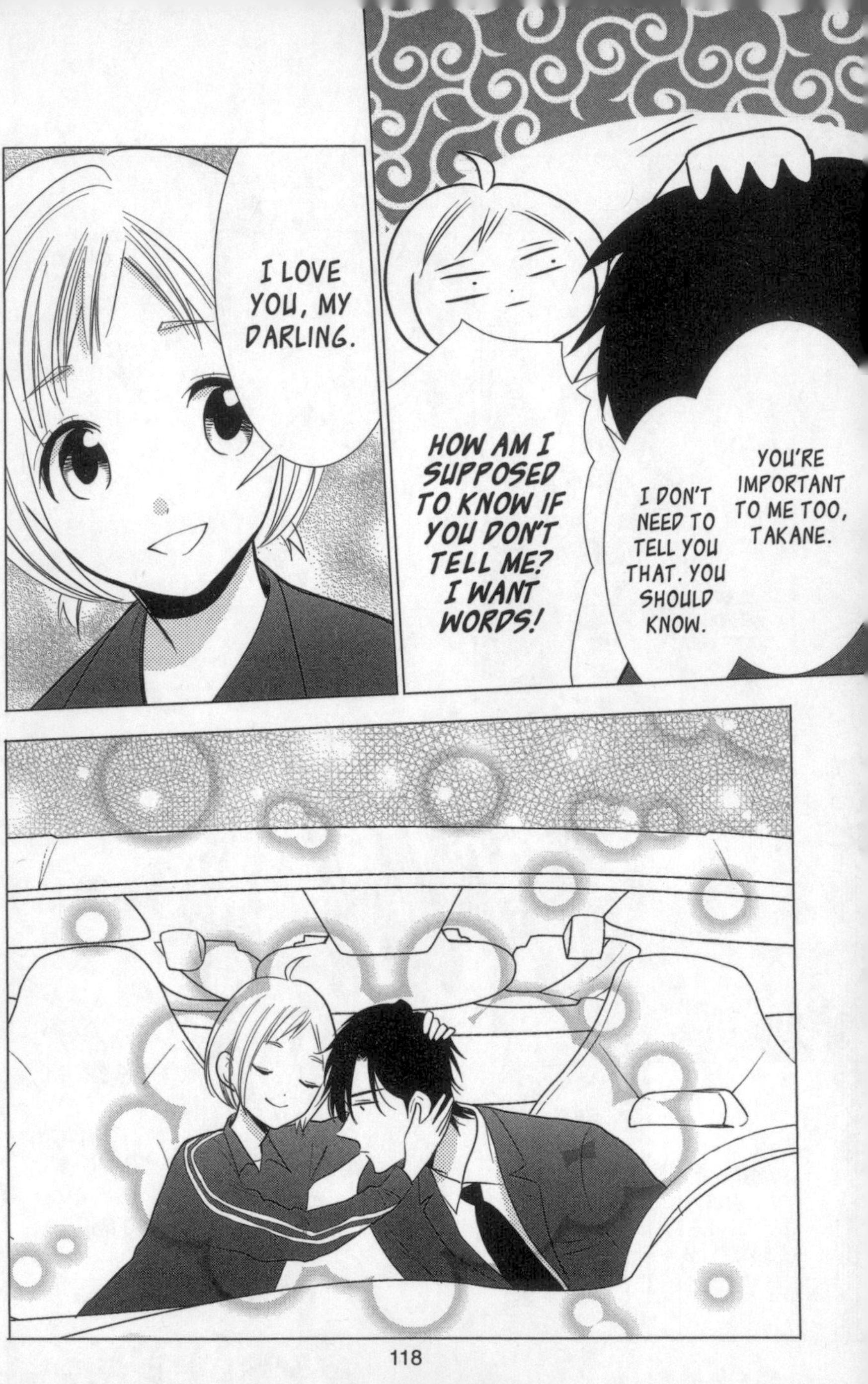
YOU'RE IMPORTANT TO ME TOO, TAKANE.
I DON'T NEED TO TELL YOU THAT. YOU SHOULD KNOW.
HOW AM I SUPPOSED TO KNOW IF YOU DON'T TELL ME? I WANT WORDS!
I LOVE YOU, MY DARLING.

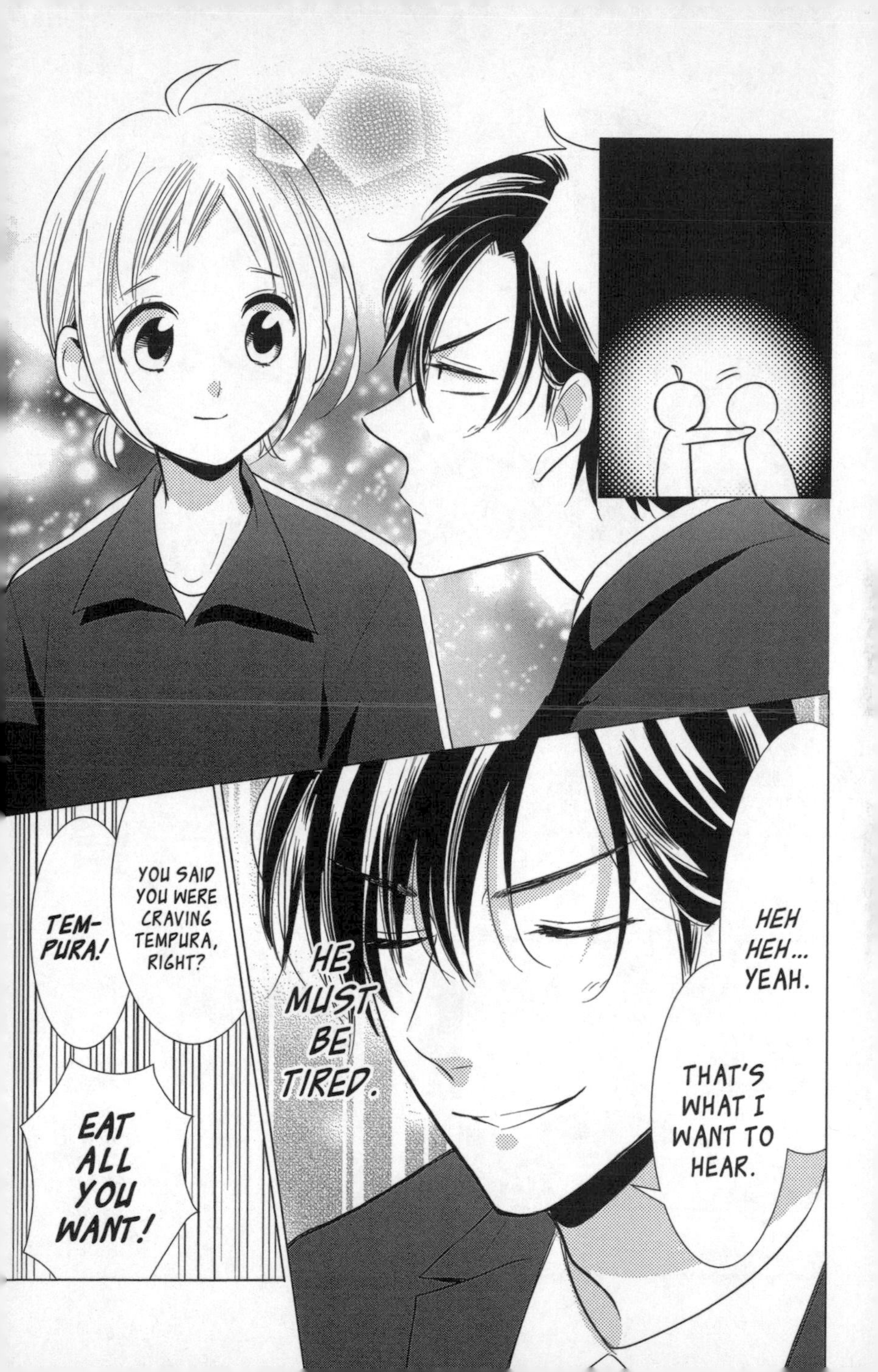
HEH HEH... YEAH.
THAT'S WHAT I WANT TO HEAR.
HE MUST BE TIRED.
YOU SAID YOU WERE CRAVING TEMPURA, RIGHT?
TEM-PURA!
EAT ALL YOU WANT!

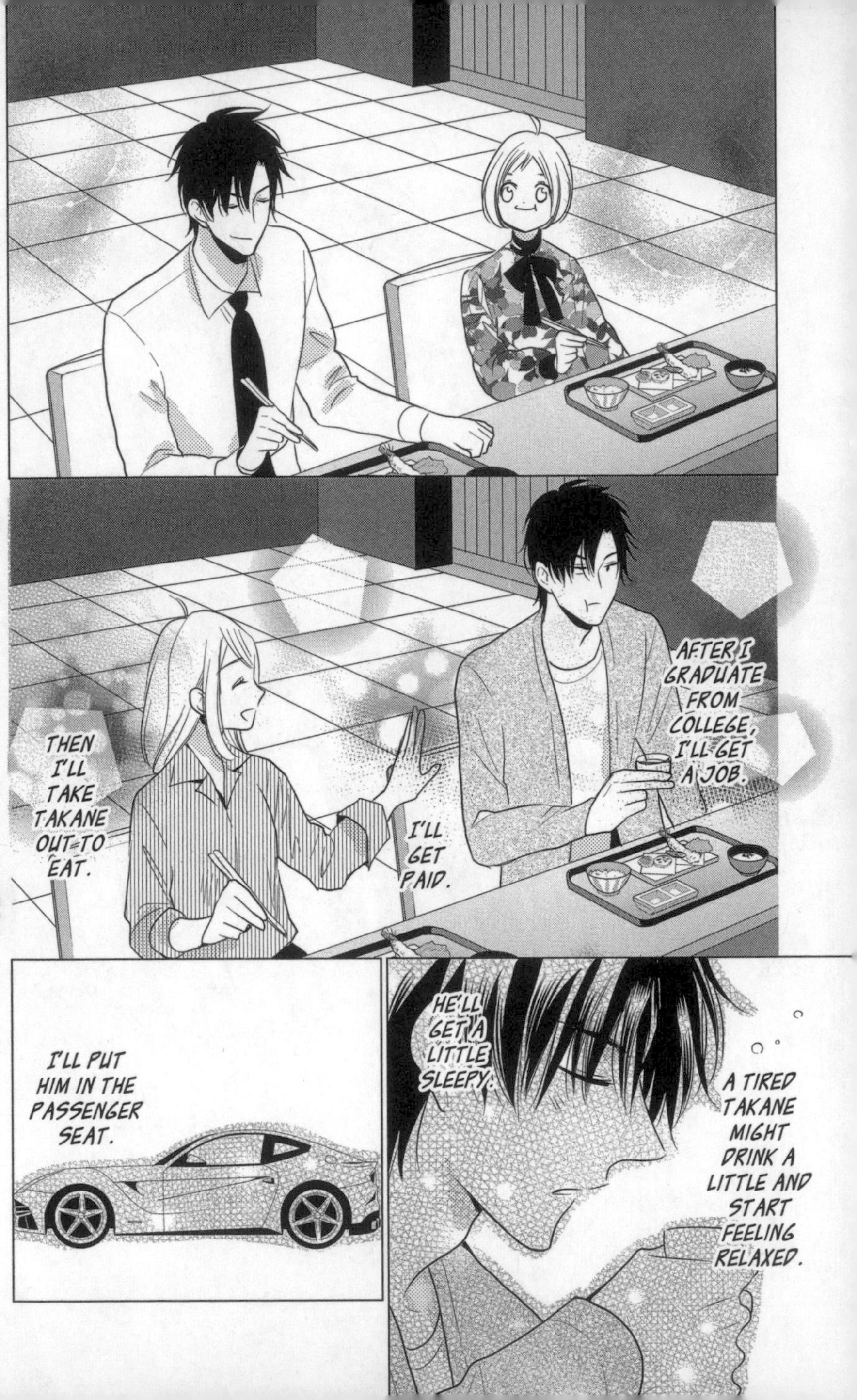
AFTER I GRADUATE FROM COLLEGE, I'LL GET A JOB.
I'LL GET PAID.
THEN I'LL TAKE TAKANE OUT TO EAT.
A TIRED TAKANE MIGHT DRINK A LITTLE AND START FEELING RELAXED.
HE'LL GET A LITTLE SLEEPY.
I'LL PUT HIM IN THE PASSENGER SEAT.

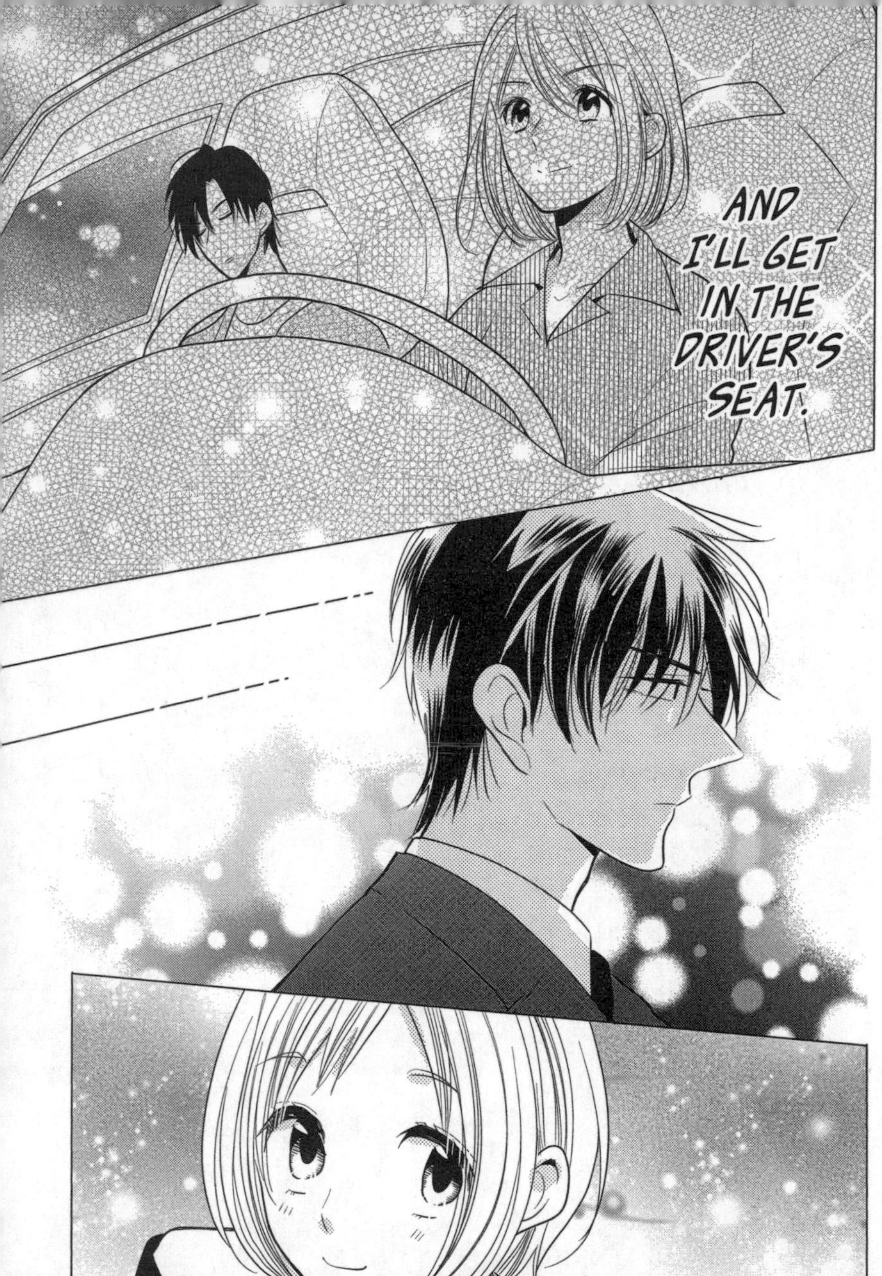
AND I'LL GET IN THE DRIVER'S SEAT.

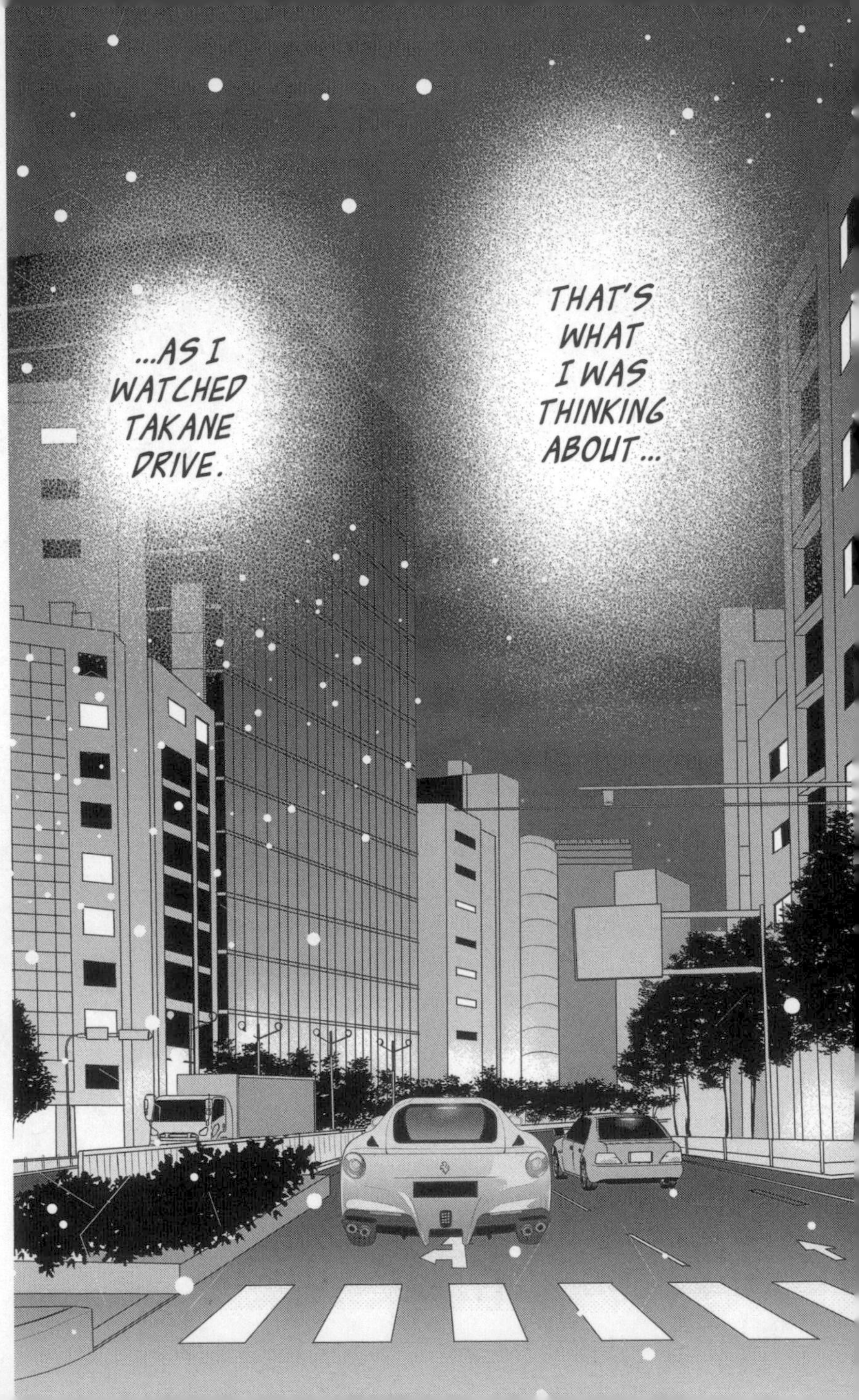
THAT'S WHAT I WAS THINKING ABOUT...
...AS I WATCHED TAKANE DRIVE.

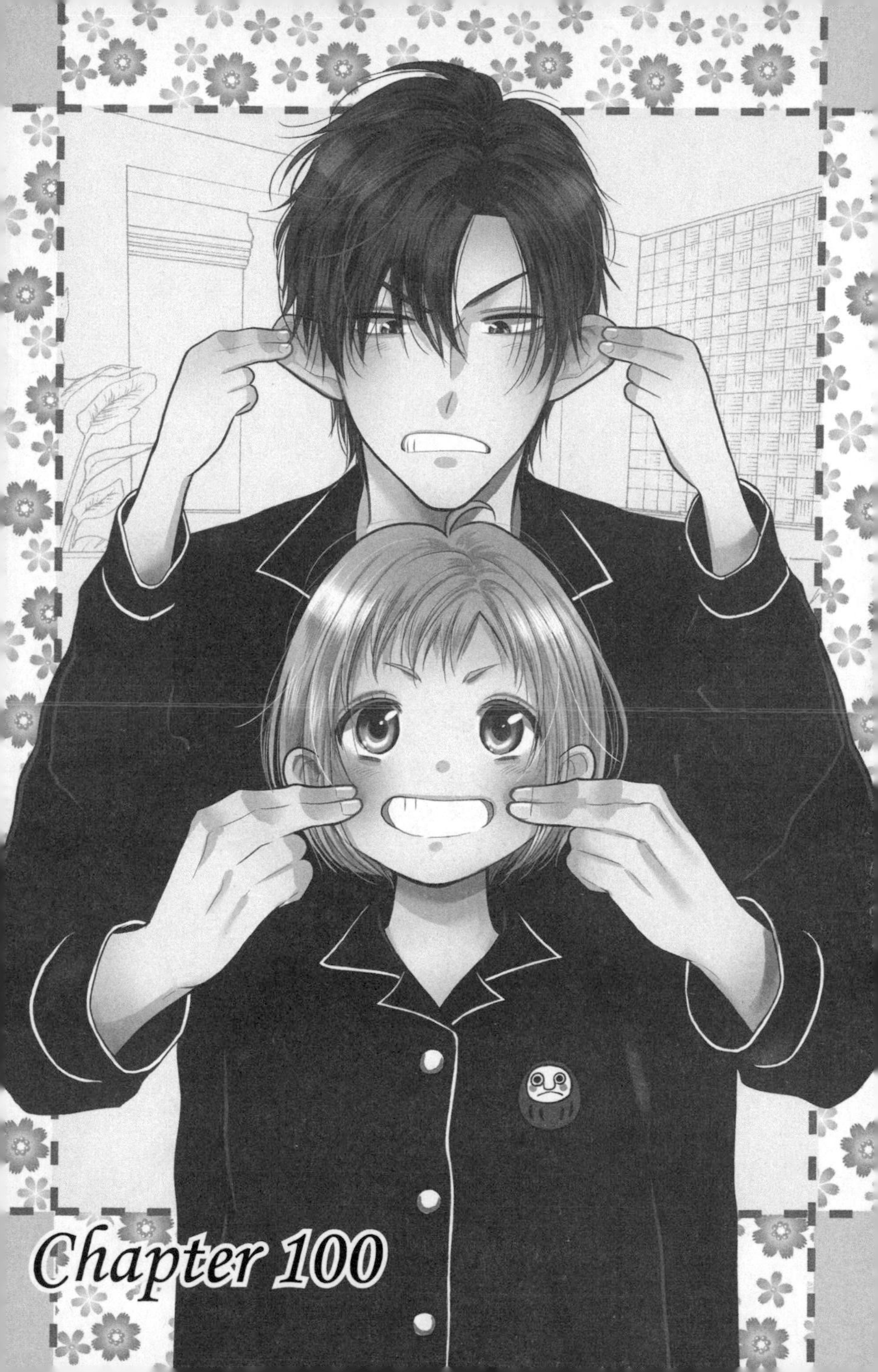
Chapter 100

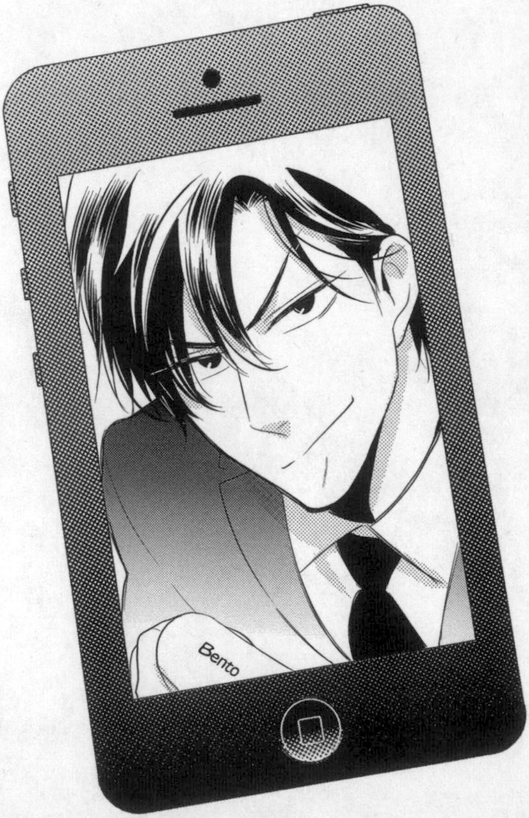
Bento

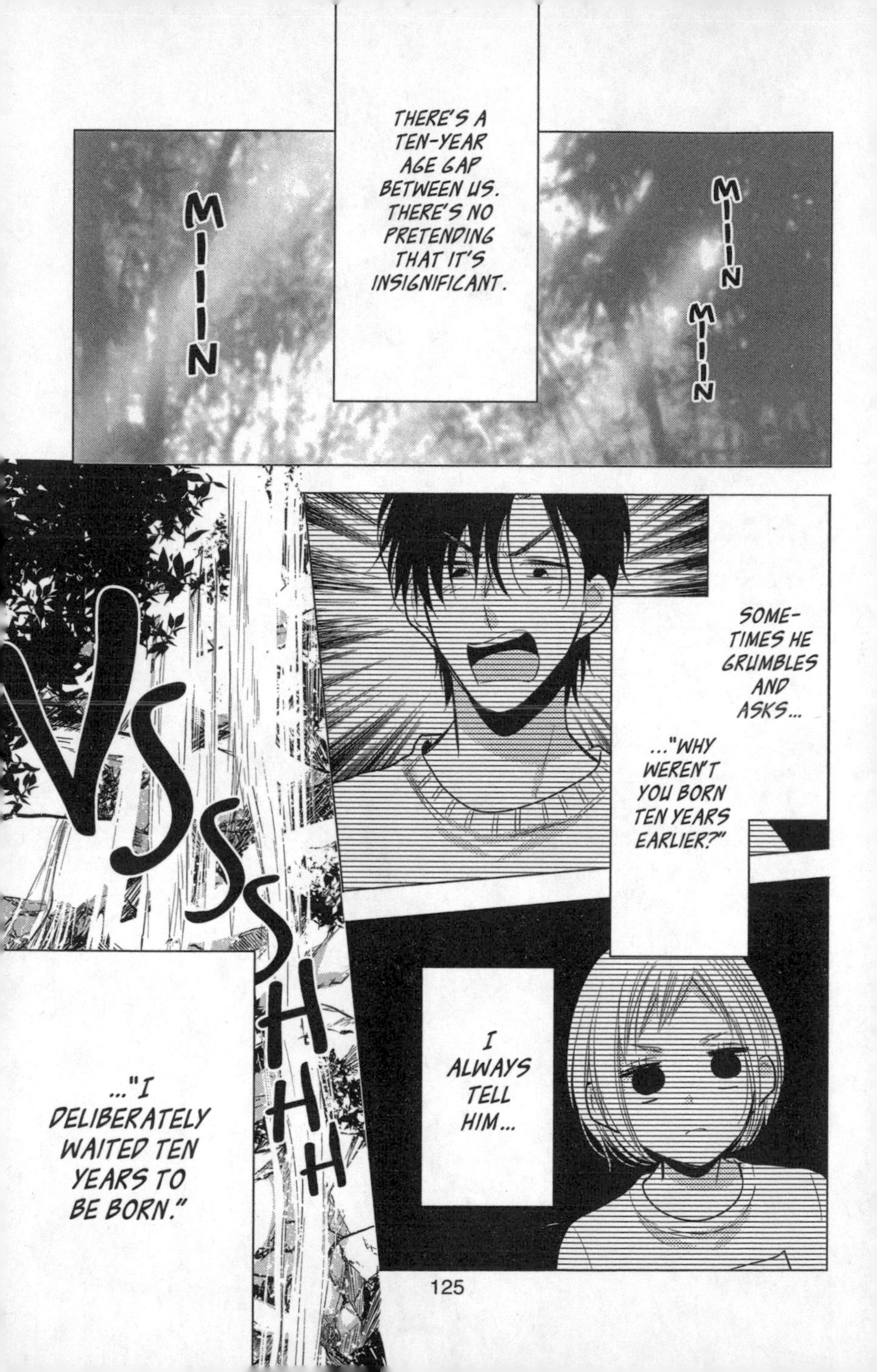
THERE'S A TEN-YEAR AGE GAP BETWEEN US. THERE'S NO PRETENDING THAT IT'S INSIGNIFICANT.
MIIIN
MIIN
MIIIN
SOME-TIMES HE GRUMBLES AND ASKS...
..."WHY WEREN'T YOU BORN TEN YEARS EARLIER?"
VSSSHHH
I ALWAYS TELL HIM...
..."I DELIBERATELY WAITED TEN YEARS TO BE BORN."

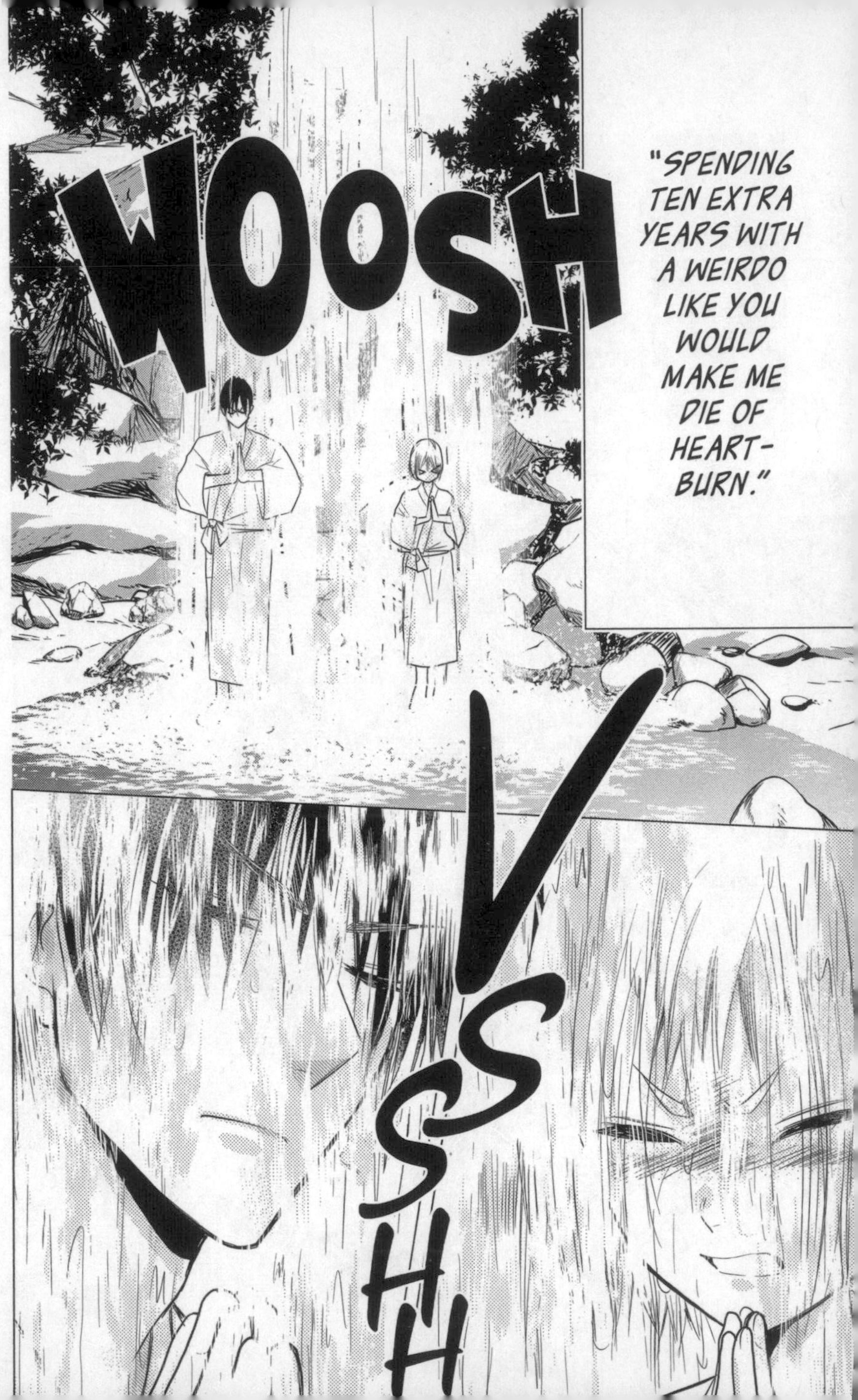
"SPENDING TEN EXTRA YEARS WITH A WEIRDO LIKE YOU WOULD MAKE ME DIE OF HEART-BURN."
WOOSH
VSSHH

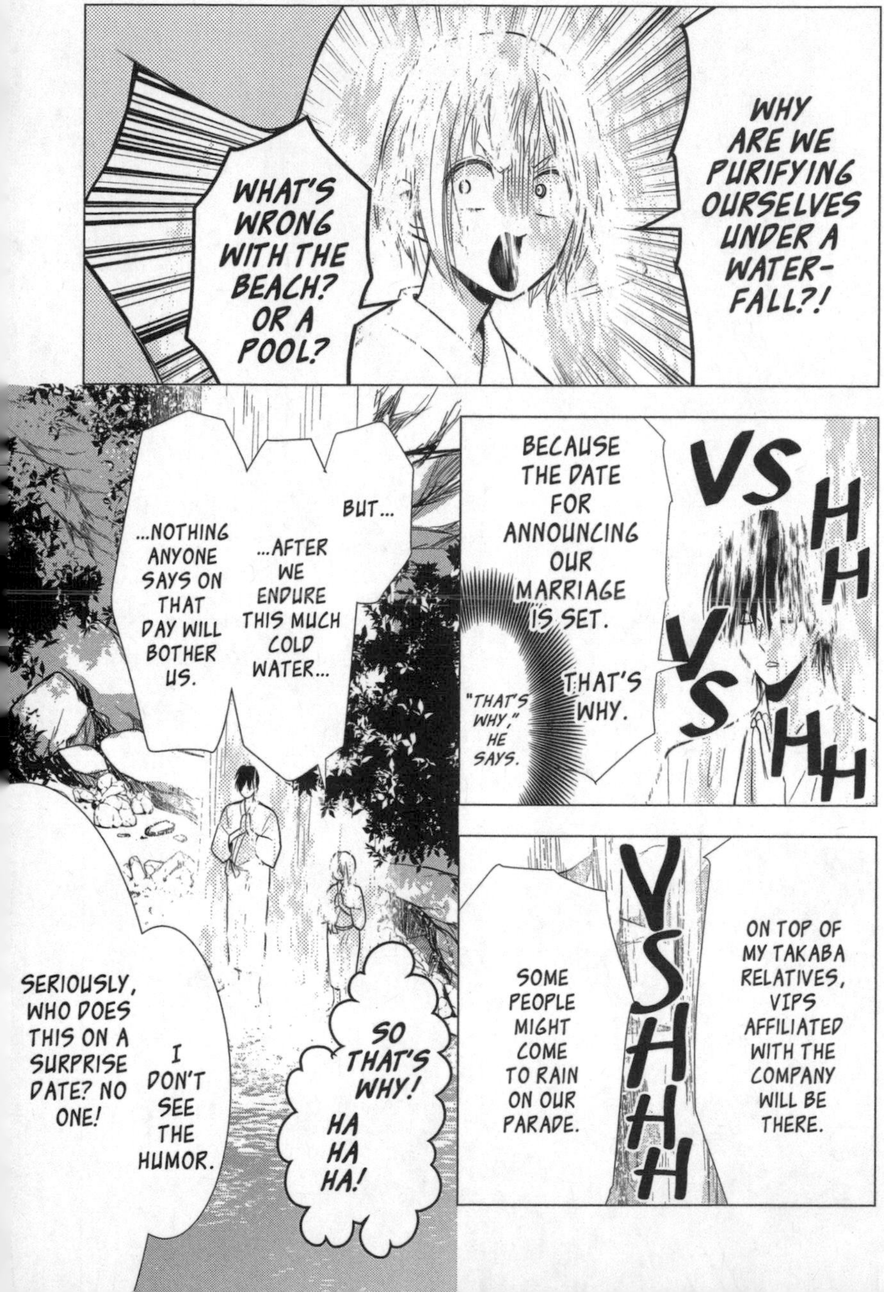
WHY ARE WE PURIFYING OURSELVES UNDER A WATER-FALL?!
WHAT'S WRONG WITH THE BEACH? OR A POOL?
BECAUSE THE DATE FOR ANNOUNCING OUR MARRIAGE IS SET.
VSHH
VSHH
THAT'S WHY.
"THAT'S WHY," HE SAYS.
VSHHH
ON TOP OF MY TAKABA RELATIVES, VIPS AFFILIATED WITH THE COMPANY WILL BE THERE.
SOME PEOPLE MIGHT COME TO RAIN ON OUR PARADE.
BUT...
...AFTER WE ENDURE THIS MUCH COLD WATER...
...NOTHING ANYONE SAYS ON THAT DAY WILL BOTHER US.
SO THAT'S WHY!
HA HA HA!
I DON'T SEE THE HUMOR.
SERIOUSLY, WHO DOES THIS ON A SURPRISE DATE? NO ONE!

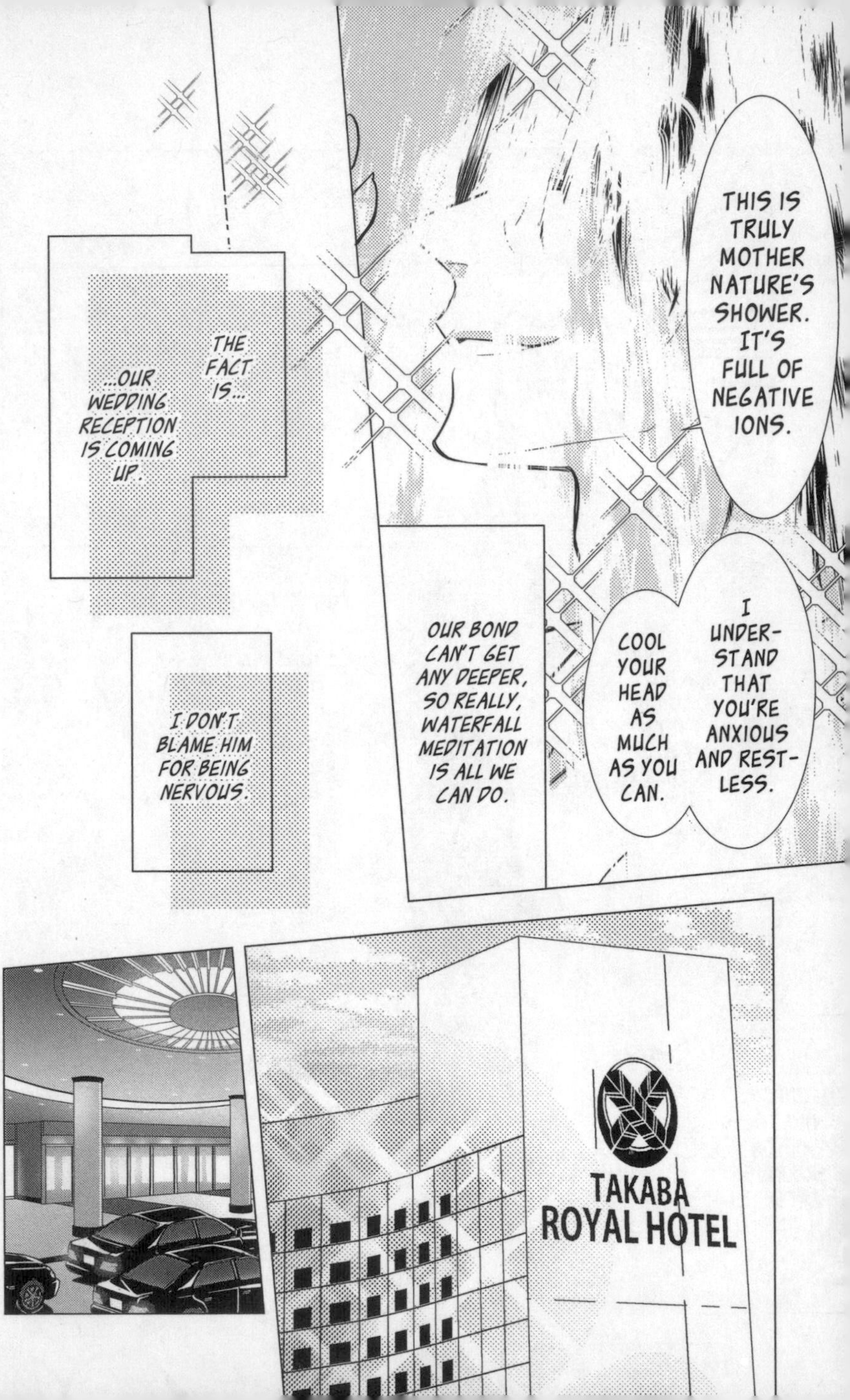
THIS IS TRULY MOTHER NATURE'S SHOWER. IT'S FULL OF NEGATIVE IONS.
I UNDER-STAND THAT YOU'RE ANXIOUS AND REST-LESS.
COOL YOUR HEAD AS MUCH AS YOU CAN.
OUR BOND CAN'T GET ANY DEEPER, SO REALLY, WATERFALL MEDITATION IS ALL WE CAN DO.
THE FACT IS...
...OUR WEDDING RECEPTION IS COMING UP.
I DON'T BLAME HIM FOR BEING NERVOUS.
TAKABA ROYAL HOTEL

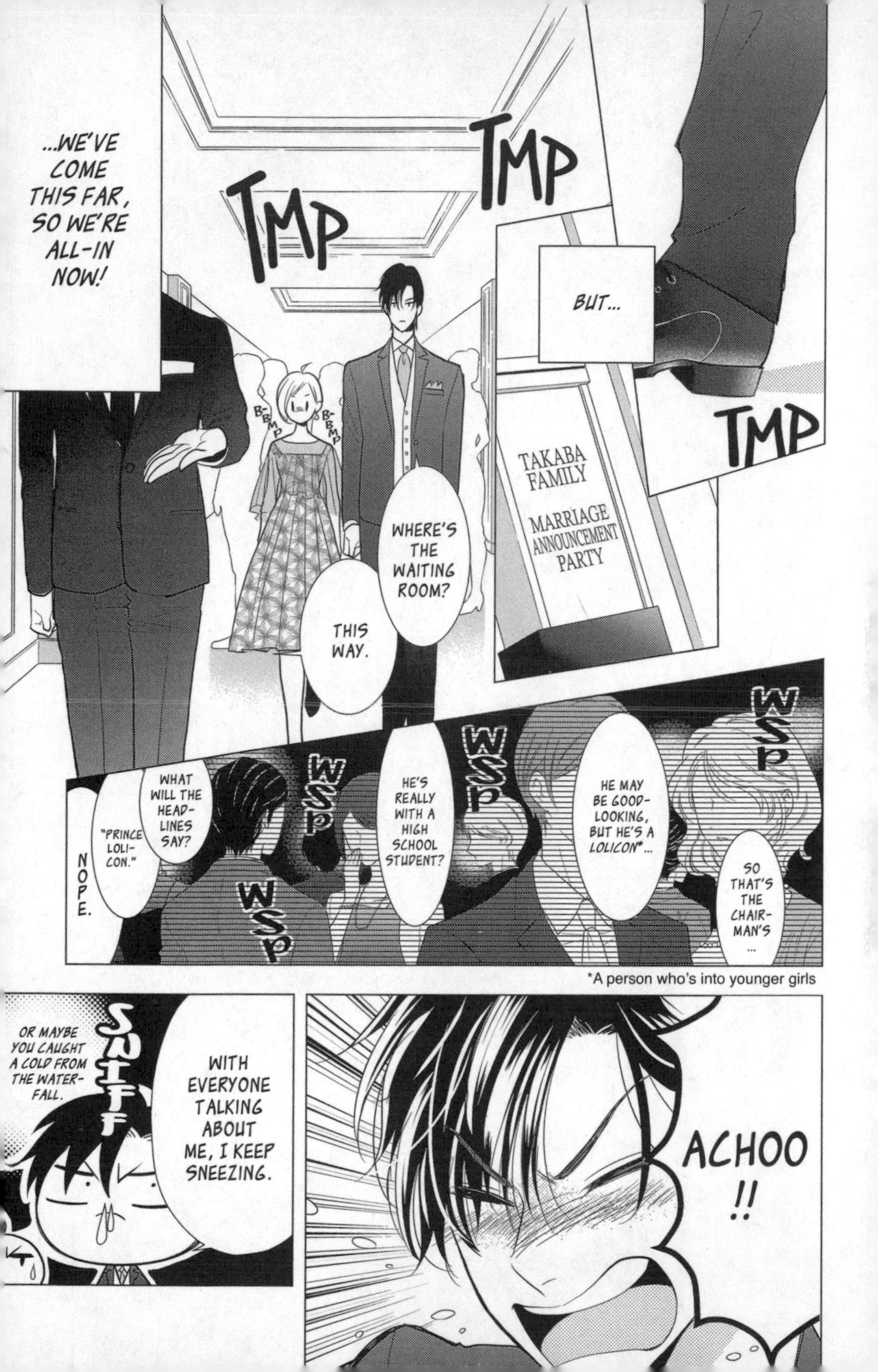
TMP
BUT...
TAKABA FAMILY
MARRIAGE ANNOUNCEMENT PARTY
...WE'VE COME THIS FAR, SO WE'RE ALL-IN NOW!
TMP
TMP
B-BMP
B-BMP
WHERE'S THE WAITING ROOM?
THIS WAY.
WSP
SO THAT'S THE CHAIRMAN'S...
HE MAY BE GOOD-LOOKING, BUT HE'S A LOLICON*...
WSP
HE'S REALLY WITH A HIGH SCHOOL STUDENT?
WSP
WSP
WHAT WILL THE HEADLINES SAY?
"PRINCE LOLICON."
NOPE.
ACHOO!!
WITH EVERYONE TALKING ABOUT ME, I KEEP SNEEZING.
SNIFF
OR MAYBE YOU CAUGHT A COLD FROM THE WATERFALL.

*A person who's into younger girls

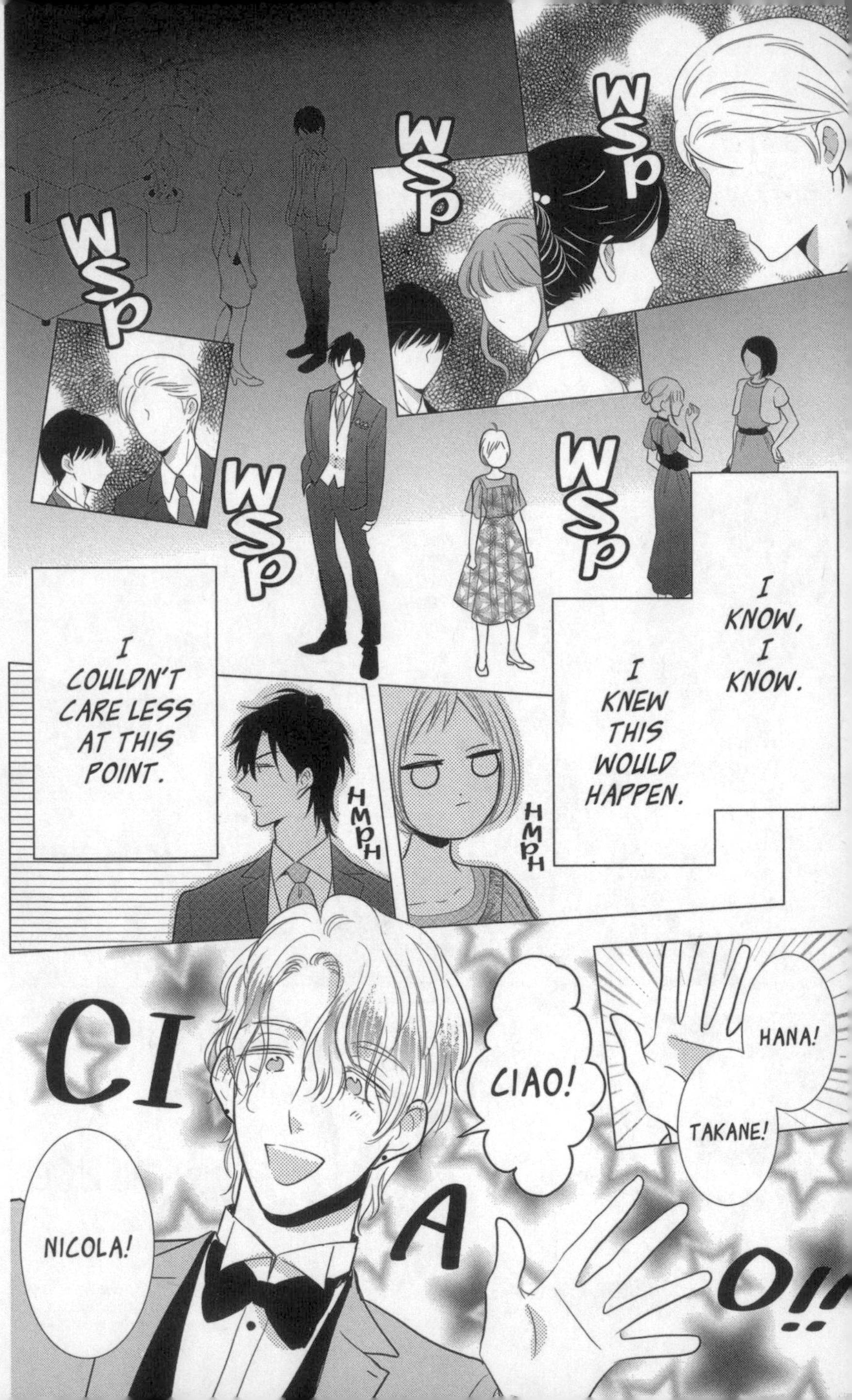
WSP
WSP
WSP
WSP
WSP
I KNOW, I KNOW.
I KNEW THIS WOULD HAPPEN.
HMPH
HMPH
I COULDN'T CARE LESS AT THIS POINT.
HANA!
TAKANE!
CIAO!
CIAO!!
NICOLA!

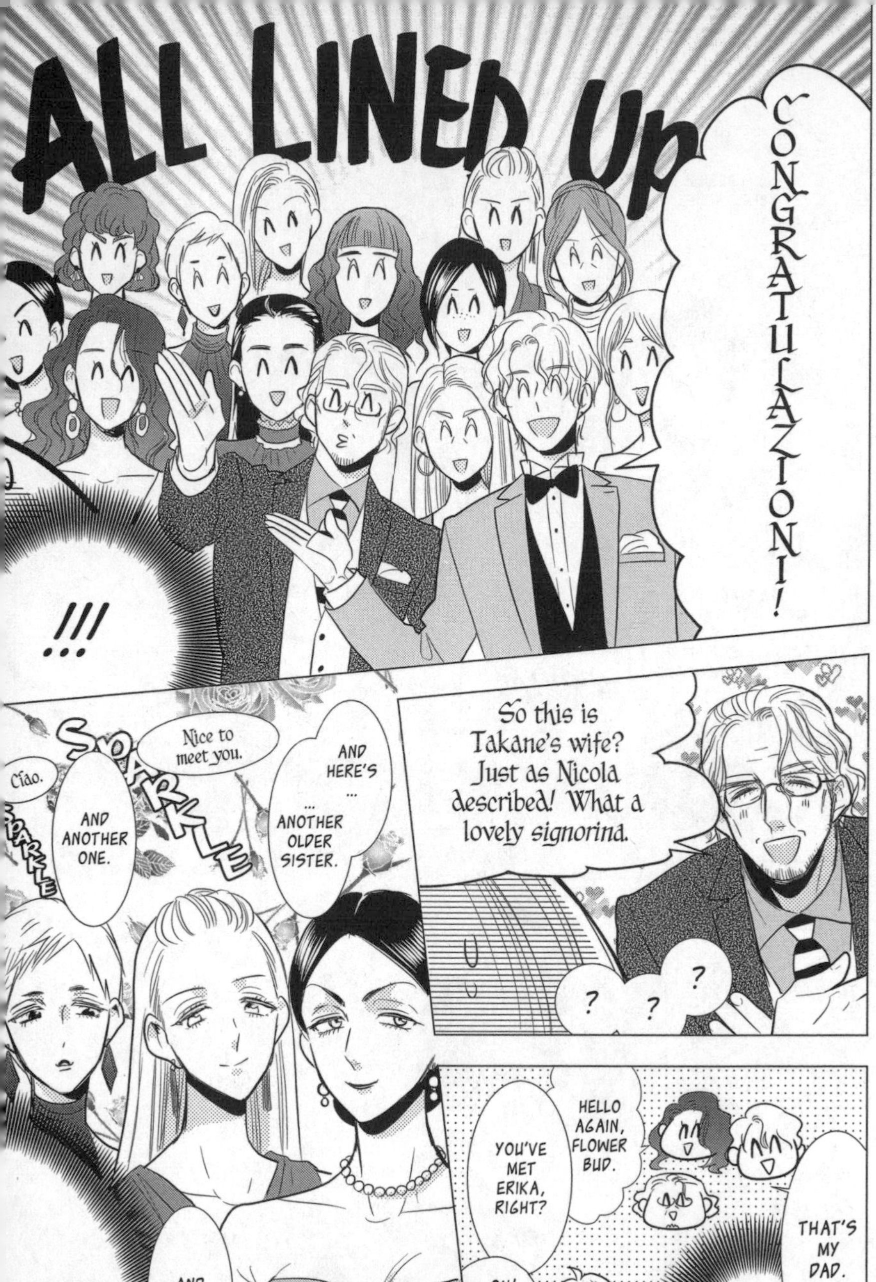
ALL LINED UP
CONGRATULAZIONI!
!!!
So this is Takane's wife? Just as Nicola described! What a lovely *signorina*.
? ? ?
THAT'S MY DAD.
LUCI PAPA.
HELLO AGAIN, FLOWER BUD.
YOU'VE MET ERIKA, RIGHT?
OH! YOUR SISTER!
AND HERE'S ... ANOTHER OLDER SISTER.
Nice to meet you.
AND ANOTHER ONE.
Ciao.
SPARKLE
SPARKLE
AND ANOTHER.
A family with droopy eyes
THEY'RE ALL SO BEAUTIFUL!

Erika = Older sister who lives in Japan

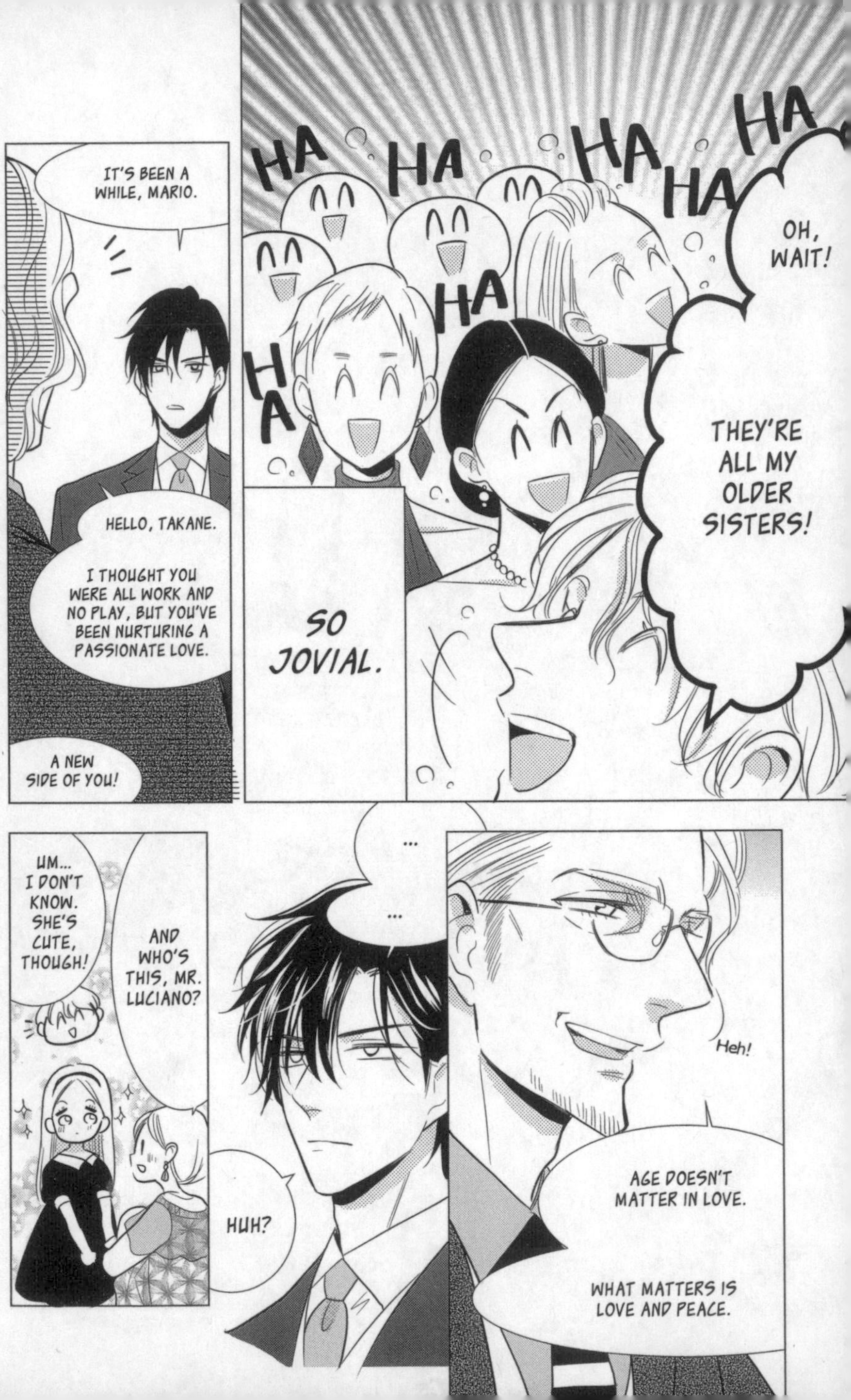
HA
HA HA
OH, WAIT!
THEY'RE ALL MY OLDER SISTERS!
HA HA
HA
HA
HA HA
SO JOVIAL.
IT'S BEEN A WHILE, MARIO.
HELLO, TAKANE.
I THOUGHT YOU WERE ALL WORK AND NO PLAY, BUT YOU'VE BEEN NURTURING A PASSIONATE LOVE.
A NEW SIDE OF YOU!
Heh!
AGE DOESN'T MATTER IN LOVE.
WHAT MATTERS IS LOVE AND PEACE.
...
...
HUH?
AND WHO'S THIS, MR. LUCIANO?
UM... I DON'T KNOW. SHE'S CUTE, THOUGH!

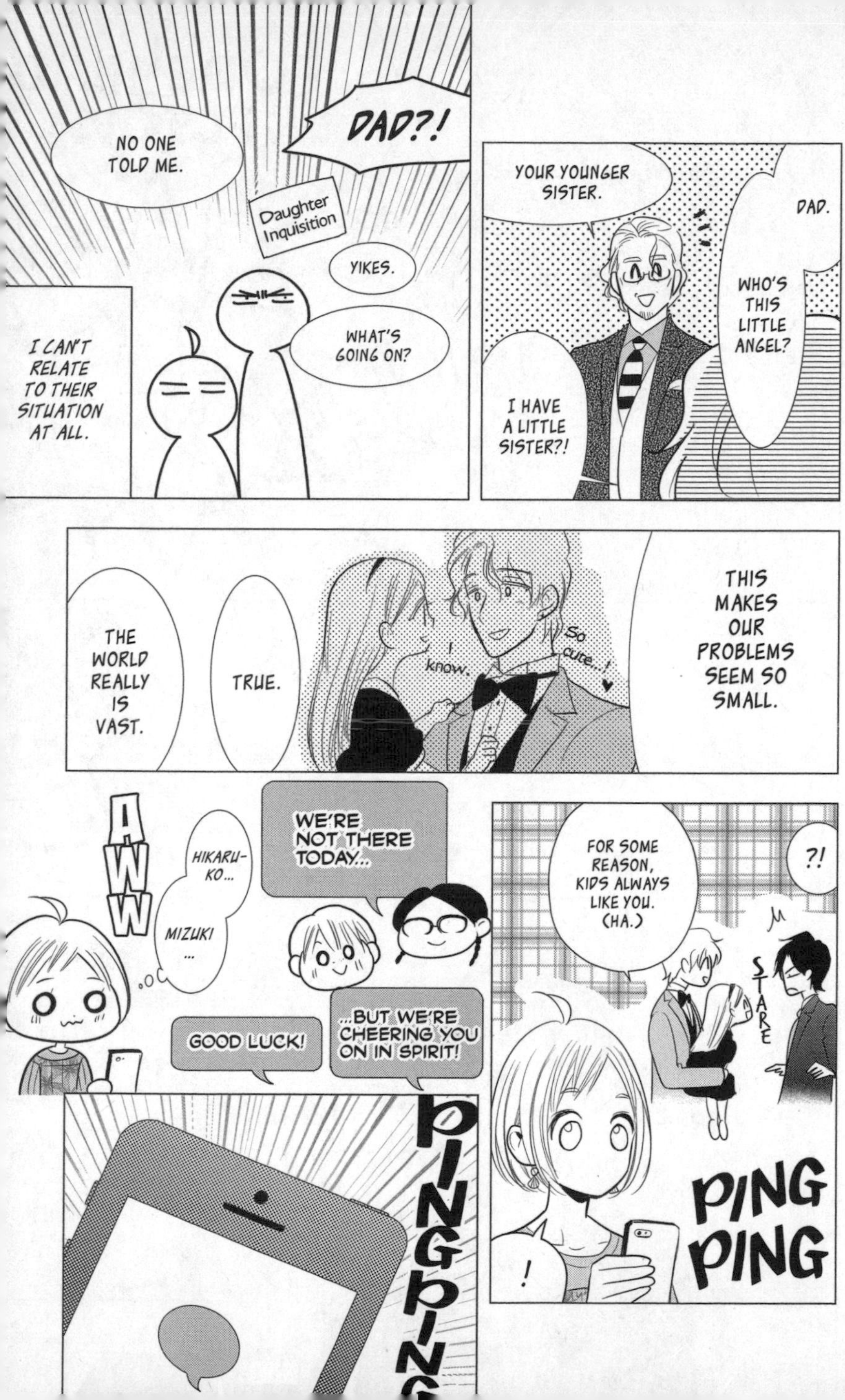
DAD.
WHO'S THIS LITTLE ANGEL?
YOUR YOUNGER SISTER.
I HAVE A LITTLE SISTER?!
DAD?!
NO ONE TOLD ME.
Daughter Inquisition
YIKES.
WHAT'S GOING ON?
I CAN'T RELATE TO THEIR SITUATION AT ALL.
THIS MAKES OUR PROBLEMS SEEM SO SMALL.
So cute...!
I know.
TRUE.
THE WORLD REALLY IS VAST.
?!
FOR SOME REASON, KIDS ALWAYS LIKE YOU. (HA.)
STARE
PING PING
!
WE'RE NOT THERE TODAY...
HIKARU-KO...
MIZUKI...
AWW
...BUT WE'RE CHEERING YOU ON IN SPIRIT!
GOOD LUCK!
PINGPING

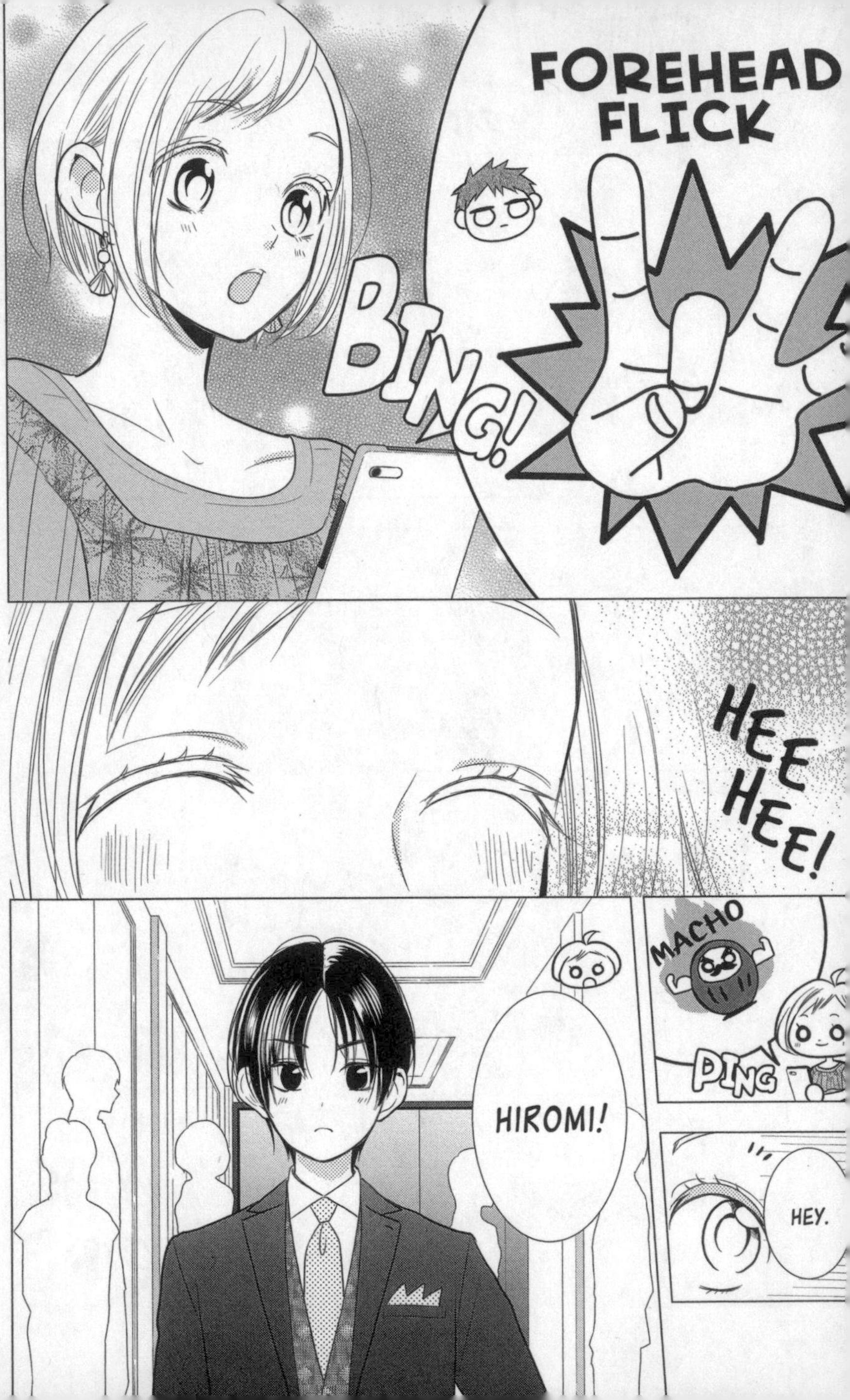
FOREHEAD FLICK
BING!
HEE HEE HEE!
MACHO
PING
HEY.
HIROMI!

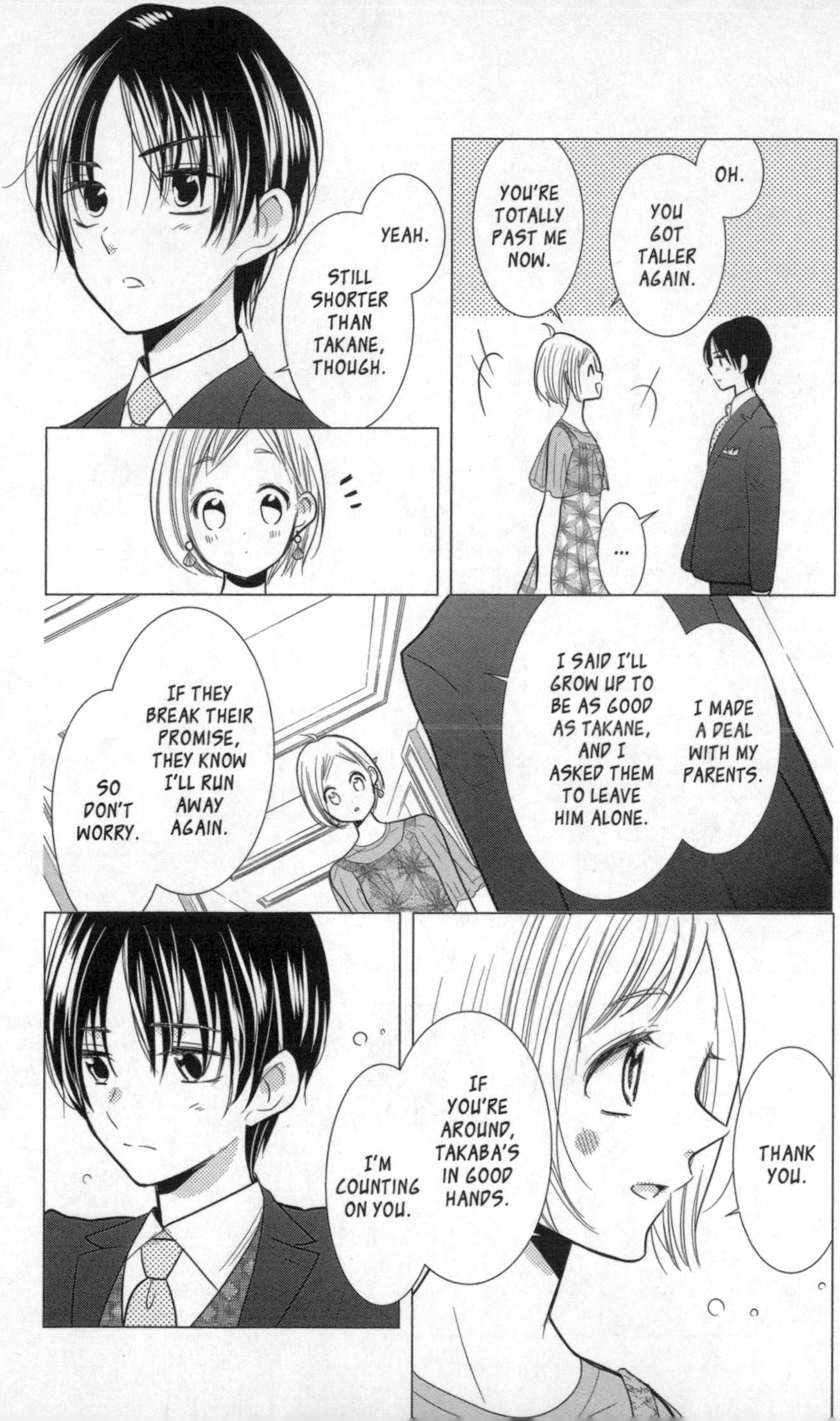
OH.
YOU GOT TALLER AGAIN.
YOU'RE TOTALLY PAST ME NOW.
...
YEAH.
STILL SHORTER THAN TAKANE, THOUGH.
I MADE A DEAL WITH MY PARENTS.
I SAID I'LL GROW UP TO BE AS GOOD AS TAKANE, AND I ASKED THEM TO LEAVE HIM ALONE.
IF THEY BREAK THEIR PROMISE, THEY KNOW I'LL RUN AWAY AGAIN.
SO DON'T WORRY.
THANK YOU.
IF YOU'RE AROUND, TAKABA'S IN GOOD HANDS.
I'M COUNTING ON YOU.

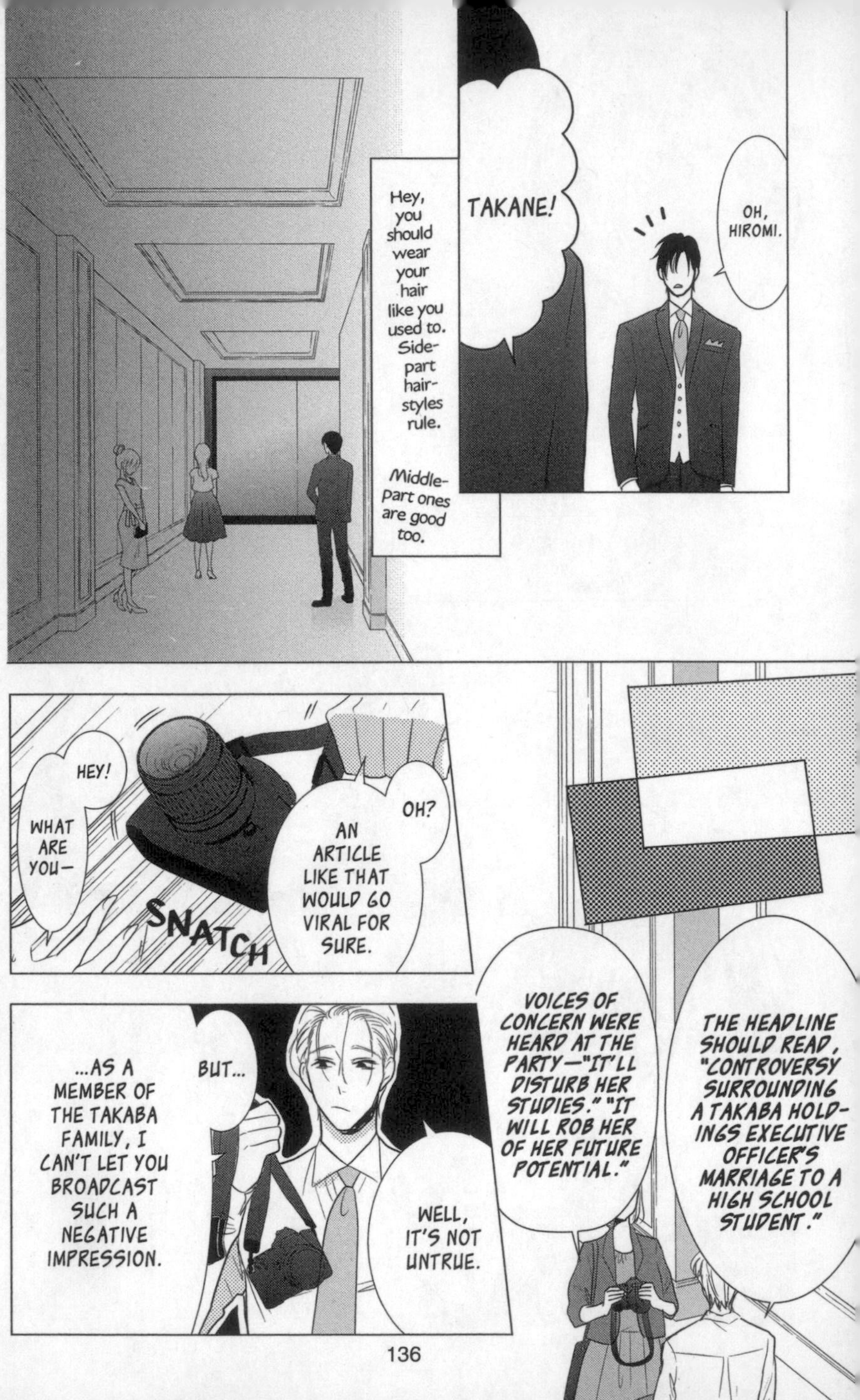
TAKANE!
OH, HIROMI.
Hey, you should wear your hair like you used to. Side-part hair-styles rule.
Middle-part ones are good too.
THE HEADLINE SHOULD READ, "CONTROVERSY SURROUNDING A TAKABA HOLD-INGS EXECUTIVE OFFICER'S MARRIAGE TO A HIGH SCHOOL STUDENT."
VOICES OF CONCERN WERE HEARD AT THE PARTY—"IT'LL DISTURB HER STUDIES." "IT WILL ROB HER OF HER FUTURE POTENTIAL."
OH?
AN ARTICLE LIKE THAT WOULD GO VIRAL FOR SURE.
SNATCH
HEY!
WHAT ARE YOU—
WELL, IT'S NOT UNTRUE.
BUT...
...AS A MEMBER OF THE TAKABA FAMILY, I CAN'T LET YOU BROADCAST SUCH A NEGATIVE IMPRESSION.

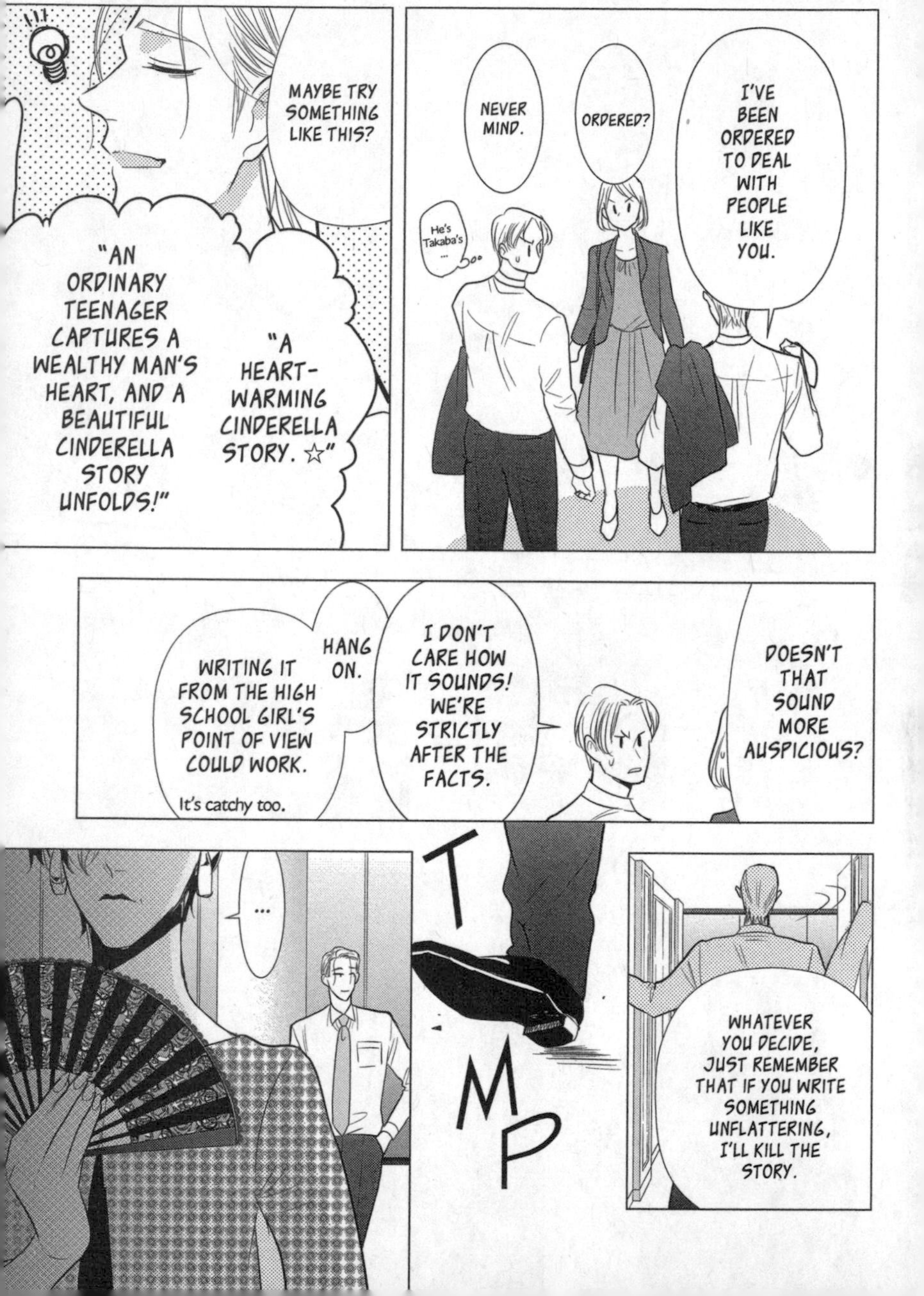
I'VE BEEN ORDERED TO DEAL WITH PEOPLE LIKE YOU.
ORDERED?
NEVER MIND.
He's Takaba's ...
MAYBE TRY SOMETHING LIKE THIS?
"A HEART-WARMING CINDERELLA STORY. ☆"
"AN ORDINARY TEENAGER CAPTURES A WEALTHY MAN'S HEART, AND A BEAUTIFUL CINDERELLA STORY UNFOLDS!"
DOESN'T THAT SOUND MORE AUSPICIOUS?
I DON'T CARE HOW IT SOUNDS! WE'RE STRICTLY AFTER THE FACTS.
HANG ON.
WRITING IT FROM THE HIGH SCHOOL GIRL'S POINT OF VIEW COULD WORK.
It's catchy too.
WHATEVER YOU DECIDE, JUST REMEMBER THAT IF YOU WRITE SOMETHING UNFLATTERING, I'LL KILL THE STORY.
TMP
...

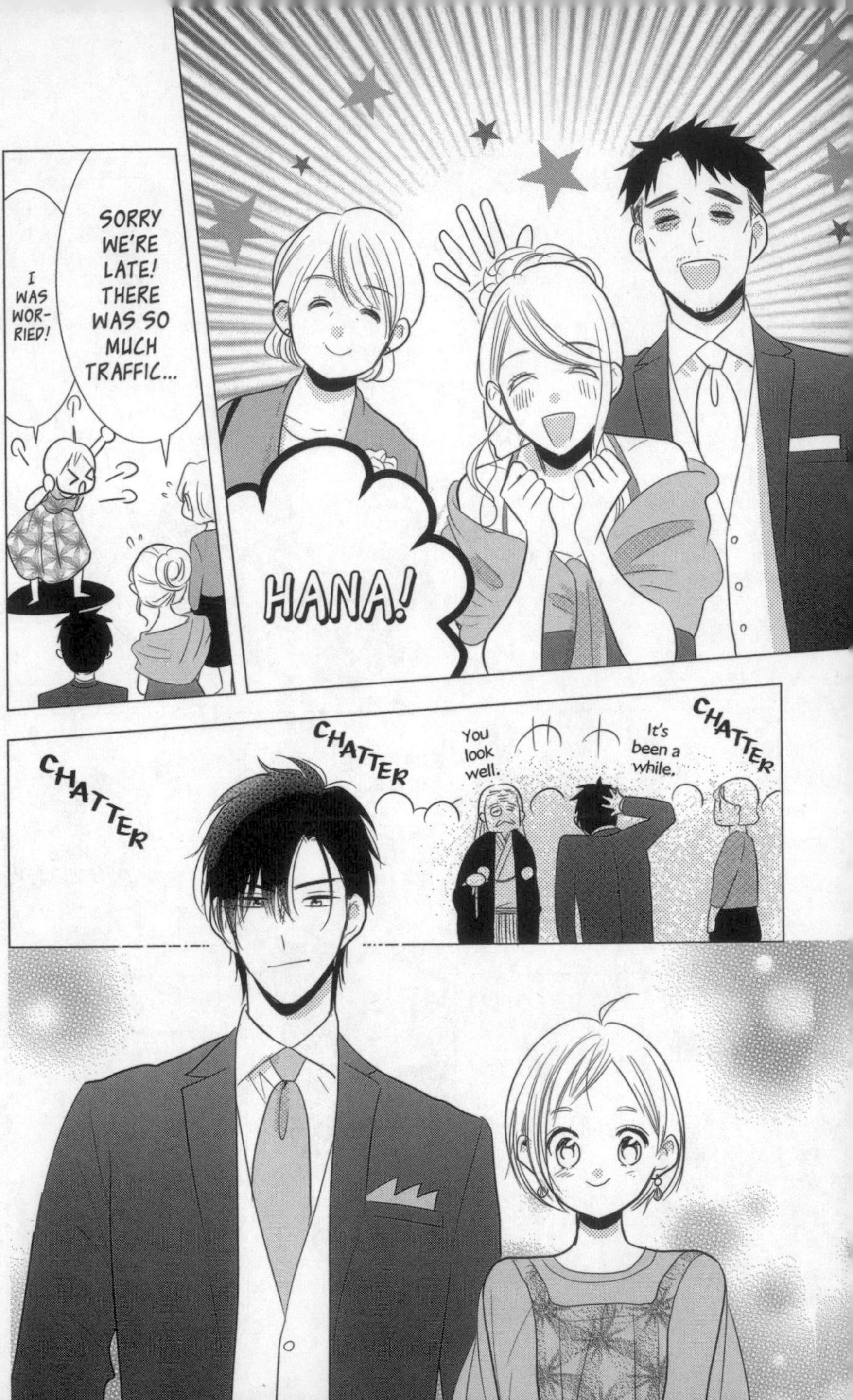
HANA!
SORRY WE'RE LATE! THERE WAS SO MUCH TRAFFIC...
I WAS WOR-RIED!
CHATTER
It's been a while.
You look well.
CHATTER
CHATTER

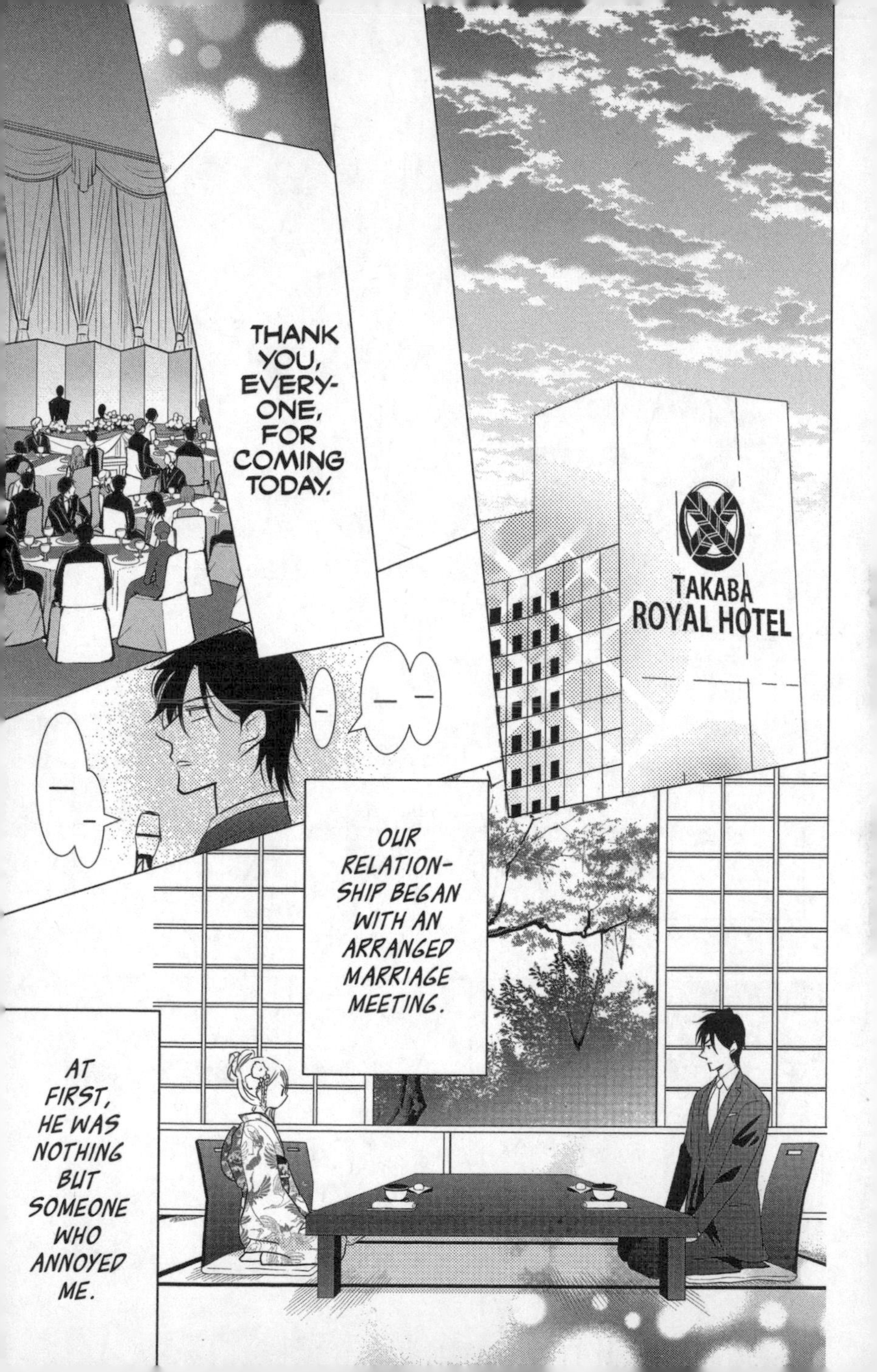
TAKABA ROYAL HOTEL
THANK YOU, EVERYONE, FOR COMING TODAY.
— —
—
— —
OUR RELATIONSHIP BEGAN WITH AN ARRANGED MARRIAGE MEETING.
AT FIRST, HE WAS NOTHING BUT SOMEONE WHO ANNOYED ME.

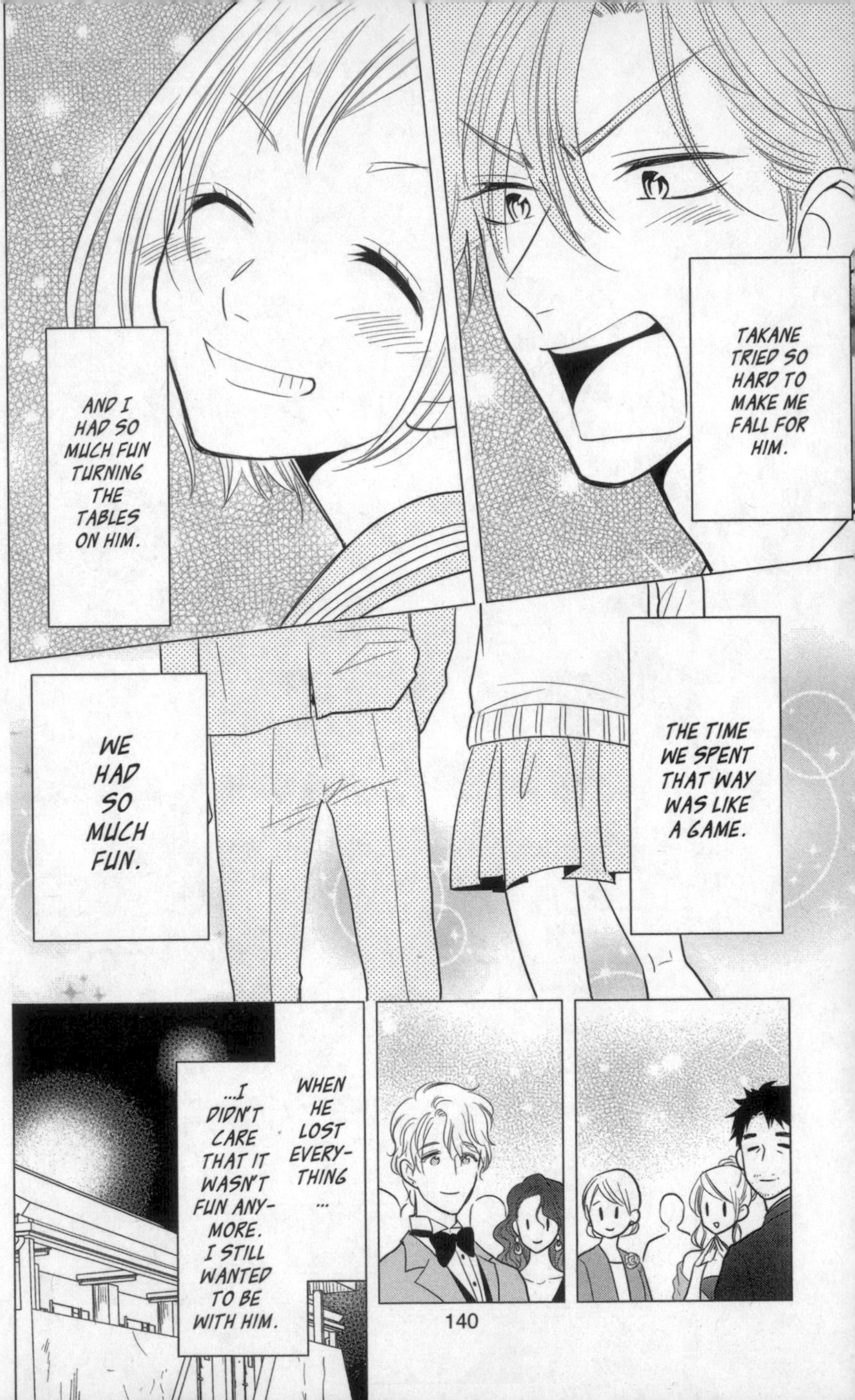
TAKANE TRIED SO HARD TO MAKE ME FALL FOR HIM.
AND I HAD SO MUCH FUN TURNING THE TABLES ON HIM.
THE TIME WE SPENT THAT WAY WAS LIKE A GAME.
WE HAD SO MUCH FUN.
WHEN HE LOST EVERY-THING...
...I DIDN'T CARE THAT IT WASN'T FUN ANY-MORE. I STILL WANTED TO BE WITH HIM.

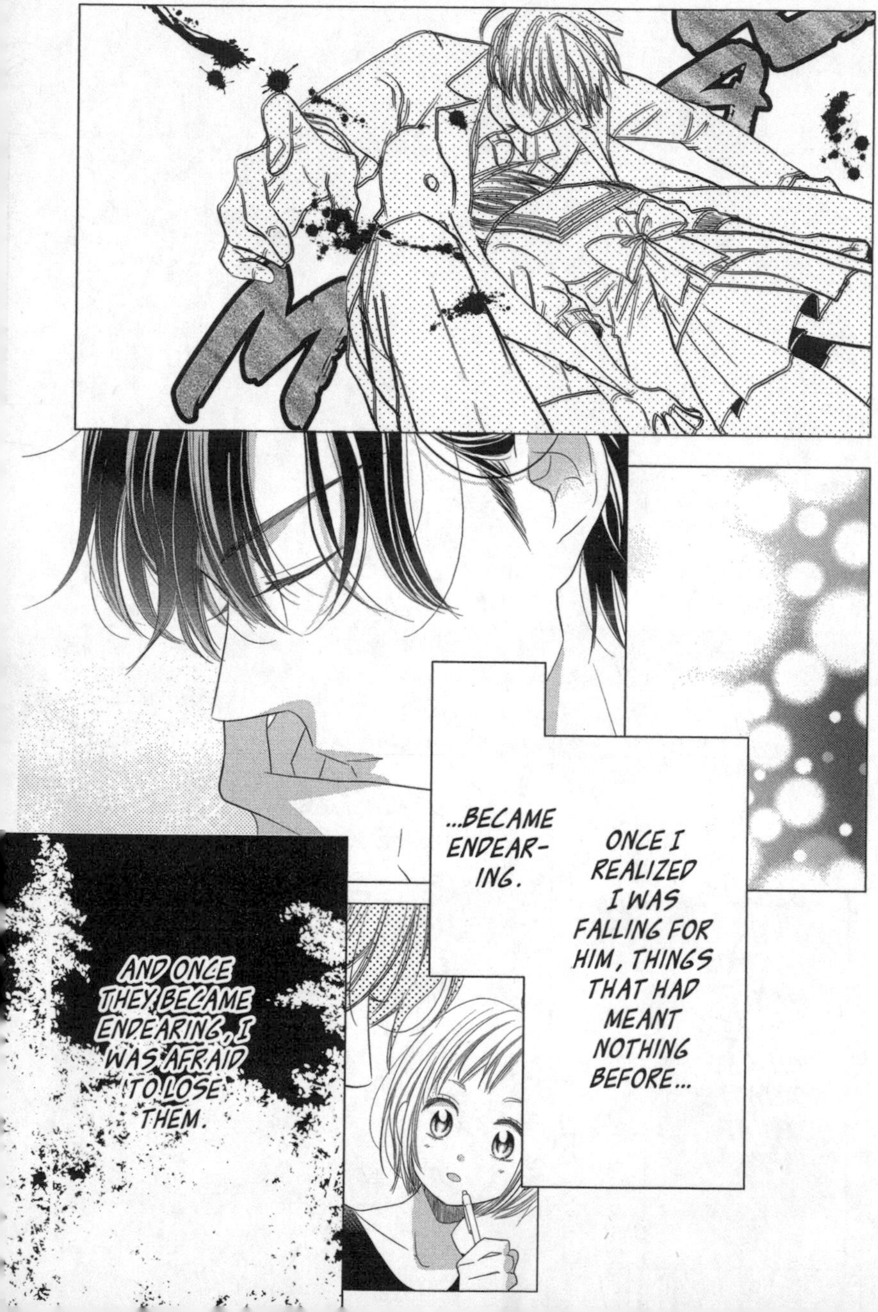
ONCE I REALIZED I WAS FALLING FOR HIM, THINGS THAT HAD MEANT NOTHING BEFORE...
...BECAME ENDEAR-ING.
AND ONCE THEY BECAME ENDEARING, I WAS AFRAID TO LOSE THEM.

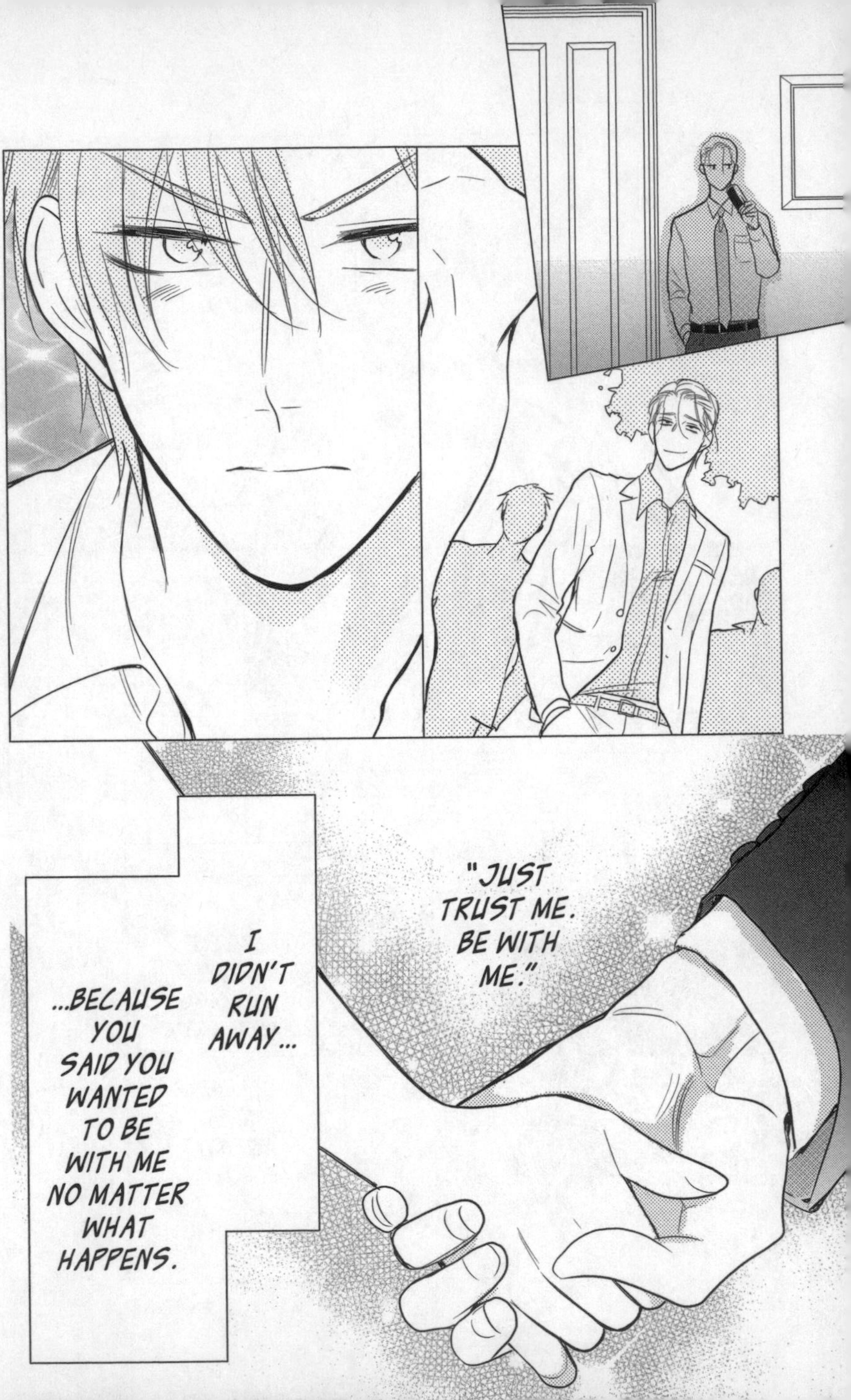
"JUST TRUST ME. BE WITH ME."
I DIDN'T RUN AWAY...
...BECAUSE YOU SAID YOU WANTED TO BE WITH ME NO MATTER WHAT HAPPENS.

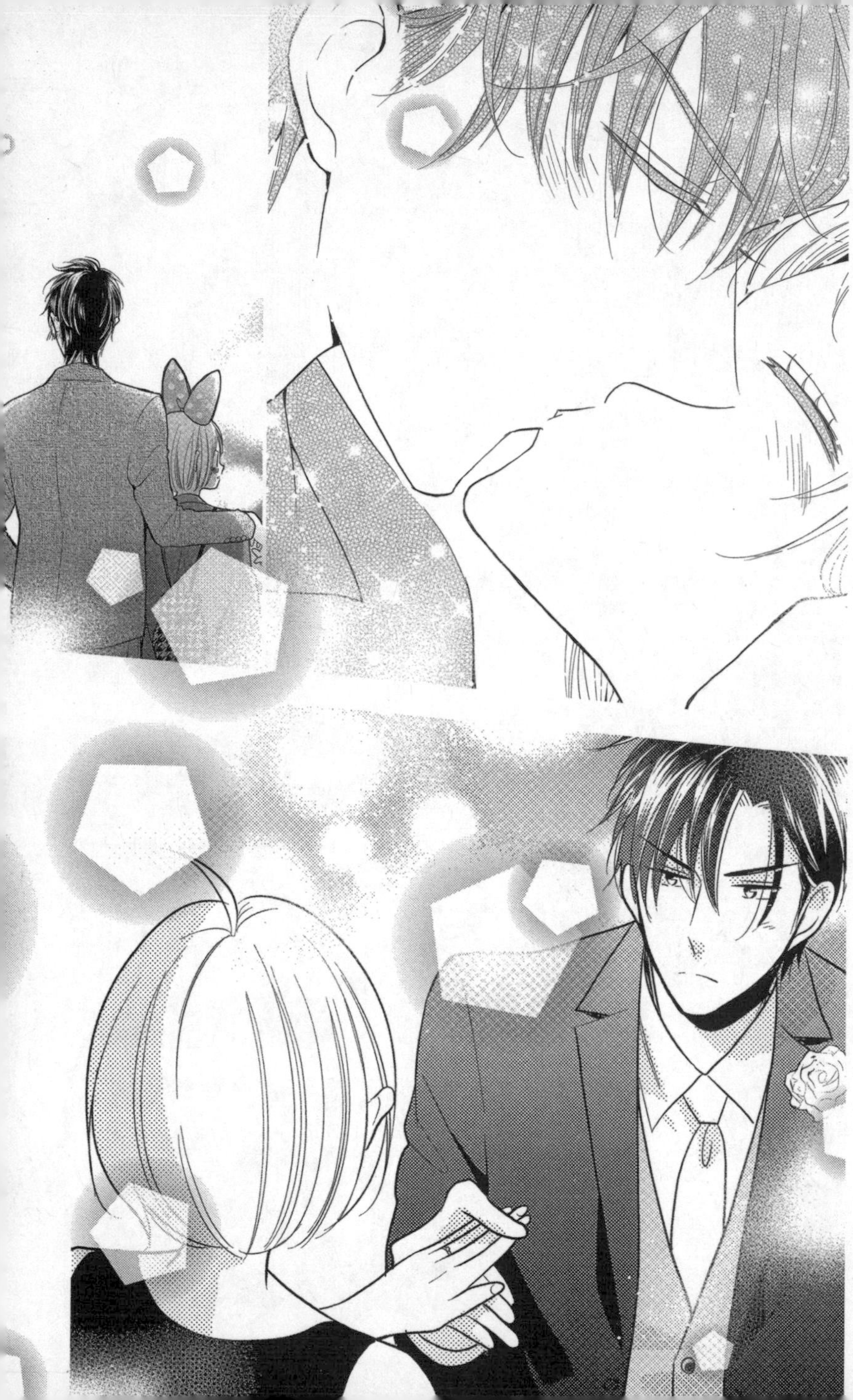

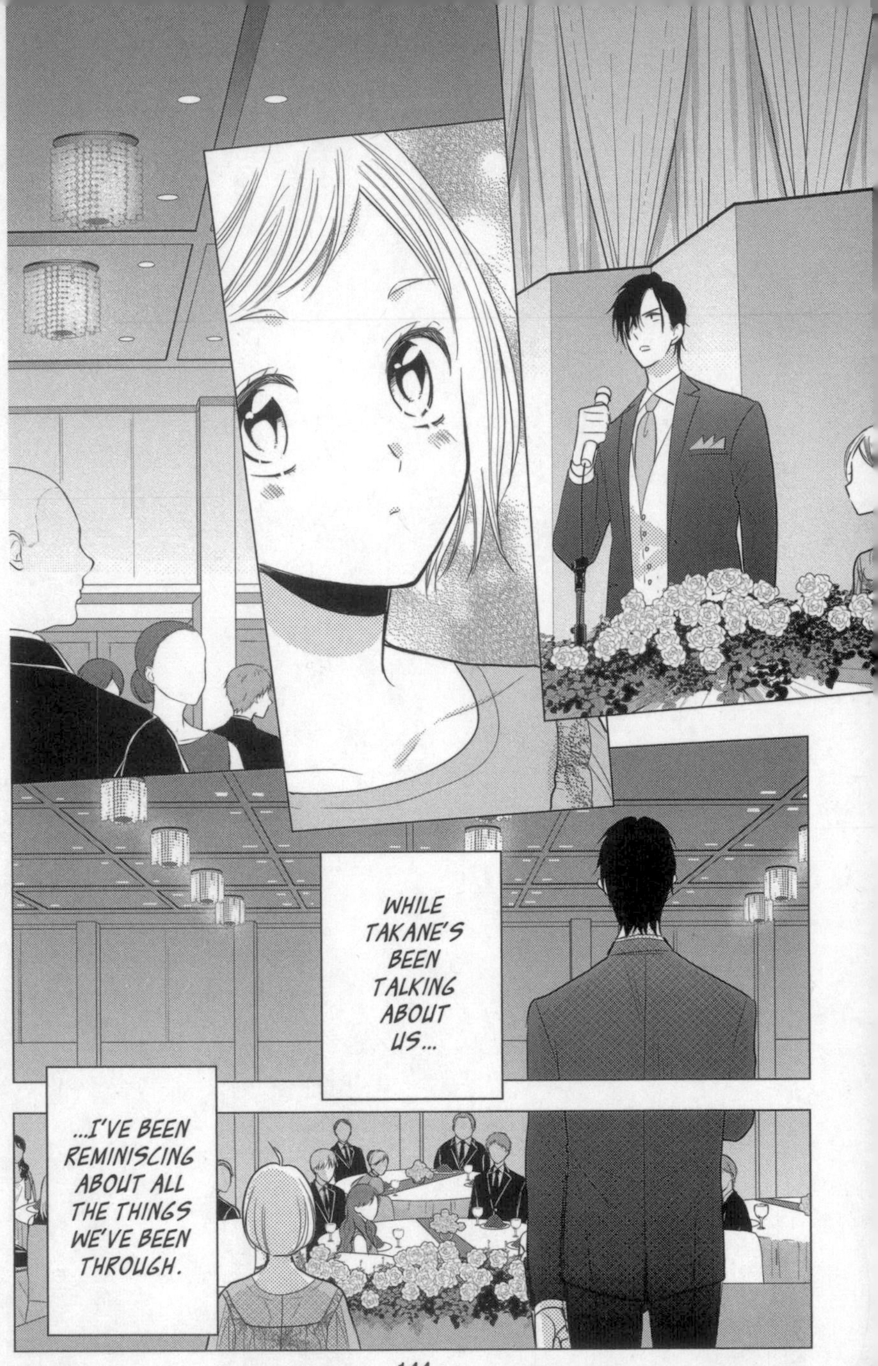
WHILE TAKANE'S BEEN TALKING ABOUT US...
...I'VE BEEN REMINISCING ABOUT ALL THE THINGS WE'VE BEEN THROUGH.

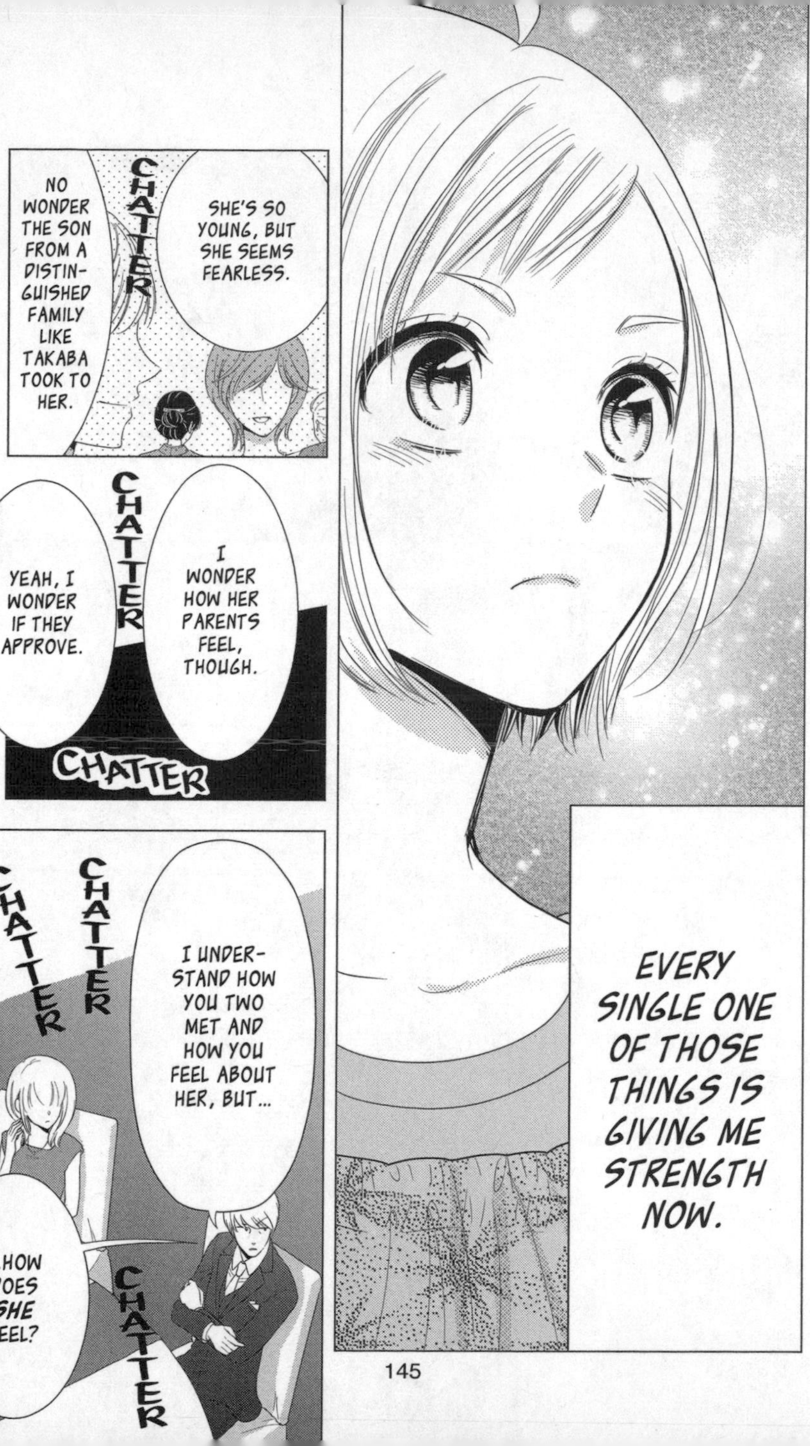
EVERY SINGLE ONE OF THOSE THINGS IS GIVING ME STRENGTH NOW.
SHE'S SO YOUNG, BUT SHE SEEMS FEARLESS.
CHATTER
NO WONDER THE SON FROM A DISTIN-GUISHED FAMILY LIKE TAKABA TOOK TO HER.
I WONDER HOW HER PARENTS FEEL, THOUGH.
CHATTER
YEAH, I WONDER IF THEY APPROVE.
CHATTER
I UNDER-STAND HOW YOU TWO MET AND HOW YOU FEEL ABOUT HER, BUT...
CHATTER
CHATTER
...HOW DOES SHE FEEL?
CHATTER

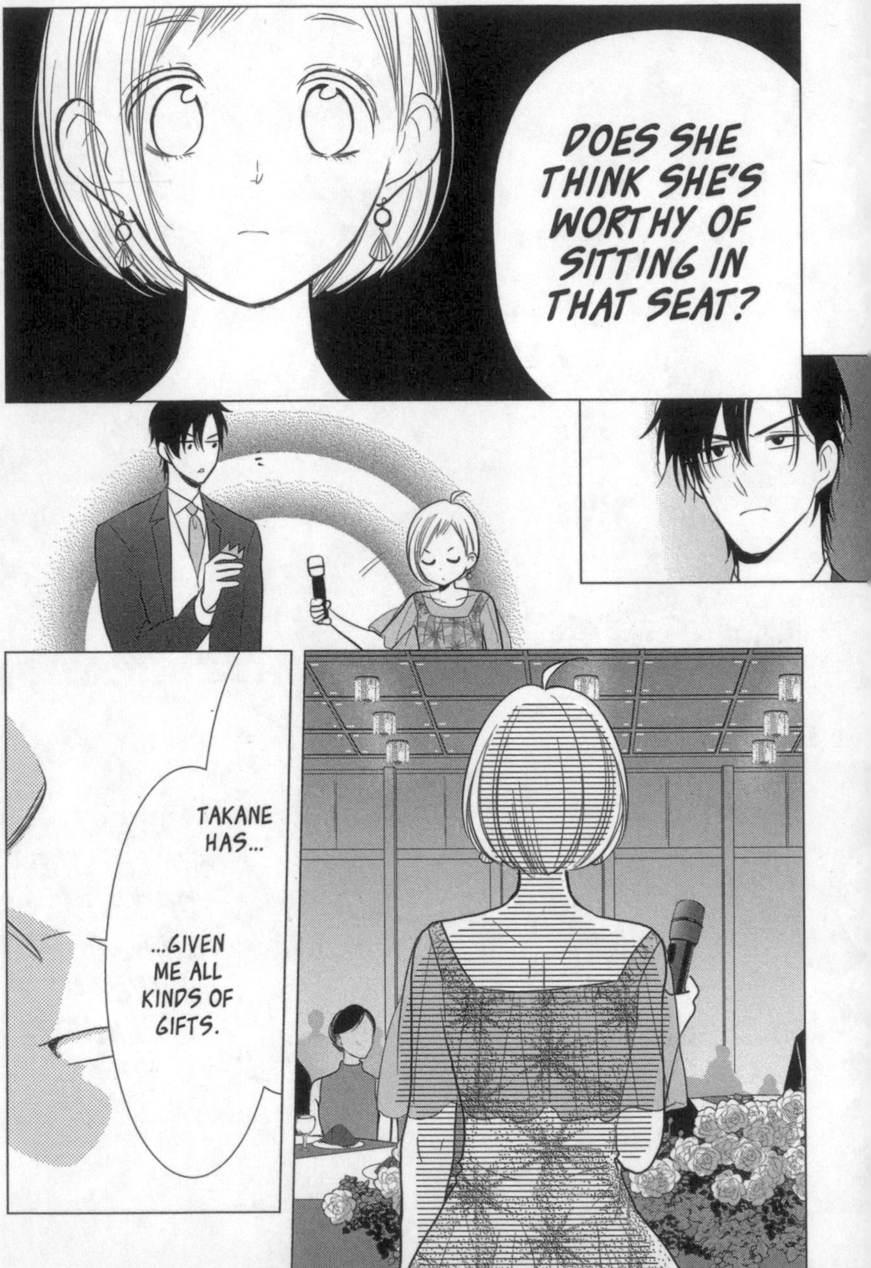
DOES SHE THINK SHE'S WORTHY OF SITTING IN THAT SEAT?
TAKANE HAS...
...GIVEN ME ALL KINDS OF GIFTS.

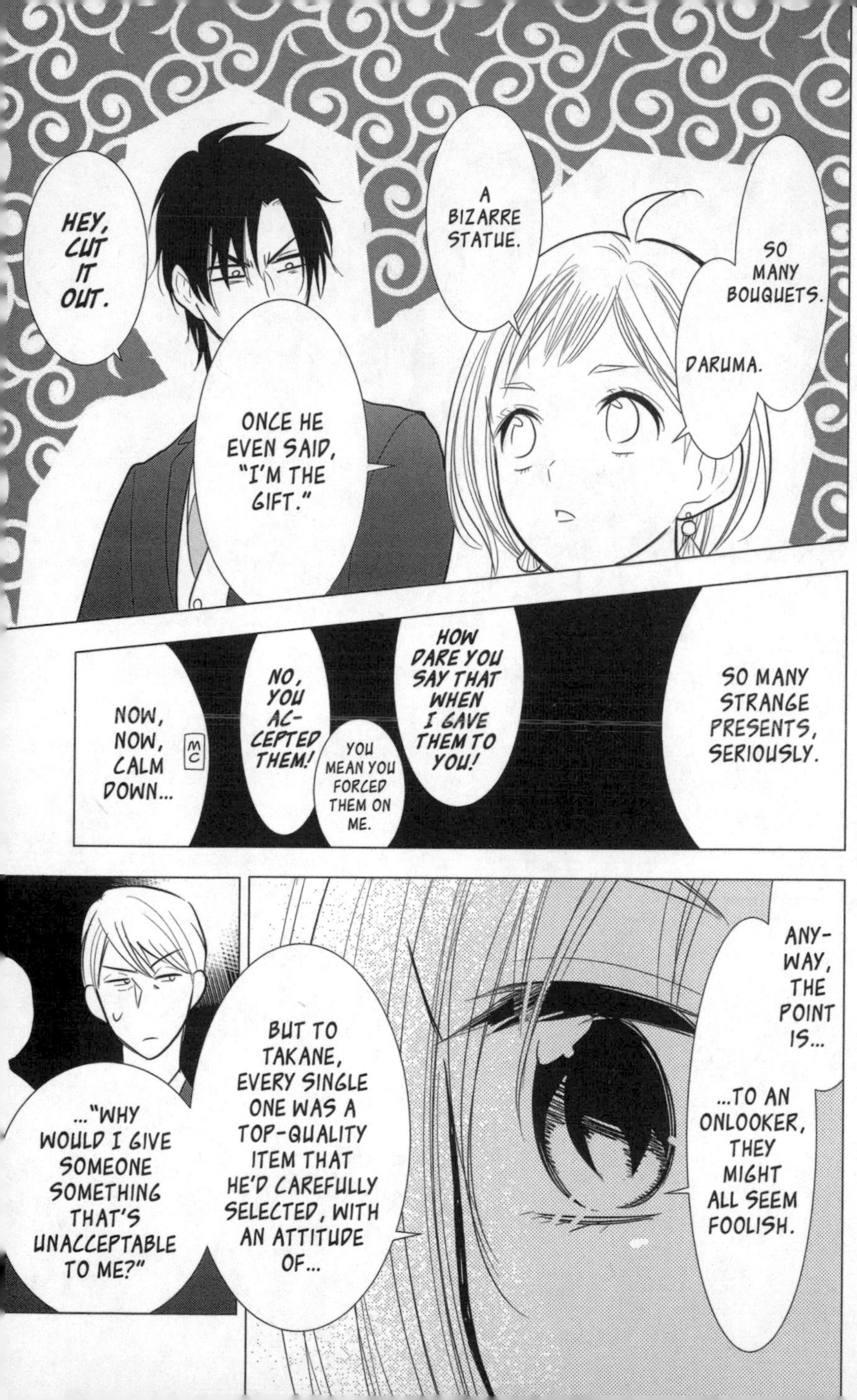
SO MANY BOUQUETS.
DARUMA.
A BIZARRE STATUE.
ONCE HE EVEN SAID, "I'M THE GIFT."
HEY, CUT IT OUT.
SO MANY STRANGE PRESENTS, SERIOUSLY.
HOW DARE YOU SAY THAT WHEN I GAVE THEM TO YOU!
YOU MEAN YOU FORCED THEM ON ME.
NO, YOU AC-CEPTED THEM!
MC
NOW, NOW, CALM DOWN...
ANY-WAY, THE POINT IS...
...TO AN ONLOOKER, THEY MIGHT ALL SEEM FOOLISH.
BUT TO TAKANE, EVERY SINGLE ONE WAS A TOP-QUALITY ITEM THAT HE'D CAREFULLY SELECTED, WITH AN ATTITUDE OF...
..."WHY WOULD I GIVE SOMEONE SOMETHING THAT'S UNACCEPTABLE TO ME?"

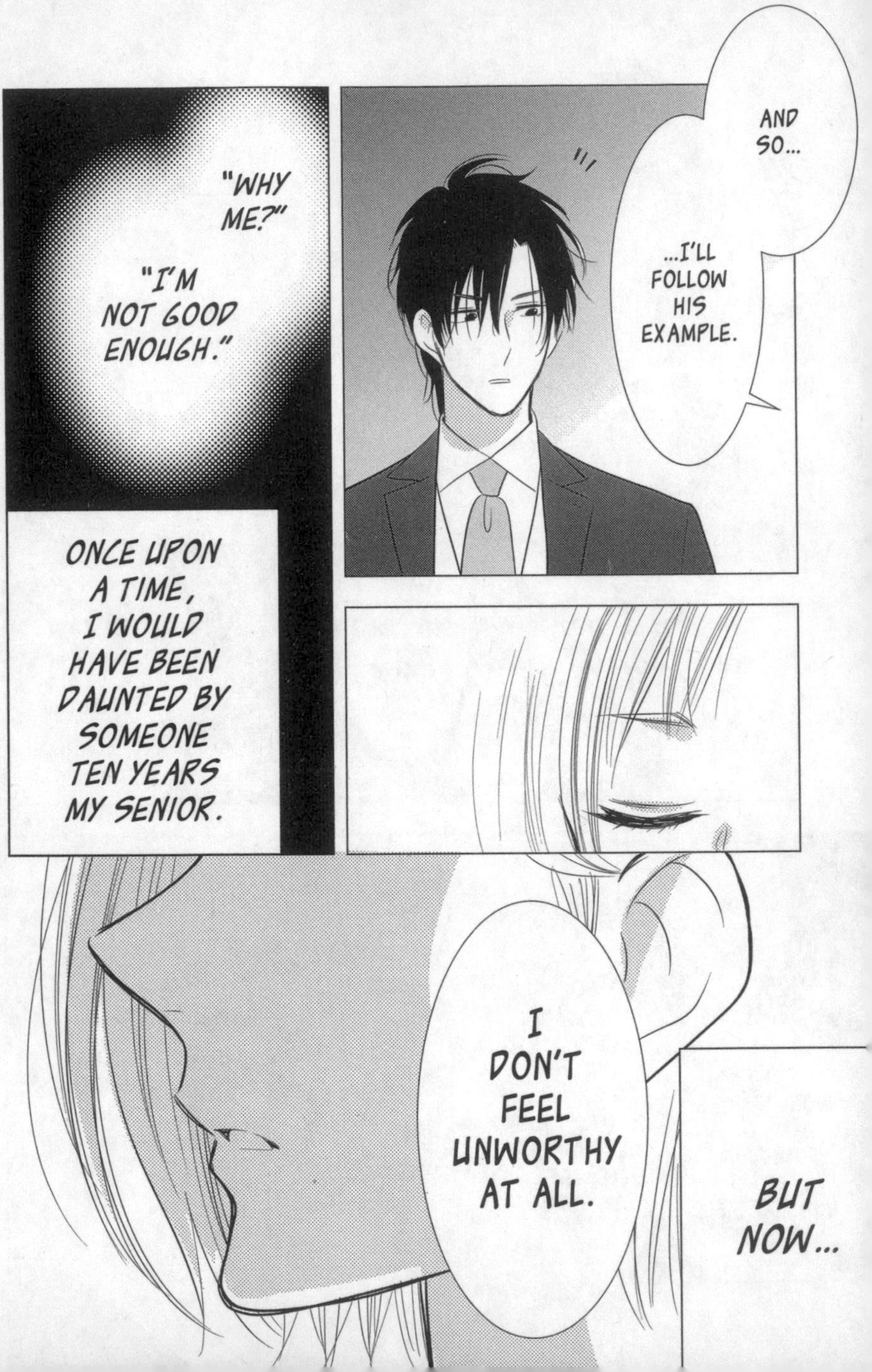
AND SO...
...I'LL FOLLOW HIS EXAMPLE.
"WHY ME?"
"I'M NOT GOOD ENOUGH."
ONCE UPON A TIME, I WOULD HAVE BEEN DAUNTED BY SOMEONE TEN YEARS MY SENIOR.
BUT NOW...
I DON'T FEEL UNWORTHY AT ALL.

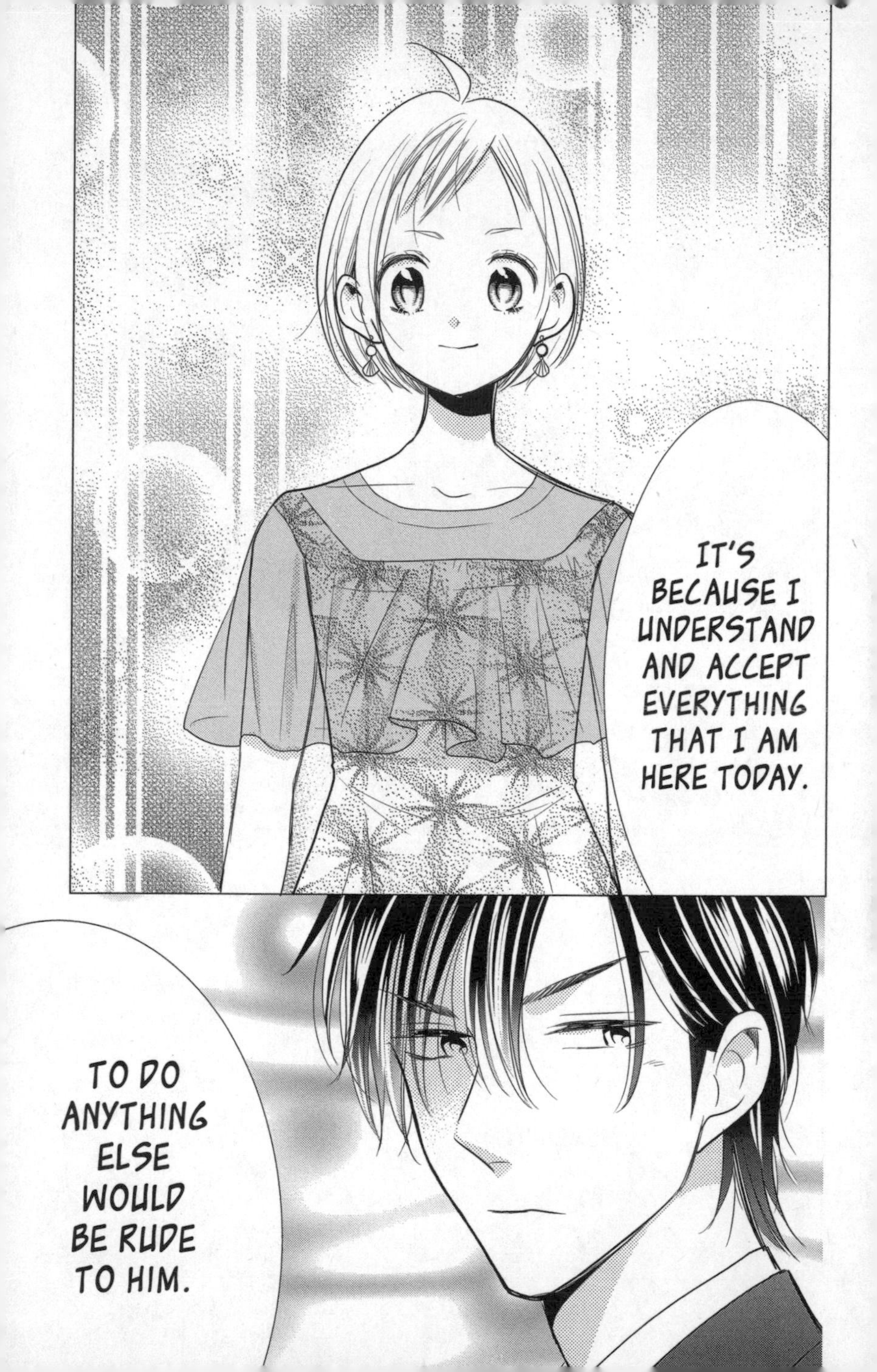
IT'S BECAUSE I UNDERSTAND AND ACCEPT EVERYTHING THAT I AM HERE TODAY.
TO DO ANYTHING ELSE WOULD BE RUDE TO HIM.

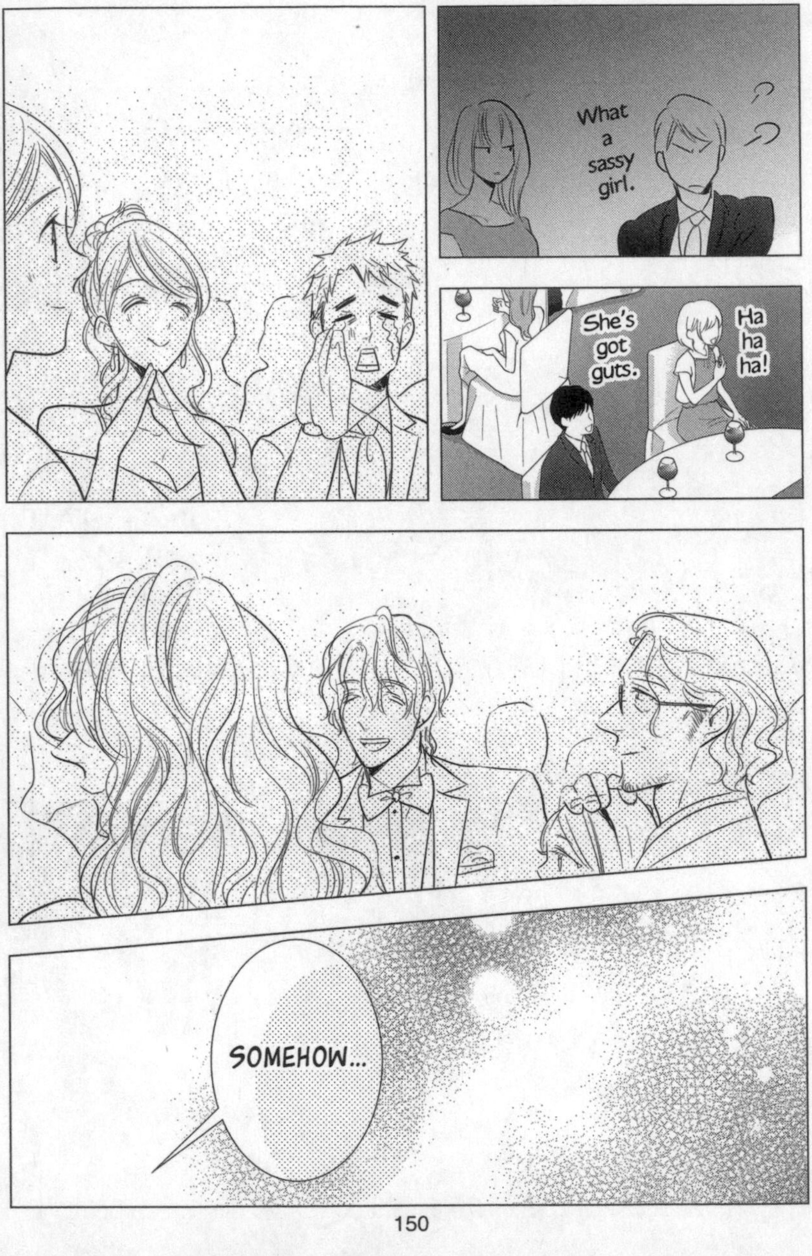
What a sassy girl.
Ha ha ha!
She's got guts.
SOMEHOW...

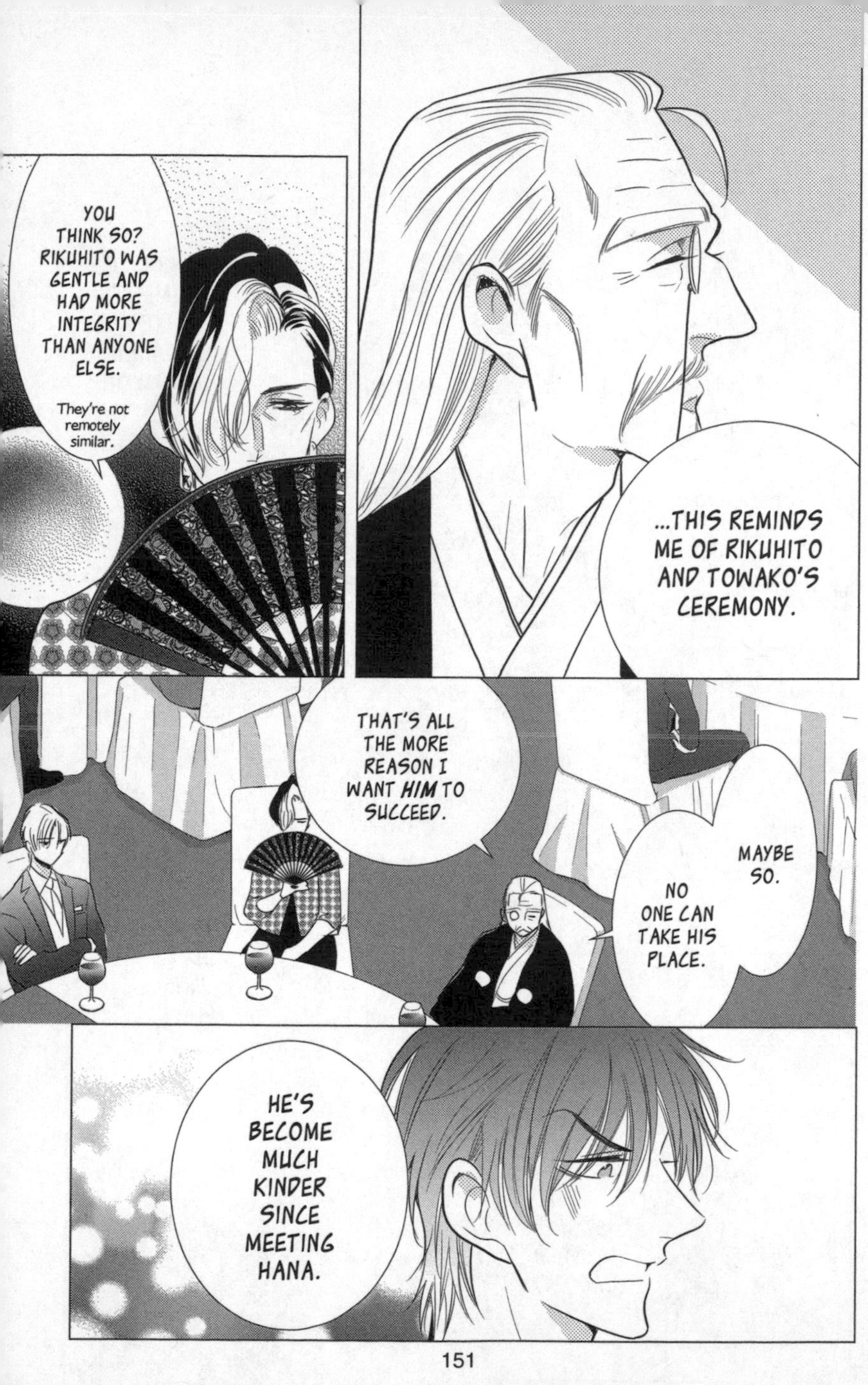
...THIS REMINDS ME OF RIKUHITO AND TOWAKO'S CEREMONY.
YOU THINK SO? RIKUHITO WAS GENTLE AND HAD MORE INTEGRITY THAN ANYONE ELSE.
They're not remotely similar.
MAYBE SO.
NO ONE CAN TAKE HIS PLACE.
THAT'S ALL THE MORE REASON I WANT HIM TO SUCCEED.
HE'S BECOME MUCH KINDER SINCE MEETING HANA.

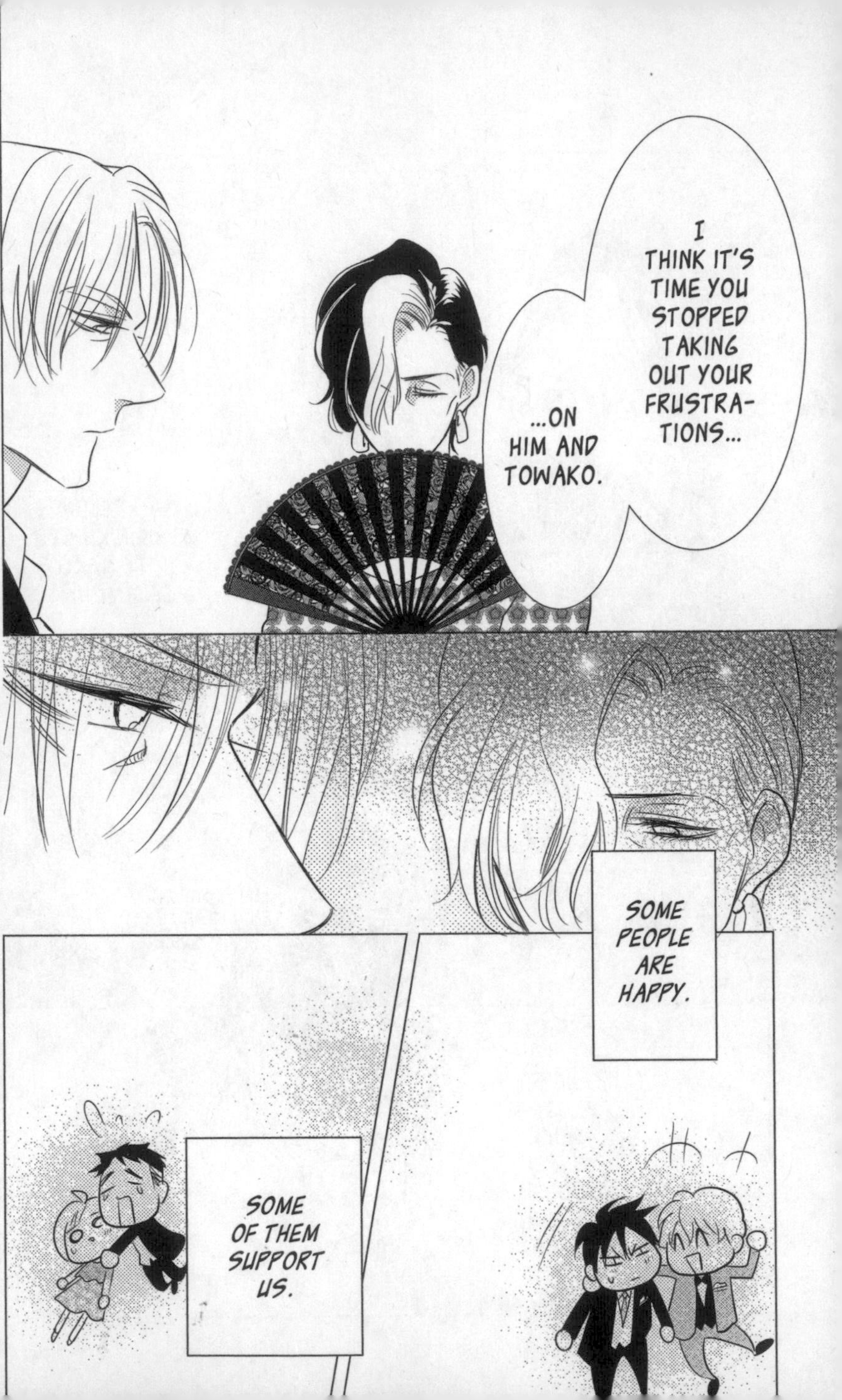
I THINK IT'S TIME YOU STOPPED TAKING OUT YOUR FRUSTRATIONS...
...ON HIM AND TOWAKO.
SOME PEOPLE ARE HAPPY.
SOME OF THEM SUPPORT US.

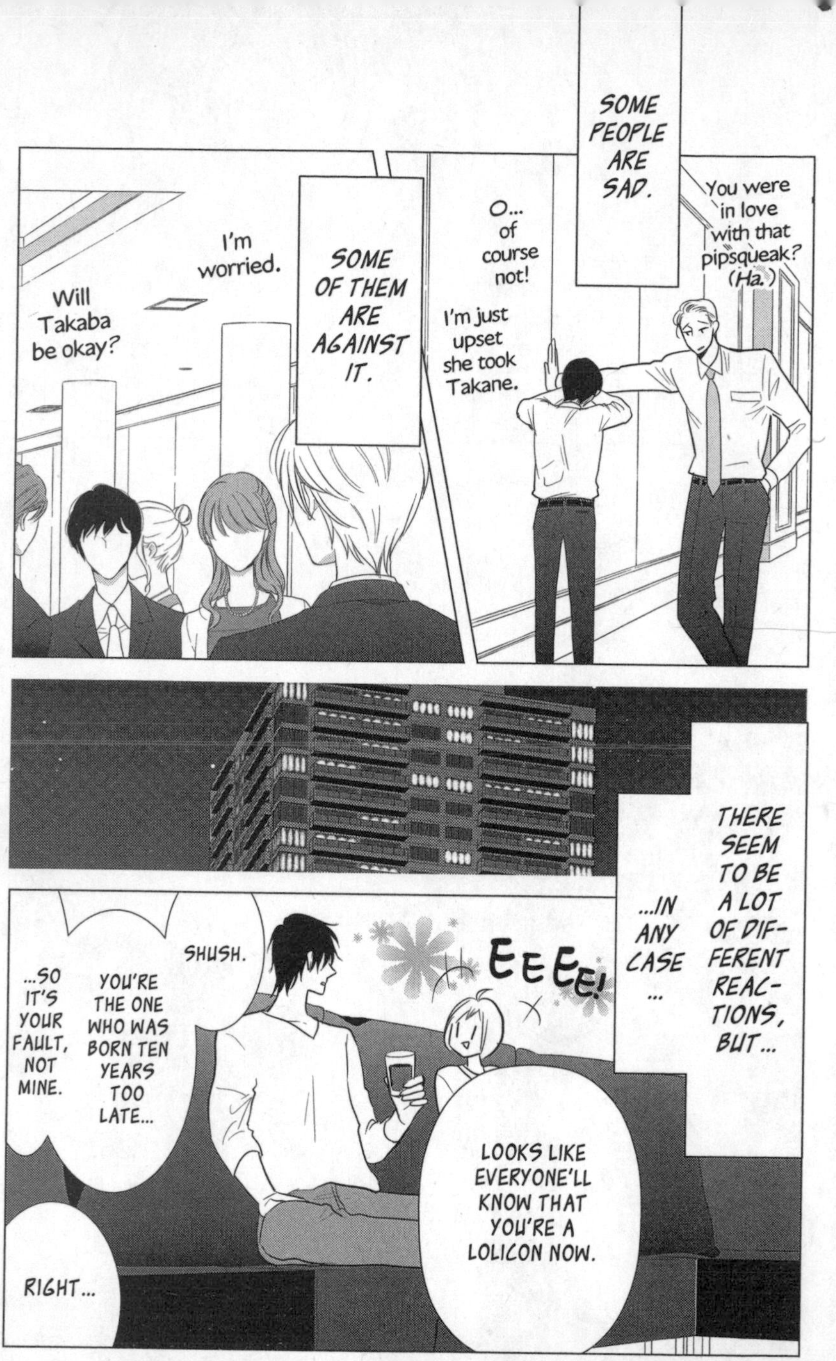
SOME PEOPLE ARE SAD.
You were in love with that pipsqueak? (Ha.)
O... of course not!
I'm just upset she took Takane.
SOME OF THEM ARE AGAINST IT.
I'm worried.
Will Takaba be okay?
THERE SEEM TO BE A LOT OF DIF-FERENT REAC-TIONS, BUT...
...IN ANY CASE...
EEEE!
LOOKS LIKE EVERYONE'LL KNOW THAT YOU'RE A LOLICON NOW.
SHUSH.
YOU'RE THE ONE WHO WAS BORN TEN YEARS TOO LATE...
...SO IT'S YOUR FAULT, NOT MINE.
RIGHT...

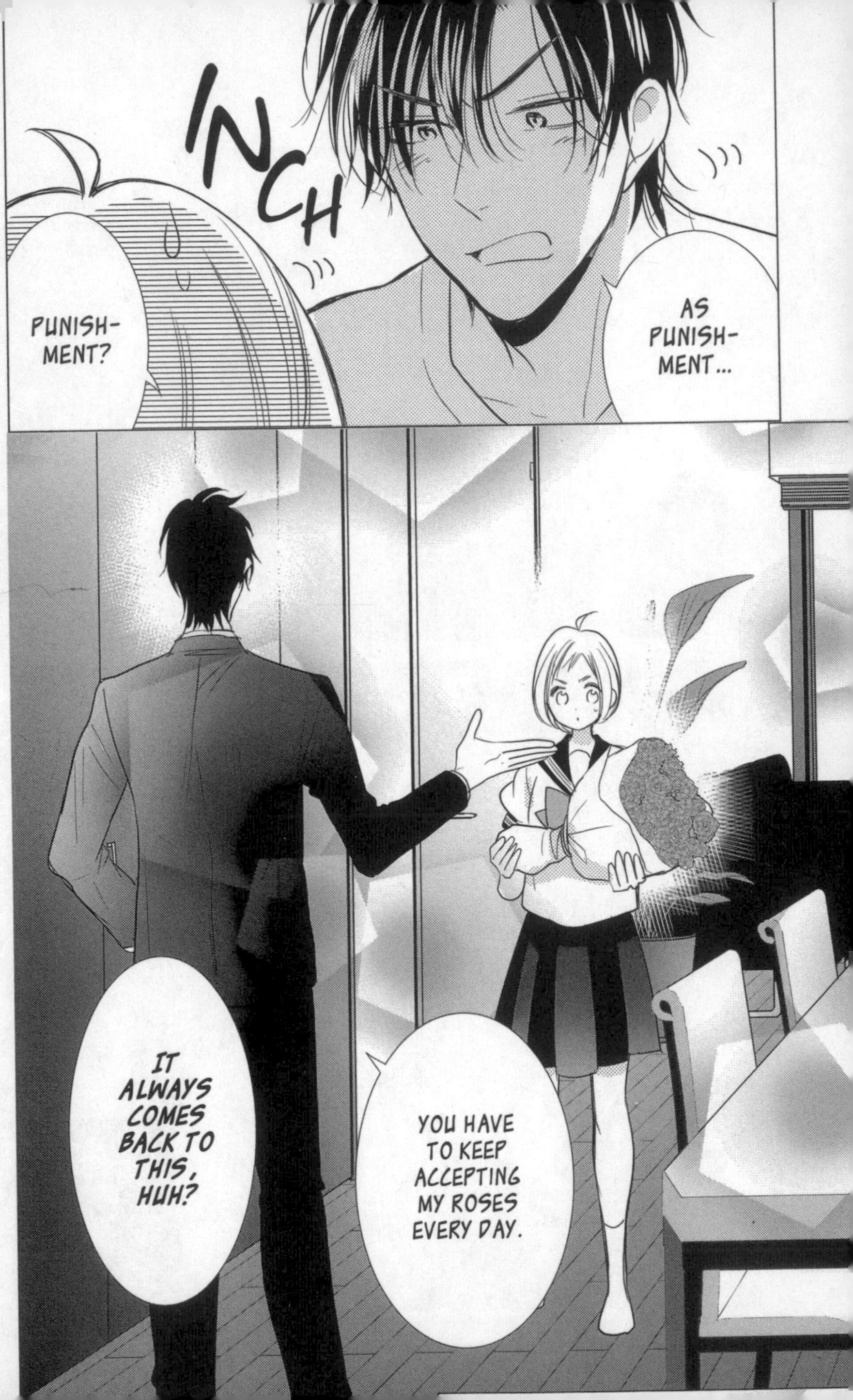
AS PUNISHMENT...
INCH
PUNISHMENT?
YOU HAVE TO KEEP ACCEPTING MY ROSES EVERY DAY.
IT ALWAYS COMES BACK TO THIS, HUH?

Buddies

YOU WERE IN LOVE WITH THAT PIPSQUEAK? (HA.)
O...OF COURSE NOT!
HERE, DRINK THIS AND CHILL OUT.
JUICE
IS IT POISON?
MAYBE.
It wasn't poison.
STARE
WHAT?
I'LL LET YOU BE A MEMBER OF THE "PRAISE TAKANE" CLUB.
WHAT'S THAT?

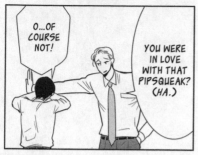

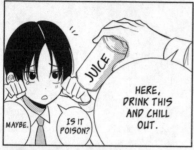

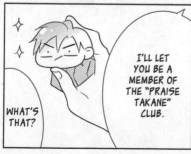

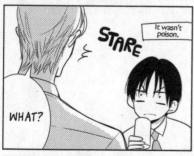

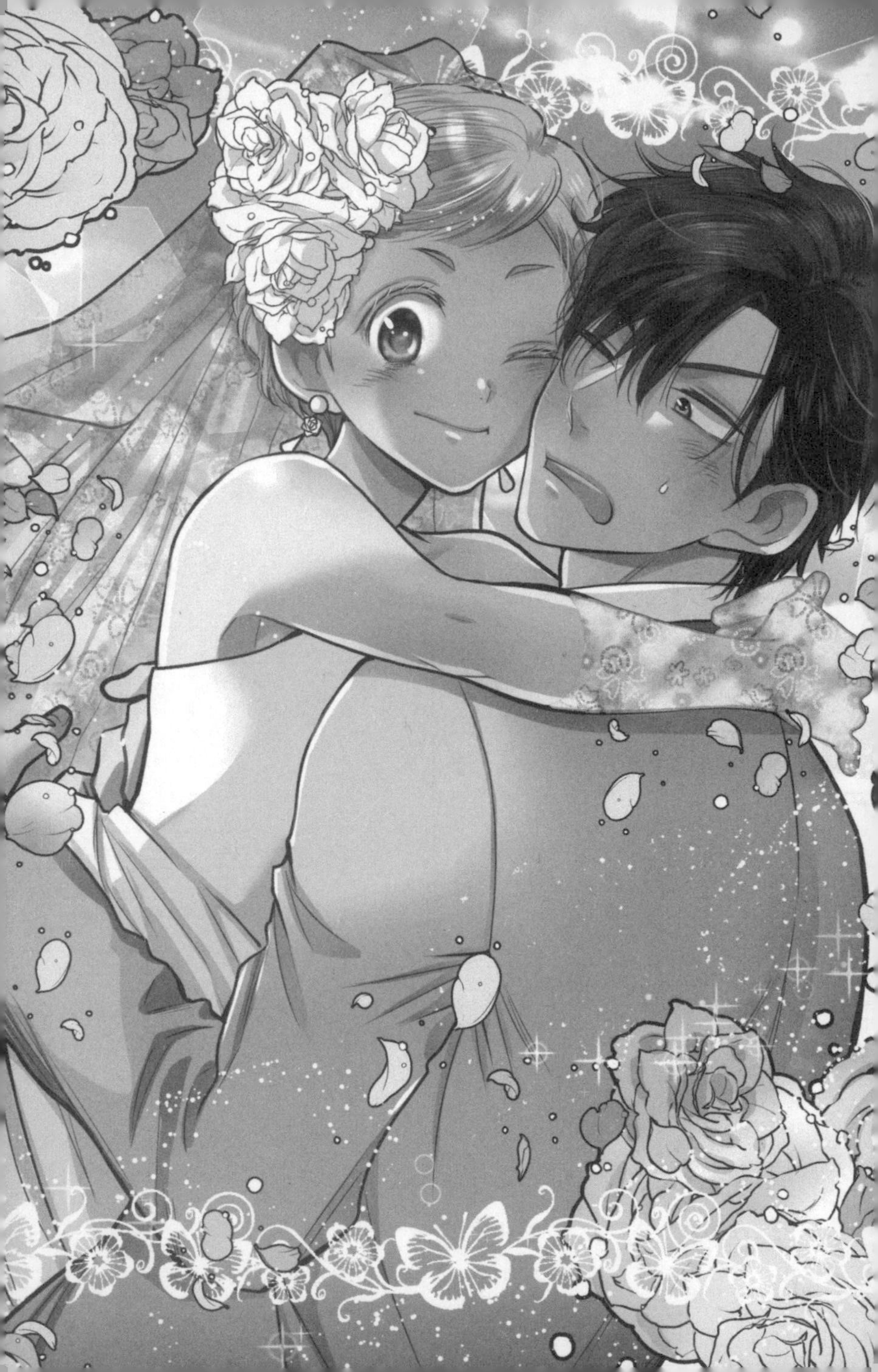

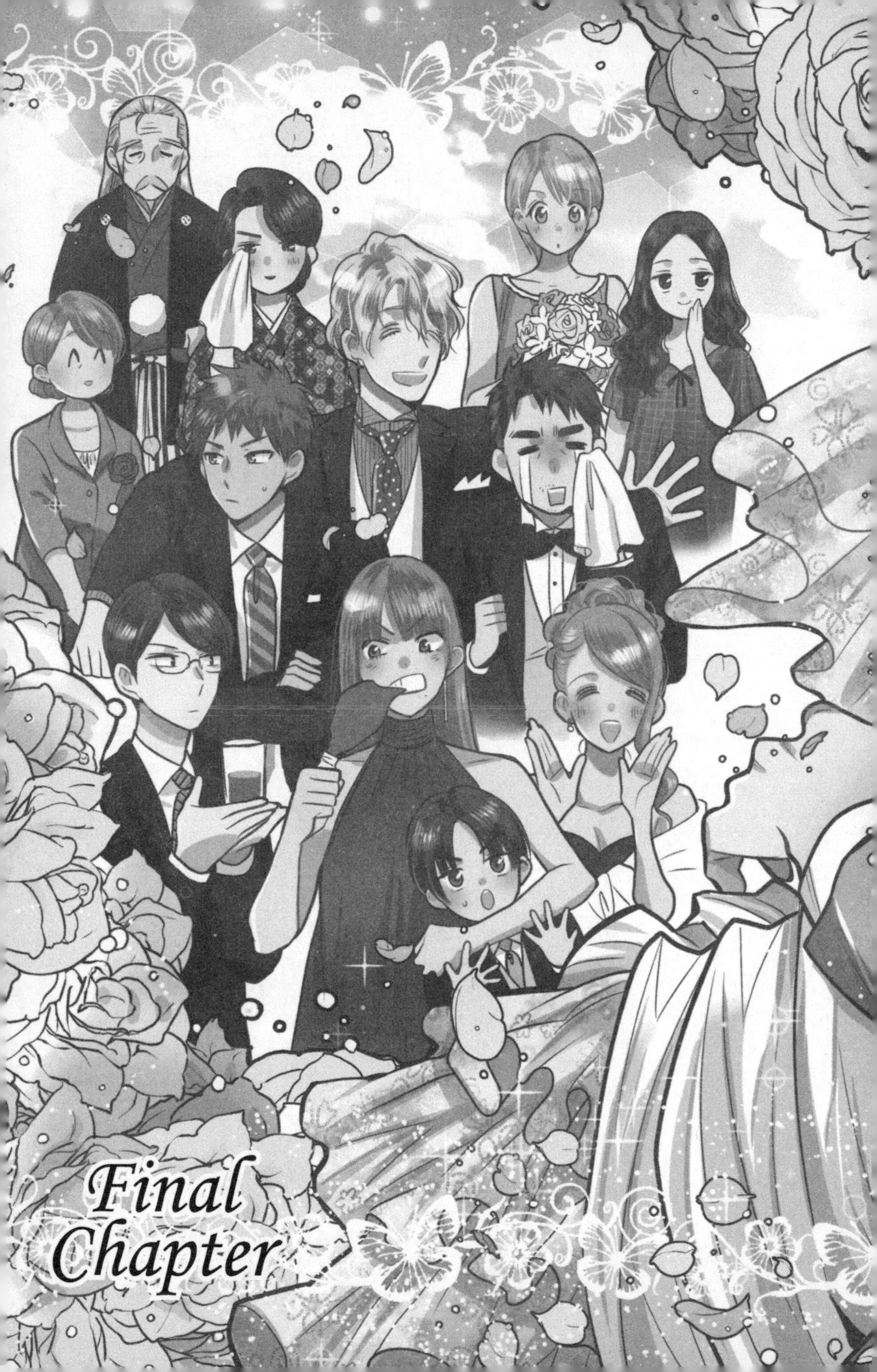
Final
Chapter

After That

"NEW MEMBERS RECEIVE A COMPLIMENTARY GIFT!"

HIS ENTHUSIASM WAS CONTAGIOUS. NEXT THING I KNEW, I WAS A MEMBER.

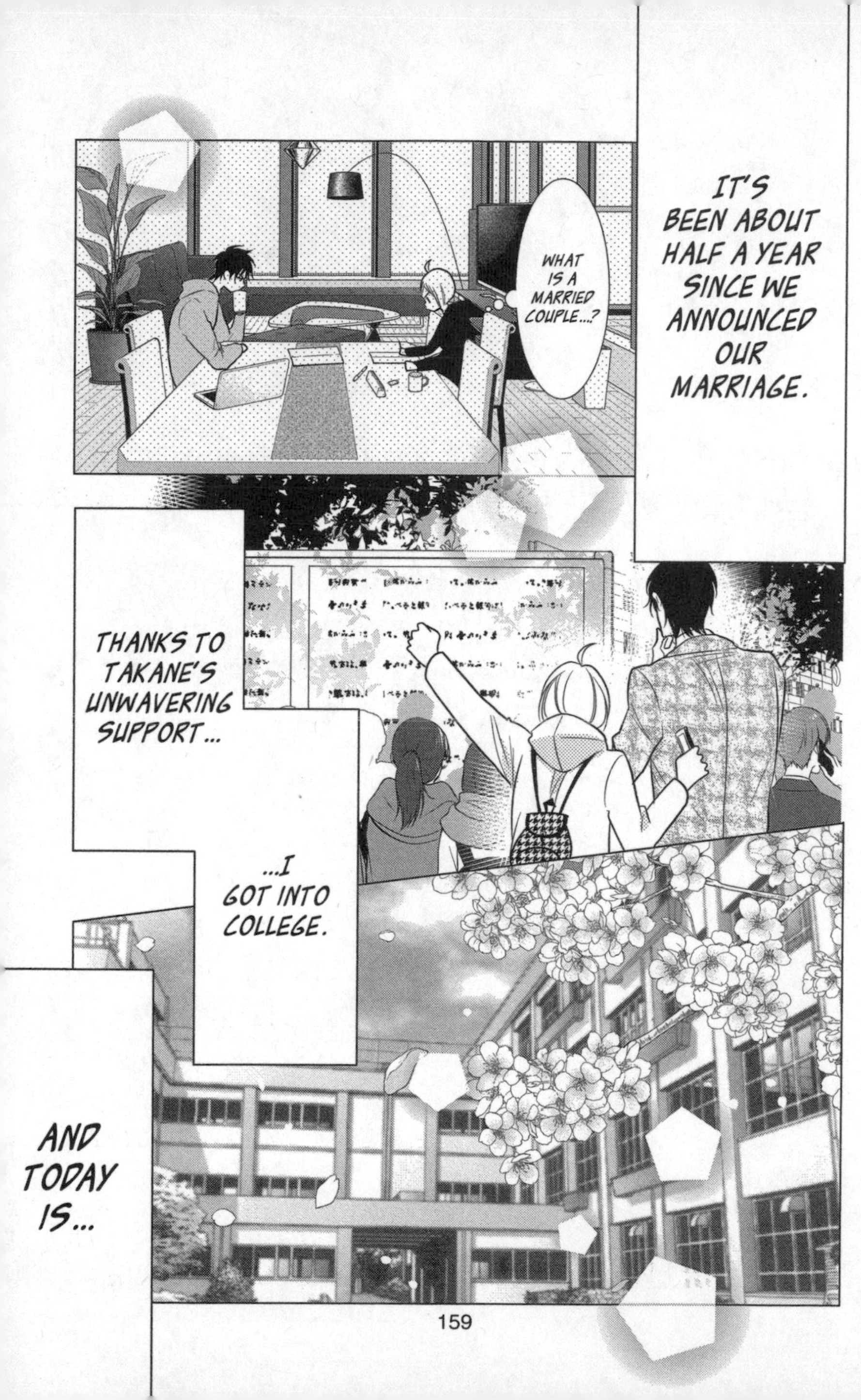
IT'S BEEN ABOUT HALF A YEAR SINCE WE ANNOUNCED OUR MARRIAGE.
WHAT IS A MARRIED COUPLE...?
THANKS TO TAKANE'S UNWAVERING SUPPORT...
...I GOT INTO COLLEGE.
AND TODAY IS...

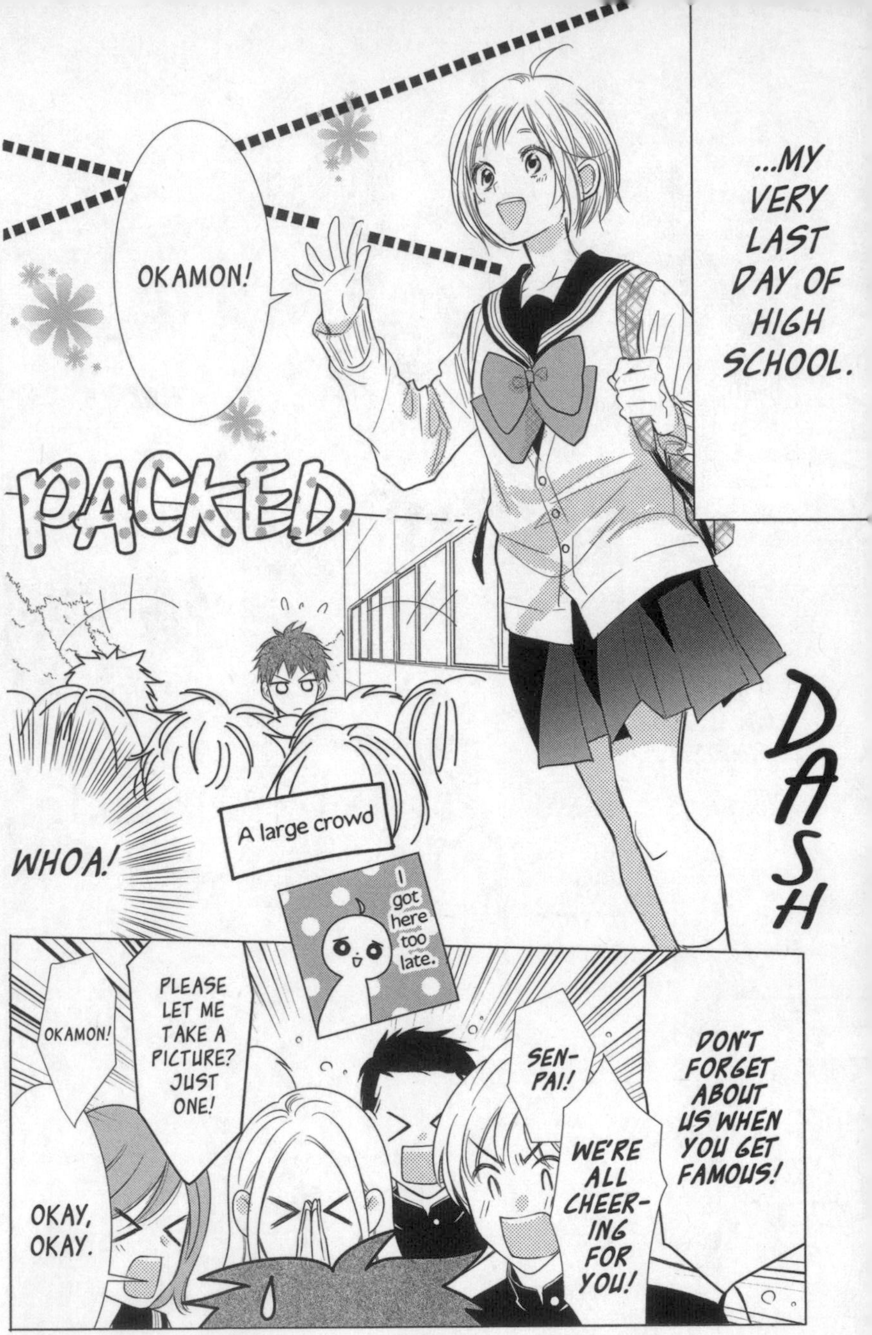
...MY VERY LAST DAY OF HIGH SCHOOL.
OKAMON!
PACKED
DASH
A large crowd
WHOA!
I got here too late.
DON'T FORGET ABOUT US WHEN YOU GET FAMOUS!
SEN-PAI!
WE'RE ALL CHEERING FOR YOU!
PLEASE LET ME TAKE A PICTURE? JUST ONE!
OKAMON!
OKAY, OKAY.

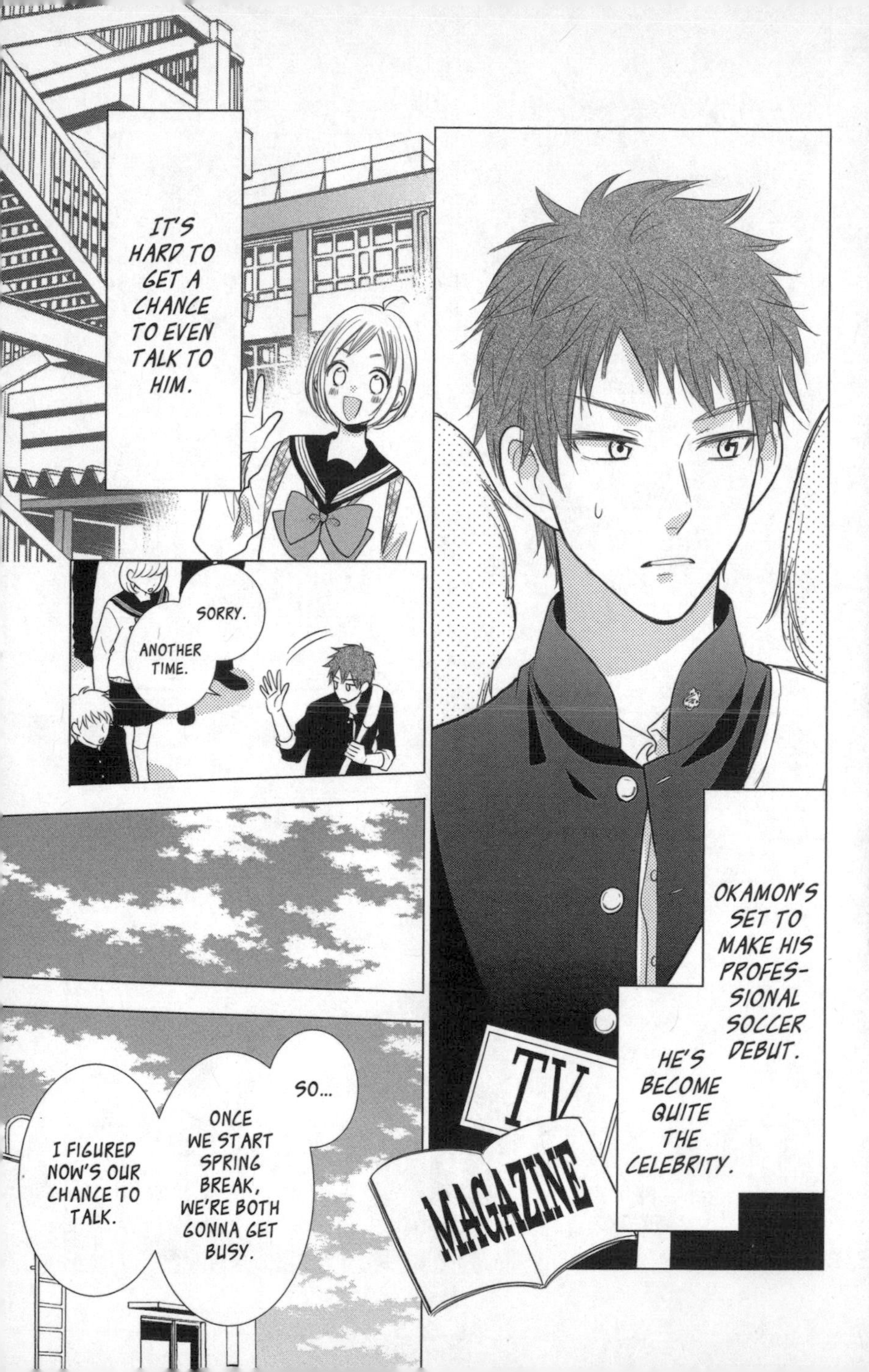
OKAMON'S SET TO MAKE HIS PROFES-SIONAL SOCCER DEBUT.
HE'S BECOME QUITE THE CELEBRITY.
TV
MAGAZINE
IT'S HARD TO GET A CHANCE TO EVEN TALK TO HIM.
SORRY.
ANOTHER TIME.
SO...
ONCE WE START SPRING BREAK, WE'RE BOTH GONNA GET BUSY.
I FIGURED NOW'S OUR CHANCE TO TALK.

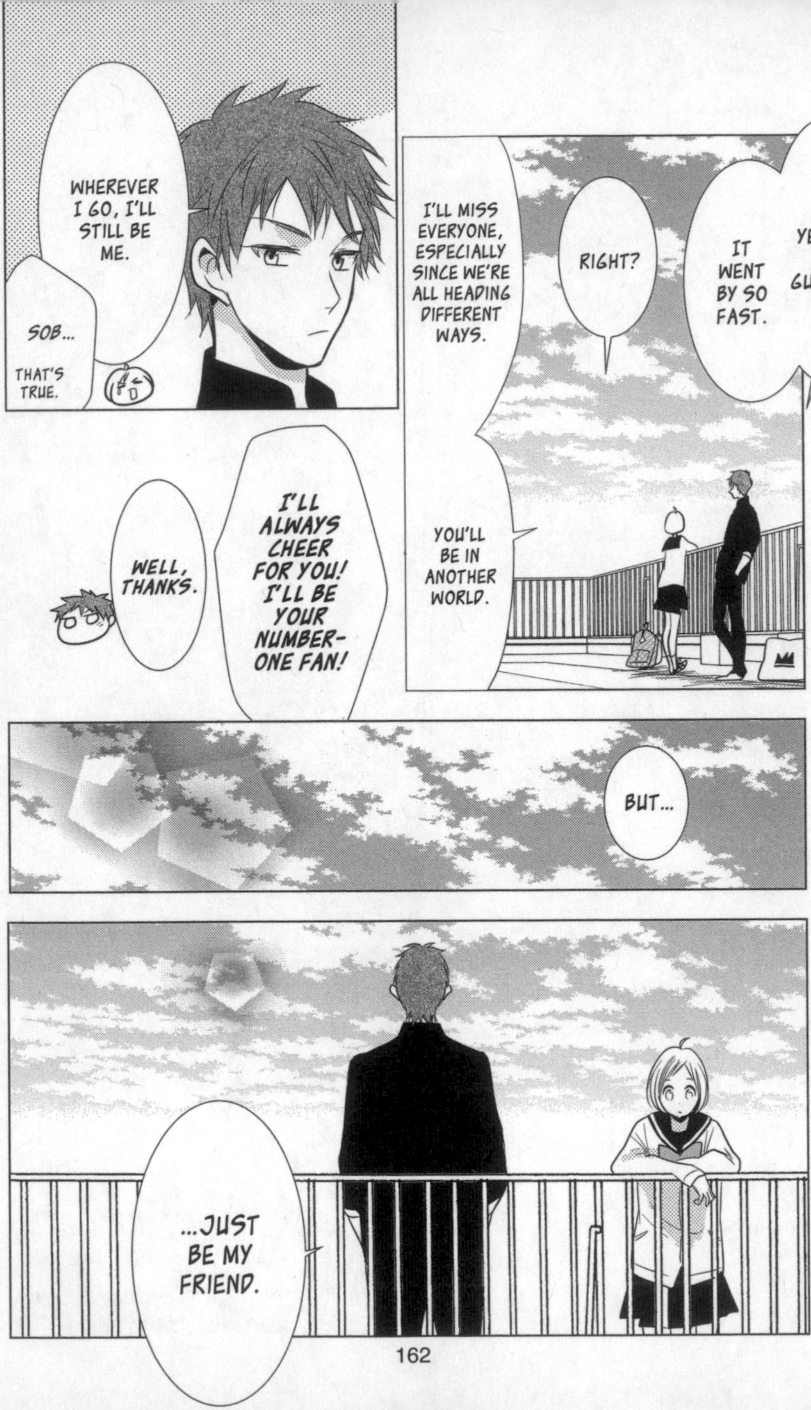
YEAH, I GUESS.
IT WENT BY SO FAST.
RIGHT?
I'LL MISS EVERYONE, ESPECIALLY SINCE WE'RE ALL HEADING DIFFERENT WAYS.
YOU'LL BE IN ANOTHER WORLD.
WHEREVER I GO, I'LL STILL BE ME.
SOB...
THAT'S TRUE.
I'LL ALWAYS CHEER FOR YOU! I'LL BE YOUR NUMBER-ONE FAN!
WELL, THANKS.
BUT...
...JUST BE MY FRIEND.

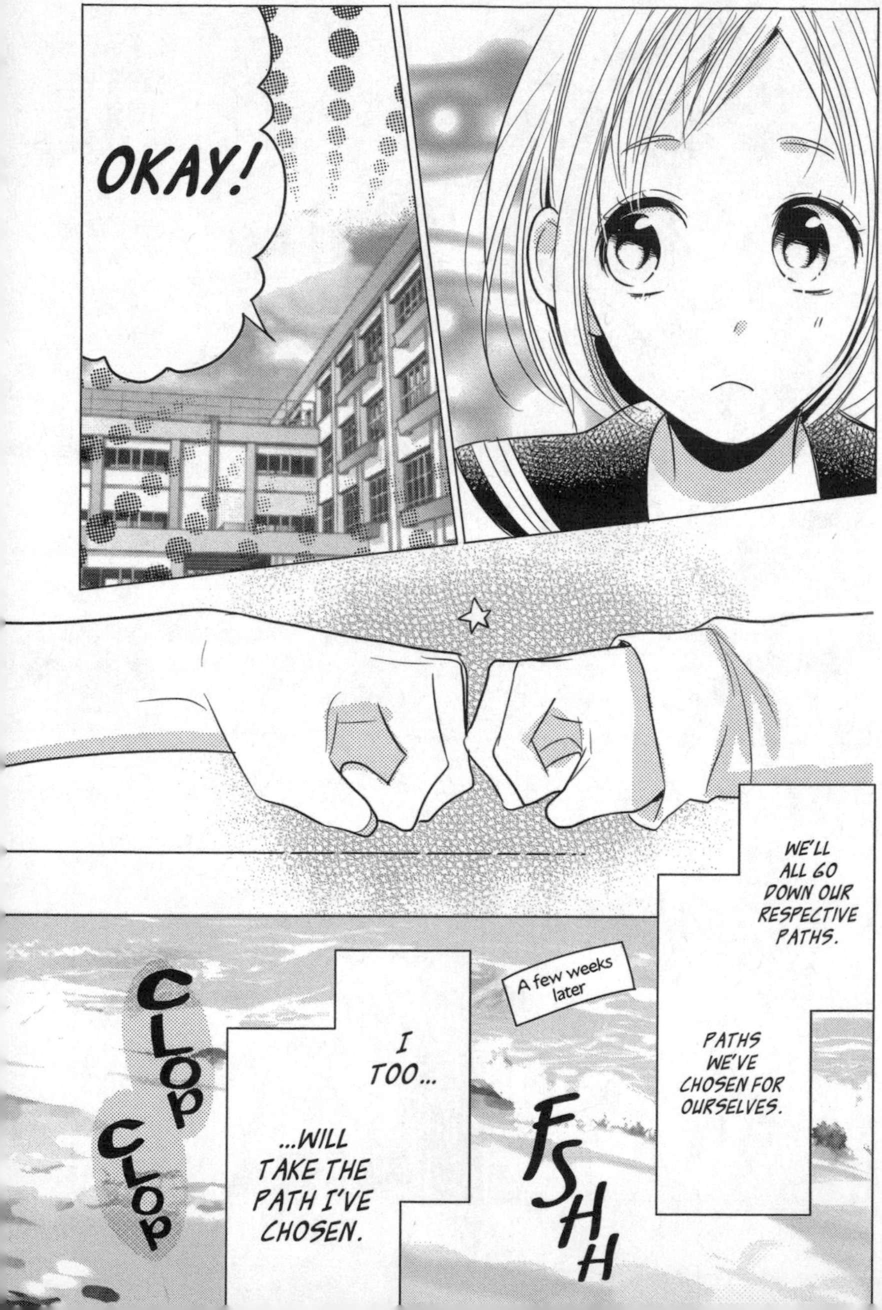
OKAY!
WE'LL ALL GO DOWN OUR RESPECTIVE PATHS.
PATHS WE'VE CHOSEN FOR OURSELVES.
A few weeks later
FSHH
I TOO...
...WILL TAKE THE PATH I'VE CHOSEN.
CLOP CLOP

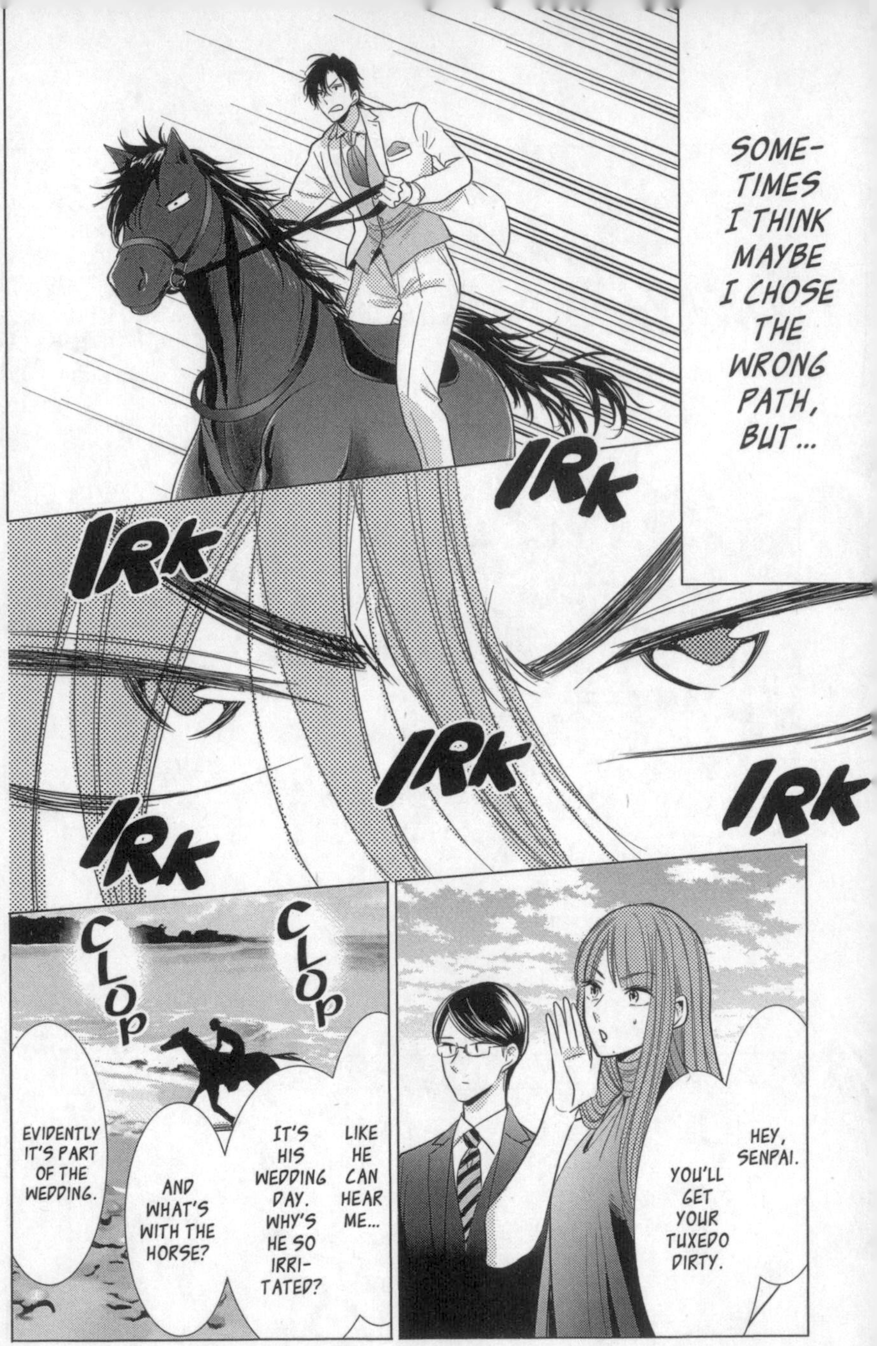
SOME-TIMES I THINK MAYBE I CHOSE THE WRONG PATH, BUT...
IRK
IRK
IRK
IRK
IRK
CLOP
CLOP
HEY, SENPAI.
YOU'LL GET YOUR TUXEDO DIRTY.
LIKE HE CAN HEAR ME...
IT'S HIS WEDDING DAY. WHY'S HE SO IRRI-TATED?
AND WHAT'S WITH THE HORSE?
EVIDENTLY IT'S PART OF THE WEDDING.

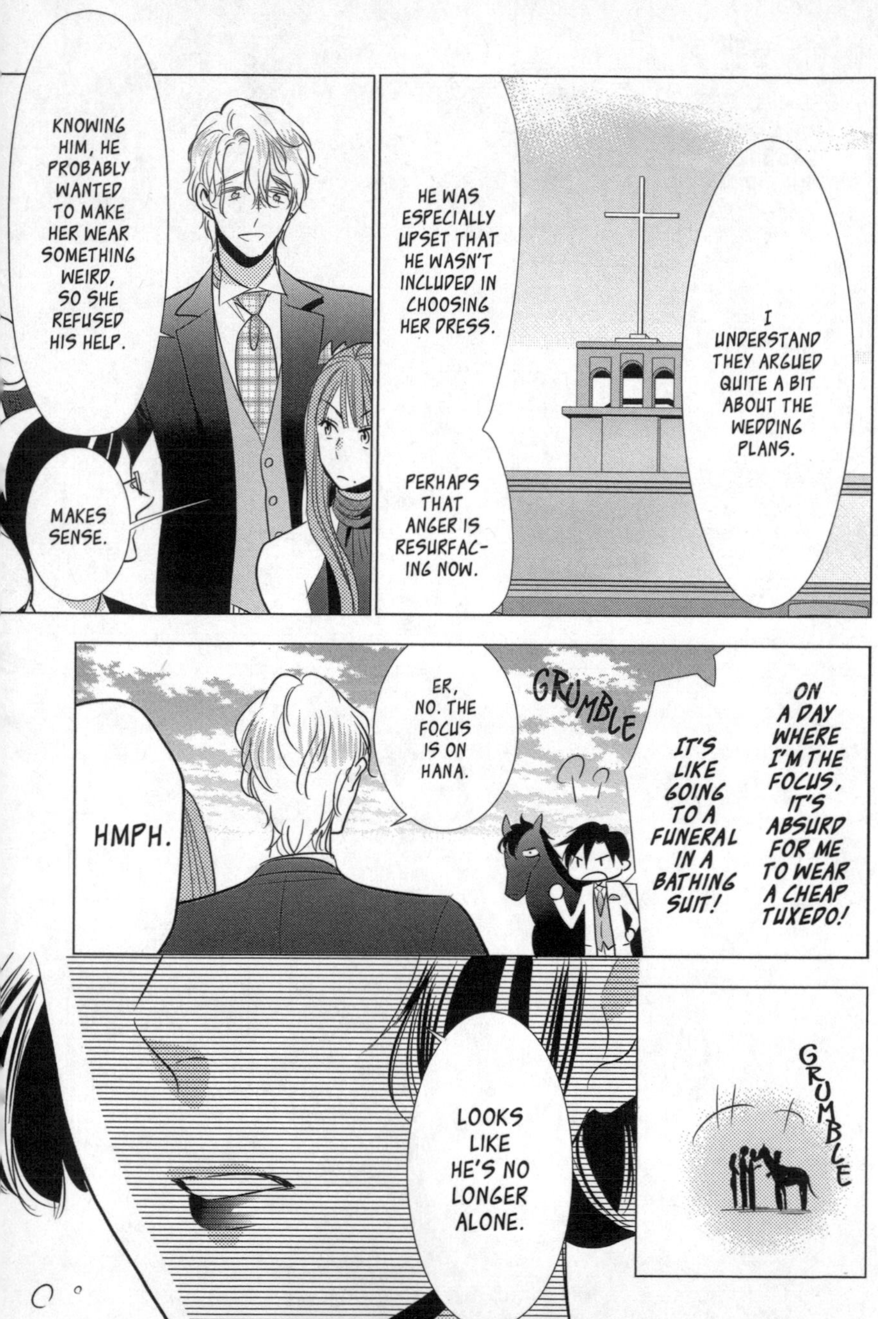
I UNDERSTAND THEY ARGUED QUITE A BIT ABOUT THE WEDDING PLANS.
HE WAS ESPECIALLY UPSET THAT HE WASN'T INCLUDED IN CHOOSING HER DRESS.
PERHAPS THAT ANGER IS RESURFACING NOW.
KNOWING HIM, HE PROBABLY WANTED TO MAKE HER WEAR SOMETHING WEIRD, SO SHE REFUSED HIS HELP.
MAKES SENSE.
ON A DAY WHERE I'M THE FOCUS, IT'S ABSURD FOR ME TO WEAR A CHEAP TUXEDO!
IT'S LIKE GOING TO A FUNERAL IN A BATHING SUIT!
GRUMBLE
ER, NO. THE FOCUS IS ON HANA.
HMPH.
GRUMBLE
LOOKS LIKE HE'S NO LONGER ALONE.

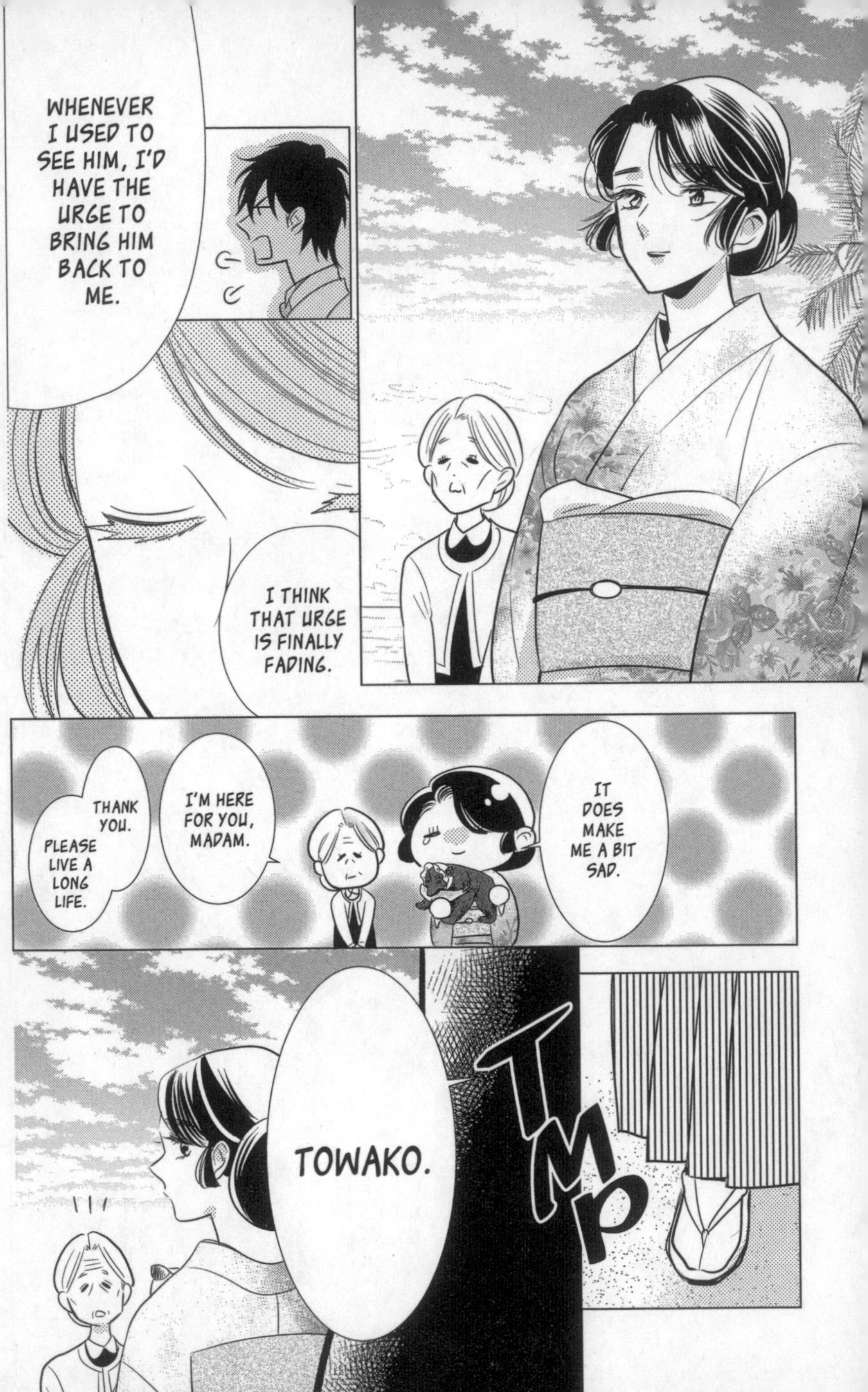
WHENEVER I USED TO SEE HIM, I'D HAVE THE URGE TO BRING HIM BACK TO ME.
I THINK THAT URGE IS FINALLY FADING.
IT DOES MAKE ME A BIT SAD.
I'M HERE FOR YOU, MADAM.
THANK YOU.
PLEASE LIVE A LONG LIFE.
TMP
TOWAKO.

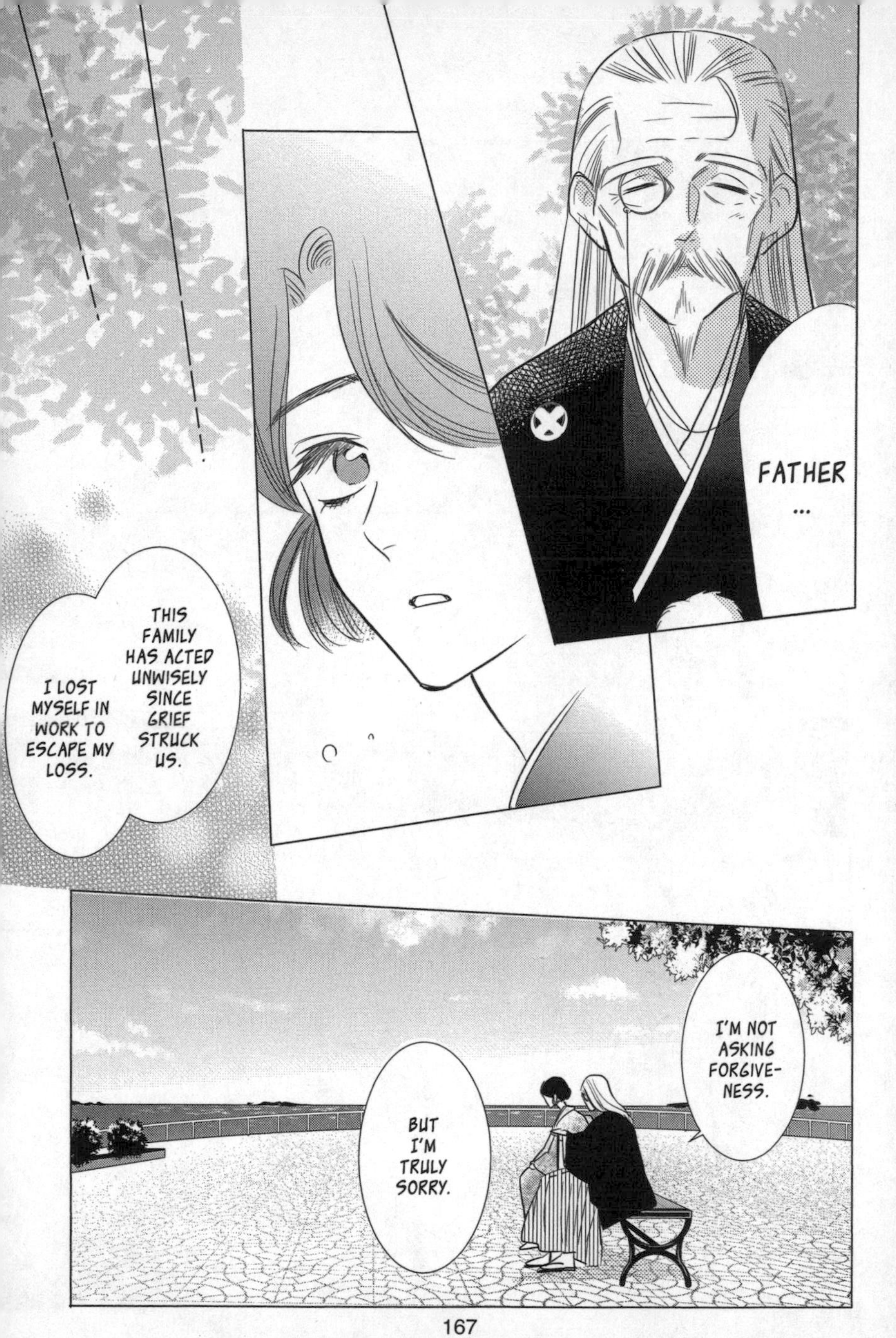
FATHER ...
THIS FAMILY HAS ACTED UNWISELY SINCE GRIEF STRUCK US.
I LOST MYSELF IN WORK TO ESCAPE MY LOSS.
I'M NOT ASKING FORGIVE-NESS.
BUT I'M TRULY SORRY.

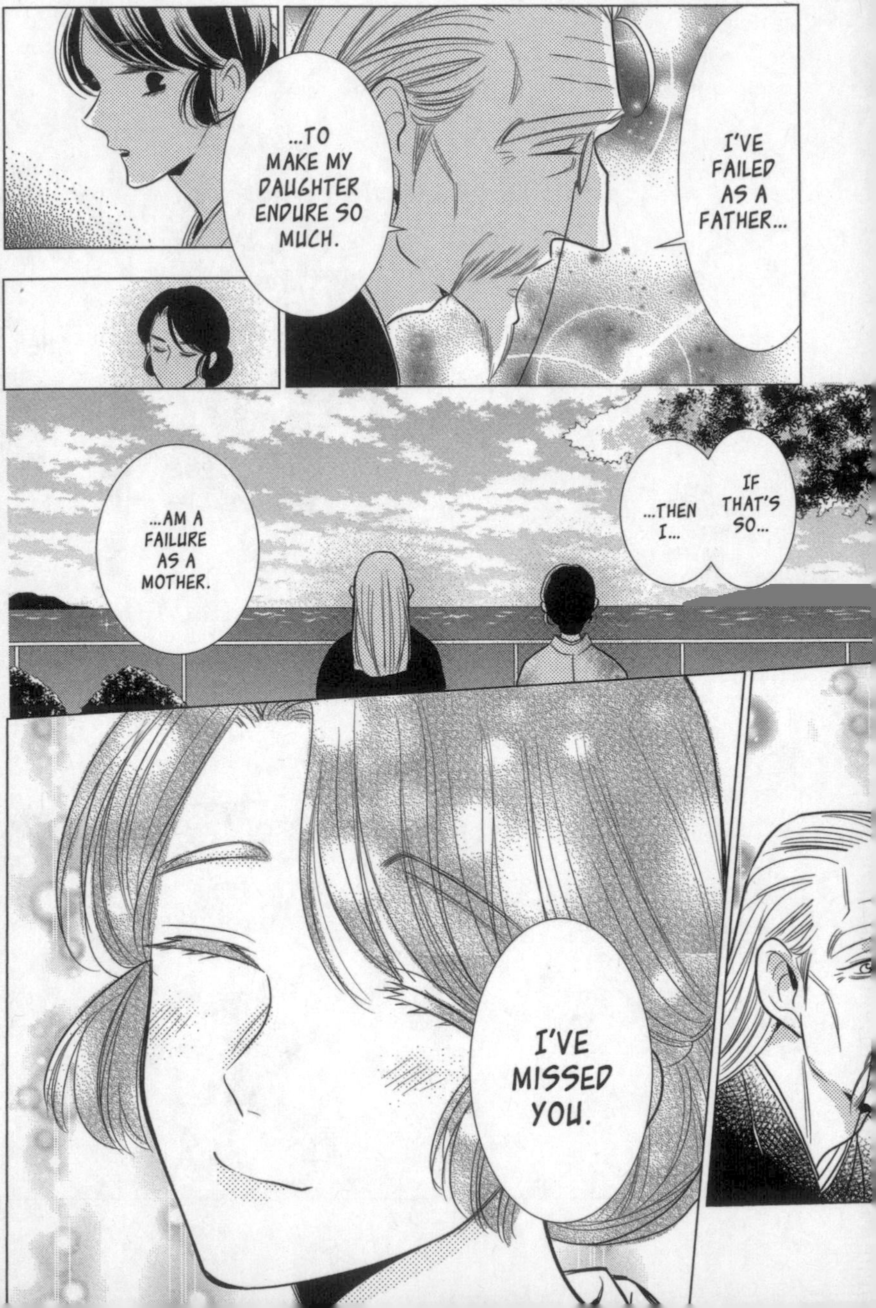
I'VE FAILED AS A FATHER...
...TO MAKE MY DAUGHTER ENDURE SO MUCH.
IF THAT'S SO...
...THEN I...
...AM A FAILURE AS A MOTHER.
I'VE MISSED YOU.

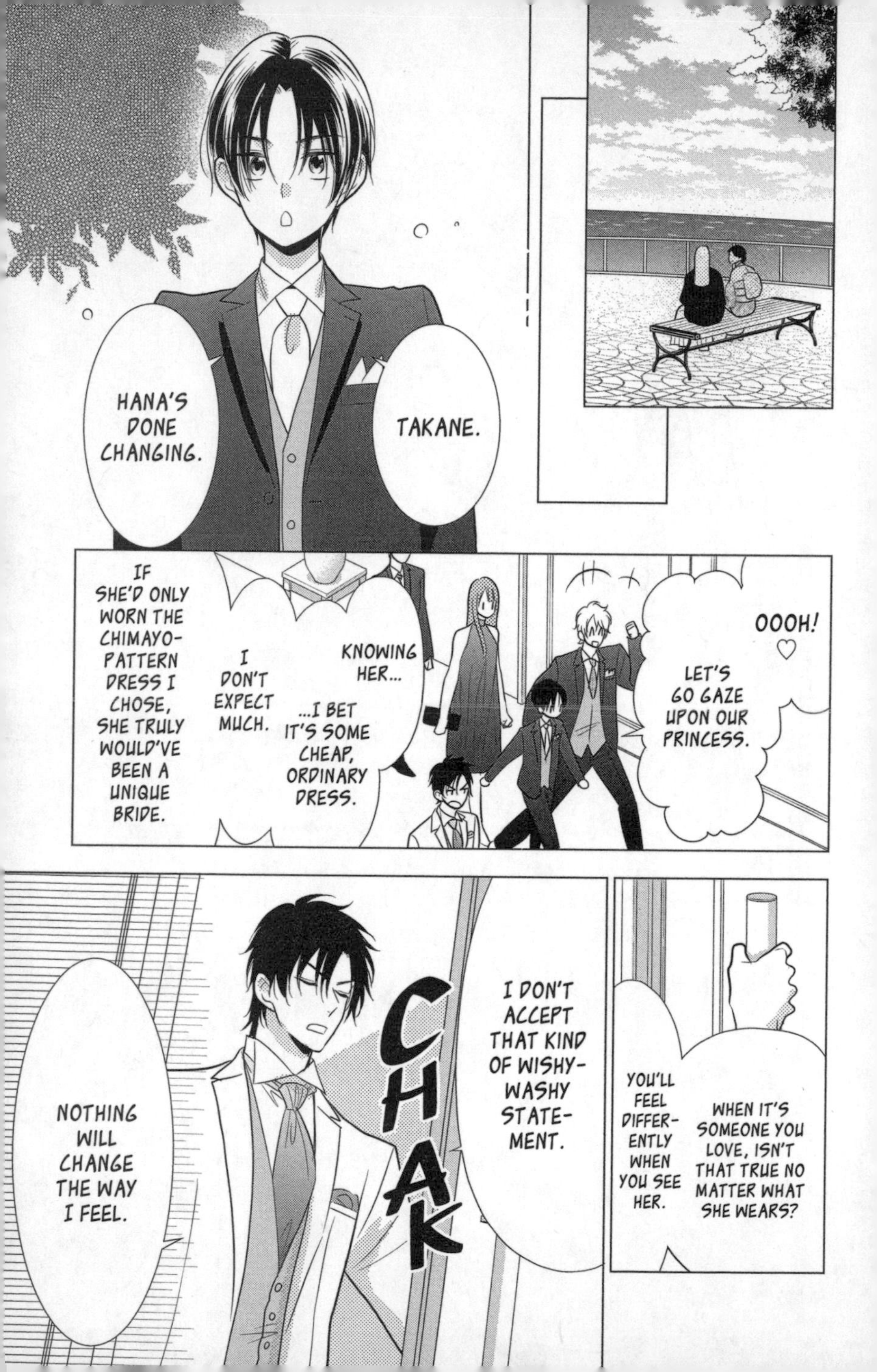
TAKANE.
HANA'S DONE CHANGING.
OOOH! ♡
LET'S GO GAZE UPON OUR PRINCESS.
KNOWING HER...
...I BET IT'S SOME CHEAP, ORDINARY DRESS.
I DON'T EXPECT MUCH.
IF SHE'D ONLY WORN THE CHIMAYO-PATTERN DRESS I CHOSE, SHE TRULY WOULD'VE BEEN A UNIQUE BRIDE.
WHEN IT'S SOMEONE YOU LOVE, ISN'T THAT TRUE NO MATTER WHAT SHE WEARS?
YOU'LL FEEL DIFFERENTLY WHEN YOU SEE HER.
I DON'T ACCEPT THAT KIND OF WISHY-WASHY STATEMENT.
CHAK
NOTHING WILL CHANGE THE WAY I FEEL.

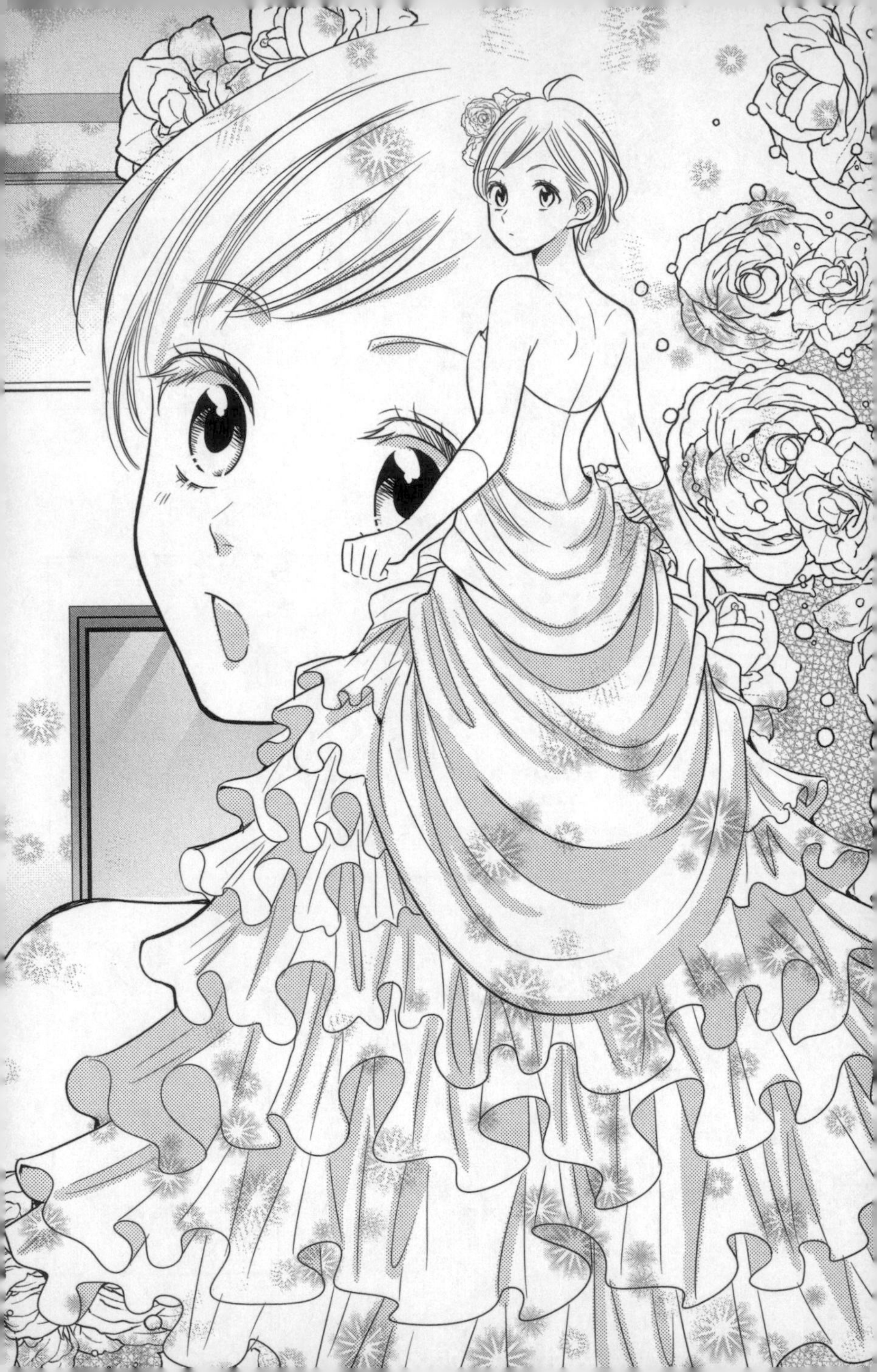

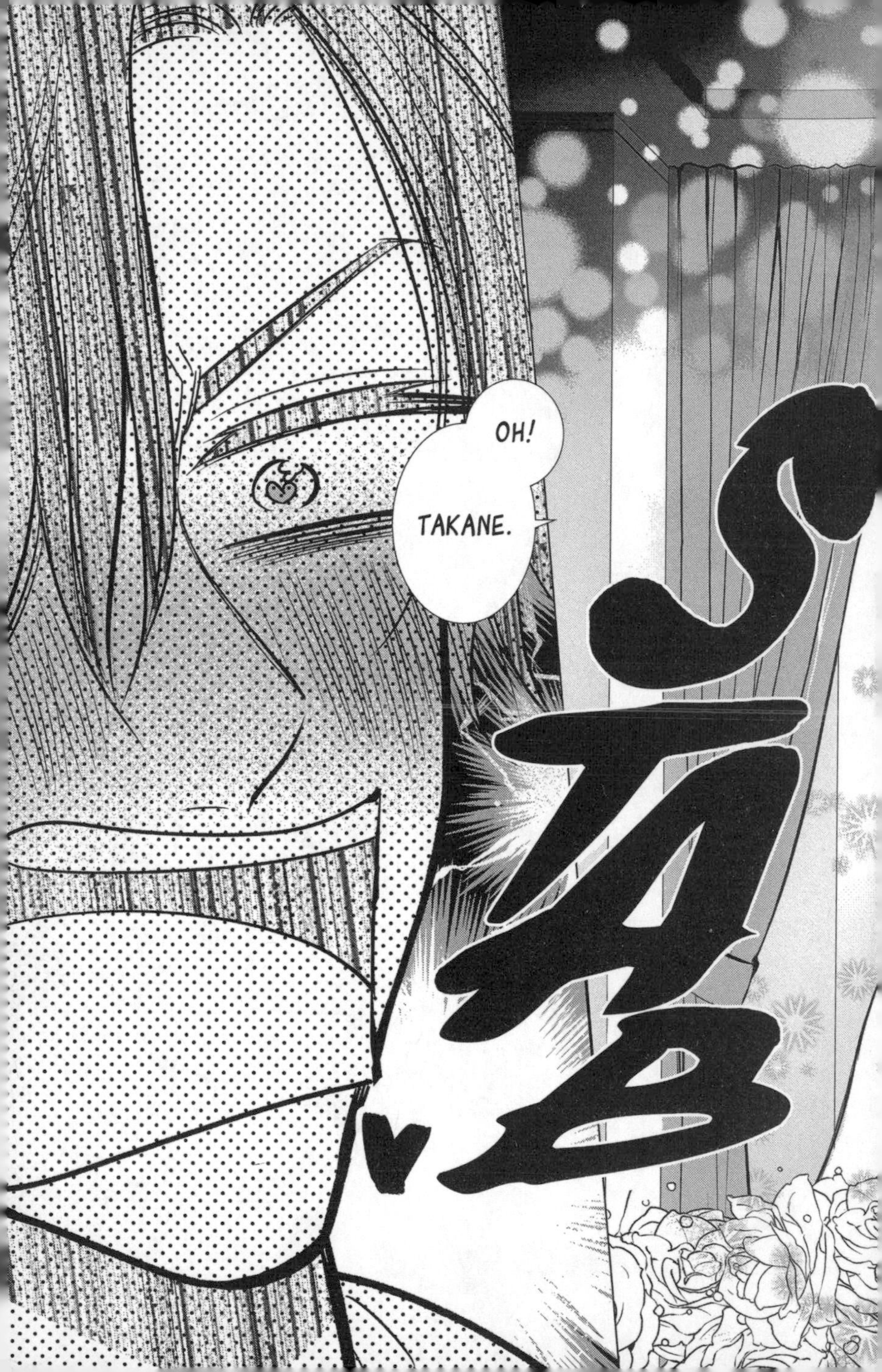
OH!
TAKANE.

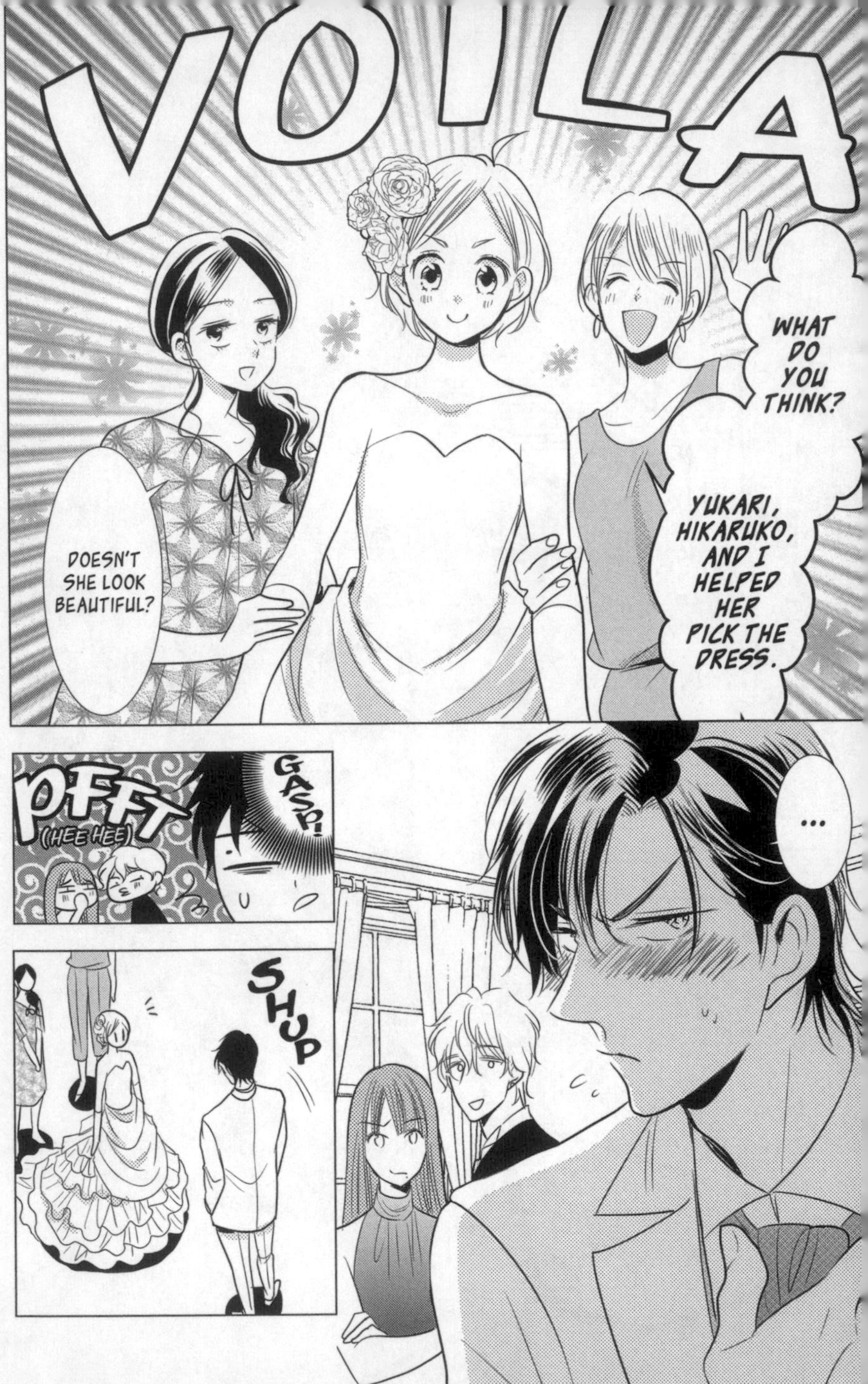
VOILA
WHAT DO YOU THINK?
YUKARI, HIKARUKO, AND I HELPED HER PICK THE DRESS.
DOESN'T SHE LOOK BEAUTIFUL?
...
GASP!
PFFT
(HEE HEE)
SHUP

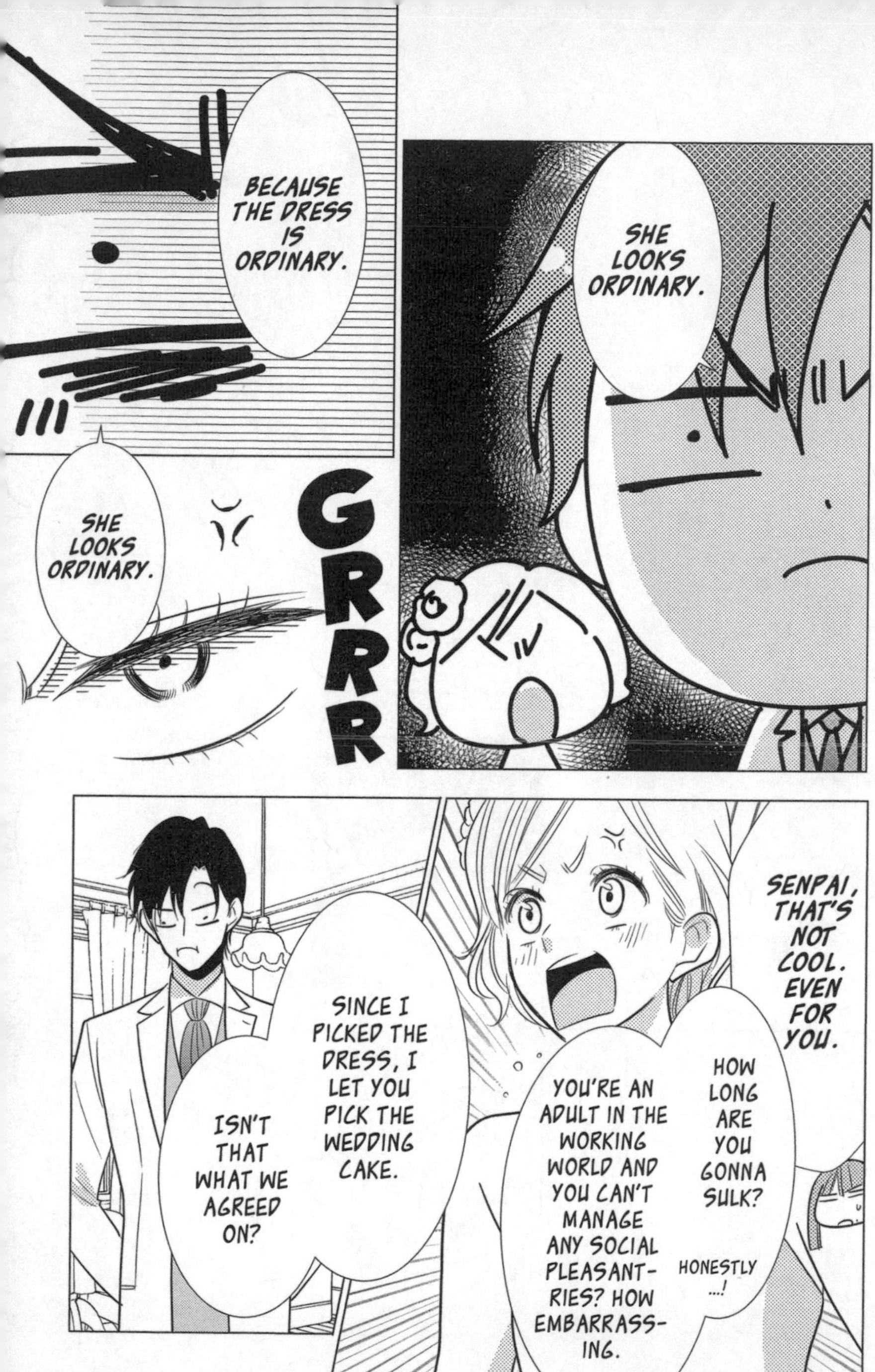
SHE LOOKS ORDINARY.
BECAUSE THE DRESS IS ORDINARY.
GRRR
SHE LOOKS ORDINARY.
SENPAI, THAT'S NOT COOL. EVEN FOR YOU.
HOW LONG ARE YOU GONNA SULK?
HONESTLY ...!
YOU'RE AN ADULT IN THE WORKING WORLD AND YOU CAN'T MANAGE ANY SOCIAL PLEASANT-RIES? HOW EMBARRASS-ING.
SINCE I PICKED THE DRESS, I LET YOU PICK THE WEDDING CAKE.
ISN'T THAT WHAT WE AGREED ON?

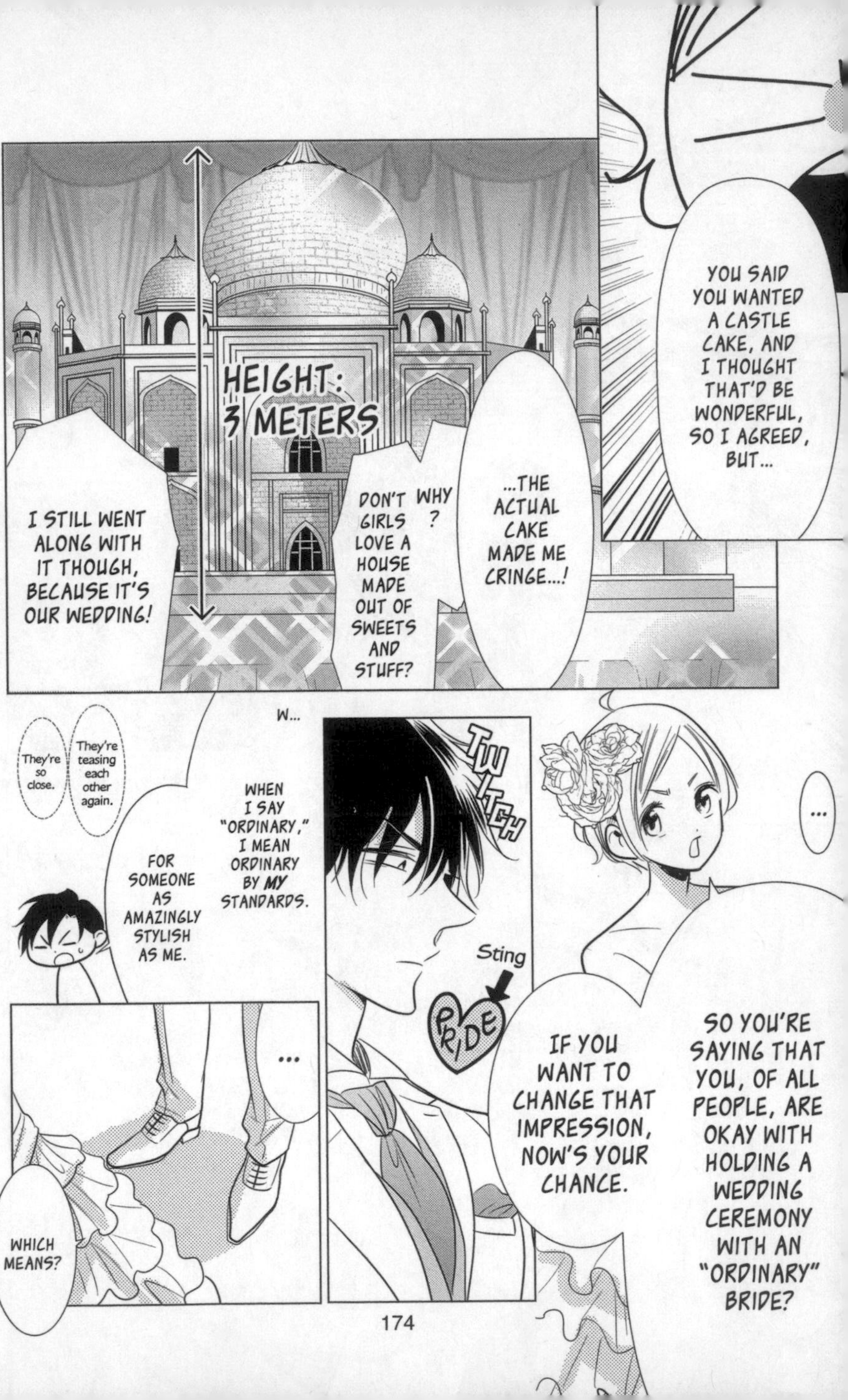
YOU SAID YOU WANTED A CASTLE CAKE, AND I THOUGHT THAT'D BE WONDERFUL, SO I AGREED, BUT...
...THE ACTUAL CAKE MADE ME CRINGE...!
HEIGHT: 3 METERS
WHY?
DON'T GIRLS LOVE A HOUSE MADE OUT OF SWEETS AND STUFF?
I STILL WENT ALONG WITH IT THOUGH, BECAUSE IT'S OUR WEDDING!
...
SO YOU'RE SAYING THAT YOU, OF ALL PEOPLE, ARE OKAY WITH HOLDING A WEDDING CEREMONY WITH AN "ORDINARY" BRIDE?
IF YOU WANT TO CHANGE THAT IMPRESSION, NOW'S YOUR CHANCE.
TWITCH
Sting
PRIDE
W...
WHEN I SAY "ORDINARY," I MEAN ORDINARY BY *MY* STANDARDS.
FOR SOMEONE AS AMAZINGLY STYLISH AS ME.
They're teasing each other again.
They're so close.
...
WHICH MEANS?

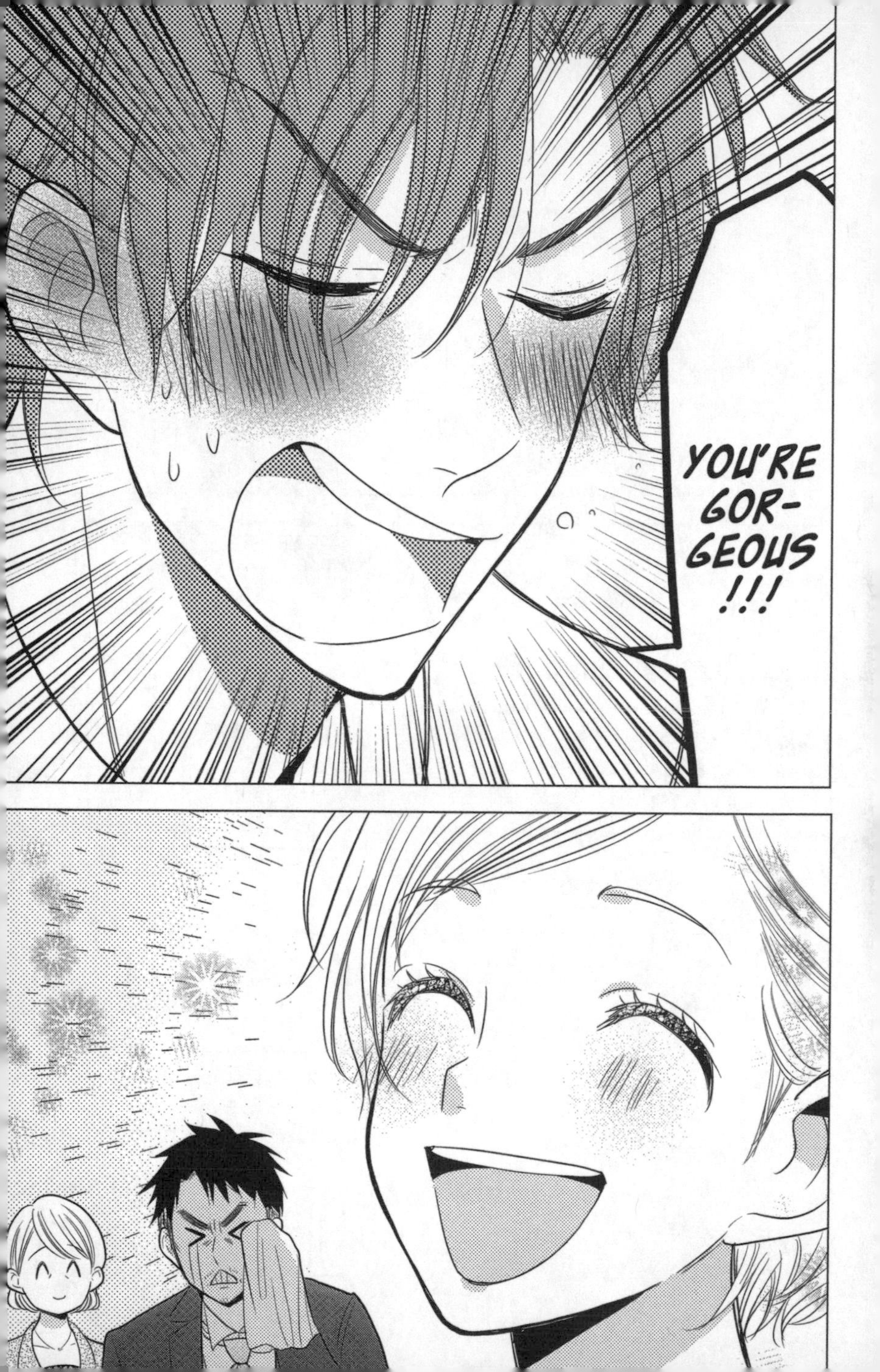
YOU'RE GOR-GEOUS!!!

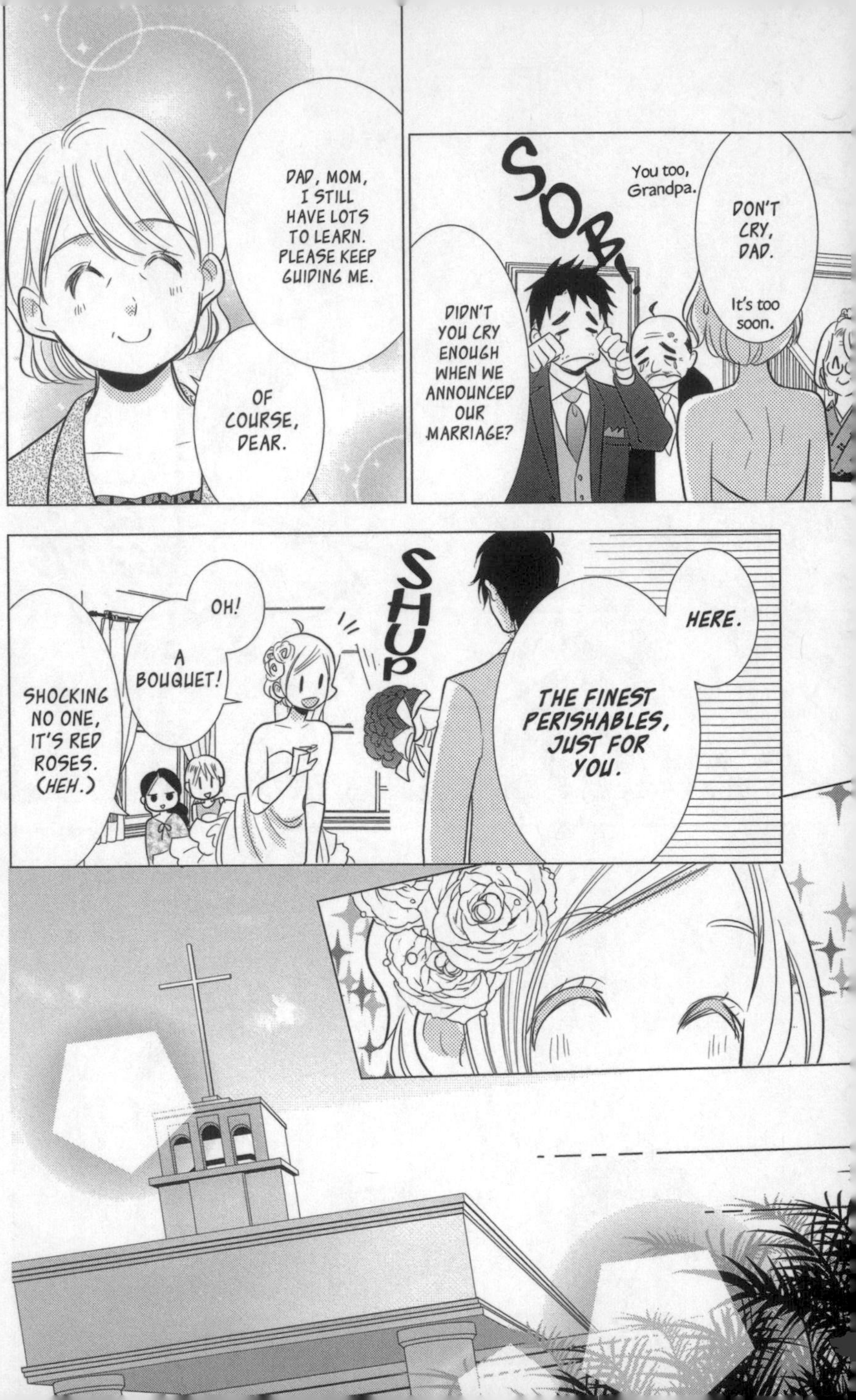
DON'T CRY, DAD.
It's too soon.
You too, Grandpa.
SOB!
DIDN'T YOU CRY ENOUGH WHEN WE ANNOUNCED OUR MARRIAGE?
DAD, MOM, I STILL HAVE LOTS TO LEARN. PLEASE KEEP GUIDING ME.
OF COURSE, DEAR.
HERE.
THE FINEST PERISHABLES, JUST FOR YOU.
SHUP
OH!
A BOUQUET!
SHOCKING NO ONE, IT'S RED ROSES. (HEH.)

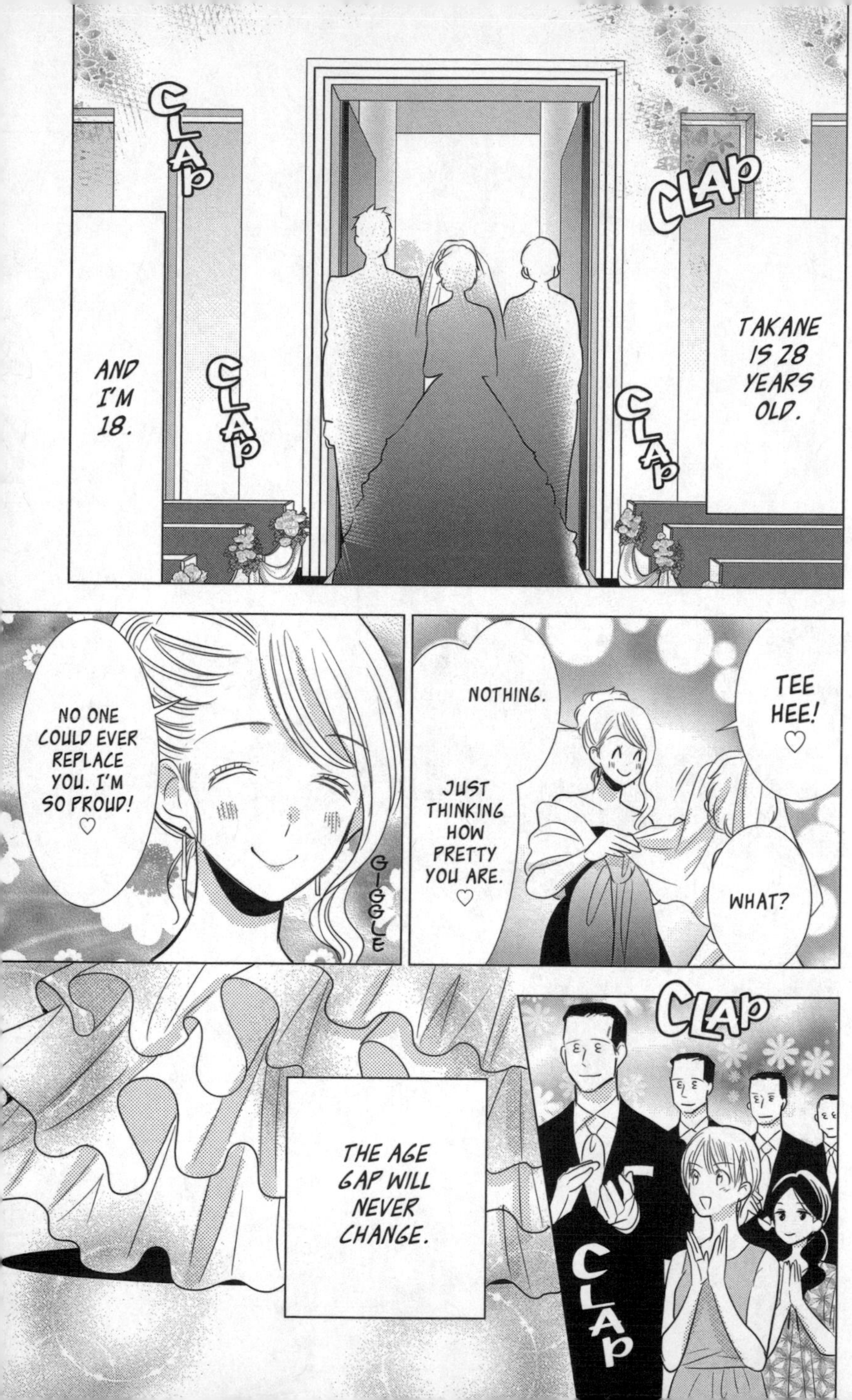
CLAP
TAKANE IS 28 YEARS OLD.
CLAP
CLAP
CLAP
AND I'M 18.
TEE HEE! ♡
WHAT?
NOTHING.
JUST THINKING HOW PRETTY YOU ARE. ♡
NO ONE COULD EVER REPLACE YOU. I'M SO PROUD! ♡
GIGGLE
CLAP
CLAP
THE AGE GAP WILL NEVER CHANGE.

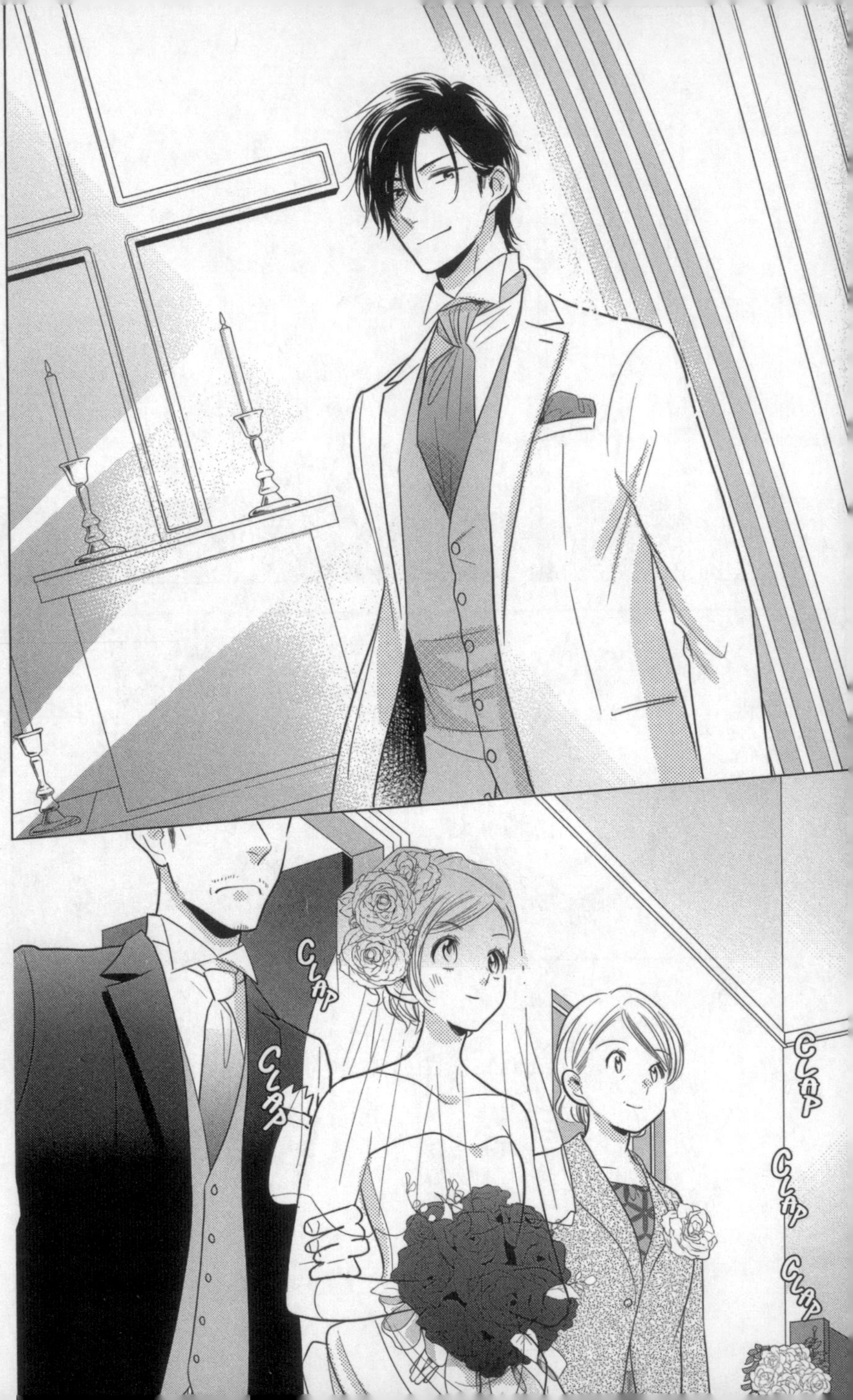
CLAP
CLAP
CLAP
CLAP
CLAP
CLAP
CLAP

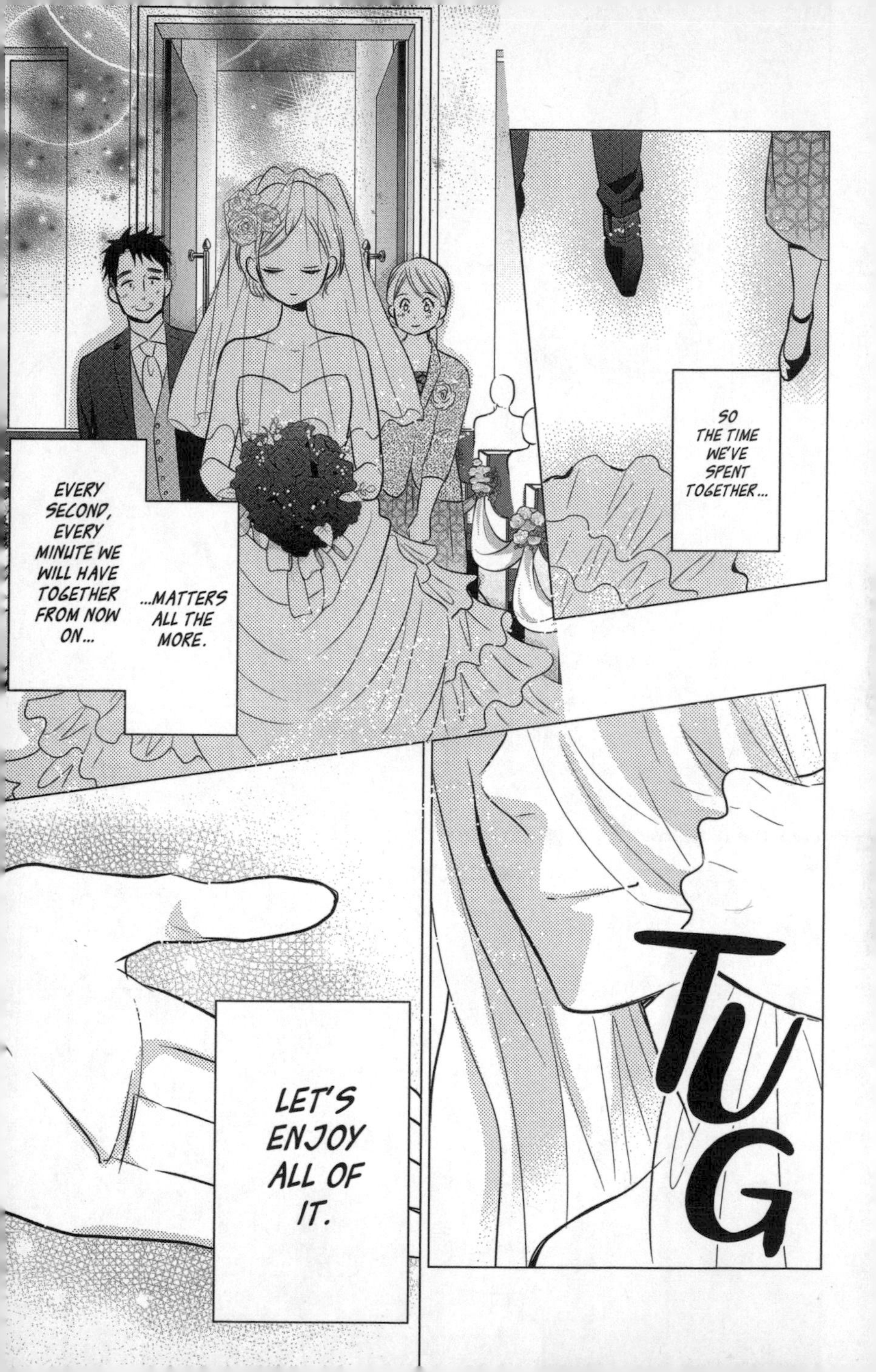
SO THE TIME WE'VE SPENT TOGETHER...
EVERY SECOND, EVERY MINUTE WE WILL HAVE TOGETHER FROM NOW ON...
...MATTERS ALL THE MORE.
TUG
LET'S ENJOY ALL OF IT.

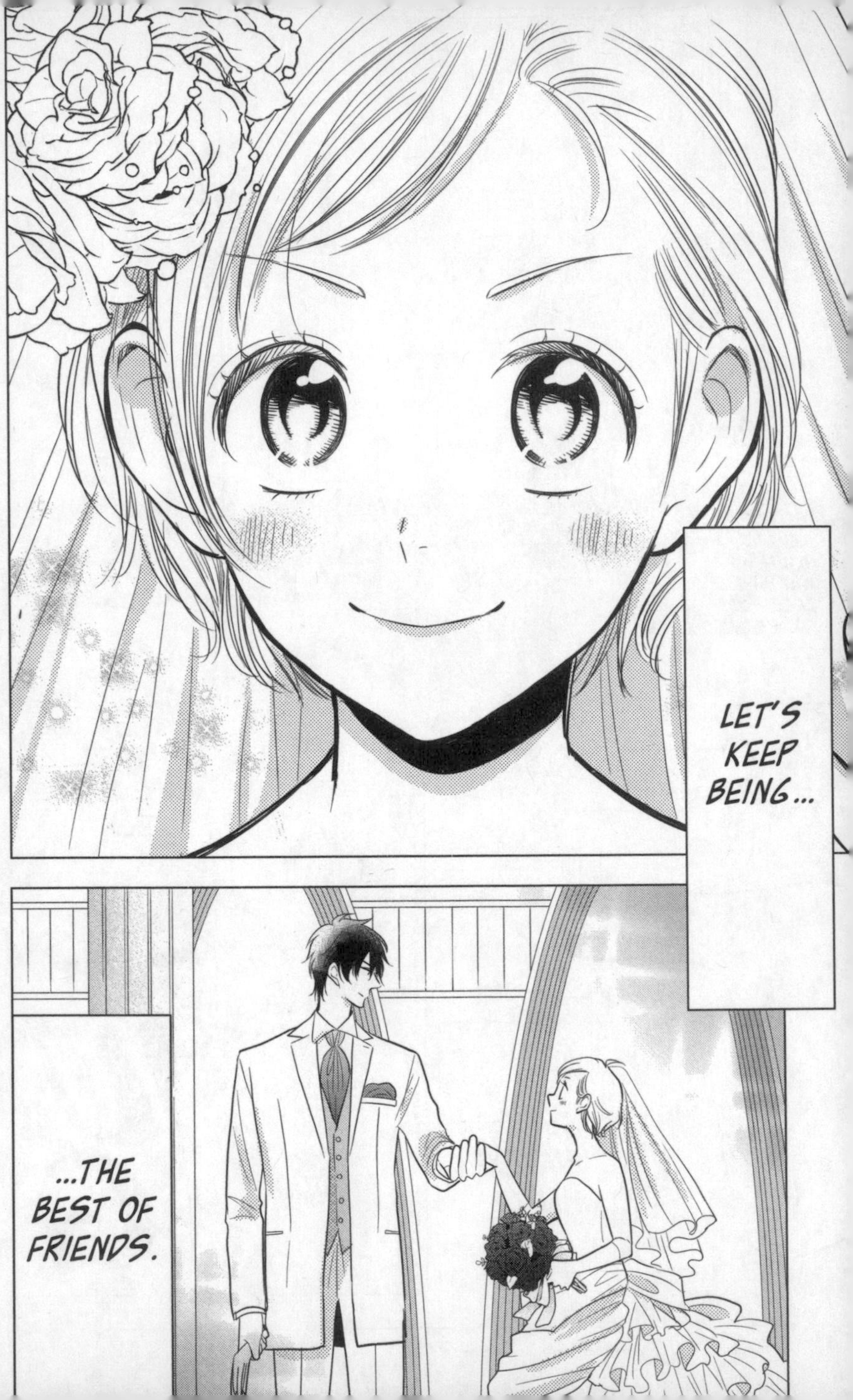
LET'S KEEP BEING...
...THE BEST OF FRIENDS.

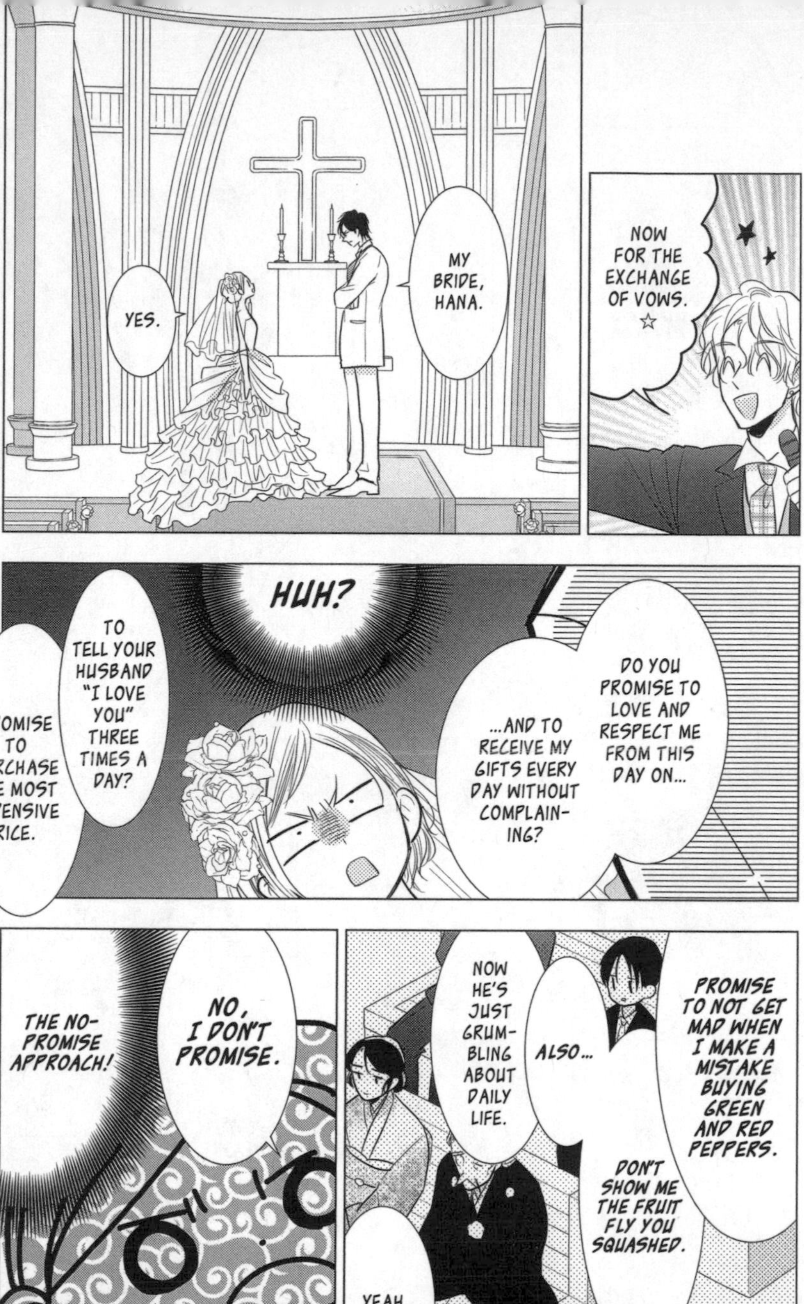
NOW FOR THE EXCHANGE OF VOWS. ☆
MY BRIDE, HANA.
YES.
DO YOU PROMISE TO LOVE AND RESPECT ME FROM THIS DAY ON...
...AND TO RECEIVE MY GIFTS EVERY DAY WITHOUT COMPLAIN-ING?
HUH?
TO TELL YOUR HUSBAND "I LOVE YOU" THREE TIMES A DAY?
PROMISE TO PURCHASE THE MOST EXPENSIVE RICE.
PROMISE TO NOT GET MAD WHEN I MAKE A MISTAKE BUYING GREEN AND RED PEPPERS.
ALSO...
NOW HE'S JUST GRUM-BLING ABOUT DAILY LIFE.
DON'T SHOW ME THE FRUIT FLY YOU SQUASHED.
YEAH...
NO, I DON'T PROMISE.
THE NO-PROMISE APPROACH!

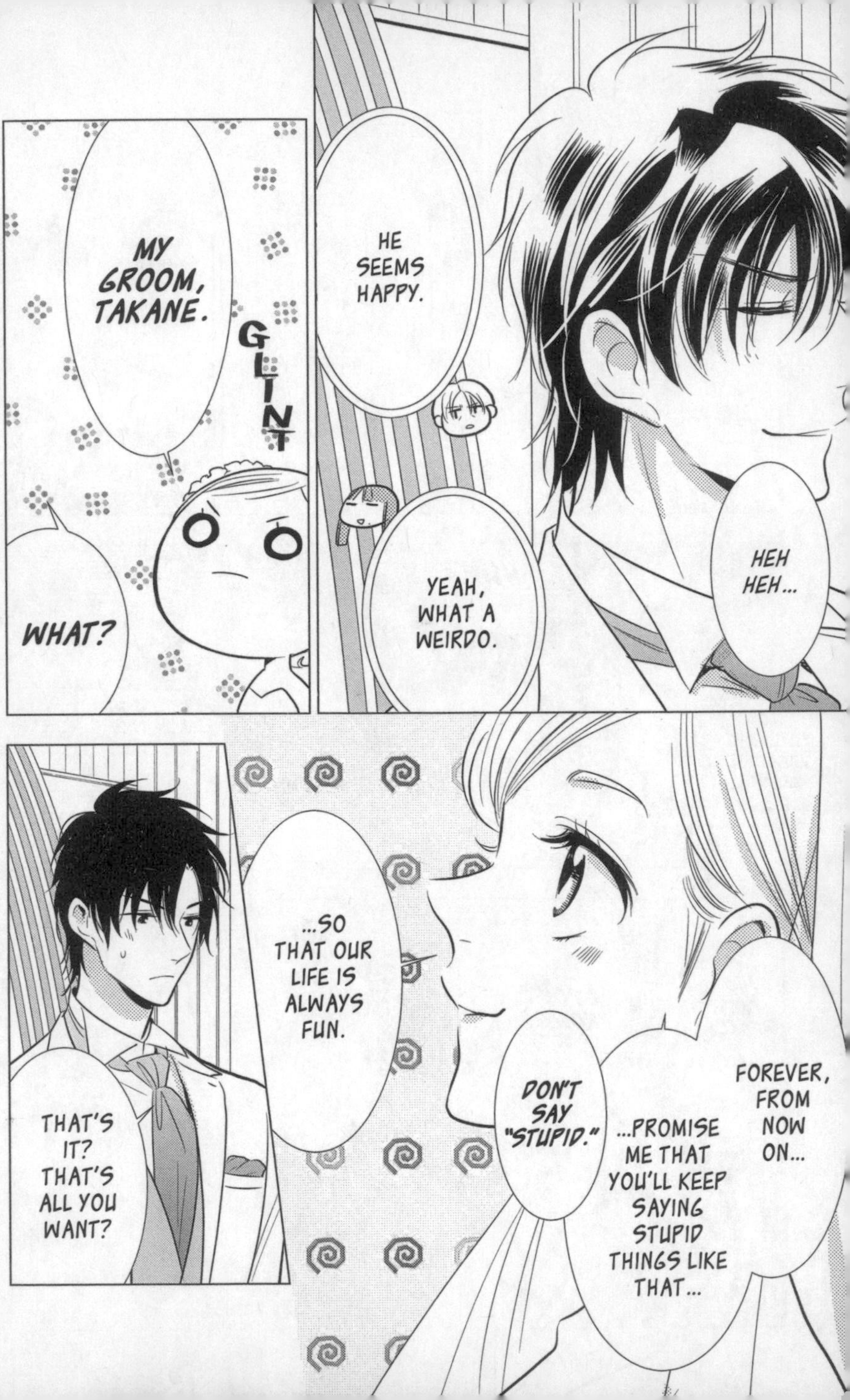
HEH HEH...
HE SEEMS HAPPY.
YEAH, WHAT A WEIRDO.
MY GROOM, TAKANE.
GLINT
WHAT?
FOREVER, FROM NOW ON...
...PROMISE ME THAT YOU'LL KEEP SAYING STUPID THINGS LIKE THAT...
DON'T SAY "STUPID."
...SO THAT OUR LIFE IS ALWAYS FUN.
THAT'S IT? THAT'S ALL YOU WANT?

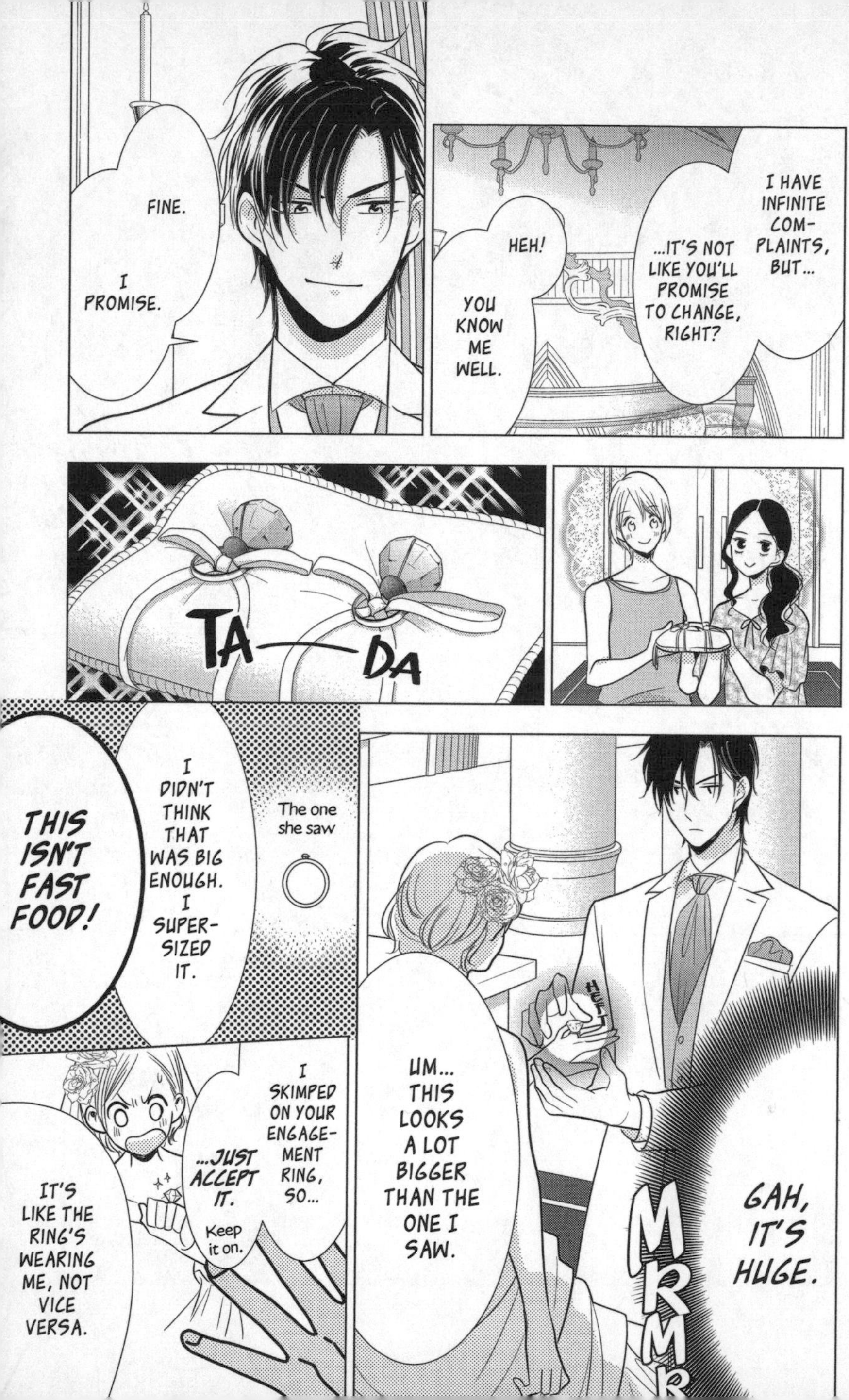

I HAVE INFINITE COM-PLAINTS, BUT...
...IT'S NOT LIKE YOU'LL PROMISE TO CHANGE, RIGHT?
HEH!
YOU KNOW ME WELL.
FINE.
I PROMISE.
TA—DA
GAH, IT'S HUGE.
MRMR
HEFT
UM... THIS LOOKS A LOT BIGGER THAN THE ONE I SAW.
I DIDN'T THINK THAT WAS BIG ENOUGH. I SUPER-SIZED IT.
The one she saw
THIS ISN'T FAST FOOD!
I SKIMPED ON YOUR ENGAGE-MENT RING, SO...
...JUST ACCEPT IT.
Keep it on.
IT'S LIKE THE RING'S WEARING ME, NOT VICE VERSA.

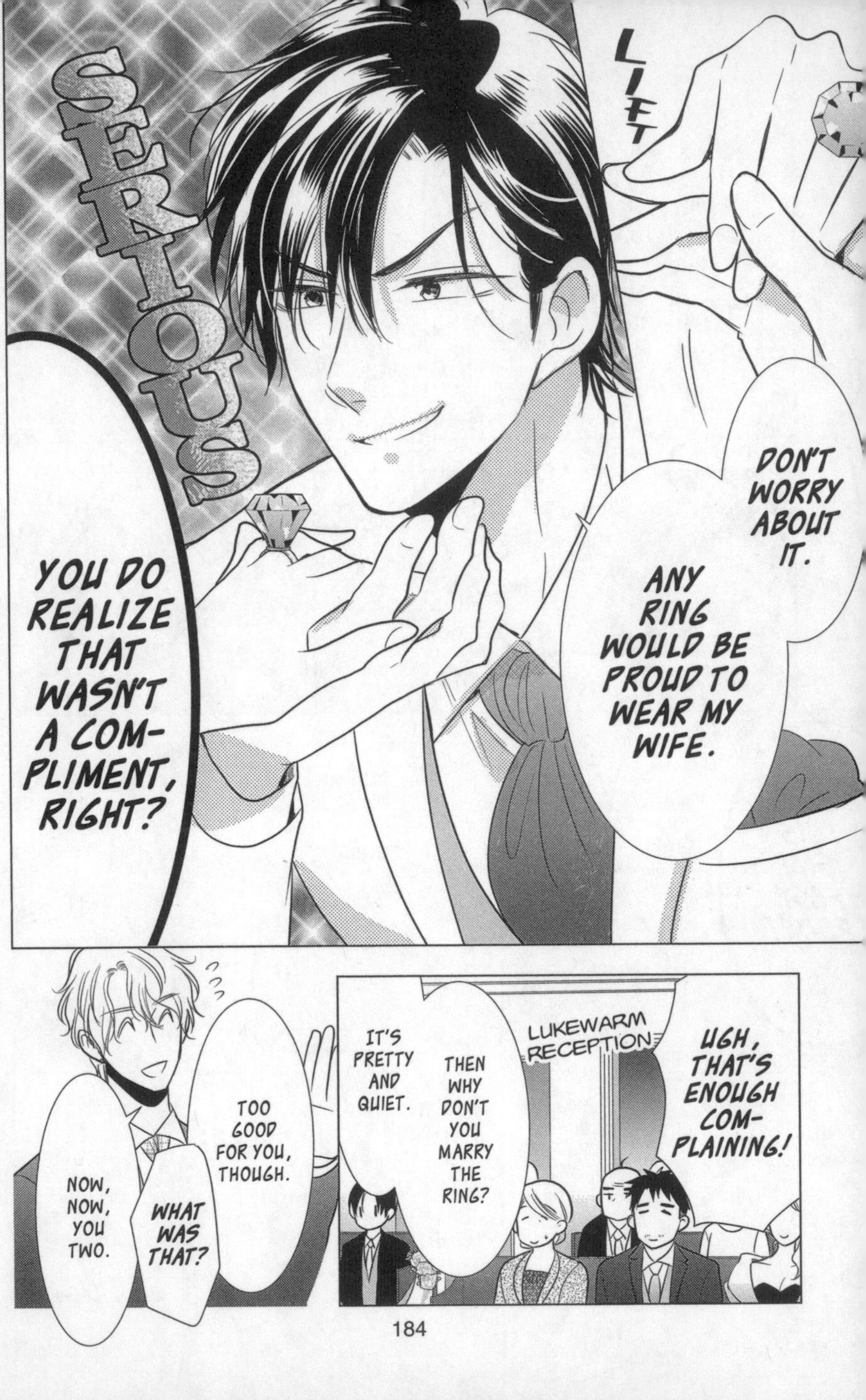
LIFT
DON'T WORRY ABOUT IT.
ANY RING WOULD BE PROUD TO WEAR MY WIFE.
SERIOUS
YOU DO REALIZE THAT WASN'T A COMPLIMENT, RIGHT?
UGH, THAT'S ENOUGH COMPLAINING!
LUKEWARM RECEPTION
THEN WHY DON'T YOU MARRY THE RING?
IT'S PRETTY AND QUIET.
TOO GOOD FOR YOU, THOUGH.
WHAT WAS THAT?
NOW, NOW, YOU TWO.

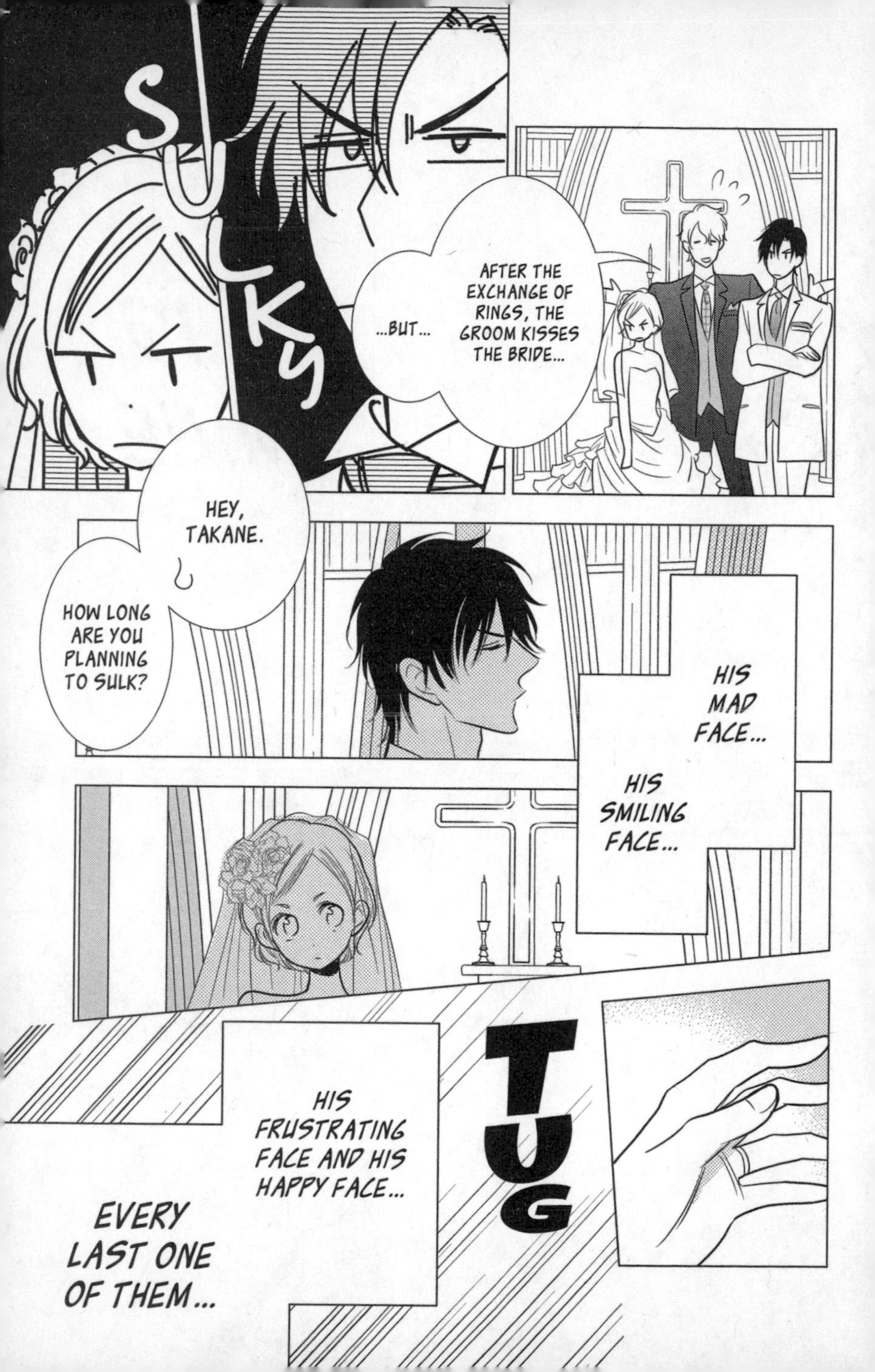
AFTER THE EXCHANGE OF RINGS, THE GROOM KISSES THE BRIDE...
...BUT...
SULKY
HEY, TAKANE.
HOW LONG ARE YOU PLANNING TO SULK?
HIS MAD FACE...
HIS SMILING FACE...
TUG
HIS FRUSTRATING FACE AND HIS HAPPY FACE...
EVERY LAST ONE OF THEM...

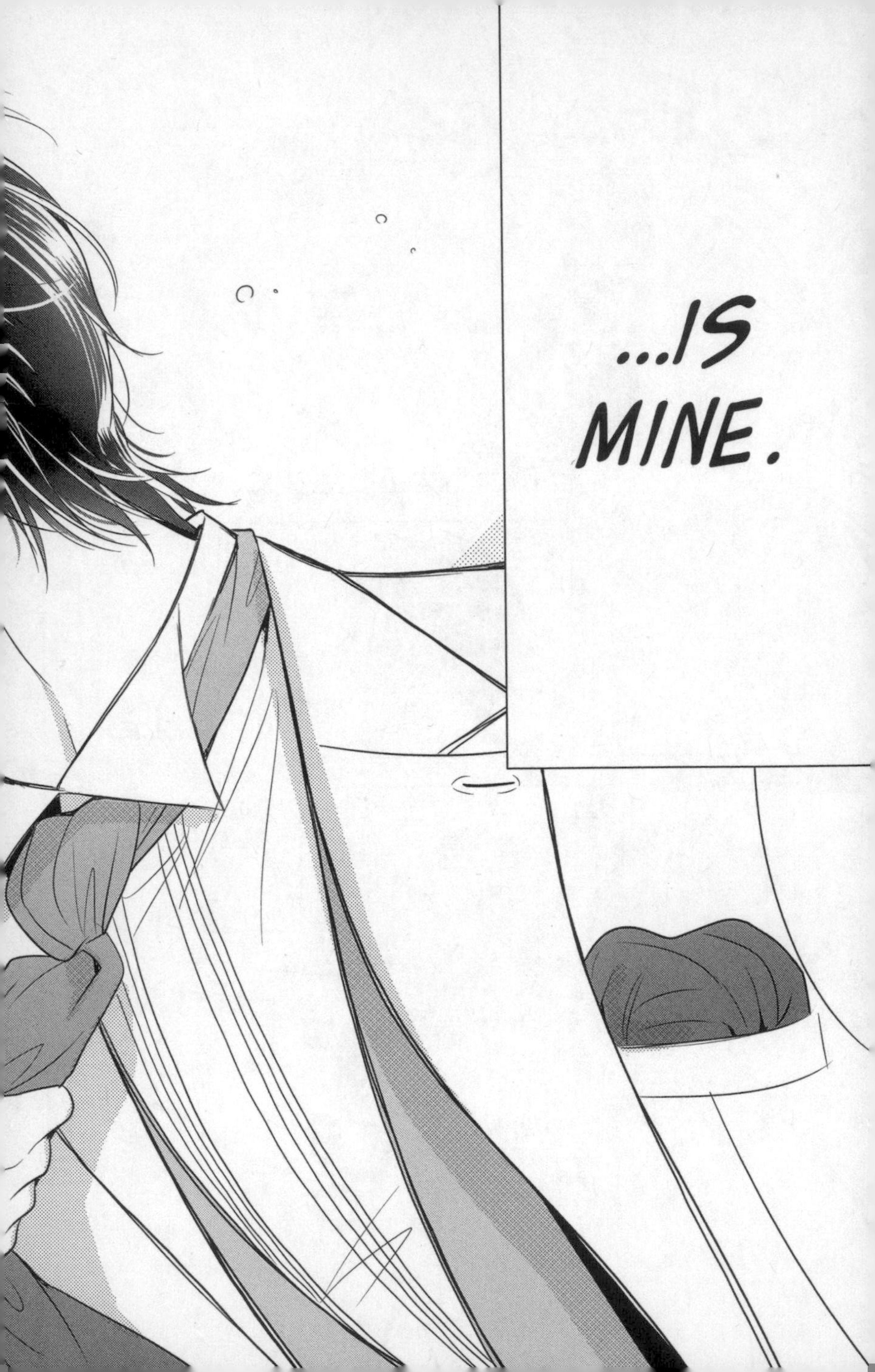
...IS MINE.

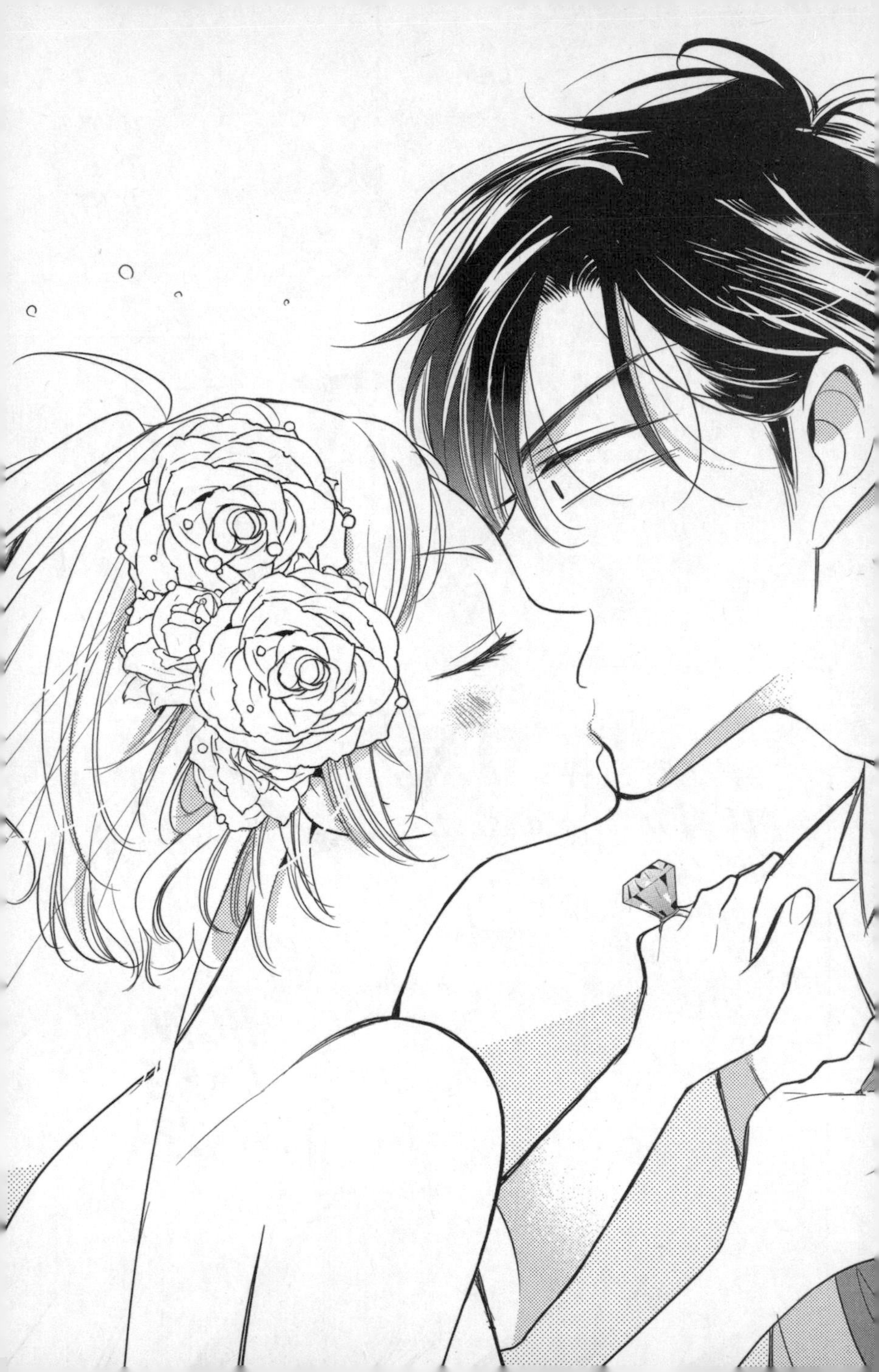

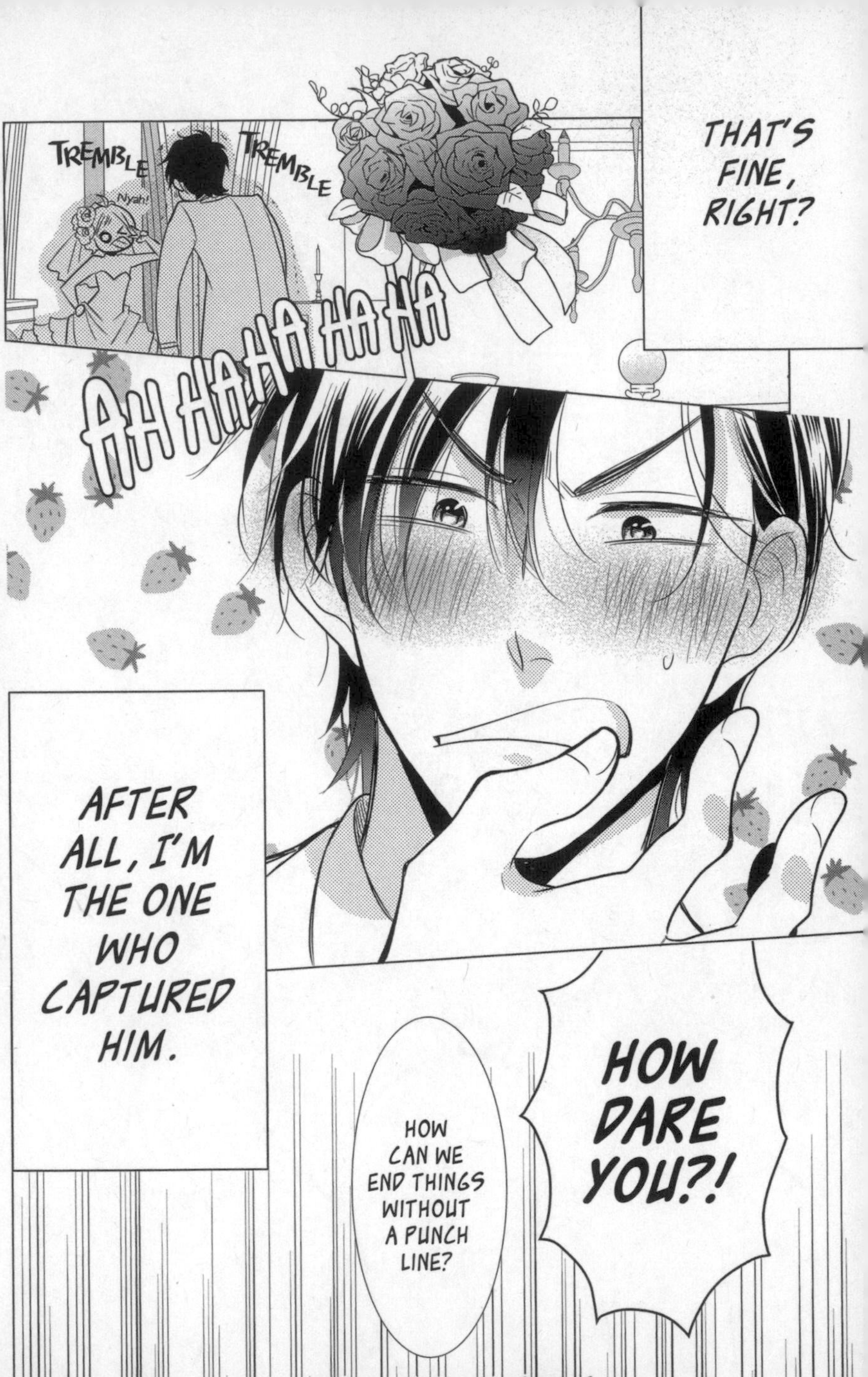
THAT'S FINE, RIGHT?
TREMBLE
TREMBLE
Nyah!
AH HAHA HA HA
AFTER ALL, I'M THE ONE WHO CAPTURED HIM.
HOW DARE YOU?!
HOW CAN WE END THINGS WITHOUT A PUNCH LINE?

Takane & Hana / The End

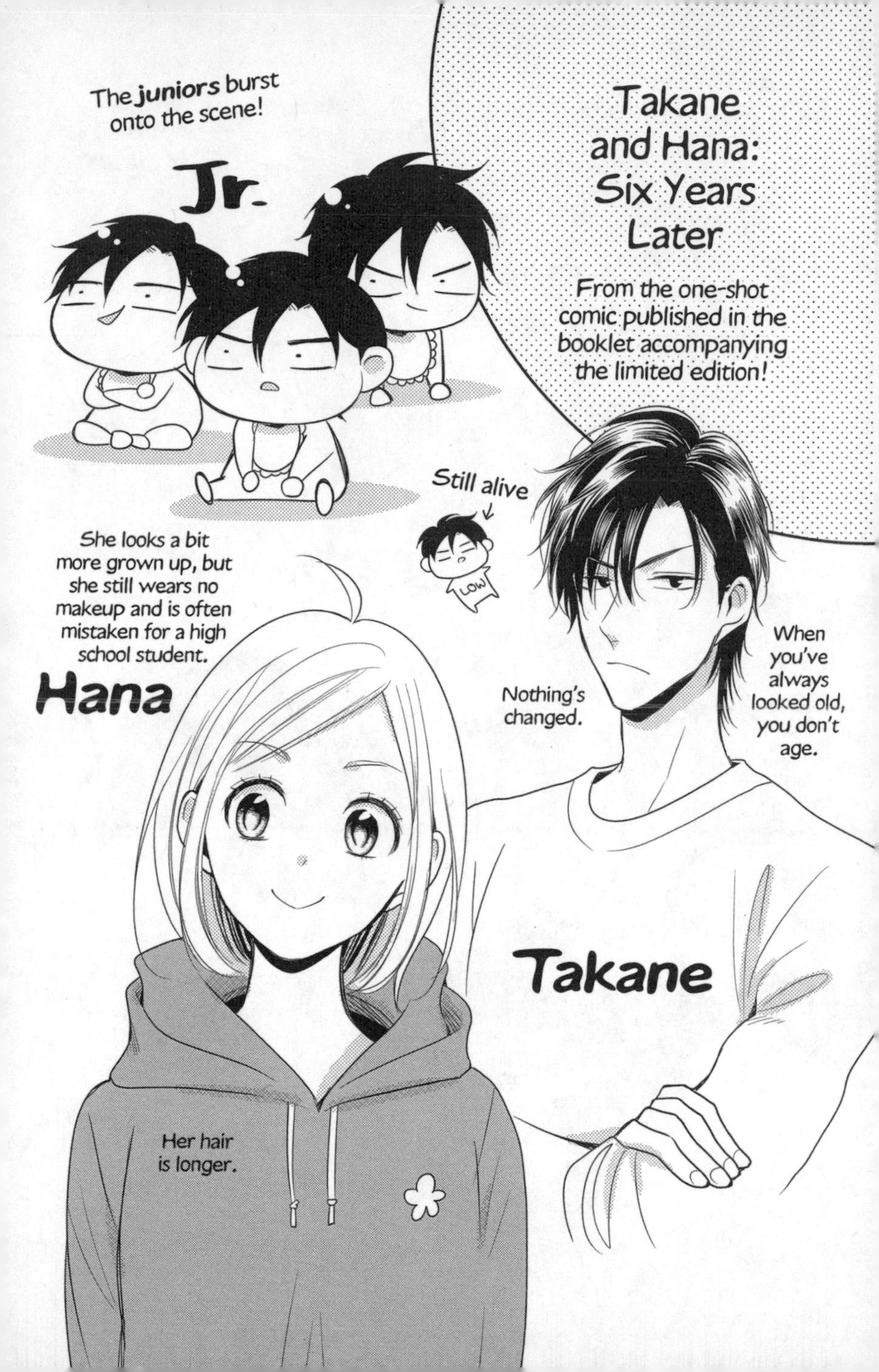
Takane and Hana: Six Years Later
From the one-shot comic published in the booklet accompanying the limited edition!
The juniors burst onto the scene!
Jr.
Still alive
LOW
When you've always looked old, you don't age.
Nothing's changed.
Takane
She looks a bit more grown up, but she still wears no makeup and is often mistaken for a high school student.
Hana
Her hair is longer.

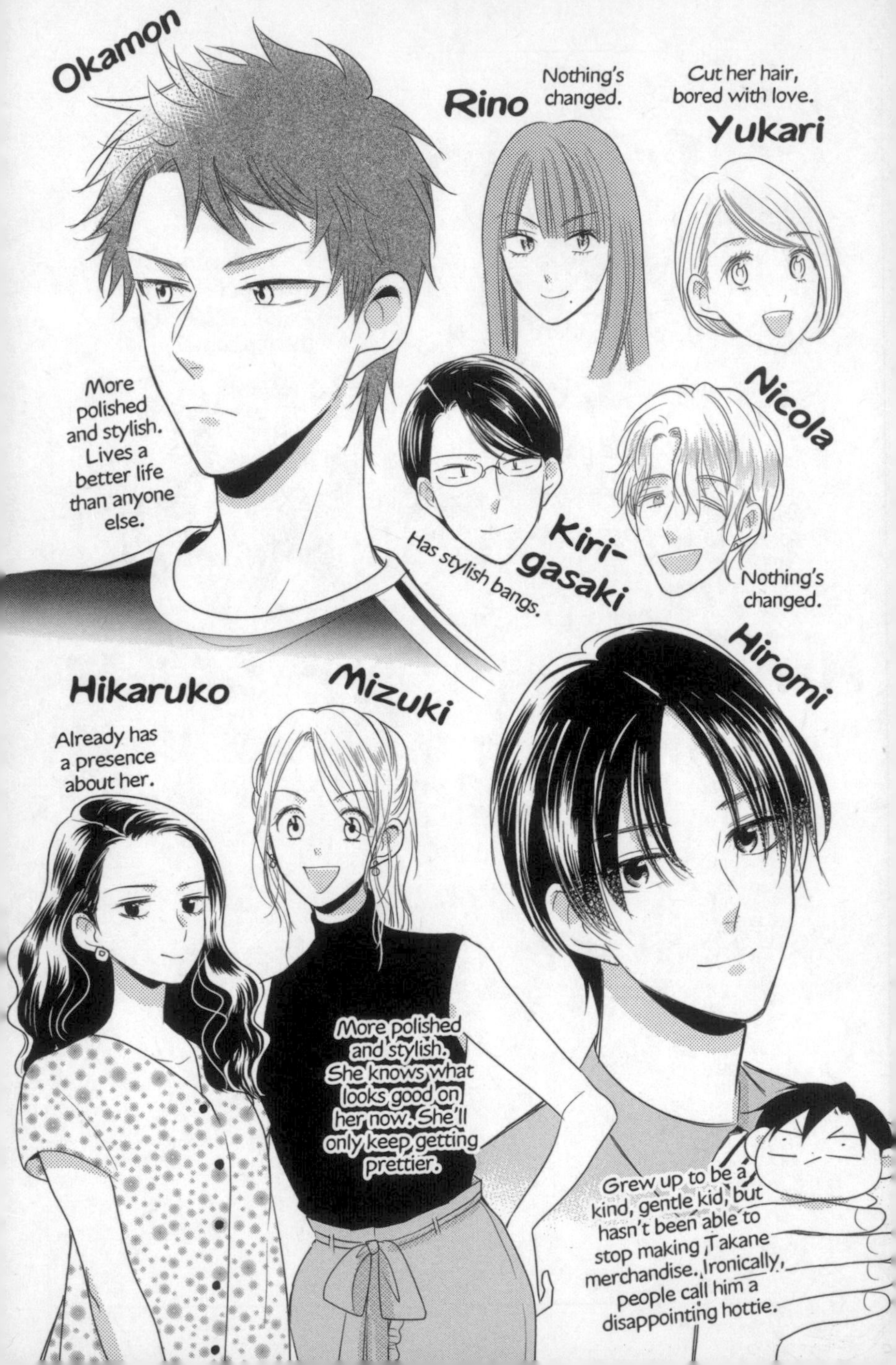
Yukari
Cut her hair, bored with love.
Rino
Nothing's changed.
Okamon
More polished and stylish. Lives a better life than anyone else.
Nicola
Nothing's changed.
Kiri-gasaki
Has stylish bangs.
Hiromi
Grew up to be a kind, gentle kid, but hasn't been able to stop making Takane merchandise. Ironically, people call him a disappointing hottie.
Mizuki
More polished and stylish. She knows what looks good on her now. She'll only keep getting prettier.
Hikaruko
Already has a presence about her.

Happy Wedding

I looked back to my inital first page of volume 1, and this is what it said:

> "Once upon a time, there was a high school girl and a rich businessman." That's the gist of it.

That's all I had in the beginning. But as the volumes progressed, multiple themes were layered in, and the **characters** stopped being just characters and became ***people***.

This may sound weird, but there were times when a character I drew influenced me into changing my way of thinking.

Since my creative well is always dried up and my brain is dried out, I struggled with every chapter. But thankfully, Takane and Hana have a happy ending, which made me feel like Shigeru (Hana's father) in a way. (*Ha.*)

Thank you for the past six years, Takane and Hana! I wish you nothing but happiness!

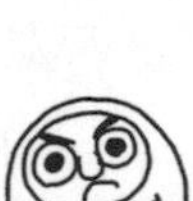
Best wishes

Yuki Shiwasu

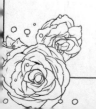

This last cover has roses. Thank you
for your support of Takane and Hana!

—YUKI SHIWASU

Born on March 7 in Fukuoka Prefecture, Japan,
Yuki Shiwasu began her career as a manga artist
after winning the top prize in the Hakusensha Athena
Newcomers' Awards from *Hana to Yume* magazine. She
is also the author of *Furou Kyoudai* (Immortal Siblings),
which was published by Hakusensha in Japan.

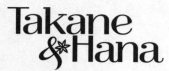

Takane & Hana

VOLUME 18
SHOJO BEAT EDITION

STORY & ART BY **YUKI SHIWASU**

ENGLISH ADAPTATION **Ysabet Reinhardt MacFarlane**
TRANSLATION **JN Productions**
TOUCH-UP ART & LETTERING **Annaliese "Ace" Christman**
DESIGN **Shawn Carrico**
EDITOR **Amy Yu**

Takane to Hana by Yuki Shiwasu

First published in Japan in 2020 by HAKUSENSHA, Inc., Tokyo.
English language translation rights arranged with HAKUSENSHA, Inc., Tokyo.

Printed in the U.S.A.

Published by VIZ Media, LLC
P.O. Box 77010
San Francisco, CA 94107

10 9 8 7 6 5 4 3 2 1
First printing, November 2021

PARENTAL ADVISORY
TAKANE & HANA is rated T for Teen and is recommended for ages 13 and up. This volume contains suggestive themes.

ratings.viz.com RATED T TEEN

VIZ MEDIA
viz.com

Shojo Beat
shojobeat.com

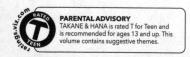

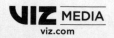

IDOL dreams

STORY & ART BY
ARINA TANEMURA

At age 31, office worker Chikage Deguchi feels she missed her chances at love and success. When word gets out that she's a virgin, Chikage is humiliated and wishes she could turn back time to when she was still young and popular. She takes an experimental drug that changes her appearance back to when she was 15. Now Chikage is determined to pursue everything she missed out on all those years ago—including becoming a star!

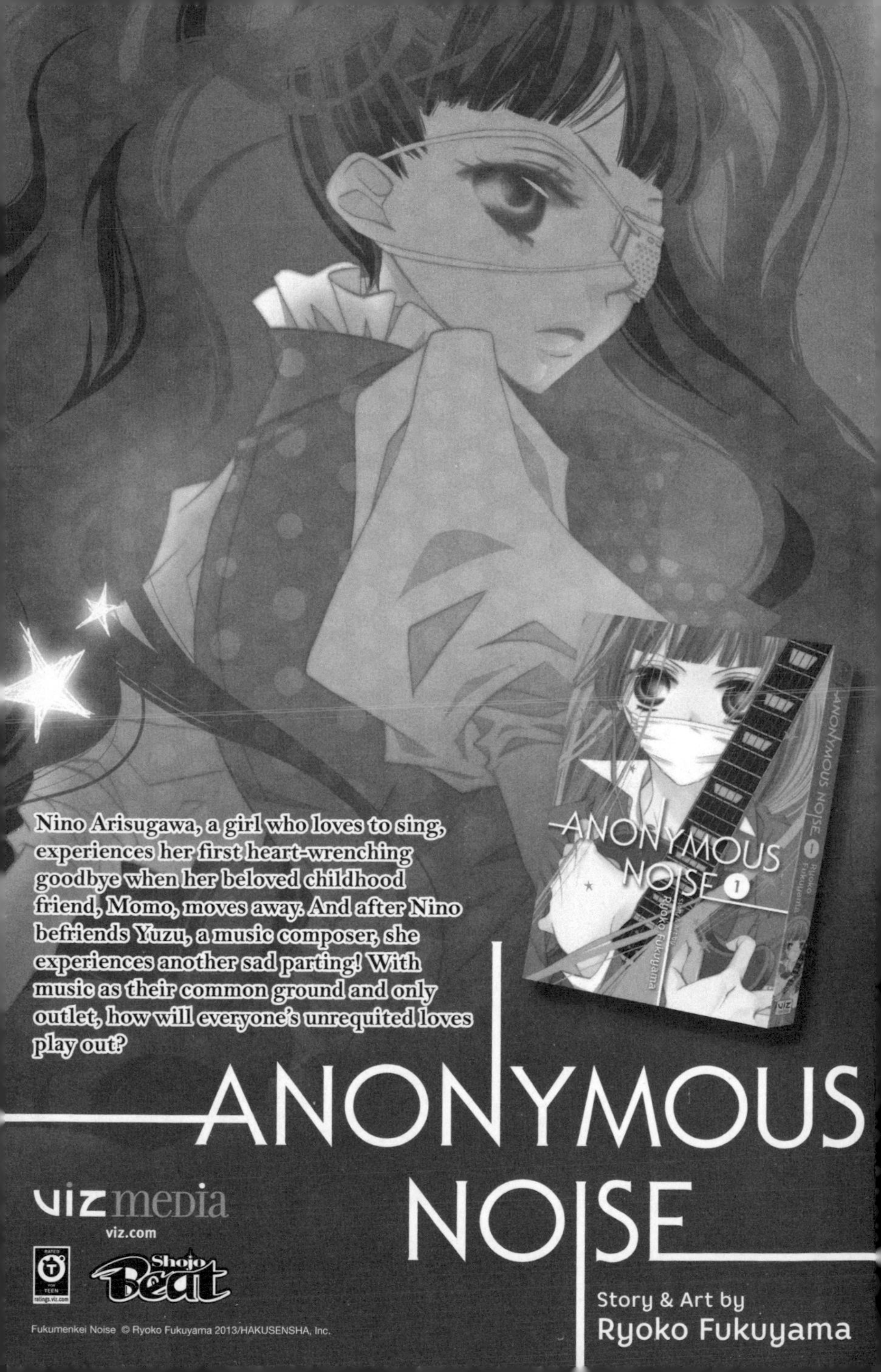
Nino Arisugawa, a girl who loves to sing, experiences her first heart-wrenching goodbye when her beloved childhood friend, Momo, moves away. And after Nino befriends Yuzu, a music composer, she experiences another sad parting! With music as their common ground and only outlet, how will everyone's unrequited loves play out?
ANONYMOUS NOISE 1
Ryoko Fukuyama
ANONYMOUS NOISE
Story & Art by
Ryoko Fukuyama
viz media
viz.com
RATED T FOR TEEN
ratings.viz.com
Shojo Beat
Fukumenkei Noise © Ryoko Fukuyama 2013/HAKUSENSHA, Inc.

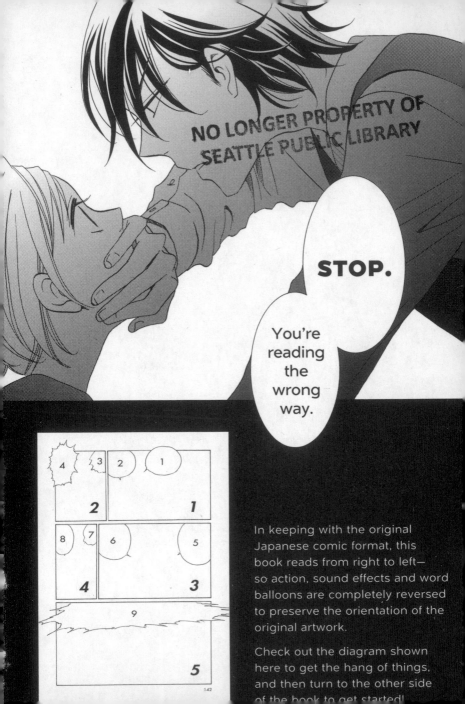

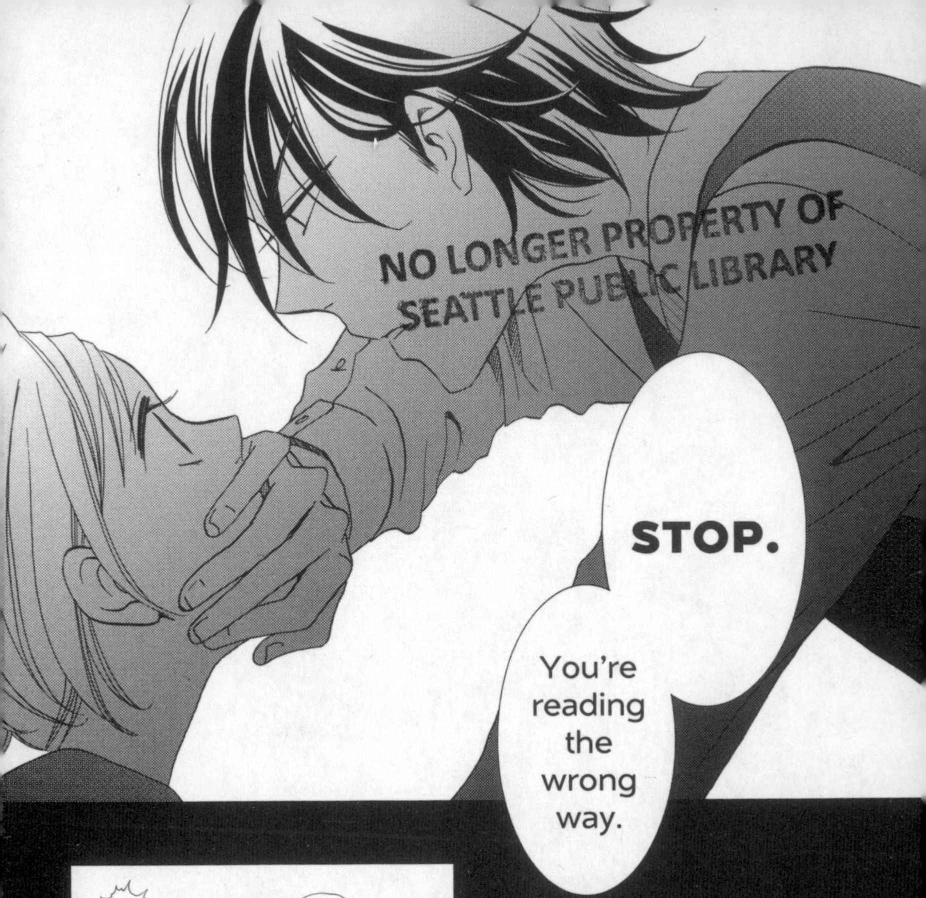
STOP.
You're reading the wrong way.

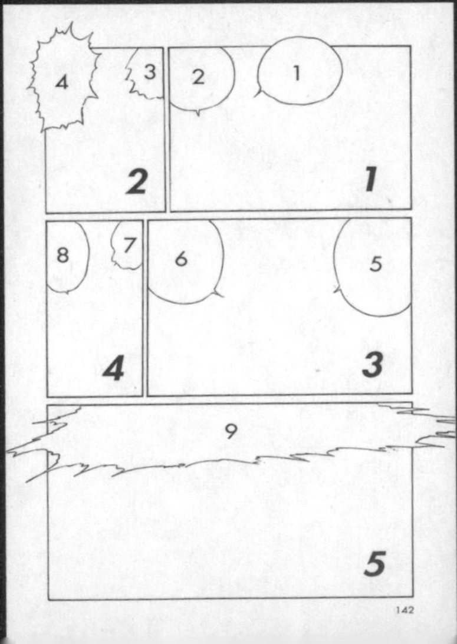

In keeping with the original Japanese comic format, this book reads from right to left—so action, sound effects and word balloons are completely reversed to preserve the orientation of the original artwork.

Check out the diagram shown here to get the hang of things, and then turn to the other side of the book to get started!